Property and Persuasion

New Perspectives on Law, Culture, and Society

Robert W. Gordon and Margaret Jane Radin,
Series Editors

Property and Persuasion: Essays on the History, Theory, and Rhetoric of Ownership, Carol M. Rose

Failed Revolutions: Social Reform and the Limits of Legal Imagination, Richard Delgado and Jean Stefancic

Words That Wound: Critical Race Theory, Assaultive Speech, and the First Amendment, Mari J. Matsuda, Charles R. Lawrence III, Richard Delgado, and Kimberlè Williams Crenshaw

Mind, Machine, and Metaphor: An Essay on Artificial Intelligence and Legal Reasoning, Alexander E. Silverman

Rebellious Lawyering: One Chicano's Vision of Progressive Law Practice, Gerald P. López

Wittgenstein and Legal Theory, edited by Dennis M. Patterson

Pragmatism in Law and Society, edited by Michael Brint and William Weaver

Feminist Legal Theory: Readings in Law and Gender, edited by Katharine T. Bartlett and Rosanne Kennedy

FORTHCOMING

Intellect and Craft: Writings of Justice Hans Linde, edited by Robert F. Nagel

The Philosophy of International Law: A Human Rights Approach, Fernando R. Teson

Thinking Like a Lawyer, Kenneth J. Vandevelde

A Guide to Contemporary Legal Theory, edited by Robert W. Gordon and Margaret Jane Radin

Progressive Corporate Law, edited by Lawrence E. Mitchell

Property and Persuasion

Essays on the History, Theory, and Rhetoric of Ownership

Carol M. Rose

Westview Press
BOULDER • SAN FRANCISCO • OXFORD

New Perspectives on Law, Culture, and Society

Photos courtesy of Library of Congress, Farm Security Administration Collection. Photo 1: Dorothea Lange. Photo 2 and cover: Russell Lee.

Published in 1994 in the United States of America by Westview Press, Inc., 5500 Central Avenue, Boulder, Colorado 80301-2877, and in the United Kingdom by Westview Press, 36 Lonsdale Road, Summertown, Oxford OX2 7EW

Library of Congress Cataloging-in-Publication Data
Rose, Carol M.
Property and persuasion : essays on the history, theory, and
rhetoric of ownership / Carol M. Rose
p. cm. — (New perspectives on law, culture, and society)
Includes bibliographical references and index.
ISBN 0-8133-8554-7 (hc). — ISBN 0-8133-8555-5 (pb)
1. Property. I. Title. II. Series.
K720.R67 1994
306.3′dc20 94-10741
CIP

Printed and bound in the United States of America

The paper used in this publication meets the requirements of the American National Standard for Permanence of Paper for Printed Library Materials Z39.48-1984.

10 9 8 7 6 5 4 3 2 1

Contents

Acknowledgments

Most of the essays in this book initially appeared elsewhere, in somewhat different form. No doubt some readers will be astonished to learn that in the originals the notes were even more copious, though somewhat less up-to-date, reflecting their earlier publication; in any event, readers searching for lengthier and more precise annotation should consult the originals. All these essays benefited from many, many comments and suggestions. I would like to thank here my steadiest and most indefatigable readers and critics over the years: Bruce Ackerman, Greg Alexander, Ian Ayres, Martha Fineman, Mark Grady, Tom Grey, Tom Merrill, Phyllis Palmer, Dan Polsby, Roberta Romano, Cass Sunstein, David Van Zandt, and especially Robert Ellickson. In writing these essays, I further benefited greatly from colleagues' comments in presentations (mainly in law schools) at Boston University, Case Western, the University of Chicago, Chicago-Kent, the University of Connecticut, Cornell, Duke, George Washington, Harvard, the University of Iowa, the University of Kentucky, New York Law School, New York University, Northwestern, the University of Pennsylvania, the University of Tennessee, the University of Texas, Tulane, the University of Virginia, and Yale. I also had the help of several very able research assistants, including Peter McCutchen, Martha Hirschfeld, Mary Alcock, Colleen Westbrook, and Darren Hutchinson. Many other individuals assisted me, and I am grateful to them all. And finally, I wish to thank Northwestern University and Yale University for generous support during the years I wrote these essays.

Carol M. Rose

Introduction: Approaching Property

Picture property. Use your mind's eye: what do you see? Perhaps a bank vault full of money or a house or maybe a fence—all common images in musings about property.

In fact, a fence might well occur to you because you have seen one on the cover of this book, or if you have riffled through the pages, you might have seen the same photo on page 276. True, the dilapidated object in the picture does not look like much of a fence, but it certainly does assert something about property. It says pretty clearly, "This is *mine.*"

You might think that this is not much of an attitude, either, particularly as applied to the pathetic little hardscrabble patch that the fence rather shakily protects. You might even think it a bit sad that such crabbed assertions of property come from the obviously lowly dirt farmer (actually a woman tenant farmer) who erected this ramshackle structure. That fence, with its splayed posts and its bedboard that substitutes for a real gate, makes the whole idea of property seem the worse for wear.

Or does it? On second glance you may find a kind of optimism in that tumbledown fence and a kind of openness to the world in that relatively grand "gate." If this little scrap of ground is somebody's property, then maybe property is not just something for the big shots after all, with their Rockefeller Centers and Trump Towers and all the other edifices they name after themselves. This scrap, too, is somebody's property, even if only for the term of her tenancy, and she intends to do something with it.

Her apparent hopefulness about such a modest claim raises a very large general question in modern thinking about property: is the idea of property now worn out, or is it a source of continuing optimism? For quite a while a number of respectable scholars have suggested that property's day is over, at least as most people know it. One version of this argument appeared at the beginning of the twentieth century, when Wesley Newcomb Hohfeld pointed out that larger entitlements could be analyzed as a series of claims and obligations of varying sorts among persons; when the dust settled on all Hohfeld's various "jural relations," hardly any independent *thing* that anybody could call "property" was left.[1] Considerably later in the century, Bruce Ackerman, following Hohfeld's lead, subdivided the notion of property into (unconsidered) lay notions and (scientific) Hohfeld-like propositions about entitlements.[2] However important and useful "scientific" property might remain under this analysis, the distinction did not bode well for the lay claimant, like the farmer with her fence and gate. Thomas Grey noticed this portent and followed with the dual observations that (1) later capitalism requires the Ackerman/Hohfeld "scientific" analysis of property but that (2) this analysis squeezes all the moral and intuitive sense out of the concept of property.[3]

An earlier and more sinister version of property's hollowness harks back to the protestations of the nineteenth-century Left. The best-known protagonist is undoubtedly Karl Marx, though the best catchphrase about property is attributable to Pierre-Joseph Proudhon, who said that property is theft. To simplify greatly, the general view is that "property rights" as they are commonly known are at most an artificial construct, masking the force and oppression of the powerful few and duping the rest of us into going along with their hegemonic pretensions.[4] Similar ideas have appeared in the work of some scholars of the Critical Legal Studies school. For example, Mark Tushnet has taken this view about rights in general—that is, that the notion of "rights" is more or less window dressing for the assertion of power by those who already dominate. A charge like this, of course, easily incorporates the more specific claims of property rights.[5]

On either account the woman farmer with the fence and gate appears to be in trouble. On one account, she is living in a dream world, supposing that her fence encloses anything other than a thin Hohfeldian "jural relation" or two. On the other, and even worse, she is dreaming someone else's dream: she is the victim of false consciousness, and her pitiful little fence perpetuates the very myths by which the powerful steal her efforts, dignity, and humanity.

What a surprise, then, that a number of people have started to take an optimistic view and to suppose that her fence and gate might do something quite important for her—and more generally, that property concepts might give at least a limited purchase on some of the most critical problems of the day. A spectacular example of the resurgence in the notion of property arises from the breakup of the old Soviet hegemony in Eastern Europe, where an absolutely critical issue for economic and political reform has turned out to be the reestablishment of a regime of private property.[6] An only slightly less dramatic example lies in the turn toward property approaches to environmental problems, even those of national or global significance. These approaches include such ideas as creating property-like, tradeable pollution permits in order to enlist market forces in reducing the airborne emissions that lead to acid rain and its devasting deforestations;[7] or preserving tropical rainforests and wild animal stocks by defining quite sophisticated versions of property rights in local communities or among indigenous peoples so that they have a stake in the proceeds of preservation.[8]

These developments are not entirely novel in property theory, as they seem to vindicate a particular way of looking at property that was perhaps most clearly expressed by the eighteenth-century philosopher Jeremy Bentham: property is designed to *do* something, and what it is supposed to do is to tap individual energies in order to make us all more prosperous.[9] Modern scholars of a neo-utilitarian bent, including that modern maven of law-and-economics Richard Posner, have been attracted to this version of property;[10] indeed, there is quite a burgeoning literature on property rights in this neo-utilitarian style, and readers will brush against some of it in this book.

Very briefly, the neo-utilitarian view asserts that property rights are a good thing because they encourage people to invest their efforts in things they claim (since each owner reaps the rewards of investment decisions as well as bearing the costs) and because they encourage trade (since clear entitlements are a precondition to trade). All this activity and trade, of course, makes us collectively wealthier. So if we want to reach that result of collective well-being (and who would not, other things being equal?), we need to have clear and secure property rights; the more valuable the resources at stake, the clearer and more secure the property rights should be.

Security of property is the political message in all this, and of course much of this literature is neoconservative. As such, it is closely allied with libertarian views like those of Robert Nozick or more recently Richard Epstein, even though the libertarians' rights-based approaches sometimes cause important breaks with the wealth-based utilitarian approaches.[11] But both libertarian and neo-utilitarian scholars are generally friendly to classical economics, and members of both schools often give the impression of an almost defiantly exuberant celebration of individual self-interest, with a concomitant rejection of common interests as anything other than the sum of individual preference satisfactions.

Readers of this book will see that I am extremely interested in this literature, particularly the notion of property as a wealth-producing institution. Almost all the essays here reflect that interest, because the idea seems to me to have powerful explanatory force in addressing many of our institutions of property. But as the essays here also reflect, I think that there is a problem in much of this literature. The problem is that individualized property rights are not necessarily the most wealth-enhancing form of property, even taking utilitarian arguments on their own terms. More generally, as I stress in these essays, self-interest has some distinct limitations as a basis for property regimes, a point to which I will return shortly.

To some degree in reaction to the economics-oriented property-rights thinkers, a number of other writers have stressed that property regimes are located in and managed by *communities.* These works are extremely varied, but there are some unifying themes: that property is itself a kind of regulatory regime; that such regimes are managed by a larger community to which the constituent members have some responsibilities; and that in particular, the wealthier members may have responsibilities to the poorer.[12] The more analytically inclined writers in this genre often draw some link between property and the work of John Rawls, citing Rawls' argument about the "difference principle" that rational people would supposedly choose in creating a just society: that is, the well-off members of a society should not gain from some institutional change unless the least well-off gain at least as much or more.[13] The more historically oriented writers in this group often relate property to the history of "civic republicanism," as it has appeared in the historical writings of J.G.A. Pocock and Gordon Wood, among others.[14]

Once again, readers of these essays will see that I am very interested in this communitarian literature, because I think that it correctly draws attention to the intensely social nature of property. Here again, though, I think there is a problem: a number of communitarian writers too easily marginalize the powerful utilitarian arguments for property as a wealth-producing institution and too readily suppose that property can be redistributed at will, without disrupting incentives to industrious behavior—the very behavior that helped to create whatever wealth is to be redistributed.[15]

There is another problematic aspect to some of the communitarian literature, but to describe it I need to come back to the self-interest posited by the neo-utilitarian group. As some of these essays discuss at greater length, modern game theory literature suggests that self-interest alone cannot be a basis for trade and commerce or, as it turns out, for property regimes either. Despite their various heroic efforts to bypass this conundrum, the theorists must always posit someone who gets the ball rolling and starts a course of dealing by cooperating—by being "nice" when self-interest would suggest cheating instead. A crowd of cheaters, a gaggle of purely "rationally" self-interested types, could never create a property regime; they just would not trust each other enough to make the necessary first moves, and so no one would make these moves at all.

At this juncture, of course, communitarian writers can collectively say, "Aha! Property depends on the larger community, not just on self-interested individuals." But at that point communitarians also sometimes make a problematic move of their own: they jump straight from this insight to the regulatory state, seemingly attributing all property regimes to formal regulation. This is unduly statist, because in fact, as my colleague Robert Ellickson has illustrated with innumerable colorful examples, people concoct all sorts of collective property regimes for their things, with or without the help of formal political regimes.[16] Just consider the way that you and others take a place in line at a ticket booth and the way you resent the line jumpers: that, too, is a kind of property regime, albeit a temporary one.

Indeed, even John Locke, the master property theorist himself, depicted property as something people acquired before they thought up a state.[17] One need not think that Locke was simply planting a proto-libertarian time bomb in order to make property seem a "prepolitical" right that should be preserved from legislative redistribution; he may instead have made the quite ordinary observation that people can come up with informal common norms for property even without formal political ordering. In a way it is too bad that Locke did not pursue the issue further, because some modern institutional scholars think that formal regulatory interventions all too often only disrupt the perfectly satisfactory property arrangements that groups have constructed informally for themselves.[18]

This of course is yet another line of modern property scholarship, suggesting that cooperative efforts—including the establishment and maintenance of property regimes—can be based on informal norms without necessarily implicating a central state. Here again there is quite a budding literature in political science and economic history, with analyses of norm-based property regimes running from the medieval commons to lobster fishing in Maine and irrigation systems in developing countries.[19]

A bright thread through this literature is the argument that contrary to much neoconservative thinking, property does not have to be individually owned to be efficient; instead, communities can govern *common* property on the basis of *common* norms. Indeed some resources seem to call for some sort of common management rather than individual ownership, a theme that I explore in several of these essays. More than that, one of my own arguments is that a regime of individual property is itself a kind of collective property or metaproperty; a private property regime holds together only on the basis of common beliefs and understandings.[20]

In fact, most of the essays in this book are in some measure an effort to learn from the insights and the lapses of both economic-based and communitarian approaches to property—and, even more important, to bridge the gap between them. The main components for building the bridge are norms and narration, and these materials are already linked to one another. Community norms—the common beliefs, understandings, and culture that hold property regimes together—raise the issue of persuasion. Where do people get those understandings about property anyway, and what gets them over that peculiar gap between property-as-thing and property-as-relationship? Just as important, what persuades people to ease up on self-interest or convinces them to pay attention to the norms that let them manage property regimes as a whole, and in so doing become more prosperous? How do people *change* norms to accommodate different property arrangements that might enhance their well-being? Here is where narrative matters: stories, allegories, and metaphors can change minds. Through narratives, or so it is said, people can create a kind of narrative community in which the storyteller can suggest the possibility that things could be different and perhaps better (or, alternatively, worse).[21]

In contemporary legal scholarship, much of the interest in narrative is located in constitutional interpretation and in feminist jurisprudence and other "out-group" scholarship.[22] These are quite glamorous topics, to be sure, especially by comparison with dowdy old property. But surely even a prosaic subject might make a contribution to this line of inquiry. From a narrative perspective, property is not really as lackluster as people tend to think. Property regimes and even individual property holdings are by no means self-evident constructs; there are many property arrangements that people have quite consciously talked themselves into (as in the emergent examples mentioned earlier from Eastern Europe and environmental law). Then, too, there are other property arrangements, like "first possession," that seem as much a part of nature as the summer sun—even if, as I suspect, people have talked themselves into those understandings as well. All these practices offer a very rich lode for narrative theory and indeed for the theory of culture, and they open up the question of the ways our aesthetic sensibilities bear on practical life. In fact, if (as I argue) property regimes cannot get over the self-interest problem without imparting some sense of a common good, then narratives, stories, and rhetorical devices may be essential in persuading people of that common good—hence the title of this book, *Property and Persuasion.*

What this book is about, then, is the various ways in which people make up and change their minds about property, and the strategies and arguments they use in persuading others to do the same. Sometimes, as in the first and last essays, "Possession as the Origin of Property" and "Seeing Property," the subject is the kinds of things people "say" to make particular claims within an overall system that everyone thinks is natural—"statements" like the rickety but somehow emphatic fence and the bedpost gate of the picture. Needless to say, that sort of statement reveals a good deal about the culture within which it is made. Several other essays concern much more conscious assertions about whole property regimes; these are, notably, the essays on storytelling (Chapter 2), the practices of property (Chapter 3), and the ancient constitution (Chapter 4). Here readers will find plenty of stories aimed at getting others to agree on the kind of economic and political regimes that should be adopted, as well as the regimes that are to be rejected and why (and, by the way, the enhancement of wealth looms large in these stories, but so do some other issues). Some other essays, like those on the comedy of the commons (Chapter 5) and common law water rights (Chapter 6) are about historically mixed property regimes, where the resources themselves (and the things we want to do with them) seem to dictate that these resources will be most fruitful if they are held in part individually, in part communally, or in part by the public at large.[23] The ambiguously titled "Crystals and Mud" (Chapter 7) concerns inconclusive property regimes, where property arrangements seem to wobble between opposite poles; the essay on women and property, in contrast, concerns one-sided regimes, where bargaining strategies mesh unevenly, with rather serious consequences for the distribution of property and even for total social wealth. Finally, because differing property arrangements may seem "natural" to different people, some essays also raise the issue of misunderstandings and losses that come from force as well as persuasion, or from acquiescence rather than conviction.[24] There is much persuasion in property, but there are breakdowns too, and one hopes that they reveal by contrast what persuasion was supposed to be about—though sometimes the breakdowns instead suggest just how ambiguous persuasion can be.

Notes

1. Hohfeld, "Some Fundamental Legal Conceptions as Applied in Judicial Reasoning," 23 *Yale L. J.* 16 (1913).

2. Bruce A. Ackerman, *Private Property and the Constitution* 10–11, 194 n. 15 (1977).

3. Grey, "The Disintegration of Property," 22 *Nomos* 69 (1980).

4. See Karl Marx, *Capital,* in *Marx* 354–55 et seq. (M. Adler ed. 1955).

5. Tushnet, "An Essay on Rights," 62 *Tex. L. Rev.* 1363 (1982). For some applications to property in the CLS mode, see Kenneth Vandevelde, "The New Property of the Nineteenth Century: The Development of the Modern Concept of Property," 29 *Buff. L. Rev.* 325 (1980); and the discussion of property in James L. Kainen, "Nineteenth Century Interpretations of the Federal Contract Clause: The Transformation from Vested to Substantive Rights Against the State," 31 *Buff. L. Rev.* 381, 445–51 (1982). Interestingly enough, both these essays relate elite domination to the development of Hohfeld's non-thing-like explication of property.

6. Cass Sunstein, "On Property and Constitutionalism," 14 *Cardozo L. Rev.* 907 (1993).

7. Clean Air Act Amendments of 1990, secs. 401–416 (tradeable emission permits to control acid rain); see generally Richard B. Stewart, "Controlling Environmental Risks Through Economic Incentives," 13 *Col. J. Envt'l L.* 153 (1988).

8. See Lee Breckinridge, "Protection of Biological and Cultural Diversity: Emerging Recognition of Local Community Rights in Ecosystems Under International Environmental Law," 59 *Tenn. L. Rev.* 735 (1992).

9. Bentham, *Principles of the Civil Code,* in *Theory of Legislation,* at 109–122 (1987; reprint of C. K. Ogden ed. 1931).

10. Posner, *Economic Analysis of Law* 30 (3d ed. 1986).

11. Robert Nozick, *Anarchy, State, and Utopia* (1974); Richard A. Epstein, *Takings: Private Property and the Power of Eminent Domain* (1985).

12. See, e.g., Frank Michelman, "Ethics, Economics, and the Law of Property," 24 *Nomos* 3 (1982); Margaret Jane Radin, "Market-Inalienability," 100 *Harv. L. Rev.* 1849 (1987); Jennifer Nedelsky, *Private Property and the Constitution* (1990).

13. Rawls, *A Theory of Justice* (1971); on property, see, e.g. Stephen R. Munzer, *A Theory of Property* (1990); Jeremy Waldron, *The Right to Private Property* (1988).

14. Pocock, *The Machiavellian Moment: Florentine Political Thought and the Atlantic Republican Tradition* (1975); Wood, *The Creation of the American Republic, 1776–1787* (1969); for property scholars, see, e.g. Gregory Alexander, "Time and Property in the American Republican Legal Culture," 66 *N.Y.U. L. Rev.* 273 (1991); Laura Underkuffler, "On Property: An Essay," 100 *Yale L. J.* 127 (1990).

15. See Thomas Merrill, "Zero-Sum Madison" (review), 90 *Mich. L. Rev.* 1392, 1400 n. 26 (1992). Some of these problems are explored in greater length in an essay not reproduced here: Rose, "'Enough and as Good' of What?" 81 *Nw. U. L. Rev.* 417 (1987).

16. See generally Ellickson, *Order Without Law* (1991); "Property in Land," 102 *Yale L. J.* 1315 (1993).

17. Locke, *Second Treatise of Government*, secs. 45–51, in *Two Treatises of Government* (P. Laslett rev. 1963; 1st ed. 1690).

18. See, e.g., Elinor Ostrom, *Governing the Commons: The Evolution of Institutions for Collective Action* 149–57 (1990); James Acheson, "The Lobster Fiefs Revisited: Economic and Ecological Effects of Territoriality in Maine Lobster Fishing," in Bonnie J. McCay and James Acheson, eds., *The Question of the Commons: The Culture and Ecology of Communal Resources* 37, 46 (1987).

19. See, e.g., Ostrom, supra note 18; Acheson, supra note 18; Carl Dahlman, *The Open Field and Beyond: A Property Rights Analysis of an Economic Institution* (1980); Jon Elster, *The Cement of Society: A Study of Social Order* (1989); Edna Ullman-Margolit, *The Emergence of Norms* (1978).

20. See the essays "Property as Storytelling" and "The Comedy of the Commons."

21. See David Carr, *Time, Narrative and History* 146 et seq. (1986).

22. See, e.g., Robert Cover, "The Supreme Court, 1982 Term: *Nomos* and Narrative," 97 *Harv. L. Rev.* 4 (1983); Robin West, "Economic Man and Literary Woman: One Contrast," 39 *Mercer L. Rev.* 867 (1988); Robert A. Williams, Jr., *The American Indian in Western Legal Thought: The Discourses of Conquest* (1990).

23. Readers may also find an analogy in regional political organization in "Ancient Constitution versus Federalist Empire" later in this volume.

24. "Possession as the Origin of Property"; "Women and Property"; "Seeing Property."

PART ONE

Initial Persuasions: Talk About Property

These two essays are about some very basic ways in which property revolves around persuasion. The first, "Possession as the Origin of Property," traces out what seems to be property's quintessential moment of chutzpah: the act of establishing individual property for one's self simply by taking something out of the great commons of unowned resources. The common law of property, through its variously named doctrines of "first possession," recognizes such self-created entitlements, but as the essay shows, the necessary moves add up to a great deal of persuasion—or, some might say, bluff.

The second essay, on property and storytelling, is about some considerably more generalized persuasive efforts aimed at talking everyone into recognizing property *institutions,* as opposed to this or that specific property claim. In the essay I ask why so many analytic property theorists have lapsed into stories at crucial spots, and I show what the stories do for the theorists—and what they tell the rest of us about the theories.

1

Possession as the Origin of Property

How do things get to be owned? This is a fundamental puzzle for anyone who thinks about property. One buys things from other owners, to be sure, but how did the other owners get those things? Back at the beginning, someone must have acquired the thing, whatever it is, without buying it from anyone else. That is, someone had to do something to anchor the very first link in the chain of ownership. The puzzle is, What was that action that anchored the chain and made an owned thing out of an unowned one? John Locke's theory, once described as "the standard bourgeois theory,"[1] is perhaps the most familiar to Americans. Locke argued that the original owner is the one who mixes his (or her) labor with the previously unowned thing, and by commingling labor to the thing, establishes ownership in it.[2]

This labor theory is appealing because it seems to rest on desert, but unfortunately it creates still more puzzles. For one, without a prior theory of ownership, what makes it so clear that anyone owns the labor that he or she mixes with something else?[3] For another, even if one does own the labor that one performs, what is the scope of the right that one establishes by mixing the owned thing (one's labor) with something else? Robert Nozick pinpoints this issue with a clever hypothetical question: suppose I own a can of tomato juice and pour it into the ocean. Do I now take title to the seas?[4]

A number of thinkers more or less contemporary to Locke proposed a different theory of ownership. According to this theory, the original owner got title through the consent of the rest of humanity (who were, taken together, the first recipients from God, the genuine original owner).[5] But here too there are some problems, notably those that the modern law-and-

The original version of this essay appeared in 52 *University of Chicago Law Review*, 73–88 (1985). Reprinted by permission of *University of Chicago Law Review*.

economics writers would call "administrative costs": how does everyone get together to consent to the division of things among individuals?[6]

The common law has a third approach, which shares some characteristics of the labor and consent theories but is still sufficiently distinct to warrant a different label. For the common law, *possession* or "occupancy" is the origin of property.[7] This notion runs through a number of fascinating old cases in property law. To be sure, a modern reader may entertain some doubts about the current usefulness of such chestnuts, which are all about acquiring title in such arguably unowned oddities as wild animals and abandoned treasure. How many times, after all, may we expect to get into disputes about our ownership of stray moose or long-buried pieces of eight?

In fact, though, these old cases are not entirely academic. People still do find treasure-laden old vessels,[8] and now more than ever, statesmen do have to consider whether someone's acts might support a claim to own the moon, for example, or the mineral nodes at the bottom of the sea.[9] Analogies to the capture of wild animals have popped up time and again when courts have had to deal with some "fugitive" resource that is being reduced to property for the first time: oil and gas, for example, or groundwater or space on the spectrum of radio frequencies.[10]

With these more up-to-date claims in mind, then, let us turn to that homily of the common law, that first possession is the root of title. But merely to state the maxim is to pose two critical questions: first, what counts as possession? and second, why does possession count as a claim to title?[11] In exploring the quaint old cases' answers to these questions, we hit on some fundamental views about the nature and purposes of a property regime.

Consider *Pierson v. Post*,[12] a classic wild animal case from the early nineteenth century. Post was hunting a fox one day on an unowned beach, and he almost had the beast in his sights when an interloper appeared, killed the fox, and ran off with the carcass. The indignant Post sued on the theory that his pursuit established his property right to the fox.

Not so, said the court's majority. It cited a long list of learned authorities to the effect that "occupancy" or "possession" went to the one who killed the animal or who at least wounded it mortally or caught it in a net; these acts brought the animal within the "certain control" that gives rise to possession and hence a claim to ownership.

Possession thus means a clear act, whereby all the world understands that the pursuer has "an unequivocal intention of appropriating the animal to his individual use."[13] A clear rule of this sort should be applied, said the court's majority, because it prevents confusions and quarrels among hunters (and coincidentally makes the judges' tasks easier when hunters do get into quarrels).

The dissenting Judge Livingston somewhat flippantly commented that the best way to handle this matter would be to leave it to a panel of sportsmen, who would presumably cook the goose of the interloper. According to Livingston, the majority's rule would discourage the useful activity of fox hunting. Who would bother to go to all the trouble of keeping dogs and tramping after the fox if the reward is up for grabs to any "saucy intruder"?[14] If we really want to see that foxes don't overrun the countryside, we will allocate a property right—and thus the ultimate reward—to the hunter at an earlier moment, so as to encourage his useful investment in keeping hounds and his useful labor in flushing out the fox.

The problem of assigning "possession" prior to the kill, of course, is that we don't quite know when to assign it. Shall we assign it when the hunt begins? When the hunter assembles his dogs for the hunt? When the hunter buys his dogs?

Pierson thus presents two great principles for defining possession, but they are seemingly at odds: (1) notice to the world through a clear act and (2) reward to useful labor. The latter principle, of course, suggests a labor theory of property: the owner gets the prize when he "mixes in his labor" by hunting. On the other hand, the "clear act" principle suggests at least a weak form of the consent theory, insofar as the world at large might be thought to acquiesce in individual ownership when the claim is clear and no one objects.

On closer examination, however, the two positions do not seem so far apart. In *Pierson,* each side acknowledged the importance of the other's principle. Although the majority came down for a clear rule, it tacitly conceded the value of rewarding useful labor; its rule for possession would in fact reward the original hunter most of the time, unless we suppose that the woods are thick with "saucy intruders." And on the other side, the dissenting Livingston also wanted some definiteness in the rule of possession. He simply thought the rule would be best understood if the relevant community decided for itself the acts sufficient for possession—the relevant community being hunters and "sportsmen," who after all were the people most often involved in the chase. Perhaps, then, there is some way to reconcile the clear-act and the reward-to-labor principles.

The clear-act principle suggests that the common law defines acts of possession as some kind of *statement.* As Blackstone said, the acts must be a *declaration* of one's intent to appropriate.[15] Let us consider this possibility in a later-nineteenth-century case involving possession of land. *Brumagim v. Bradshaw*[16] involved two claimants to a considerable amount of land that had become, by the time the litigation was brought, the residential and commercial Potrero district of San Francisco. Each party claimed to own land through a title extending back to an original "possessor" of the land, raising the question as to who had really been there first. More precisely, the issue was whether the first of these purported possessors, one George Treat, had really "possessed" the land at all. If he had not, his successors in interest could not claim ownership through him, and title would go to those claiming through a later "first possessor."

Those who claimed through Treat put a number of facts before the jury to establish his original possession. They particularly noted that Treat had repaired a fence across the neck of the Potrero peninsula—to which the other side rejoined that outsiders could still land in boats, and, besides, there was a gap in the fence. Well, then, the Treat claimants went on, Treat pastured livestock on the land—to which the other side replied that the land had not been suitable for cattle even then, because San Francisco was expanding in that direction. The court ruled that the matter was one for the jury to decide, and that in making its decision, the jury should consider whether Treat's acts gave sufficient notice to the public that he had appropriated the property.[17]

Now this emphasis on notice-giving seems to come down pretty firmly for the clear-act theory of possession. But that theory leaves out some elements of the evidence. To be sure, all the talk about Treat's fence suggests that the first possessor is the first to inform the public of his claim. But the parties' arguments over "suitable use" seem to bear on the reward to useful labor; that is, the first possession rule should give the property to the first one to make good use of the soil. Why then did the court's jury instruction ignore the value of rewarding useful labor?

The answer may well be that suitable use is also a form of notice. If outsiders would think that a large area near a growing city was an abandoned lot because it was vacant except for a few cows, they might enter on the land and claim some prime waterfront footage for themselves. In other words, if the use that Treat made was unsuitable, his use would not give notice to others of his claim. Thus to ask whether Treat used the land suitably is just another way of asking whether he informed others of his claim, particularly those others who might be interested either in buying the land from Treat or settling it for themselves. We are all worst off where claims are vague: if no one knows whether she can safely use the land or from whom she should buy it if it is already claimed, the land may end up being used by too many people or by none at all.

Possession now begins to look even more like something that requires a kind of communication, and the original claim to the property looks like a kind of speech, with the audience composed of all others who might be interested in claiming the object in question. Moreover, some venerable statutory law requires the acquirer to *keep on* speaking, lest she lose title through the odd but fascinating doctrine of adverse possession.

Adverse possession is a common law interpretation of statutes of limitation for actions to recover real property.[18] Suppose I own a lot in the mountains, and some stranger to me, without my permission, builds a house on the land, clears the woods, and farms the lot continuously for a given period, say twenty years. During that time, I am entitled to go to court to force him off the lot. But if I have not done so at the end of twenty years or some other period fixed by statute, not only can I not sue him for recovery of what was my land, but the law recognizes him as the title owner.[19] The doctrine of adverse possession thus transfers property from the title owner to another who is essentially a trespasser, if the trespasser's presence is open to everyone and lasts continuously for a given period of time, and so long as the title owner takes no action to get rid of him during that time.

Here again we seem to have a wonderful example of reward to useful labor, at the expense of the sluggard. But the doctrine is susceptible to another interpretation as well; it is not so much designed to reward the useful laborer as to require the title owner publicly to assert her right. It requires her to clarify that she, and not the trespasser, is the person to deal with if anyone should wish to buy the property or use some portion of it.

Courts have chewed over at some length the elements that make up adverse possession. Is grazing livestock a continuous use, so as to entitle a livestock grazier to claim full ownership as an adverse possessor?[20] How about farming, where intensive use is merely seasonal, or what about merely taking care of a lawn?[21] Is a cave that encroaches deep under my land something that is obvious to me, so that I should be required to kick out the trespasser who operates it as a commercial attraction?[22] No matter how much the doctrine of adverse possession seems to reward the one who performs useful labor on land, over against the lazy owner who does nothing, the crucial element in all these situations is once again communication. What "possession" means is acts that "'apprise the community[,] ... arrest attention, and put others claiming title upon inquiry.'"[23]

In Illinois, for example, an adverse possessor may establish his claim by doing no more than paying taxes on the property, at least over against an owner who is familiar with real estate practice and records.[24] Why is this? Naturally the community likes to have taxes paid and is favorably disposed toward one who pays them. But more important, payment of taxes is a matter of public record, and the owner whose taxes are paid should be aware that something peculiar is happening.[25] Just as important, the *public* is very likely to view the taxpayer as the owner. If someone is paying taxes on my vacant lot or empty house, any third person who wants to buy the house is very likely to think that the taxpayer is the owner; and if I want to keep my land I had better correct the misimpression. Adverse possession, then, once again serves to make sure that the public can rely upon its reasonable perceptions, and any owner who fails to correct misleading appearances is apt to find his title lost to the one who speaks loudly and clearly, even though erroneously.

Possession as the basis of property ownership, then, seems to amount to something like yelling loudly enough to all who may be interested. The first to say, "This is mine," in a way that the public understands, gets the prize, and the law will help him keep it against someone else who says, "No, it is *mine.*" But if the original communicator dallies too long and allows the public to believe the interloper, he will find that the interloper has stepped into his shoes and has become the owner.

Similar ideas of the importance of communication, or as it is more commonly called, "notice," are implicit in our recording statutes and in a variety of other devices that force a property claimant to make a public record of her claims, on pain of losing them altogether.[26] Indeed, notice plays a part in the most mundane property-like claims to things that the law does not even recognize as capable of ownership. "Would you please save my place?" you say to your neighbor in the movie line, to make sure that everyone knows that you are coming back and not relinquishing your claim.[27] Or in my former hometown of Chicago, one may shovel away the snow in a parking place on the street, but in order to establish a claim to it one must put a chair or some other object in the cleared space.

Why, then, is it so important that property owners make and keep their communications clear? Economists have an answer: clear titles facilitate trade and minimize resource-wasting conflict. If I am careless about who comes on to a corner of my property, I effectively permit others to make mistakes and to waste their labor on improvements to what I have allowed them to think is theirs. I thus invite a free-for-all on my ambiguously held claims, and I encourage contention, insecurity, and litigation—all of which waste everyone's time and energy and may result in underuse or overuse of resources. But if I keep my property claims clear, others will know that they should deal with me directly if they want to use my property. We can bargain rather than fight; and through trade, all items will come to rest in the hands of those who value them most. If property lines are clear, then, anyone who can make better use of my property than I can will buy or rent it from me and turn the property to his better use. In short, we will all be richer when property claims are unequivocal, because that unequivocal status enables property to be traded and used in its highest value.[28]

Thus, it turns out that the common law of first possession, in rewarding the one who communicates a claim, *does* reward useful labor: the useful labor is the very act of speaking clearly and distinctly about one's claims to property. Naturally, this must be in a language that is understood, and the acts of "possession" that communicate a claim will vary according to the audience. Thus, to go back to *Pierson v. Post,* the dissenting Judge Livingston may well have thought that the fox hunters are the only relevant audience for a claim to a fox; they are the only ones who have regular contact with the subject matter. By the same token, the mid-nineteenth-century California courts gave much deference to the mining camp customs in recognizing various gold rush claims; the forty-niners themselves, as the persons most closely involved with the subject matter, could best communicate and interpret the signs of property claims and would be particularly well served by a stable system of symbols that enabled them to fend off disputes.[29]

The point, then, is that "acts of possession" are, in the now fashionable term, a "text"; and the common law rewards the author of that text. But as students of hermeneutics know, the clearest text may have ambiguous subtexts.[30] In connection with the text of first possession, there are several subtexts that are especially worthy of note. One such subtext is the tacit implication that the text will be "read" by the relevant audience at the appropriate time. But it is not always easy to establish a symbolic structure in which the text of first possession can be "published" at such a time as to be useful to anyone. Once again, *Pierson v. Post* illustrates the problem that occurs when a clear sign (killing the fox) comes only relatively late in the game, after the relevant parties may have already expended overlapping efforts and embroiled themselves in a dispute. Similar problems occurred from time to time in the whaling industry in the nineteenth century. The courts expended some effort to locate signs of "possession" that were comprehensible to whalers from their own customs, and that—like the whalers' own usual signals—came at a point in the chase that allowed the parties to avoid wasted efforts and the ensuing mutual recriminations.[31]

Some objects of property claims indeed seem to resist clear demarcation altogether—ideas, for example.[32] To establish property rights in such disembodied items, we may be reduced to translating the property claims into sets of secondary symbols that are cognizable in our culture. In patent and copyright systems, for example, one establishes an entitlement to an idea's expression by translating the idea into a written document and going through a registration process—though from the unending litigation over ownership of these expressions and over which notions can or cannot be subject to patent or copyright, we might conclude that these secondary symbolic systems do not always yield universally understood "markings."[33] We also make up secondary symbols for physical objects that would seem to be much easier to mark out than ideas; even a property claim to land, that most massively physical of things, is now at its weightiest in the form of written records.

It is expensive to make up these elaborate structures of secondary symbols, as indeed it may be expensive even to establish a structure derived from direct sensory symbols of possession. The economists once again have performed a useful service in pointing out the costs entailed in establishing *any* property system.[34] Indeed, we may not even establish such systems at all, unless our need for secure investment and trade is greater than the costs of creating the necessary symbols of possession.

There is a second and perhaps even more important subtext to the "text" of first possession: the tacit supposition that there is such a thing as a "clear act" unequivocally proclaiming to the world at large that one is appropriating this or that—that is, the supposition that there are in fact unequivocal acts of possession that any relevant audience will naturally and easily interpret as property claims. Literary theorists of late have written a great deal about the instability of texts. They have written too much for us to accept uncritically the idea that a "text" about property has a natural meaning, independent of some group constituting an "interpretative community," or independent of a range of other "texts" and cultural artifacts that together form a symbolic system, within which a given text may make sense.[35] It is not enough, then, for the property claimant to say simply, "It's mine," through some act or gesture; in order for the statement to have any force, some relevant world must understand the claim it makes and take that claim seriously.

Thus in defining the acts of possession that make up a claim to property, the law not only rewards the author of the "text"; it also puts an imprimatur on a particular symbolic system and on the audience that uses this system. Thus for *Pierson*'s dissenting judge, who would have made the definition of first possession depend on a decision of hunters, the rule of first possession would have put the force of law behind the mores of a particular subgroup. The majority's clear-act rule undoubtedly referred to a wider audience and a more widely shared set of symbols. But even on the majority's rule, the definition of first possession depended on a particular audience and its chosen symbolic context. Some audiences win, others lose.

In the history of American territorial expansion, a pointed example of the common law's choice among audiences occurred in an instance in which one group did not play the approved language game and refused to get into the business of publishing or reading the accepted texts about property. The result was one of the most arresting decisions of the early republic: *Johnson v. M'Intosh*,[36] a John Marshall opinion concerning the validity of opposing claims to land in what is now a large area of Illinois and Indiana. The plaintiffs in this case claimed through Indian tribes, on the basis of deeds made out in the 1770s; the defendants claimed under titles that came from the United States. The Court found for the defendants, holding that the claims through the Indians were invalid for reasons derived largely from international law rather than the law of first possession. But tucked away in the case was a first possession argument that Marshall passed over. The Indians, according to an argument of the claimants from the United States, could not have passed title to the opposing side's predecessors because "[b]y the law of nature," the Indians themselves had never done acts on the land sufficient to establish property in it. That is to say, the Indians had never really undertaken those acts of possession that gave rise to a property right.[37]

Although Marshall based his decision on other grounds,[38] there was indeed something to the argument from the point of view of the common law of first possession. Insofar as the Indian tribes moved from place to place, they left few traces to indicate that they claimed the land (if indeed they did). From an eighteenth-century political economist's point of view, the results were horrifying. The absence of distinct claims to land merely invited disputes, it was said, which in turn meant a constant disruption and dissipation of energy in warfare. In addition, uncertainty as to claims meant that no one would make any productive use of the land, since there is no incentive to plant when one does not know that one will still have the land and its fruits at harvest time. From this classical economic perspective, the Indians' alleged indifference to well-defined property lines in land was part and parcel of what seemed to be their relatively unproductive use of the earth.[39]

Now it may well be that North American Indian tribes were not so indifferent to marking out landed property as eighteenth-century European commentators supposed.[40] Or it may be that at least some tribes found landed property less important to their security than other forms of property—in migratory animals, for example—and thus felt no need to assert claims of property to land.[41] But however anachronistic the *Johnson* parties' (ultimately mooted) argument may now seem, it is a particularly striking example of the relativity of the "text" of possession to the interpretative community for that text. It is doubtful whether the claims of *any* nomadic population could ever meet the common law requirements for establishing property in land. Thus the audience presupposed by the common law of first possession is an agrarian or a commercial people—a people whose activities with respect to the objects around them require an unequivocal delineation of lasting control so that those objects can be either managed or traded.

Marxists would doubtless see in these common law property doctrines still further proof of the relativity of ideas to economic substructure. The law of first possession—the rule that a clear and visible demarcation of my claim should confer some right—would appear to be just another item in the intellectual baggage of capitalist production.

But perhaps the deepest aspect of the common law text of possession lies in the attitude that this text strikes with respect to the relationship between human beings and nature. At least some Indians professed bewilderment at the concept of owning the land. Indeed they prided themselves on not marking the land but rather on moving lightly through it, living with the land and with its creatures as members of the same family rather than as strangers who visited only to conquer the objects of nature.[42] The doctrine of first possession, quite to the contrary, reflects the attitude that human beings are outsiders to nature. It gives the earth and its creatures over to those who mark them so clearly as to transform them, so that no one else will mistake them for unsubdued nature. The metaphor of the law of first possession is, after all, death and transfiguration; to own a fox the hunter must slay it, so that he or someone else can turn it into a coat.

To be sure, we may admire nature and enjoy wildness.[43] But those sentiments find little resonance in the doctrine of first possession. Its texts are those of cultivation, manufacture, and development. We cannot have our fish both loose and fast, as Herman Melville might put it.[44] The common law of first possession makes a choice. The common law gives preference to those who convince the world that they can catch the fish and hold it fast. This may be a reward to useful labor, but it is more precisely the articulation of a specific vocabulary within a structure of symbols understood by a commercial people. It is this commonly understood and shared set of symbols that gives significance and form to what might seem the quintessentially individualistic act: the claim that one has, by "possession," separated for one's self property from the great commons of unowned things.

Notes

1. Richard Schlatter, *Private Property: The History of an Idea* 151 (1974).

2. John Locke, *Second Treatise of Government,* sec. 25, in *Two Treatises of Government* (P. Laslett rev. ed. 1963; 1st ed. 1690).

3. Locke's cryptic assertion that one owns one's labor appears to rest on the equally cryptic assertion that one owns one's body and thus its exertions. See Locke, supra note 2, secs. 27–28. Richard Epstein argues that for Locke, one owns one's body because one occupies or possesses it, and thus the labor theory rests on first possession; Epstein, "Possession as the Root of Title," 13 *Ga. L. Rev.* 1221, 1227–28 (1979). This, of course, leaves open the questions of why possession establishes ownership and what constitutes possession.

4. Robert Nozick, *Anarchy, State, and Utopia* 175 (1974).

5. See, e.g., Hugo Grotius, *On the Law of War and Peace,* bk. 2, ch. 2, paras. 1, 4–5 (Kelsey trans. 1925; 1st ed. 1646). In the next century, Blackstone noted the conflict between consent and labor theorists with the remark, "A dispute that savours too much of nice and scholastic refinement!" 2 William Blackstone, *Commentaries on the Laws of England* 8 (1979; reproduction of 1766 ed.).

6. Locke, supra note 2, sec. 28, at 330 noticed the problem too, commenting, "If such a consent [of all mankind] was necessary, Man had starved, notwithstanding the Plenty God had given him." Robert Filmer, against whose work Locke directed

his *Treatises,* had also noticed the difficulty. See the edition of Filmer's *Patriarcha* in John Locke, *Two Treatises on Civil Government* 249–308 (T. Cook ed. 1947).

7. 2 Blackstone, supra note 5, at 8.

8. See, e.g., Treasure Salvors, Inc. v. Unidentified Wrecked & Abandoned Sailing Vessel, 569 F.2d 330 (5th cir. 1978).

9. For the "global commons," including the high seas, the polar regions, and outer space, see Alexandra M. Post, *Deepsea Mining and the Law of the Sea* ch. 6 (1983).

10. For oil, see Jones v. Forest Oil C., 44 A. 1074 (Pa. 1899); for gas, Westmoreland & Cambria Natural Gas C. v. DeWill, 18 A. 724, 725 (Pa. 1889); for groundwater, Adams v. Grigsby, 152 So.2d 619, 624 (La. App.), cert. refused 153 So.2d 880 (La. 1963); for the radio spectrum, see Frank S. Rowley, "Problems in the Law of Radio Communication," 1 *U. Cin. L. Rev.* 1, 27–31 (1927), disputing what was apparently a current analogy to wild animals.

11. For a somewhat different approach, see Epstein, supra note 3, at 1225.

12. 3 Cai. R. 175 (N.Y. Sup. Ct. 1805).

13. Id. at 178.

14. Id. at 189–81.

15. 2 Blackstone, supra note 5, at 9, 258.

16. 39 Cal. 24 (1870).

17. Id. at 30, 41–42, 51.

18. 7 Richard Powell, *The Law of Real Property* par. 1012 (P. Rohan rev. ed. 1984).

19. Id. par. 1025; Henry W. Ballantine, "Title by Adverse Possession," 32 *Harvard L. Rev.* 135, 141 (1918).

20. See Halsey v. Humble Oil & Refining Co., 66 S.W.2d 1082, 1087 (Tex. Civ. App. 1933) (yes); cf. McShan v. Pitts, 554 S.W.2d 759, 763–64 (Tex. Civ. App. 1977) (no, when the grazing was merely "casual").

21. Cutting grass was enough in Ramapo Mfg. Co. v. Mapes, 110 N.E. 772, 776 (N.Y. 1915).

22. See Marengo Cave v. Ross, 10 N.E.2d 917 (Ind. 1937) (no, because occupancy was not open and notorious).

23. Slatin's Properties, Inc. v. Hassler, 291 N.E.2d 641, 643 (Ill. 1972), quoting Chicago Title & Trust Co. v. Drobnick, 20 169 N.E.2d 792, 796 (Ill. 1960).

24. Slatin's Properties, Inc. v. Hassler, 291 N.E.2d 641, 644 Ill. (1972); see also Limitations Act sec. 7, *Ill. Rev. Stat.* ch. 110, secs. 13–110 (1983). Some western states disallow adverse possession *unless* taxes are paid, which may have aimed at protecting the railroads' huge landholdings. See Comment, "Payment of Taxes as a Condition of Title by Adverse Possession: A Nineteenth Century Anachronism," 9 *Santa Clara L. Rev.* 244 (1969).

25. Interestingly enough, if the owners are children or mental incompetents or are otherwise incapable of receiving or acting upon such "communications" of others' claims, adverse possession does not run against them. See, e.g., *N.J. Rev. Stat.* sec. 2A:14–32 (1952), including persons out of the country among the immune.

26. For more on recording statutes, see the essay "Crystals and Mud in Property Law" in this volume.

27. See "On the Pressures and Policies of Waiting in Line," *N.Y. Times*, Feb. 11, 1982, at C1, C7, noting that claims are staked by "saving places" and leaving objects; one enterpriser distributes numbered tickets for places in the standing-room line at the opera.

28. Richard A. Posner, *Economic Analysis of Law* 30–33 (3d ed. 1986). For a critique of this line of analysis, see Duncan Kennedy and Frank Michelman, "Are Property and Contract Efficient?" 6 *Hofstra L. Rev.* 771 (1980); Frank Michelman, "Ethics, Economics and the Law of Property," 24 *Nomos* 3 (1982).

29. Charles McCurdy, "Stephen J. Field and Public Land Law Development in California, 1850–1866: A Case Study of Judicial Resource Allocation in Nineteenth Century America," 10 *Law & Soc'y Rev.* 235, 239–41 (1976); see also John Umbeck, "A Theory of Contract Choice and the California Gold Rush," 20 *J. L. & Econ.* 421 (1977).

30. See, e.g., Stanley Fish, *Is There a Text in This Class?* 29 (1980).

31. See, e.g., Swift v. Gifford, 23 Fed. Cas. 558 (D. Mass. 1872); Aberdeen Arctic Co. v. Sutter, 149 Rev. Rep. 358 (H.L. 1862) (Scot.); Hogarth v. Jackson, 172 Eng. Rep. 271 (K.B. 1827); Fennings v. Grenville, 127 Eng. Rep. 825 (C.P. 1808). See also Robert Ellickson, *Order Without Law: How Neighbors Settle Disputes* 191–93, 196–204 (1990), stressing the efficacy of whalers' norms and the merely secondary role of law.

32. See, e.g., Millar v. Taylor, 98 Eng. Rep. 201, 230–31 (K.B. 1769) (Yeates, J., dissenting, saying that mere ideas, being incorporeal, cannot be subject to possession or ownership).

33. For a classic case, see Arnstein v. Porter, 154 F.2d 464 (2d cir. 1946) (plaintiff entitled to trial on charge that Cole Porter's "Begin the Beguine" infringed copyright on plaintiff's tunes "The Lord Is My Shepherd" and "A Mother's Prayer"). For a newer version of these problems, see Apple Computer, Inc. v. Franklin Computer Corp. 714 F.2d 1240 (3rd cir. 1983), cert. dismissed, 104 S.Ct. 690 (1984) (computer operating system software may be copyrighted).

34. For an extensive study, see Gary D. Libecap, *Contracting for Property Rights* (1989); see also Carol M. Rose, "Rethinking Environmental Controls: Management Strategies for Common Resources," 1991 *Duke L. J.* 1, 8–24.

35. See Terry Eagleton, *Literary Theory* 74–88, 127–50 (1983); Fish, supra note 30, at 239–44; Christopher Norris, *Deconstruction: Theory and Practice* 24–32 (1982).

36. 21 U.S. (8 Wheat.) 543 (1823).

37. Id. at 569–70. For a discussion of the background arguments over Indian land claims, see Robert A. Williams, Jr., *The American Indian in Western Legal Thought: The Discourses of Conquest* 271–75, 288–89, 308–317 (1990).

38. *Johnson*, 21 U.S. (8 Wheat.) at 588 (1823) ("We will not enter into the controversy, whether agriculturalists, merchants, and manufacturers, have a right, on abstract principles, to expel hunters from the territory they possess. ... Conquest gives a title which the courts of the Conqueror cannot deny.").

39. See Jeremy Bentham, *Principles of the Civil Code*, in *Theory of Legislation*, at 118 (1987; reprint of C. K. Ogden ed. 1931); Locke, supra note 2, sec. 37, at 335–36. Both compared what they saw as the Indians' wild and unproductive land to the productive lands of settled property owners.

40. At the time of English settlement a number of eastern tribes farmed and lived in villages, practices that elicited a limited English recognition of property rights. See R. C. Simmons, *The American Colonies from Settlement to Independence* 156 (1976); William Cronon, *Changes in the Land: Indians, Colonists, and the Ecology of New England* 53, 56–57 (1983). For a survey of historic North American native land and resource claims, see Linda Parker, *Native American Estate: The Struggle over Indian and Hawaiian Lands* (1989).

41. One example came in the discussions of the Alaska Native Claims Settlement Act of 1971, 43 U.S.C. secs. 1601–1624, where some native groups objected to land settlements because they feared that this might preclude their following migratory herds. See Michael Parfit, "Alaska's Natives Are Bringing Off the Biggest Corporate Takeover," *Smithsonian Mag.*, Aug. 1981, at 30. Note that settled land ownership, from this perspective, appeared to cause *insecurity.*

42. See, e.g., a letter from an elderly Indian chief to President Franklin Pierce in 1855, described in Charles Haar and Lance Liebman, *Property and Law* 15 (1977). However, Indians did do a good deal to transform the landscape, notably through fires. See Stephen J. Pyne, *Fire in America: A Cultural History of Wildland and Rural Fire* 71–83 (1982).

43. For the history of this attitude, see Roderick Nash, *Wilderness and the American Mind* (1973).

44. Herman Melville, *Moby-Dick* ch. 89 ("Fast-Fish and Loose-Fish"), describing a legal conflict between whalers about the distinction between a whale marked as owned, or "fast-fish," and one that had escaped and become once again an unowned "loose-fish"; Melville went on to a figurative comparison of fast-fish (including serfs and mortgages) and loose-fish (including ideas and pre-discovery America).

2

Property as Storytelling: Perspectives from Game Theory, Narrative Theory, Feminist Theory

Introduction

In the preceding essay I presented the claim of ownership as a kind of assertion or story, told within a culture that shapes the story's content and meaning. That is, the would-be "possessor" has to send a message that others in the culture understand and that they find persuasive as grounds for the claim asserted.

In the present essay I take up another kind of property story—indeed an even bigger story. The stories in this essay are not just about a particular piece of property in the sense of claims to this thing or that. The stories that follow are instead about the very institution of property.

In a way, these big-picture property stories seem quite surprising and peculiar because they have often been told by theorists who usually eschew the storytelling form as a means of conveying knowledge. Several of these theorists are the same seventeenth- and eighteenth-century thinkers who have been so influential in our modern conceptions not just of property but also of economics and politics generally—thinkers who, like Thomas Hobbes, hoped to ground the study of "political economy" on a firmly scientific basis. As Hobbes put it, political knowledge "consisteth in certain rules, as doth Arithmetique and Geometry; not (as Tennis-play) on Practice onely."[1]

Given the analogy to "Arithmetique and Geometry," one might surmise that such theorists would wish to account for the institution of prop-

The original version of this essay appeared in 2 *Yale Journal of Law and the Humanities*, 37–57 (1990). Reprinted by permission of *Yale Journal of Law and the Humanities*.

erty in a purely analytic way as well. That is to say, one might expect an explanatory mode that the linguistic scholars describe as "synchronic" (as opposed to "diachronic"). A synchronic account would treat its subject as if all the parts occur at once, in an interlocking whole whose various aspects can be logically inferred and empirically verified, without reference to time-related, "diachronic" matters that unfold and transform over the course of the chronology.[2] To be sure, in a synchronic account one might indeed perceive that things change as time passes, but if one has a proper grip on the overall analytic framework, one sees that changes occur according to set patterns, so that future states are predictable from past states. The synchronic account would be, more or less, the systematic and scientific explanatory mode: all changes in a given system are predictable from a proper analysis of the system itself.

But however much the early modern theorists hoped to ground political economy as a science, a reader cannot help but notice that their discussions of property at some point take a striking turn toward a narrative or diachronic explanatory mode, where—as in Hobbes' dismissive example of "Tennis-play"—time and cumulative experience play essential roles.[3] Such accounts treat property regimes as if they had origins and as if their subsequent elements emerged over time. Locke is undoubtedly the most influential of the classic property theorists,[4] and whatever the demands of scientific explanation, Locke used a narrative account in his famous discussion of property in the *Second Treatise of Government.* Although the parts are somewhat scattered, the *Treatise* clearly unfolds a story line, beginning in a plenteous state of nature, carrying through the growing individual appropriation of goods, then proceeding to the development of a trading money economy, and culminating in the creation of government to safeguard property.[5] Indeed Locke's choice of a narrative mode is all the more striking because he appears to have been quite indifferent to the factual accuracy of the story as a genuine history.[6]

Almost a century later, William Blackstone launched into a quite similar pseudohistory in explaining property as an institution with an origin and evolution: he, too, described human beings as beginning in a state of plenty, gradually accumulating personal and landed property, and finally creating government and laws to protect property.[7] And in more recent days, the modern economist Harold Demsetz has chosen to illustrate his theory of property rights by reference to a narrative history of an evolving property regime among fur-hunting Indians on the American continent.[8]

Why have these theorists turned to storytelling to discuss property? Why have they choosen a narrative explanatory mode, which often diverges from science and prediction and instead envisions events as unfolding in ways that are, arguably, understandable only after the fact? That is the subject of this essay, or at least it is one of the subjects. The larger subject-behind-the-subject is of course the relation of property to storytelling generally: this essay asks why, in our general discussions of who has what and how property gets distributed, we turn to narratives instead of looking exclusively to scientific or predictive analytic approaches. In treating that problem, the following pages borrow especially from game theory, narrative theory, and feminist theory.

The first part of the essay outlines the classical theory of property and in particular identifies the kinds of rational utility-maximizing preference orderings that this classical theory assumes in individuals. The next part of the essay poses some practical difficulties for the classical theory; it sets out a series of thought experiments on preference orderings and identifies some quite familiar preference orderings that deviate from the classical model. These "deviant" preference patterns are most interesting because they are not simply "natural" or "just there" in an assumed human nature of rational utility maximization. Instead, they seem to require some post hoc narrative explanation of how the preference-holders got that way.

The third part of the essay begins to explain why a property regime needs the rhetorical mode of narrative and storytelling, a mode that seeks to account for events only after the fact and that seems to assume a certain freedom among actors that is at least somewhat at odds with a logical predictive account. This part uses game theory to argue that the classic property theory itself has a kind of explanatory glitch: for property regimes to function, some of us have to have other-regarding preference orderings. These are preference orderings that the classical property theory would not predict and can only explain post hoc, through a story.

The last part of the essay offsets game theory with feminist theory and the theory of narrative. Game theory suggests some reasons why the utility-maximizing preference orderings seem more "natural" than others—even though everyone knows that there are lots of non-utility-maximizing preferences out there in the real world. But feminist theory and narrative theory use storytelling to counteract the impulses that we see in game theory. That is, we use storytelling to break the spell of individual maximization, even among those more powerful than we; we tell tales to create a community in which cooperation is possible. Finally, the essay returns to the narrativity of classical property theory and links the storytelling of classical property theory to a kind of moral discourse; it treats narrative as an exhortation to the listener to overcome a game-theoretic, self-interested "nature" and to follow instead the cooperative preference orderings that a property regime requires.

I. Preference Orderings in the Classical Analysis of Property

We often think of property as some version of entitlement to things: I have a right to this thing or that.[9] In a more sophisticated version of property, of course, we see property as a way of defining our relationships with other people.[10] On such versions, my right to this thing or that isn't about controlling the "thing" so much as it is about my relationship with *you*, and with everybody else in the world: if I have a property right to this thing or that, I can keep you from exercising any control over it or having any access to it at all. That was Blackstone's benchmark for property: property was not just a "sole and despotic dominion," but it was a dominion that empowered the holder to the "total exclusion of the right of any other individual in the universe."[11]

In fact, that is the garden-variety economic version of property: as an institution, property revolves around the desire for resources themselves, but it also revolves around the desire to control others' access to those resources, at least when the resources are scarce. On this classical view, the institution of property mediates peoples' conflicting desires about resources, and it does so by allocating exclusive rights. If there were no property rights in the berry patch, all of us would just have to fight all the time for the berries. But instead, a property regime allocates this part of the patch to X and that part to Y; and this (or any other) allocation gives each owner a sense of security, so that she invests in cultivating and tending the plants—which she won't do if she thinks she is going to wind up having to share the berries later with a lot of interloping loafers.[12] Besides that, exclusive property rights identify who has what, making trades possible among owners. As a result, everything gets more valuable. Why? Because the property regime encourages us to work on the resources we have and then to trade the results of our work, instead of wasting time and effort in bickering and fighting.

That is a very standard version of the virtues of property, and when we break it down, we find several critical points. The first point is that desire—that is, a desire for resources—is at the center of the whole institution of property. The second point is that in order to satisfy our desire for resources, we need the capacity to shut out others from those resources, at least when the resources we want become scarce. And the third point, of course, is that by allocating exclusive control of resources to individuals, a property regime winds up by satisfying even more desires, because it mediates conflicts between individuals and encourages everyone to work and trade instead of fighting, thus making possible an even greater satisfaction of desires.

There is another element hidden in this analysis, though: it is the idea that we already know, at least roughly, how people are going to order their desires or, more technically, their *preferences* about themselves and others and about their respective access to desired resources.

What is that understood ordering? Well, it comes to us, again like many of our interesting ideas in this area, from the seventeenth century, and most particularly from Hobbes first and later Locke. Hobbes' major point about human preferences is that individuals want to *live.*[13] Our desire to stay alive is just *there,* omnipresent and undeniable; it needs no further explanation. When push comes to shove, Hobbes thought, we will prefer our own lives over other people's,[14] and by and large, we will also prefer our lives over high-falutin' causes, however noble. That is why in battle, for example, as Hobbes so succinctly put it, "There is on one side, or both, a running away."[15] Locke's major addendum to this picture was to show the relevance of property to the desire to live. He pointed out that life depends on property in a very primitive sense; if one cannot literally *appropriate* those berries and fruits, one will simply die.[16]

And so acquisitiveness, the desire to have property, is "just there" too, also universal and omnipresent. Thus one can always predict a human desire to have things for one's self or, as some say more recently, the human propensity to be a self-interested, rational utility maximizer.[17] This propensity is just a kind of fact of life, and the eighteenth-century political economists took it for granted, rejecting as unrealistic the earlier condemnations of acquisitiveness. They attempted instead to carry forward the new science of political economy on the firm ground of irreducible self-interest, and indeed they toned down the language of "avarice" into that of the more benign "interest."[18]

Indeed, if we do take these preferences for life and acquisition as givens, then economics can make a bid to be a kind of logical science for politics and law. With these preferences understood, we can sensibly talk about how the law gives people incentives to do this thing and that, and we can manipulate future welfare by institutionalizing the proper ex ante approaches.[19] Shifts of entitlements become predictable too, because we know how people order their preferences; with that knowlege, we can predict their responses and moves under different states of affairs.

That is what modern neoclassical economists do, more or less taking these utility-maximizing preference orderings for granted and using them to perform some very powerful and sophisticated predictions of property-related behavior under varying circumstances. For example, they make predictions about the production or consumption shifts that follow from changes in costs, and they may predict something like a lowered provision of rental housing in the wake of added landlord repair costs.[20] Underlying such predictions is an idea that people prefer more for themselves rather than less, and that this preference ordering is an irreducible fact that needs no further explanation—it is just there.[21]

Note, however, that if we do *not* have that starting point of a predictable set of preferences for "more" rather than "less," then the ways that people trade and otherwise shift their entitlements will be a little weird and unpredictable. That means that in talking about property, and about the ways people deal with it, at least sometimes we may have to turn to post hoc explanatory approaches to supplement our logical predictions. That is, we may only be able to understand property arrangements through narrative discourses like literature and history, discourses that construct a story of how things got to be that way—a story in which there were genuine choices along the way and in which things were not really predictable in advance and did not have to wind up the way they did.[22]

That brings me to the next part of this essay.

II. The Humdrum and the Weird; or, Predictable and Unpredictable Preferences

This part of the essay questions the idea that any given preference orderings are "just there," as they seem to be in the standard classical and neoclassical economic view. It suggests instead that even if one is quite sympathetic to the classical view of self-interest, there are a lot of leftover preference orderings that would not be predicted and that have to be explained in some way through an after-the-fact story. This section makes that point through a series of thought experiments on the ways that people order their preferences about their own and other people's access to resources.

These thought experiments present scenarios about preference orderings in a situation where there are two people (you and I) and some Resource X that both of us desire. The scenarios presume five possible outcomes, to wit:

- I get a lot of X, and so do you
- I get pretty much X (where "pretty much" is something over one-half of "a lot"), and so do you
- I get a little X, and so do you
- I get a lot of X, and you get nothing
- I get nothing, and you get a lot of X

Obviously, these outcomes would not be exhaustive in the real world, but they are enough to work with for now. In each of the following scenarios, "I" order my preferences among these possible outcomes, beginning with the outcome that I desire most and moving downward to the outcome that I desire least. Again, there is some mathematically large number of ways that people might line up these outcomes, but I have chosen six that are probably familiar to most readers and have given them names so that they can be identified more easily. Here they are:

Number 1: John Doe (JD). This perfectly ordinary person has the following ordering of preferences:

Choice 1: I get a lot, you get a lot
2: I get a lot, you get zip
3: I get pretty much, you get pretty much
4: I get a little, you get a little
5: I get zip, you get a lot

JD seems to be quite compatible with classical property thinking. His order of preferences is based on a kind of self-interest that is "just there." He is not mean and is happy to have you get a lot of X where there is plenty to be had, but not if your share cuts into his. And in general, he basically just prefers getting more over getting less, no matter what you get.[23]

Number 2: King of the Mountain (KOM). A somewhat more competitive type orders his preferences as follows:

Choice 1: I get a lot, you get zip
2: I get a lot, you get a lot
3: I get pretty much, you get pretty much
4: I get a little, you get a little
5: I get zip, you get a lot

KOM is getting a bit slippery, from the point of view of the standard predicted preferences. He reverses John Doe's first and second preferences: he doesn't prefer the situation of maximum combined utility (both get a lot), but rather prefers the situation where he is the only winner. Still, economic prediction might be able to accommodate KOM; after all, KOM is just like JD insofar as he maximizes his own take and his choices always put getting *more* over getting *less*. He just competes a bit more with the other guy. A little later, I will argue that with respect to property, JD and KOM are pretty much identical.

Number 3: Malice Aforethought (MA). This is a nastier character:

Choice 1: I get a lot, you get zip
2: I get a little, you get a little
3: I get pretty much, you get pretty much
4: I get a lot, you get a lot
5: I get zip, you get a lot

MA is *very* slippery. MA would rather lose a great deal than have the other guy win; his preference ordering is based on keeping the other guy down.

He is not looking very self-interested any more, at least in the usual sense. The reason is that he is "distracted" by interpersonal matters.

Number 4: Mom (or Good Citizen). Mom is a more comfortable figure, and orders her preferences this way:

Choice 1: I get a lot, you get a lot
2: I get pretty much, you get pretty much
3: I get zip, you get a lot
4: I get a lot, you get zip (?)
5: I get a little, you get a little (?)

Interestingly enough, Mom too is out of line for a prediction based on self-interest. Her first choice is like JD's (both get a lot), but after that she prefers that both get a reasonably good deal, and thereafter she puts the other person first. Why would a self-interested utility maximizer do that? She wouldn't. Again, Mom seems to be distracted by interpersonal matters. But note, Mom's orderings choose highest *joint* utility first, the next highest next, and so forth. As for the question marks by 4 and 5: if Mom gets a lot, maybe she can give you some; if she can't do that, she might prefer 5 to 4.

Number 5: Portnoy's Mom (PM). She will be the first to tell you that her order of preference is:

Choice 1: I get zip, you get a lot
2: I get a lot, you get a lot
3: I get pretty much, you get pretty much
4: I get a little, you get a little
5: I get a lot, you get zip

PM is even more out of line with a predicted preference ordering of self-interested maximization. She would rather have the other person come in first—but she's not completely crazy, either, since her second choice is to do well herself, as long as other guy does too.

Number 6: Hit Me. This is a kind of natural victim:

Choice 1: I get zip, you get a lot
2: I get a little, you get a little
3: I get pretty much, you get pretty much
4: I get a lot, you get a lot
5: I get a lot, you get zip

This character is out of the economic predictor's ballpark. She is a mirror image of Malice Aforethought: She wants to lose; she wants to be beaten, preferably by somebody else.

So, those are the preference orderings. I want to pause here a moment to reply to some objections. The first objection is that pleasure (or pain) about others' gains (or losses) are a part of a person's preference orderings; for example, if I care about you, I always get a "lot" when you do. Now, this may be so, but it trivializes the whole idea of ordering preferences: getting a lot would always come first, by definition.[24] So, to preserve the meaning of ordering preferences about one's own "take" in these two-party situations, I am using preference about one's self in a narrower (and I think more ordinary) sense of what one gets of Resource X.

The second and somewhat related objection is that a utilitarian/economic position is agnostic about preference orderings; economists can construct a demand schedule for any ordering of preferences. Perhaps that is true, but if so, it means that economics loses its claim to predictive power; e.g., in a world of Hit Me's, we would see a *higher* demand for goods as costs rise, offsetting the self-interest of John Doe.[25] An economist might be able to set the demand schedule *if he knows* the relative numbers of Hit Me's, JDs, etc., but that knowledge would have to come from some other source.

Now I want to return to the main argument. Which of our preference orderings can be predicted on the classical assumptions of self-interested maximization? John Doe certainly can be, and King of the Mountain too, if we assume that self-interest simply means indifference about others. Both are maximizing their own "take," and both consistently choose more over less; preference orderings like that are assumed to be "just there," without any need for further explanation.

But how about the others? However odd they are and however small their numbers, characters with the offbeat and unpredicted preference orderings of Numbers 3 to 6 do indeed seem to be around too, at least in most people's repertoire of experience. How do we know that? Well, for one thing, these characters show up constantly in actual narratives, both historical and fictional. In Shakespeare's Iago or Gibbon's Commodus, to take just two illustrious examples, we see full-blown examples of Malice Aforethought in all his vengeance and spite; more recently, we have been seeing computer hackers who implant viruses for no apparent reasons other than pride and meanness. Mom and the Good Citizen might be less dramatic, but they too are all over the place in heroic novels and tales; indeed, according to feminist literature, the cooperative, helpful character is really quite common.[26] Phillip Roth of course told the story of Portnoy's Mom[27] in a way that is readily recognizable by a substantial segment of the population, and feminist literature has a good deal to say about Hit Me and about victimization generally.[28]

Those other characters certainly make themselves felt in the law as well. Here as in literature and history, some of the most interesting examples revolve about the Malice Aforethought character. In property law there is a whole category of cases about people who build the so-called spite fence; their story revolves about some character who goes to very considerable expense to wall in a neighbor's windows or put up some repulsive object to ruin the neighbor's view of the sunset.[29] An example from a few years ago involved a disappointed Vermont landowner whose neighbors blocked his efforts to rezone his lot for motel use; he decided to use the property for a piggery instead.[30] One needs to know the story, the narrative, to figure out how such people got that way.

Much sadder are the cases of Hit Me's, the victims. The criminal law is now seeing persons who give away all they have, even their lives, and appear consistently to defer to some others in what seems to be a kind of pathology of other-regarding behavior. Perhaps such persons are not very common and perhaps their motives are exceedingly complex, but their plight does seem to attract an extraordinary level of popular fascination and perhaps self-comparison.[31]

The Good Citizen or Mom is another category that shows up constantly in law, and, generally speaking, the law tries to encourage her cooperative behavior. The law allows people to set up all kinds of cooperative arrangements; people can form contracts and partnerships, hold joint bank accounts, and own property in various forms of common tenure.[32] The law also polices cooperative arrangements and disfavors those in which one person seems to take advantage of another, even though the advantage-taking may fall within the formal terms of a given agreement.[33] Moreover, while the law does not generally require that anyone assist another who is in trouble, it does recognize that some people will volunteer anyway and protects those Good Samaritans. Thus if John Doe's carelessness causes an accident, and Mom stops to assist the victim, tort law may make John Doe responsible for Mom as well as the original victim, on the theory that he should have realized that she would try to help.[34]

The point of all this is that legal doctrines reflect the knowledge that these other preference orderings exist; certainly there is no monolithic legal expectation that everyone will behave as an individual self-interested utility maximizer. The further point is that all these offbeat preference orderings suggest an element of indeterminacy in the ways that people use property, trade it, transfer it. There is no single ordering of preferences in the real world, and everyone knows it. Even supposing that most people are indeed like John Doe, the rest throw in a kind of chaos factor that may have odd effects in the world of property-holding.

What does that mean? It means that even if we think the classical property view is generally true, we are going to have to make some allowances for oddities in the way people actually do order their preferences. And that in turn means that the way we fix and trade entitlements is not going to be perfectly predictable, from a set of maximizing preferences that are "just there." At least some of the time, in order to figure out how entitlements have shifted and settled as they have, we are going to have to have to explain things after the fact, post hoc—that is, we are going to have to tell a story.

III. Narrativity and the Property Regime

I want to go now to the point where the weakness of a single ordering of preferences is most telling. That point has to do with the very regime of property itself. But to get to that point, I have to begin with an explanation of a particular kind of property, that is, common property.

Common property is a kind of property system that often emerges when it is impractical or expensive to have individualized property in a given resource. For example, it might be awfully expensive to establish and police individual rights to the fish in a large lake. At the same time, though, the stock of fish is a finite resource, and it might be important to restrain the total "take" of this resource, so that the fishery doesn't get overused or ruined and so that the fish can regenerate. What our fishermen have to do, then, is to agree on some way that they can limit the times they fish or the numbers they take or the way they restock the lake—or do something else to protect the fish against decimation.[35]

Note that our fishermen now cannot follow the preference choice "I get a lot, you get a lot," and just let all the fishermen take all the fish they want. That is the choice of plenty, and these fish are not infinitely plentiful; they are a limited resource. But the fishery resource is not easily divided up among the fishermen either; it would be most productively conserved and used if all the parties were simply to exercise some forbearance. And so they could be faced with what is conventionally called the prisoners' dilemma: all parties have to give up something for the sake of a higher long-term collective total, but it is not at all clear that they will do so, especially since each has some individual motive to cheat on any cooperative arrangement.[36]

Now, this common-property problem creates a modification of the way we can picture the preference choices that were available to our earlier cast of characters. If we rule out the choice of plenty (i.e., "I get a lot, you get a lot"), the remaining options fall into the familiar prisoners' dilemma square shown in the accompanying diagram.

	You cooperate	*You cheat*
I cooperate	(A) I get pretty much, you get pretty much	(B) I get zip, you get lots
I cheat	(C) I get lots, you get zip	(D) I get little, you get little

The best choice from the point of view of joint utility maximization is of course Box (A), where each fisherman cooperates and curtails some of his fishing for the sake of preserving the resource indefinitely for the whole group. That choice would mean that everyone would get pretty much over the long run, and the total fish taken would be maximized because the underlying resource would be able to renew itself. But for each fisherman, the *individual's* maximizing choice would be Box (C), in which he cheats while the others cooperate; thus he would prefer that all the others follow the rules and cooperate to curtail overfishing, while he "defects," or cheats, and takes all he can. But if each fisherman chooses this strategy of cheating, the whole system is driven toward Box (D), where all parties cheat, and the joint product winds up at a relatively puny level because the fish are too depleted to regenerate. Thus the "cheating" choice can turn a renewable resource—a "positive-sum" resource where there are gains from cooperation—into an wasting asset, a "zero-sum" resource in which all individual gains are at the expense of others, and in which the resource eventually depletes, to the ultimate detriment of all the players.

Now let us review the choices of our cast of characters. How would each character choose, if we rule out the option of plenty ("I get a lot, you get a lot")? And most important, would any of these characters be able to sustain a cooperative arrangement and chose the optimal Box (A), where everyone acts to get "pretty much" but not the individual maximum?

First and most important, John Doe and King of the Mountain would not choose this cooperative Box (A). Where the option of plenty is gone, these two characters would have identical preference orderings. In a situation of finite or scarce resources, when we have to strike out the preference for everyone getting a lot, we see for both JD and KOM the following ordering:

#1 (C) I get lots, you get zip
#2 (A) I get pretty much, you get pretty much
#3 (D) I get a little, you get a little
#4 (B) I get zip, you get lots

When resources are limited, the cooperative management of common property is a second choice for both John Doe and King of the Mountain. Instead, in this situation of scarcity, they both have the same first choice: to take "the mostest fustest." Hence the standard political economists' prediction, which is based on these characters, is what is often called the tragedy of the commons: unless restrained by some outside compulsion, each tries to get the most for himself, and in the ensuing race, a resource that could be renewable is driven instead toward ruination.[37]

Malice Aforethought wouldn't put Box (A) first either. Striking the option of plenty makes no difference to his first choice, which is (C), "I get lots, you get zip." In this he is like John Doe and KOM, even though his next choices would diverge from theirs. Mrs. Portnoy wouldn't choose box (A) either: her first choice remains (B) ("I get zip, you get lots"), which of course just encourages Malice Aforethought. And Hit Me is like Portnoy's Mom in putting choice (B) first.

The heroine of the piece, then, is Mom (or the Good Citizen), who does not put her own well-being above yours but is not a fool about needless self-sacrifice either. After the ruled-out choice of plenty ("I get a lot, you get a lot"), her next—and now first—choice is the cooperative choice (A) ("I get pretty much, you get pretty much"). This is the most productive choice in a world where scarce resources have to be managed cooperatively; it is the choice that forbears to take the largest individual portion and instead maximizes the joint product.

Now, here is the kicker. The larger implication of all this is that a property *regime* generally, taken as an entire system, has the same structure as a common property.[38] This is most notable at the formative stage. At the outset of private property, people have to cooperate to set up the system—they have to get themselves organized, go to the meetings, discuss the options, figure out who gets what and how the entitlements will be protected.[39] Even if the property regime is just a matter of customary practices that develop over time, the participants have to cooperate to the extent of recognizing and abiding by the indicia of ownership that their customs set out.[40] And indeed, even after a property regime is in place, people have to respect each other's individual entitlements out of cooperative impulses, because it is impossible to have a continuous system of policing and/or retaliation for cheating. Thus a property system depends on people not stealing, cheating, and so forth, even when they have the chance. That is to say, all the participants, or at least a substantial number of them, have to cooperate to make a property regime work.[41]

A property regime, in short, presupposes a kind of character who is *not* predicted in the standard story about property. And that, I suggest, is why the classic theories of property turned to narrative at crucial moments, particularly in explaining the origin of property regimes, where the need for cooperation is most obvious. Their narrative stories allowed them to slide smoothly over the cooperative gap in their systematic analyses of self-interest.

One can see the point in the various parts of Locke's story about property. He starts off with a tale of people in a state of nature, acquiring natural products like acorns and apples through the very labor of gathering them; then realizing that wealth could be stored through the collection of durables (like nuts and little pieces of gold); and finally, growing nervous at the "very unsafe, very unsecure" enjoyment of property in the state of nature and joining with others to establish the civil society that will protect everyone's hard-earned property.[42]

Hold it right there: joining with others? Just how did they form that civil society and its government anyway? Who put in the time and effort of schmoozing and getting the special committees together and hammering out the terms? Why didn't they all just loaf around, as John Doe would, choosing Box (C) in the hopes that other people would do all the organizing work? And if they did let George do it, who is this George character anyway? If there is a George, he looks an awful lot like Mom or the Good Citizen—somebody who would be willing to do some work for the sake of the common good.

Blackstone's story is a more connected narrative, but it slides over the point even more easily. After a long tale about the way in which people started to hold onto increasing numbers of objects for themselves, as they became more talented and numerous, he points out that the "earth would not produce her fruits in sufficient quantities, without the assistance of tillage: but who would be at the pains of tilling it, if another might watch an opportunity to seize upon and enjoy the product of his industry, art and labour?"[43] Here is the very next sentence: "Necessity begat property, and in order to insure that property, recourse was had to civil society." And that's it.

Now wait a minute: if nobody would be at pains of tilling unless they could capture the rewards, why should they be at pains of setting up a civil society? Why don't Blackstone's characters sit around waiting for George too?

In short, there is a gap between the kind of self-interested individual who needs exclusive property to induce him to labor and the kind of individual who has to be there to create, maintain, and protect a property regime. The existence of a property regime is not in the least predictable from a starting point of rational self-interest; and consequently, from that perspective, property needs a tale, a story, a post hoc explanation.

That, I think, is one reason Locke and Blackstone and their modern-day successors are so fond of telling stories when they talk about the origin of property. It is the story that fills the gap in the classical theory, and that, as Hayden White might put it, makes property "plausible."[44] Narrative gives us a smooth tale of property as an institution that could come about through time, effort, and above all, cooperative choices.

Cooperation, then, is a preference ordering that the classical property theorists weren't counting on in theory but that they can't do without. And so they have to tell a story to explain it, and rely on our imaginative reconstruction from narrative to paint a plausible picture about how we got these property regimes in the first place.

IV. Reprise: The "Naturalness" of Self-Interest and the "Moralness" of the Property Story

Quite aside from the thought experiments we have run through and quite aside from the striking case of the cooperative preferences that we need for the institution of property itself, it should be pretty obvious that John Doe's self-interested preference ordering is only one among a number of options. In the real world, his orderings have to be explained too; they have a history too and need a story just like anybody else's. The Critical Legal Studies movement has been around long enough to get across the idea that John Doe is just another story; it is instead the endless repetition of JD's "naturalness" that has made us think that his preferences are "just there," needing no further explanation or narration.[45]

Feminist theorists have made the point in another way: at least since Carol Gilligan, and really for some time before, we have realized that Mom or the Good Citizen—the caring, cooperative person generally—is just as much "there" as the indifferent noncooperator John Doe.[46] Indeed, feminist theorists have pointed out the importance of narrative in arriving at preference choices: Mom talks things over and arrives at her preference orderings through discussion and negotiation[47]—perhaps at least sometimes because she has little to begin with and hence little capacity to retaliate against noncooperators. Presumably, from Mom's (or Good Citizen George's) perspective, cooperation would be the predictable set of preferences, while John Doe's self-interest would be the oddity, and John Doe would have to be explained by some kind of story about how he got that way.

So why is cooperation the preference ordering that seems to need the story? There is, of course, the point that is made so tellingly by critical theory and even more so by feminist theory: the dominant storyteller can make his position seem to be the natural one.[48] It is not too hard to envision the bland John Doe (or perhaps the more competitive King of the Mountain) as the surrogate for the liberal, the dominating storyteller and bête noire of the Crits; while Malice Aforethought could stand in for the patriarch, another dominating storyteller and nemesis in feminist theory. And one should note that John Doe, King of the Mountain, and Malice Aforethought all have a disturbing similarity in their patterns of preferences: where there is not enough to go around, where plenty is ruled out as an option, each of these characters prefers as a first choice "I get a lot, you get nothing." Perhaps this is why it is sometimes difficult to tell these characters apart.

But there is more to be said about these characters than their identity as a dominating group of storytellers. Consider Mom's big problem: suppose that she encounters John Doe, the blandest of these three noncooperating characters. However much she may prefer cooperative solutions, when she meets this noncooperator, she has to choose between two roles she does not want. One of her choices is to be a Hit Me victim, since her choice to cooperate would only meet John Doe's choice to cheat, which would put her in the worst of all possible positions. Her other choice is to mimic John Doe himself by choosing mutual noncooperation—but that is a role that she realizes would lead to a collective loss, which she also does not want. Thus unless she is dealing with another Mom, another cooperator, she is stuck with a choice between Box (B) or (D): the choice between cooperating and the great risk of domination or of cheating and the certainty of the relative mutual impoverishment of "I get a little, you get a little."

And that, I would suggest, is a big reason why John Doe seems like nature, like something that is "just there," while Mom seems to need a narrative. John Doe chooses the safe route, the route that might lead to the jackpot if the opposite number is a cooperator/sucker, and that at least lets him get a little bit if the other guy is another noncooperative John Doe.[49]

But Mom the cooperator takes risks for a common good. When it works, everyone is better off, but when it doesn't, she may lose horribly. And she makes you wonder—how did she get that way? Why didn't she take the safe route and cheat, like John Doe? Why does she hang in there, hoping the frog will become a prince? What gives her the nerve to take a risk that the other guy might be a cooperator too? More importantly, is it really a matter of her nerve at all, or only of having no alternatives—of using imagination in the face of hopelessness, of creativity when she has no leverage for retaliation? *What's her story, anyway?*

Thus we are back to storytelling. What's more, we need to consider not just the story *about* Mom but also the story that *she herself can tell.* Mom's storytelling both can create a sense of commonality and can reorder her audience's ways of dealing with the world. According to the narrative theorists, the teller of the tales has a vision of some kind of community, even if it is only a community of two. The storyteller places herself with the audience experiencing the tale; she takes a clutch of occurrences and through narrative reveals them for her audience as *actions,* with beginnings, middles, and ends—actions in which the audience can imagine themselves as common participants or common observers.[50]

When Mom tells us, "Here is what we (or they) did and how we (or they) did it," she transforms events into our experienced or imagined actions and in the process tells us who we are. This is the way the storyteller, by structuring the audience's experience and imagination, helps to turn her audience into a moral community.[51] Moreover, by giving shape to our experience of events, the storyteller in effect constructs our memories and consciousness, so that we can draw on this new stock in the future. In this sense, narratives change our minds and give us an opportunity to reconsider and reorder our approach to events. We can recollect them as actions taken and not taken, and act differently in the future, instead of endlessly repeating some formulaic, repetitive, and predictable response, as rocks respond to gravity.[52]

Perhaps this is what Mom is aiming at: narrative theory coincides with feminist theory in suggesting that preference orderings don't just come out of nowhere. They may be constructs of narrative and negotiation and may change over time, as we digest the stories of the places that our preferences have led us, or may lead us in the future, unless we act to lead them instead.

Thus as the feminist theorist Robin West has pointed out—though in somewhat different terms—narrative gives Mom a way to get John Doe to exercise a little imagination and get him to take a chance on cooperating too, for the sake of a larger good. She can tell him a story, she can let him know that things don't have to be the way they are; she can put together a narrative to show how it feels to be in the other guy's shoes and how it is that mutual trust and cooperative efforts are not only possible but preferable from everyone's point of view.[53] In fact, there is even a story about this storytelling endeavor, in a way: it is the tale of Scheherazade. But even that is a particularly haunting story-of-storytelling, since the captive Scheherazade had no weapons but her wits, and her tale suggests that storytelling may begin in weakness, telling tales to power.

Perhaps now we can take another guess at why Locke and Blackstone and their successors have all told those siren tales about property, too. Their theoretical self-interest had a fatal weakness too when it came to establishing a property regime. But if their tales could just get us John Does over the hump of our conservative, unimaginative, play-it-safe self-interest, they might get us to establish property regimes; they might get us to recognize that if we all respect each other's claims, we can encourage everyone to expend labor on the resources of the world, and we all will be better off in the end.

And maybe that is the real story about why they told those stories and why their successors continue to tell them. They may have been right or wrong in their argument that property improves the lot of humankind; and their smooth tales of property's cooperative origins may well have slighted the emotional context in which cooperation takes place.[54] But those tales are moral ones all the same, just as much as Aesop's fables, speaking to and constituting a kind of moral community and urging that community to change its ways.

Notes

1. Thomas Hobbes, *Leviathan,* ch. 20, at 261 (C. B. McPherson ed. 1968; 1st ed. 1651); see also John Locke, *Two Treatises of Government,* editor's introduction at 104 (P. Laslett rev. ed. 1963); James McCosh, *The Scottish Philosophy,* 2–3 (1875); Alfred Hirschman, *The Passions and the Interests,* 12–20 (1977).

2. This use of "synchronic" derives from Ferdinand de Saussure, *Course in General Linguistics* 81, 90–95 (C. Bally and A. Sechehaye eds., W. Baskin trans. 1959; from Saussure's 1916 *Cours de linguistique générale*); see also Peter Goodrich, "Law and Language: An Historical and Critical Introduction," 11 *J. Law & Soc'y* 173, 177, 179–82 (1984).

3. Saussure, supra note 2, at 81, 90–95 contrasted diachronic to synchronic treatment as accidental and unsystematic. See also E. E. Evans-Pritchard, *Social Anthropology,* iii, 161 (1964), describing social science as synchronic, history as diachronic.

4. Locke continues to be central in modern discussions of property. See, e.g., Richard Epstein, *Takings* 9–16 (1985); but see Thomas Grey, "The Malthusian Constitution," 41 *U. Miami L. Rev.* 21, 31–32 (1986) (criticizing Epstein, contrasting to Locke); Robert Nozick, *Anarchy, State, and Utopia* 174–82 (1974); John T. Sanders, "Justice and the Initial Acquisition of Property," 10 *Harv. J. of Law & Pub. Pol'y* 366 (1987) and comment thereto by Geoffrey Miller, "Economic Efficiency and the Lockean Proviso," id. at 401; see also Carol Rose, "'Enough and as Good' of What?" 81 *Nw. U. L. Rev.* 423–25, 430 (1987), and authorities cited therein.

5. Locke, supra note 1, *Second Treatise,* at secs. 31, 36–38, 45–48, 123–24.

6. Id., editor's introduction, at 82, 89, 91, 111–12.

7. 2 William Blackstone, *Commentaries on the Laws of England* 3–9 (1979; reproduction of 1766 ed.).

8. Harold Demsetz, "Toward a Theory of Property Rights," 57 *Am. Econ. Rev.* (Papers & Proceedings) 347 (1967).

9. Thomas Grey, "The Disintegration of Property," 22 *Nomos* 69 (1980); Bruce Ackerman, *Private Property and the Constitution* 116–17 (1977).

10. A pivotal article was Wesley Newcomb Hohfeld, "Some Fundamental Legal Conceptions as Applied in Judicial Reasoning," 23 *Yale L. J.* 16 (1913).

11. 2 Blackstone, supra note 7, at 2.

12. For a classic statement, see Jeremy Bentham, *Principles of the Civil Code,* in *Theory of Legislation* 109–119 (1987; reprint of C. K. Ogden ed. 1931). See also 2 Blackstone, supra note 7, at 4, stating that property helps avoid "innumerable tumults" that occur when many vie for the same things.

13. Hobbes, supra note 1, ch. 14, at 189.

14. Id., ch. 13, at 184: when two persons want the same thing and both cannot have it, they become enemies and "endeavour to destroy, or subdue one an other." See also his defense of his view of the mutual enmity between persons: "Let [the

doubter] consider with himselfe, when taking a journey, he armes himselfe ...; when going to sleep, he locks his dores; when even in his house he locks his chests; ... what opinion he has of his fellow subjects, when he rides armed; of his fellow Citizens, when he locks his dores; and of his children, and servants, when he locks his chests. Does he not there as much accuse mankind by his actions, as I do by my words?"

15. Hobbes, supra note 1, ch. 21, at 270.

16. Locke, supra note 1, *Second Treatise,* at sec. 28.

17. See, e.g., Fred McChesney, "Rent Extraction and Rent Creation in the Economic Theory of Regulation," 16 *J. Leg. Stud.* 101, 102–103 (1987), describing political actors as self-interested utility maximizers.

18. Hirschman, supra note 1, at 54–65 (1977).

19. Alternatively, of course, we can collectively impoverish ourselves by giving people the wrong incentives. See, e.g., Frank H. Easterbrook, "The Supreme Court—Foreword: The Court and the Economic System," 98 *Harv. L. Rev.* 4, 10–13 (1984).

20. See, e.g., Charles Meyers, "The Covenant of Habitability and the American Law Institute," 27 *Stan. L. Rev.* 879 (1975); for a critique, see Duncan Kennedy, "The Effect of the Warranty of Habitabililty on Low Income Housing: 'Milking' and Class Violence," 15 *Fla. St. U. L. Rev.* 485, 506, 519 (1987).

21. Economists do not generally purport to predict preferences for any specific things but rather treat such preferences as givens (or "exogenous"); see, e.g., Charles J. Meyers, "An Introduction to Environmental Thought: Some Sources and Some Criticisms," 50 *Ind. L. J.* 426, 450–52 (1975); Dwight R. Lee, "Politics, Ideology and the Power of Choice," 74 *Va. L. Rev.* 191, 193–94 (1988). This could change in light of work on "preference formation" or adaptive preferences; see Cass R. Sunstein, "Legal Interference with Private Preferences," 53 *U. Chi. L. Rev.* 1129, 1145–58 (1986).

22. For the view that human events may be intractable to scientific ex ante prediction and only understandable through post hoc narration or interpretation, see Charles Taylor, "Interpretation and the Sciences of Man," in *Understanding and Social Inquiry* 101, 104–106, 129 (F. R. Dallmayr and T. A. McCarthy eds. 1977); 1 Paul Ricoeur, *Time and Narrative* 147, 156–57 (1984).

23. Of course, even JD can become satiated with X after a while, if, for example, X is ice cream. But even if JD doesn't want a particular item for his own consumption, he does want it so that he can trade it to you, take the proceeds you give him, and go down to Bloomies to get something else that he *does* want.

24. For a similar view, see Daniel A. Farber and Phillip F. Frickey, "The Jurisprudence of Public Choice," 65 *Tex. L. Rev.* 873, 894, n. 129 (1987). Cf. Richard A. Posner, "Gratuitous Promises in Economics and Law," 6 *J. Legal Stud.* 411–12 (1977).

25. Cf., e.g., Lee, supra note 21, at 193–94, arguing that economics or public choice theory can accommodate any value set but generally implying that as the cost of a given activity rises, people will engage in it less.

26. See Carol Gilligan, *In a Different Voice* (1982). This character is fairly common in ordinary life as well; see, e.g., "What's in a Neighborhood?" *N.Y. Times,* July 10,

1988, sec. 1, at 20 (local citizens, often women, may assist newcomers and organize neighborhood services).

27. Phillip Roth, *Portnoy's Complaint* (1969).

28. See, e.g., Elizabeth M. Schneider, "Describing and Changing: Women's Self-defense Work and the Problem of Expert Testimony on Battering," 9 *Women's Rts. L. Rep.* 195 (1986). See also the essay "Women and Property" later in this volume.

29. See, e.g., Erickson v. Hudson, 249 P.2d 523 (Wyo. 1952); De Cecco v. Beach, 381 A.2d 543 (Conn. 1977) (10-foot stockade placed in such a way as to destroy neighbor's view of river); see also Comment, "Spite Fences and Spite Wells: Relevancy of Motive in the Relations of Adjoining Landowners," 26 *Cal. L. Rev.* 691 (1938).

30. "With Motel Blocked, Developer Starts a Pig Farm," *N.Y. Times,* Dec. 19, 1982, sec. 1, at 42.

31. See, e.g., "Why Hedda Nussbaum So Compels the Public's Interest," *N.Y. Times,* Dec. 9, 1988, sec. 2, at B1, concerning a witness at a battering trial; for further discussion of battered women, see the essay "Women and Property" later in this volume.

32. Our legal institutions, however, disfavor certain types of cooperation that victimize others, e.g., criminal conspiracy or monopolistic cartels.

33. For further discussion, see the essay "Crystals and Mud in Property Law" later in this volume.

34. See, e.g., William L. Prosser and & W. Page Keaton, *The Law of Torts* 307–308 (5th ed. 1984) (liability to rescuers).

35. The classic article is Scott Gordon, "The Economic Theory of a Common-Property Resource: The Fishery," 62 *J. Pol. Econ.* 124 (1954); for a series of variants on this problem, see Carol M. Rose, "Rethinking Environmental Controls: Management Strategies for Common Resources," 1991 *Duke L.* J. 1.

36. For a good explanation of this much-discussed problem, see Jack Hirschleifer, "Evolutionary Models in Economics and Law: Cooperation Versus Conflict Strategies," 4 *Res. L. & Econ.* 1, 14 (1982).

37. Garrett Hardin, "The Tragedy of the Commons," 162 *Science* 1243 (1968); for examples concerning the environment, William Ophuls, *Ecology and the Politics of Scarcity* 145–55 (1984).

38. See Rose, supra note 4, at 438–39; Frank Michelman, "Ethics, Economics, and the Law of Property," 24 *Nomos* 3, 30–31 (1982); James Krier, "The Tragedy of the Commons, Part Two," 15 *Harv. J. Law & Pub. Pol'y* 325, 337–39 (1992).

39. See Russell Hardin, *Collective Action* 34–37 (1982), arguing that although political entrepreneurship explains some organizing activity, motivations for contribution to collective action are weakest at opening stages.

40. See the essays "Possession as the Origin of Property" earlier in this volume and "The Comedy of the Commons" later.

41. Robert Axelrod, among others, has argued that the possibility of retaliation ("tit for tat") preserves a cooperative regime on a basis of self-interest; see his book *The Evolution of Cooperation* (1984). The difficulties are that (a) someone must make an initial cooperative move based on trust; (b) monitoring of the different parties' successive moves may be difficult; and (c) each party must continue to cooperate, disregarding the prospect of a last move on which a sheerly self-interested player

would cheat (a prospect that would lead to cheating on the next-to-last move and so on back). For variations on these problems, Anthony de Jasay, *Social Contract, Free Ride: A Study of the Public Goods Problem* 63–66 (1989).

42. Locke, supra note 1, *Second Treatise,* secs. 28, 37, 48, 123 (quotation from sec. 123).

43. 2 Blackstone, 7, at 2–8 (quotation at 8).

44. White, *The Content of the Form: Narrative Discourse and Historical Representation* 93–94, 193 (1987); see also 1 Ricoeur, supra note 22, at 150, who describes narrative conclusions as acceptable rather than predictable.

45. See, e.g., James L. Kainen, "Nineteenth Century Interpretations of the Federal Contract Clause: The Transformation from Vested to Substantive Rights Against the State," 31 *Buff. L. Rev.* 381, 399–402, 451, 461 (1982), arguing that a legal elite presented self-serving legal doctrines as "natural"; for similar critiques of the partiality in "rights," see Mark Kelman, *A Guide to Critical Legal Studies* 270–71, 282 (1987); Mark Tushnet, "An Essay on Rights," 62 *Tex L. Rev.* 1363, 1392–93 (1984).

46. Gilligan, supra note 26; Joan C. Tronto, "Beyond Gender Difference to a Theory of Care," 12 *Signs* 644, 649–51 (1987) (identifying ethic of care in variety of social groups).

47. Gilligan, supra note 26, at 28–30; Marilyn Friedman, "Feminism and Modern Friendship: Dislocating the Community," 99 *Ethics* 275, 279–80 (1989); for women's narration, Robin West, "Economic Man and Literary Woman: One Contrast," 39 *Mercer L. Rev.* 867, 873–74 (1988); on the feminist tradition of consciousness-raising through narratives of experience, see also Jo Freeman, *The Politics of Women's Liberation* 116–19 (1975).

48. See, e.g., Robin West, "Jurisprudence and Gender," 55 *U. Chi. L. Rev.* 1, 64–65 (1988). For the self-fulfilling behavioral feedback effects of hypotheses of self-interest, see also Geoffrey Brennan and James M. Buchanan, "Is Public Choice Immoral? The Case for the 'Nobel' Lie," 74 *Va. L. Rev.* 179, 183–84 (1988); Margaret Radin, "Market-Inalienability," 100 *Harv. L. Rev.* 1849, 1877–81 (1987); Alan Ryan, "Distrusting Economics" (review), *N.Y. Rev.* May 18, 1989, at 25, 26.

49. JD may be using a maximin strategy, which involves making choices that minimize his maximum loss. This conservative strategy may be appropriate for zero-sum games, but it is inappropriate in the positive-sum prisoners' dilemma, where the greatest joint game emerges from riskier choices. See Edna Ullmann-Margalit, *The Emergence of Norms* 20, n. 1 (1977).

50. David Carr, *Time, Narrative and History,* 48–50, 61–62, 153–56 (1986).

51. Id. at 156–57; see also White, supra note 44, at 25.

52. Cf. Taylor, supra note 22, at 128–29 (distinguishing prediction of repetitive events from post hoc interpretive understanding of human ones, where conceptual innovation transforms what counts as reality); Carr, supra note 50, at 60–62.

53. West, supra note 47 at 868–89, 870.

54. See West, supra note 48, at 65; see also Robert H. Frank, *Passions Within Reason: The Strategic Role of the Emotions* (1988), generally arguing that emotion is essential to cooperation.

PART TWO

Wealth and Community, Then and Now

In the two essays in this part, I locate some modern property issues in the history of political institutions of the Atlantic world, and I illustrate the historical relativity of our standard understanding of property as an institution to enhance wealth. In the essay "'Takings' and the Practices of Property," I consider a modern constitutional issue; in so doing I contrast the wealth-enhancing notion of property with the ideas of an earlier time–a time in which property was thought to be a means to foster and recognize "propriety," in the sense of a "proper" ordering of social and political life.

With the second essay, "Ancient Constitution," I turn to an example from the American past, that is, the Antifederalist understanding of the "proper" political order, including property's place within it. I pursue this seemingly archaic understanding of "civic republican" order and its critique of currently mainstream ideas; I then follow the Antifederalist tracks as they continue to cross our political paths, especially in modern local government in the United States.

3

"Takings" and the Practices of Property: Property as Wealth, Property as "Propriety"

Introduction

Among the problems of the modern law of property, a certain group of issues must place high on almost any ranking: those that are collectively known as the "takings" issue. Takings problems swirl around the legitimacy of governmental regulation of individually held property, particularly when a regulation affects the interests claimed by one or a small number of property holders. Under some circumstances, it is said, governmental regulation may legitimately limit or channel the owner's use of property; but under other circumstances it may not do so unless the government buys and pays for the private rights affected by the regulation. It is the latter set of circumstances that agitates the voluminous case law of takings, in which courts attempt to define just when a governmental action turns as if from Dr. Jekyll into Mr. Hyde, from legitimate regulation on the one hand into illegitimate, uncompensated taking of private property on the other.

Scholars have joined judges in spilling a great deal of ink over takings, with what sometimes seems to be maddeningly little coherence.[1] Part of the reason may be that the takings issue masks a logically prior question of some difficulty: that is, in order to say when governmental action "takes" someone's property, we must have some idea about what rights are included in property in the first place. Without such an underlying idea, we cannot really tell what measures might even affect individual

---

The original version of this essay appeared in 33 *NOMOS*, 223–247 (1991). Reprinted by permission of *NOMOS*.

property rights, whether for good or ill, and certainly we cannot tell what would count as compensation for any ill effects on property rights.

This point is amply illustrated in a number of examples from well-known takings law, particularly in the defenses that governmental bodies raise when someone charges that a given regulation takes private property. For example, one common governmental defense is the argument that the regulation merely prevents nuisances: your property is not taken, this reasoning goes, if the regulation in question merely prevents you from perpetrating a nuisance.[2] The idea here is that your property right never included the nuisance activity in the first place, and hence you have had nothing taken through the regulation. A second traditional takings defense recites the governmental purpose of restraining monopoly: your property is not taken if a regulation simply imposes some restraints on the returns from your monopoly enterprise and instead limits you to a reasonable return on your investment.[3] The theory of this defense is that your property rights never included a right to charge monopoly prices, which give you extraordinarily high returns at the consumers' expense, and thus nothing within your property right is disturbed by the regulation requiring reasonable rates.

There are more takings defenses, and I will come back to some of them later in this essay. All of them raise further questions, but the specific ways that these defenses are used, followed, or rejected is not the point. The point is that these defenses show that in a very practical way, takings jurisprudence depends on some underlying conception of what your property rights entitle you to have and what they do not. You can only claim that you should be compensated for adverse effects to something that is within your property right. One might start, then, with the question, What "takes" your property? But simply by looking at some cases, one quickly arrives at a more general question, namely, What does your property right include?

But then to answer this second question, we have to ask a third and even larger one: what are we trying to accomplish with a property *regime?* If we know the answer to this most general question about property, we can begin to understand what we include in property and why, and what we leave out and why, and thus what kinds of governmental actions we deem to take property and why we so deem them. Though these questions clearly involve issues of theory, they are also intensely practical; and practice itself should yield some information about which theory or theories best inform our general vision of property.

In this essay I am going to approach this most general question—that is, what we are trying to accomplish with a property regime—by reflecting on an interesting theoretical approach put forth by the jurisprudence scholar Stephen Munzer. While his approach is provocative and informative, I think that it bypasses certain conceptions that in fact have been most important to our historic property practices. What I am going to do is to contrast Munzer's property theory to two other conceptions of property, each of which seems to me to have had considerably greater impact on the things we have really had in mind in dealing with property.

But first, Munzer: in a single pithy article, Munzer summarizes the applicability to takings of a general typology of property that he has developed at length in his book, *A Theory of Property*.[4] On that theory, property can be understood on the basis of three principles that give it direction. Those principles are (a) preference satisfaction (that is, a combined version of efficiency and utility),[5] (b) justice and equality, and (c) desert. According to Munzer, these three principles are pluralistic in the sense that no one principle can be reduced to any of the others.[6] But my own view is that these principles are not necessarily pluralistic at all, and the reasons bring us back to the crucial issue—the purposes a property regime is supposed to serve.

Munzer's principles certainly look divergent enough. Why then might they not be pluralist—that is, how could any one reduce to any of the others? One hint is that the principle Munzer calls "preference satisfaction" comes first in his typology: on a closer look, it is entirely possible to do something that Munzer himself does not do, that is, to construct a unitary model within which his second principle (justice) and third principle (desert) are entirely reduced to the first and all-powerful principle of preference satisfaction. That model of a property regime is very familiar in the context of modern practices and in fact should already be familiar to readers of this book. It outlines a property regime whose dominating concern is generally the enhancement of total social wealth, because that is what preference satisfaction is all about. Indeed, not only is it *possible* to construct a unitary preference-satisfying or wealth-enhancing model out of the three principles, it is almost difficult to *avoid* doing so, given the power and dominance of this familiar conception of property's role in our practical political economy.

All the same, this wealth-enhancing or preference-satisfying conception of property is not the only one available in our Western historical tradition; there is another and far older traditional vision of property as a practical social institution. On this traditional understanding, the implicit aim of the institution of property is to secure to each person that which is "proper" to him or her, in relation to each person's role in the commonwealth.

This essay will outline these two visions of the purposes of property, visions I believe have had a substantial impact on property practice. I will begin by discussing the dominating, wealth-enhancing or preference-satisfying view and will do so by arguing that on this approach, Munzer's three principles are not necessarily pluralistic but can rather be subsumed easily into this single cluster of moral and political ideas. I will then reach back to the older but far less systematically articulated vision of property as "propriety"—securing to each the entitlements "proper" to that person's role.

My argument will be that there is indeed a pluralism inherent in our property practices, but it does not derive from any inevitable clash of the preference satisfaction principle with either the principle of justice or the principle of desert. Instead the real pluralism—which indeed constantly refuels our endless discussions of takings—derives from the very disparate overall conceptions of property that have historically informed our jurisprudential practices. Our system is pluralistic because we have a dominant, preference-satisfying practical understanding of property, but it is subject to constant albeit often ill-articulated intrusions from the traditional, quite divergent understanding of property as "propriety."

I. Property as Preference Satisfaction

Preference satisfaction can easily be taken as a goal of a property regime; indeed, most modern economic theorists focus on that goal. But it is worthwhile to look closely at the means by which a property regime is thought to maximize preference satisfaction. When we do so, we notice that Munzer's other principles for shaping a property regime—that is, justice on the one hand and desert on the other—need not be independent constraints on preference satisfaction at all. Rather, they fit quite neatly into the overall version of property as an institution that, first and foremost, maximizes the satisfaction of preferences by maximizing wealth.

Maximizing Preference-Satisfactions

How does the maximization of preference satisfaction occur in a property regime? One approach—which seems to be shared by a surprising number of property scholars—looks at the world as if it contained a large but finite number of good things, a kind of fixed bag of goodies whose total is not much affected by the rules of allocation.[7] Taking this fixed-bag view for a moment, if one were to try to distribute the contents so as to maximize preference satisfaction, then presumably the object would be to divvy up the goodies in a way that most people like or at least prefer in the aggregate to alternative divvying-up schemes. Thus, for example, all (or almost all) the teddy bears would go to the toddlers, whereas all the Alfa Romeos would go to my older brother and to others of like character who have proved their devoted auto-mania over the years. Perhaps, too, the streets and wilderness areas might go to the general public (since most people might prefer their common ownership), but presumably clothes and dishes would stay in private ownership, supposing that most people would rather own those items individually.[8] Naturally, given that any world is likely to contain someone like Richard Epstein along with John Rawls, one can imagine that there would be some disagreements about whether certain items should be public or private, just as there would be some disagreements, within the private sphere, about who gets the Alfa car and who gets the Omega watch, not to speak of Delta Airlines. But once we decide these issues, that is, about which things we would rather have in which hands, our fixed-bag property regime would attempt to maximize preferences by getting the appropriate things in the relevant hands and then calling the results "property rights."

This approach can be fairly quickly dispatched, and not simply because it is crazily optimistic about our collective powers of judgment about other peoples' preferences, which of course it is. The much more important reason it can be dispatched is that it entirely misses the classic economic point about property's role in maximizing preference satisfaction. On the classic view, a property regime isn't there just to divvy up the contents of the bag (though it does that too); it is supposed to make the bag *bigger* and put more things in it.[9]

How does does a property regime do that? Well, to get some idea, we can compare a property regime to a nonpropertized commons. Let's suppose some berry patch is an unowned commons. According to the classic view, the patch will be all right so long as there are a lot of berries and only a few berry-eaters.[10] But once the berry-eaters get numerous enough, they start competing, and they are likely to get into conflicts about who gets how many berries. Their competitiveness of course is one big reason why it is crazy to be overly optimistic about our abilities to calculate just-so shares when resources are finite.

But of course there is much more to the classic story: while everyone is grabbing and fighting over the berries, nobody cultivates any berry bushes. The whole patch is depleted and trampled from our mad grab, and everybody is worse off. But let's suppose we have enough sense to institute a regime of property rights—*any* individual property rights—for the patch: what happens now? Well, first of all, people stop fighting over the berries. The new property regime has allocated the patch, or parts of the patch, to one person or another—labor is a good claim, but it really doesn't matter who, just so long as everyone knows who has what. When everyone knows that, they all stop wasting resources on grabbing and fighting, or "rentseeking," as this sort of activity is now fashionably designated.[11] Second, individual owners are now secure in their little corners of the berry patch, and this security encourages each to labor on his or her corner to make it more productive. Finally, since everyone knows who has what, the various owners can trade berries, or even whole berry patches, so that the one who values the berries or the berry patches the most winds up with them. How does that person show that she wants the berries the most? The clearest signal she can give is that she offers the most for them, that is, the most acorns or straw hats or tools or whatever else her labor and foresight have allowed her to accumulate.

So the upshot of all this is that a property regime maximizes preference satisfaction not just by divvying up resources, but by making resources *more valuable.* The property regime creates a bigger bag, because in a property regime, (a) we aren't wasting time and energy on fighting; (b) we are busily investing that time and energy in our own resources and thus making them more valuable, knowing that we will get the rewards; and (c) we can trade the products of our efforts; that is, we can make a smooth set of Pareto-superior moves, whereby everybody is better off just because we all get the things we want the most. We don't need somebody else to allocate finite sets of things to us—indeed, we are better off making our own decisions, because one of the decisions that we make is the decision to work harder to get more of what we want by trading with others.

All this means that available resources themselves are not finite in value; they grow more valuable because we put our efforts into them. And why do we put our efforts into them? Because we have *property* in the resources and in their products. In a property regime, we are better off because property rights encourage us to enhance resources instead of dissipating them and because we can make gains sheerly from trading things we have for other things we want even more.

By the way, there are more public roads and other public goods in a property regime, too. Some resources are most economically produced and managed on a large scale, and because of these scale economies, they are best allocated to joint control rather than to individuals. In a well-oiled property machine, these kinds of products will wind up as joint property of some sort—perhaps family property or corporate property, or perhaps municipal or state or even national property. But we should note that this joint or public allocation also expands the total bag of goodies, because these kinds of resources are most productive in some kind of multiple ownership.

The need for larger-scale management, incidentally, is a standard reason for the power of eminent domain in our law, and this need provides a well-known example of a limitation on individual property rights. Your property does not include the right to extort a holdout price for property that is most productively managed by the public. Hence you may have to sell your property to the public at the fair market value of its private use, and you don't get compensated for any additional monopoly price you might otherwise have charged the public.[12]

Once again, then, this is the standard but very powerful story about property as a preference-satisfying institution. According to that story, a property regime satisfies preferences not by divvying up a finite bag of resources but rather by encouraging behavior that enhances resources' value, making the total bag a whole lot bigger and more diverse.

With that, I will turn to the second and third principles that Munzer locates in a property regime, namely, justice and desert. Munzer himself suggests that these principles act as pluralistic constraints on preference satisfaction. My own view is that these principles do not necessarily imply anything pluralistic or constraining at all, in the sense that they are in some way incompatible with a preference-satisfying understanding of a property regime. On the contrary, they fit quite handily with a property regime whose purpose is seen as the satisfaction of preferences.

Justice or Fairness

Munzer means by "justice" a distributional constraint on property ownership, which is evident in his calling the principle "justice and equality." But he does not mean equality across the board. Instead he takes his cues from the best-known exposition of "justice as fairness," that is, John Rawls' *Theory of Justice*.[13] Munzer too, generally following the Rawlsian tradition, treats the principle of justice as a tenet that requires not flat-out equality of holdings and instead only a certain minimum set of holdings, but these can be taken together with some acceptable level of inequality.[14]

But this understanding of justice (or fairness) is not difficult to justify on preference satisfaction grounds and hence does not necessarily constrain or conflict with a preference satisfaction principle. It all falls into place if one supposes a diminishing marginal utility of wealth. Now, that is a controversial supposition, but it is at least reasonably plausible that an additional dollar would be worth more to a poor person than to a wealthy one. Some of the classic economic thinkers, like Alfred Marshall, thought so, and the idea may be implicit in our graduated income tax as well.[15] Again, this view is not uncontroversial, but if we accept it at least hypothetically, then some wealth transfers from the rich to the poor—to bring the poor up to an appropriate minimum—will maximize the total amount of preference satisfaction, since the poor get more satisfaction than the rich out of the same resources.

On the other hand, there is a preference satisfaction limitation on such transfers. That is, we wouldn't want to take so much from the rich that they get discouraged about investing. If they do get discouraged, then the total bag of goodies shrinks too much; that is, it shrinks more than is warranted by the incremental satisfactions of the poor.

We should note that this point ties in with the idea of "demoralization costs" that Frank Michelman developed from the earlier work of Jeremy Bentham.[16] The idea is that if rich people (or any other people, really) have too many of their earnings redistributed, they will get discouraged, and ultimately they will quit working. Why will they get discouraged and quit? The basic reason is that their expectations are violated—that is, their expectations of keeping the things that they invested in and worked on. When these expectations come to naught, they get depressed, and so do others like them, who would otherwise be toiling happily away without gloomy thoughts of possible takings. This is of course another major way of thinking about justice or fairness—nobody pulls the rug out from under you.

But notice that it is the property *regime* that gives people those expectations in the first place, and it does so for utilitarian reasons.[17] We call certain things "property rights" and foster the expectation that owners can control and enjoy the things they have worked for in order to encourage both rich and poor to invest the labor, time, energy, and effort that will make resources more valuable and the total bag bigger. To go back to the takings issue, compensation is one tool we use to try to reduce the demoralization attendant upon public takings of private property, and thus takings compensation too has a utilitarian function.

But as Frank Michelman saw, our fairness and utilitarian considerations lead in the same direction.[18] It would be easy enough to imagine ourselves living under a quite different set of expectations. For example, we might expect that any time an individual acquired a significant amount of anything, he or she would have to give it all up, in a sort of modern-day, obligatory potlatch. If we lived under such a system, nobody would have her expectations violated when her things were confiscated, and the system would not be unfair or unjust in the sense of bait-and-switch or pulling the rug out from under the citizenry. Individuals in such a system wouldn't get demoralized about the confiscation of their investments. They just wouldn't invest effort and energy in the first place, which of course would mean that the system would be likely to produce a considerably smaller total bag of resources and goods. But according to the classic property theory, that result is the direct opposite of the outcome we seek in a property regime. That is why we have what we call "fair" or "just" compensation for takings of property—so that more investments will be made and more aggregate preferences will wind up being satisfied.[19]

In short, it is pretty easy to see that our concepts of justice or fairness are not necessarily constraints on a preference maximization version of property but can easily be seen as a part of the *very same* moral and political universe. We could easily look at these justice or fairness considerations as elements in a unified overall design: the overall design is that the property regime aims at encouraging investment and enterprise, and ultimately at getting more preferences satisfied, since the behavior that is encouraged creates a bigger bag of more valuable things.

Desert

The third principle in Munzer's trio, desert, is mainly aimed at reward to labor,[20] but this is even easier to justify on preference satisfaction grounds. The reward to labor is an obvious corollary to a property regime that tries to increase the bag of goodies by encouraging the investment of effort and time. We should note, for example, that it is not just *any* old labor that gets rewarded; nobody rewards anybody for sweeping sands into the ocean. On the contrary, the labor that gets rewarded is the labor that produces goods or services that people *want.* And so the reward to "deserving" labor also falls into line with preference satisfaction. The deservingness that counts is the labor that results in producing what people want.

In short, it seems entirely possible to construct a version of property, and of takings of property, that includes all three principles in Munzer's trio. The principles of preference satisfaction, justice, and desert can easily be cast as a smooth and seamless whole—a whole that is entirely dominated by maximizing preference satisfaction.

It is within the context of this whole that takings compensation is explicable. When someone's property is taken for some worthy public purpose—worthy, by the way, on the understanding that public management of certain projects is more wealth-enhancing than private management would be—we do not depart in the slightest from utilitarian considerations when we compensate the private owner. The owner is someone whose labor and investment in her property may have produced highly desirable things, and we certainly would not want to discourage this person, or others like her, by removing the incentives to make these contributions to the total wealth. You can call it justice, you can call it desert, you can call it encouragement of preference-satisfying behavior: they amount to the same thing.

By the same token, however, not all public measures raise a utilitarian occasion for compensation. No public body need compensate any owners when it prohibits a nuisance; what we call a "nuisance" is a use of property that causes more harm to the neighbors than good to the owners, and we don't count it among the owners' property rights, because to do so would give encouragement to wealth-dissipating activity. By the same token, the regulation of monopoly requires no compensation. Why not? Because it does nothing for preference satisfaction to encourage monopoly, except, perhaps, as a limited way to encourage innovators—whose efforts *do* count as property under our intellectual property laws. But monopolists generally only restrict supply and charge higher prices, and thus they restrain rather than expand total preference satisfaction. And so we try not to give them any encouragement. Instead, we regulate their earnings to some rate that would seem "reasonable" to a nonmonopolist, so that monopolistic ventures do not seem particularly attractive. As I mentioned earlier, these kinds of regulation are defensible under our standard practices in our takings law; and once again, desert and preference satisfaction do not diverge. Instead, they are part of the same strategy. The dominating partner in the strategy is preference satisfaction; the conception of "desert," like the conception of "justice" or "fairness," is tailored to encourage behavior that maximizes that goal. And, finally, it is a goal that informs a great deal of our modern legal practice about property—a great deal, but not all, which brings me to the next subject, a quite different historic conception of property.

II. Property as Propriety

I have gone through the ways in which property, viewed as a vehicle for preference satisfaction, subsumes a set of principles of justice or fairness on the one hand and desert on the other. What I want to do now is to describe a completely different understanding of a property regime. It is an understanding based on a quite different conception of what property is good for. This understanding of property can also include principles of justice and desert, but they come out quite differently from the ideas of justice and desert that are incorporated in a preference-satisfying understanding of property.

What is the purpose of property under this other understanding? The purpose is to accord to each person or entity what is "proper" or "appropriate" to him or her. Indeed, this understanding of property historically made no strong distinction between "property" and "propriety," and one finds the terminology mixed up to a very considerable degree in historical texts.[21] And what is "proper" or appropriate, on this vision of property, is that which is needed to keep good order in the commonwealth or body politic.

Property, Propriety, and Governance

That "property" was the mainstay of "propriety" was a quite common understanding before the seventeenth and eighteenth centuries. This understanding continued, albeit in abated form, even after the great revolutions at the end of the eighteenth century. One early example is in the work of Jean Bodin, a late-sixteenth-century French political theorist. Bodin was well known in his day and was much quoted on the subject of sovereignty, an issue of great moment at the time; he was commonly regarded as a monarchist and spokesman for the able French king Henry IV.

Bodin, for all his monarchist proclivities, nevertheless thought that property was a fundamental restraint on monarchic power. We need to have property, he said, for the maintenance and rightful ordering of families; families in turn were necessary as the constituent parts of the commonwealth itself.[22]

This version of property did *not* envision property as a set of tradeable and ultimately interchangeable goods; instead, different kinds of property were associated with different kinds of roles. The family property that Bodin was talking about was almost certainly land—and not just any land, but rather the specific landholdings associated with and "proper" to a particular family. The law itself acknowledged the "properness" of landholdings to specific families and included a variety of restraints on alienation by individual family members, in effect treating those individuals as trustees for succeeding generations of their families.[23]

Moreover, in a European tradition stretching back at least as far as the Middle Ages, land was associated with males. Men might acquire control over property through their wives and female relatives, but women themselves generally lacked full control of land. Women rather had property only in movables, which meant money and transient things; even their limited landholdings were treated metaphorically as "movable." In fact, Howard Bloch, speaking of medieval France, has made the point that females *were* money: they were transient beings and the subjects of family trades, as Bloch put it, "the kind of property which circulates between men."[24] But like money, women did not represent "immovable," "real" property. The only property that counted as real was land—an attitude that continued well into the eighteenth century, when even the proponents of commerce continued to discuss trade in feminized terms.[25]

What is perhaps most important, landownership, and indeed property in general, carried with it some measure of governing authority, and this authority had notably hierarchical characteristics.[26] Indeed, property and entitlement formed the key element in what the modern Critical Legal Studies proponents might call the reproduction of hierarchy, though this phrase would not have seemed in any way damning to those who adhered to a traditional view. Quite the contrary, although it is difficult now for us to reconstruct the attitude, property as propriety was a part of a "mental world," as Robert Darnton has said of prerevolutionary France, in which "most people assumed that ... inequality was a good thing, and that it conformed to the hierarchical order built into nature by God himself."[27] Property in this world "properly" consisted in whatever resources one needed to do one's part in keeping good order; and the normal understanding of order was indeed hierarchy—in the family,[28] in the immediate community,[29] in the larger society and commonwealth,[30] in the natural world,[31] and in the relation between the natural and the spiritual worlds.[32]

A person's property fixed his location in this hierarchy. Thus a monarch had his own property in the form of the royal domains; in theory (though the practice was much attenuated), he should not need to tax the subjects, since the income from his domains would enable him, as the traditional phrase put it, to "live of his own." The idea was that his royal property would provide him the wherewithal to exercise his role, that of overall governance.[33] The members of the noble estate in turn had their own lands, on which *they* were subrulers or "co-governors"; and other subruling orders as well had the property they needed to maintain proper order within their respective jurisdictions.[34] For example, municipalities had their own endowments, which were managed by the ruling corporations of the "burghers" or "citizens," a class that by no means included all the residents of a given community but only its leading members.[35] One should note that this pattern was brought to the New World cities as well; Hendrik Hartog's history of New York centers on the city's endowed property and its management by the ruling "corporation," and his work illustrates the pattern associating property with governance well into the early nineteenth century.[36]

Elsewhere in the areas colonized by Europeans, one finds this same association of property with authority. The American colonial enterprises, as well as the East India Company, were initially organized on this principle: the proprietors and charter holders acquired not only monopolistic property rights in their respective colonial enterprises but also the right and duty to govern the colonial charges and keep them in proper order.[37] In a way, property merged with authority in American "civic republican" thinking as well, a subject to which I return shortly and elaborate on more thoroughly in the next essay.

Before the advent of modern centralized fiscal and bureaucratic techniques, the Old Regime European countries, and to a somewhat lesser extent their colonies, all had a political organization that amounted to a kind of farming-out system—a system that fused property with "proper" authority.[38] Monopolistic guild privileges governed large segments of the economy—textiles, shoes, metalwork, and on and on. In justification of their exclusive privileges, the holders of these monopolies were charged with keeping their respective enterprises in "good order and rule."[39] In France, public offices, notably judicial magistracies, could be purchased and were treated as hereditable property; as such, these magistracies became the founding property for the so-called nobility of the robe that came to dominate the French aristocracy in the eighteenth century.[40] In England too in the same era, some public offices were seen as freehold properties of the officeholders.[41] In short, in this tradition, all rights were in some measure seen as property, and property brought with it some measure of "proper" authority, to be exercised ideally as a trust for those to whom one was responsible for governing.

Now let me come to a subject that touches on the theory of takings. In the theory of governance in the Old Regime monarchies, when a ruler's ordinary revenues failed to cover the expenses of governance, the ruler had to *ask* his subjects for subsidies; even the king, it was said, could not just take their property as he wished.[42] But the reason was quite different from the reasons that are given by preference satisfaction theories. It was not so much that confiscations of subjects' property would discourage their industriousness but rather that the things that were truly the subjects' property were things that were *proper* to them—proper because the subjects' property enabled them to take their appropriate roles and to keep good order throughout each corner of the realm.[43]

Though royal practice deviated far from this theory by the eighteenth century, particularly on the Continent, a good deal of lip service was paid to the notion that the king could not simply appropriate the subjects' property. Certainly royal overreaching continued to be the subject of great bitterness, recrimination, and even rebellion; the French Revolution itself was preceded by years of complaint from various propertied classes about royal inroads on their entitlements and "liberties."[44]

American "Republicanism" and Property

In America, a version of property as propriety can be located in an historic political mentality that is now much discussed under the rubric of "civic republicanism." Republican property was not so hierarchical as monarchic property was, because it was thought that in a republic the people rule themselves, and as a consequence a much broader range of citizens needed to have property. Montesquieu's writing supported this position, and although he would never have advocated such a thing for monarchic/aristocratic France, he noted that democratic republics entailed a much wider and more equal dispersal of property.[45] The reason, repeated again and again in the early American republic, was that property lent independence to individuals and that independence enabled them to exercise the autonomous judgment necessary for their common self-rule.[46]

As to the persons who had little property or who—like married women or slaves or children or madmen—were excluded from property ownership on principle because of their purported incapacities and "dependency": republican theory had few qualms about excluding such persons from the franchise.[47] Thus republicanism had its own pyramid of hierarchy, although perhaps a more flattened one than monarchy or aristocracy. But the logic was everywhere the same: ruling authority entailed property, and vice versa. For all its rhetoric of equality, republicanism too divided the populace into rulers and ruled, and the rulers, though they might be called "the people," were actually only those citizens who had the property necessary to make them "independent" and thereby capable of participating in governance.[48]

It should be noted that in this republican idea of property, as in monarchic or aristocratic versions, not all property was alike. Jefferson's agriculturalism stemmed from the view that landed property particularly fostered independence, and Jefferson was not alone in a certain republican uneasiness about manufacturing and commercial forms of property.[49] Commerce entailed *inter*dependence: one manufacturer or trader had to depend on another and another and another. Thus the property acquired from these interdependent activities was suspect, precisely because it was not autonomous. In a way, American agrarians were not so far removed from the medieval view that land was genuine and real, while money was merely transient, dependent, effeminate, and unsturdy.

We should note as well that the republican vision of property was more or less indifferent to encouraging accumulation or aggregate wealth. Republicanism, like other "proprietarian" visions, associated property with governance and good order, but republican good order entailed a certain sturdy equality among those who counted as self-governing citizens. Great differences of wealth might corrupt republican virtue and were thus a special matter for republican alarm.[50]

Moreover, in republicanism as in all proprietarian understandings, governance and good order always included a duty of liberality to the larger community, for the sake of the common good.[51] For any version of property as propriety, it was understood that the ill fortune of others presented the propertied with a duty to assist, and not with an occasion to revile or shame those in need. Though the practice of generosity and contribution was certainly subject to the predictable limitations of personal cupidity, there was little question that generosity was a moral and political duty of the haves to the have-nots—which was the same as saying, of course, that generosity was a duty of those with authority, to those without it.[52] Although there were certainly contrary murmurings earlier, it was not until the nineteenth century, and the ascendency of a preference-satisfying moral and political theory, that political thinkers systematically argued against generosity to the poor because of potential wealth-dissipating incentives and effects; as David Ricardo was to express this viewpoint, relief to the poor should be resisted because it "invites imprudence" and only impoverishes everyone.[53]

Justice and Desert Under Property-as-Propriety

If we were to take propriety and good order as the objects of a property regime, it is quite clear that considerations of "justice/fairness" and of "desert" would have different meanings than they do where the goal of property is taken as the maximization of preference satisfaction.

"Justice" on this older understanding meant having that which is appropriate to one's station, as well as giving that which one's station demands. Property in the proprietarian version entailed governing authority in some domain; but because of that authority, property was a kind of trust as well. On such an understanding, it would not be considered unjust or unfair to request a sacrifice for the sake of a larger community, especially from those whose property extends beyond their "proper" needs or whose propertied role makes them responsible for good order in the community.[54]

"Desert" on this understanding would also be based not on useful labor but on status or station: one deserves to have that which is appropriate to one's role and station, but not more and not less. Many kinds of goods might hardly be considered very firm property at all, since they had no connection with the holder's role in keeping proper order and were thus merely "acquired" and accidental.[55] Perhaps connected with that idea, aggrandizement beyond one's station routinely met with outrage in the era before the great revolutions, as, for example, in the harsh treatment to "regrators" and hoarders in Stuart England and in colonial America as well.[56]

This set of attitudes now seems quite antiquarian, as indeed it is. But we still hear some echoes, perhaps most notably in connection with welfare law and policy. One example is Charles Reich's famous argument about the status of governmental benefits as property: his argument, among other things, is that benefit recipients are a part of the body politic and as such have a "rightful claim" to hold these benefits as property, so that they can maintain their "independence" and participate in the commonwealth.[57] Cass Sunstein has worked some of these themes in his own considerations of welfare law, and, not surprisingly, he has done so with a nod to the republican theory of seventeenth-century England and the early American republic.[58]

An attractive feature of the older view, for Sunstein and for others, is no doubt the concept of trusteeship that permeated the idea of property as propriety. Property endowed the haves not only with rights but also with responsibilities about the disposition of property; their property was theirs only in trust for family, community, and commonwealth. A much more problematic feature of this older view, for Sunstein and other civic republican revivalists, is of course the profoundly hierarchical character of the older ways of thinking about property—a flavor perhaps best captured in the ambivalence of our contemporary response to the phrase "noblesse oblige."[59]

Despite that ambivalence, one might well suspect that a substantial motivation in our welfare laws stems not so much from sophisticated preference-maximizing theory—the supposed declining marginal utility of wealth and all the rest of it—as from the older conception of property as propriety. Many who support welfare may well do so out of a sense that poverty (and perhaps great wealth too) is a kind of disorder in the republic, that our poorer citizens should have the economic means to escape this disorder, and that our wealthier citizens have a duty to help out. In some measure the sense may be that the disorder of poverty brings scandal and disgrace to our community and that the station of propertied persons obliges them to do something to remedy the situation.

"Propriety" in Modern Property Law

At this point I will return to the takings issue and to the question of which elements in takings law are pluralist and irreducible and which are not. It seems to me that the genuinely pluralistic character of our takings law stems from its reflection of two complete but different ideas about what property is good for. The first and dominating idea casts property as an engine for the maximization of preference satisfactions; the second, now a weaker but still very stubborn idea, casts property as the vehicle for propriety and decent good order.

The preference-satisfying vision of property is so common that its arguments and its takings applications seem almost self-evident. Richard Epstein's book *Takings* runs through these arguments with confident facility. The arguments really reduce to one: that uncompensated redistributions violate the very purpose of a property regime, namely, to increase the size of the bag of goods or, as Epstein puts it, the size of the pie.[60]

But property in the second sense, that is, property as propriety, as the foundation of decency and good order, appears in our property law as well. Where does this occur? Some examples appear, once again, in commonly used judicial tests for governmental takings of private property. One such test places special limitations on governmental actions that constitute "physical invasions" of individual property.[61] On a preference satisfaction view, property should be more or less all alike; a physical invasion is like any other adverse effect on property, raising only questions of dollar values and demoralization costs. But the matter looks different on a view of property as propriety: a physical invasion is particularly reprehensible because it is a special affront to the owner of the property; it is a pointed violation of his or her understanding of decency and order.

An even more telling example lies in a kind of secondary test under the rubric of "diminution in value." Generally speaking, a regulation that drastically reduces the value of a property may be equated with a taking of that property, though the line-drawing on this issue is fraught with difficulty.[62] One subtest for diminution in value has inquired whether the affected property can continue to produce a reasonable income after the regulation is in place; if so, on this test, the diminution has not crossed the line to a taking.[63]

This is a "test" that seems incomprehensible from a utilitarian or preference satisfaction point of view, where the issue should be the effect on the owner's "demoralization" and future willingness to work and invest. But the underlying idea here is not preference satisfaction at all. The presupposition is that the owner does not need more than a *decent* income, as opposed to a maximizing income, from his or her property; hence the legislature's imposition on the property may be treated as a legitimate demand on a citizen, so long as the citizen's decent and proper income is preserved.

Similarly, another common takings test balances the owner's private loss against the public's benefit. But this test is also opaque from the point of view of maximizing preference satisfaction. Large public benefits might justify a compensated taking through eminent domain but not an uncompensated taking. Why should a particular private owner lose expected rights simply because the public gains are great?[64] From the angle of vision of property as propriety, on the other hand, this balancing of public gain against private loss suggests that citizens have a duty to give up those things which their representatives think the community can use better than they. This balancing test harks back to the underlying idea of property as propriety, namely, that property carries the authority, but also the responsibility, of a trust to the larger community.

Conclusion

Summing up all this, I have been arguing for several propositions in this essay: first, that we have two major and divergent overall conceptions of the goals of a property regime, namely property for preference satisfaction and property for propriety; second, that these different postures toward property are not compatible; and third, that we can see their incompatibility at a number of practical junctures in our extremely confused law of takings.[65] Thus it is undoubtedly the case that the principles of takings compensation are pluralist or even incoherent in the sense that some elements may be in potential conflict with others. Indeed the uncertain history of our own takings law reflects that fact.

But the incompatible elements do not have to do with any necessary clash among the several guiding principles that Stephen Munzer so interestingly sets out for modern property regimes, that is, preference satisfaction, justice, and desert. On the contrary, that trio of principles can easily be subsumed under the imperial first principle of preference satisfaction. Instead, the incompatible elements in our takings law emerge from the oil-and-water mixture of a dominating preference-satisfying conception of property on the one hand, with a weaker but very different historical conception of property as propriety on the other. What we have, in short, is two quite different historical visions of the purposes for which we have a property regime in the first place. We have never entirely abandoned the one or fully embraced the other—and our takings law is left to muddle along with the consequences.

Notes

1. Probably the best-known and most-cited article in this voluminous literature is Frank Michelman, "Property, Utility, and Fairness: Comments on the Ethical Foundations of 'Just Compensation' Law," 80 *Harv. L. Rev.* 1165 (1967). For just two quite different recent accounts, see Saul Levmore, "Takings, Torts and Special Interests," 77 *Virginia L. Rev.* 1333 (1991); Jeremy Paul, "The Hidden Structure of Takings Law," 64 *S. Cal. L. Rev.* 1393 (1991). For two of my own forays into this wilderness, see "Property Rights, Regulatory Regimes and the New Takings Jurisprudence—an Evolutionary Approach," 57 *Tenn. L. Rev.* 577 (1990); and "*Mahon*" Reconstructed: Why the Takings Issue Is Still a Muddle," 57 *S. Cal. L. Rev.* 561 (1984). All have numerous further cites.

2. See, for example, Euclid v. Ambler Realty, 272 U.S. 365 (1926); compare Richard Epstein, *Takings: Private Property and the Power of Eminent Domain* 112–33 (1985). The nuisance defense reemerged explicitly in Lucas v. South Carolina Coastal Council, 112 S.Ct. 2886, 2899–2901 (1992).

3. The classic case is Munn v. Illinois, 94 U.S. 113 (1877), discussed by Harry Scheiber, "The Road to *Munn:* Eminent Domain and the Concept of Public Purpose in the State Courts," 5 *Perspectives in Am. Hist.* 329, 256 (1971).

4. Munzer, "Compensation and Government Takings of Private Property," 33 *Nomos* 195 (1991) [hereinafter Munzer]. This article collects in one location the relevant portions of his book *A Theory of Property* (1990) [hereinafter Munzer, *Theory*).

5. As Munzer points out, the difference between these two revolves around the possibility of interpersonal comparisons of utilities. Munzer, supra note 4, at 200, and Munzer, *Theory,* supra note 4, at 202–203. This is an issue important in dividing utilitarians from libertarians, but I will follow Munzer's lead in putting it to one side.

6. Munzer, supra note 4, at 200; Munzer, *Theory,* supra note 4, at 3–5; Munzer defends pluralism generally in *Theory,* 292 et seq. (ch. 11, "Conflict and Resolution").

7. For example, John Stick seems to take this view: see his "Turning Rawls into Nozick and Back Again," 81 *Nw. U. L. Rev.* 363 (1987), and my own critique, "'Enough and as Good' of What?" *81 Nw. U. L. Rev.* 417–22 (1987). So to some degree, perhaps, does John Rawls, whose work is discussed on those pages, though the matter is murky. And again, to some degree, so does Munzer, who as Thomas Merrill points out, shares with some other academics an interest in "how we cut the pie" as opposed to the ways that property might make the pie bigger. See Thomas W. Merrill, "Zero-Sum Madison" (review), 90 *Mich. L. Rev.* 1392, 1400, n. 26 (1992).

8. For some of Munzer's public-private preference examples, see *Theory,* supra note 4, at 207–11.

9. See Rose, supra note 7; Merrill, supra note 7; see also Thomas W. Merrill, "Wealth and Property," 38 *UCLA L. Rev.* 489, 495 (1990) (reviewing Munzer's *Theory of Property*).

10. John Locke, *Second Treatise of Government*, in *Two Treatises of Government* (P. Laslett rev. ed. 1963), sec. 31.

11. Jeremy Bentham, *Principles of the Civil Code*, in *Theory of Legislation* 109–14, 121 (1987; reprint of C. K. Ogden ed. 1931); on "rentseeking," see James M. Buchanan, Robert D. Tollison, and Gordon Tullock, *Toward a Theory of the Rent-Seeking Society* (1980).

12. Thomas W. Merrill, "The Economics of Public Use," 72 *Cornell L. Rev.* 61, 74–78, 82–85, 101–102 (1986).

13. Rawls, *A Theory of Justice* (1971). Rawls' work is central in Munzer's chapter "Justice and Equality"; see Munzer, *Theory*, supra note 4, at 227 et seq.

14. Munzer, supra note 4, at 201; Munzer, *Theory*, supra note 4, at 247.

15. Alfred Marshall, *Principles of Economics* 80–81 (1982; reprint of 8th ed. 1920). On the income tax, and a skeptical view of the declining marginal utility of income, see Walter Blum and Harry Kalven, *The Uneasy Case for Progressive Taxation* 56–62 (1953). For more doubts, see also Richard Posner, *Economic Analysis of Law* 434–36 (3d ed. 1986).

16. Michelman, supra note 1, at 1211–14; Bentham, supra note 11, at 115–19, describing, among other "evils" of attacks on property, the "deadening of industry."

17. Bentham, supra note 11, at 111–14.

18. Michelman, supra note 1, at 1222–24.

19. One form of this utilitarian argument has appeared in some "takings" scholars' analogy of takings compensation to insurance; for a good review and analysis, see William A. Fischel and Perry Shapiro, "Takings, Insurance, and Michelman: Comments on Economic Interpretations of 'Just Compensation' Law," 17 *J. Legal Stud.* 269 (1988).

20. Munzer, *Theory*, supra note 4, at 254 et seq.

21. See J.G.A. Pocock, "The Mobility of Property and the Rise of Eighteenth Century Sociology," in Anthony Parel and Thomas Flanagan, eds., *Theories of Property, Aristotle to the Present* 141–42 (1979). Forrest McDonald points out that even John Locke often exercised this usage; see McDonald, *Novus Ordo Seclorum: The Intellectual Origins of the Constitution* 10–11 (1985).

22. See Bodin's *Six Bookes of a Commonweale* 11–12, 110–11 (1962; reprint of 1606 English trans.); J. W. Allen, *Political Thought in the Sixteenth Century* 424–25 (rev. ed. 1960).

23. Ralph E. Giesey, "Rules of Inheritance and Strategies of Mobility in Prerevolutionary France," 82 *Am. Hist. Rev.* 271–72, 275–77 (1977). Giesey discusses the lineage property (*propres*) of commoners; aristocratic land had different rules of succession but also kept landed property in the hands of the ongoing family.

24. Howard Bloch, "Women, Property, Poetry" (unpublished manuscript on file with the author, delivered at Conference on Property and Rhetoric, Northwestern University, 1986), at 6–7.

25. Id. at 17; for discussion of commerce, see Pocock, supra note 21, at 153.

26. For some examples from the late Holy Roman Empire (Austria and Germany), see Carol Rose, "Empire and Territories at the End of the Old Reich," in J. Vann and S. Rowan, eds. *The Old Reich: Essays on German Political Institutions, 1495–1806,* at 61–63, 67–70 (1974).

27. Robert Darnton, "What Was Revolutionary About the French Revolution?" *N.Y. Rev.,* Jan. 19, 1989, at 3, 4.

28. See 1 William Blackstone, *Commentaries on the Laws of England* 416–20, 430–32 (1979, reproduction of 1765 ed.), describing head of household's authority over servants, wife, children.

29. See Peter Laslett, *The World We Have Lost: England Before the Industrial Age* 21, 62–66 (2d ed. 1971).

30. Id. at 31–32, for seventeenth-century perceptions of English gradations. The "body politic," with a governing head as well as arms, feet, and so on, was a dominating metaphor for larger social and political organization; see, for example, Conrad Russell, *The Crisis of the Parliaments: English History, 1509–1660,* at 41–43 (1971); J. R. Hale, *Renaissance Europe* 167–68 (1977). See also the essays "Ancient Constitution" and "Seeing Property" later in this volume.

31. Arthur A. Lovejoy, *The Great Chain of Being* (1936); for the eighteenth-century version of this metaphor, see 183–207 et seq.

32. See John Calvin, *Institutes of Christian Religion* (1536), in *On God and Political Duty* 47–49 (2d ed. 1956), referring to civil magistrates as God's viceregents.

33. See Roger Lockyer, *Tudor and Stuart Britain, 1471–1714,* at 27–28 (1964); Allen, supra note 22, at 418.

34. For the term "co-governor," see Dietrich Gerhard, "Problems of Representation and Delegation in the Eighteenth Century," in *Liber Memorialis Sir Maurice Powicke* 123 (1965) (quoting Roland Mousnier).

35. See, e.g., Gerald Strauss, *Nuremberg in the Sixteenth Century* 50–51, 74–84 (1966), describing city's property and patriciate.

36. Hendrik Hartog, *Public Property and Private Power: The Corporation of the City of New York in American Law* 21–22, 33–34, 40 (1983); see also Carol Rose, "Public Property, Old and New" (review), 79 *Nw. U. L. Rev.* 216, 219–22 (1984).

37. J. H. Parry, *The Age of Reconnaissance* 215 (1964); Charles M. Andrews, *The Colonial Period in American History* 28–45, 259 (1967).

38. See generally Rose, supra note 36, 219–21.

39. See 1 E. M. Heckscher, *Mercantilism* 254, 285–86 (M. Shapiro trans. 1935), quoting (at 286) a seventeenth-century English document concerning a guild lawsuit.

40. See generally Franklin L. Ford, *Robe and Sword: The Regrouping of the French Aristocracy After Louis XIV* (1953); for some nuances of sale and heritability of office, see Giesey, supra note 23, at 282–83.

41. J. H. Plumb, *The Growth of Political Stability in England 1675–1725,* at 38–39 (1969).

42. Allen, supra note 22, at 418–19; 1 Blackstone, supra note 28, at 135–36.

43. Allen, supra note 22, at 421. See also 1 Montesquieu, *The Spirit of the Laws* 260 (1984, reprint of 1751 English trans.); although Montesquieu generally argued against confiscation, he seemed to think it far less problematic to confiscate com-

mercial properties, which he saw as more or less adventitious, than family land; see, e.g., id. at 79 (favorably citing Bodin), 260.

44. See 1 Robert R. Palmer, *The Age of Democratic Revolution* 448–65 (1959). For non-French examples, see also id. at 341–48, 377–84 (Belgium, Hungary); for the repercussions of these practices on the American constitutional debates, see the next essay in this volume, "Ancient Constitution."

45. 1 Montesquieu, supra note 43, 50–53; cf. the inequalities he thought inherent in monarchies, id. at 66–67, 88–89.

46. McDonald, supra note 21, at 74–75; for an extended discussion of the republican tradition of property, see Gregory S. Alexander, "Time and Property in the Civic Republican Culture," 66 *N.Y.U. L. Rev.* 273 (1990–91); for "independence," id. at 292.

47. See generally Robert Steinfeld, "Property and Suffrage in the Early American Republic," 41 *Stan. L. Rev.* 335 (1989); see also McDonald, supra note 21, at 25–27.

48. Christopher Hill, "The Poor and the People in Seventeenth-Century England," in Frederick Krantz, *History from Below: Studies in Popular Protest and Popular Ideology* 29 et seq. (1988), notes that seventeenth-century republicanism excluded the poor from a definition of the "people."

49. Alexander, supra note 46, at 285–90; see also Lacey K. Ford, Jr., *The Origins of Southern Radicalism: The South Carolina Upcountry, 1800–1860,* at 52, 73–74 (1988).

50. 1 Montesquieu, supra note 43, 52–58, 344. Some at least mildly levelling sentiments appeared in comments of the Antifederalists; these will be discussed at greater length in the next essay, "Ancient Constitution."

51. See 1 Montesquieu, supra note 43, at 50, on republican eagerness to serve the common good; he also thought citizens in a republic were more willing to tax themselves, id. at 265.

52. See Roger Tawney, *Religion and the Rise of Capitalism* 216–19 (3d ed. 1956); for American republican attitudes, see Gordon Wood, *The Creation of the American Republic* 63–65, 68–70 (1969).

53. Tawney, supra note 52, at 219–25; David Ricardo, *Principles of Political Economy, 1 Complete Works* 105–107 (P. Sraffa ed. 1951).

54. See, e.g., Tawney, supra note 52, at 216–17; see also Erasmus' advice to Charles V, urging light taxation on the poor and heavy duties on the luxuries of the rich, cited in Hale, supra note 30, at 163; William Tyndale's *Obedience of a Christian Man* (1535), cited in Russell, supra note 30, at 43, exhorted agricultural landlords to restrain rents and fines and to "be as fathers to your tenants."

55. See text at note 43 supra, concerning Bodin's and Montesquieu's acceptance of the uncompensated taking of "acquired" goods; for similar views in the context of taxes, see Vivian Gruder, "A Mutation in Elite Political Culture: The French Notables and the Defense of Property and Participation, 1787" in 56 *J. Mod. Hist.* 598, 611–12 (1984).

56. McDonald, supra note 21, at 14.

57. Reich, "The New Property," 73 *Yale L. J.* 733, 785–86 (1964).

58. Sunstein, "Beyond the Republican Revival," 97 *Yale L. J.* 1539, 1551 (1988). See also Akhil Amar, "Republicanism and Minimal Entitlements," 11 *Geo. Mason*

U. L. Rev. 11 (1988); Frank Michelman, "The Supreme Court, 1985 Term—Foreword: Traces of Self-government," 100 *Harv. L. Rev.* 4, 40–41 (1986).

59. See Richard Epstein's criticism in "Modern Republicanism—or The Flight from Substance," 97 *Yale L. J.* 1633, 1635–36 (1988); Mark Tushnet, "The Concept of Tradition in Constitutional Historiography," 29 *Wm. & Mary L. Rev.* 93, 96–97 (1987). For an odd variant of noblesse oblige in James Madison, i.e., a supposed elitist need to protect property for the sake of the "ultimate happiness" of those without property, see Jennifer Nedelsky, *Private Property and the Limits of American Constitutionalism* 35–38, 41 (1990).

60. Epstein, supra note 2, at 3–6.

61. See, e.g., Nollan v. California Coastal Comm'n, 483 U.S. 825 (1987); Loretto v. Teleprompter Manhattan CATV Corp., 458 U.S. 419 (1982).

62. The 1992 case Lucas v. South Carolina Coastal Council, 112 S.Ct. 2886, held a complete loss of economically valuable use to be a taking unless defended in some other way, but the case leaves unanswered the question of how much, short of complete loss, constitutes a taking.

63. *Lucas* is ambiguous whether a reasonable remaining income obviates a "taking"; but see, e.g., Penn Central Transpo. Co. v. City of New York, 438 U.S. 104 (1978).

64. See Robert Ellickson and A. Dan Tarlock, *Land-Use Controls* 136, n. 3 (1982).

65. See Rose, *"Mahon,"* supra note 1, at 596; cf. Laura Underkuffler, in "An Essay on Property," 100 *Yale L. J.* 127 (1990), who argues that the early republic's conception of property combined these conceptions. While I agree with much in this interesting article, it leaves to one side the question of the consistency of these conceptions.

4

Ancient Constitution Versus Federalist Empire: Antifederalism from the Attack on "Monarchism" to Modern Localism

Introduction

Antifederalism is generally thought to represent a major road not taken in our constitutional history. The Antifederalists, after all, lost the great debate in 1787–1788, while their opponents' constitution prevailed and prospered through the years. If we had needed proof of the staggering victory of the Federalist constitutional project, the bicentennial celebrations of 1987 would certainly seem to have given it, at least insofar as victory is measured by longevity and adulation.

One of the most impressive signals of the Federalists' triumph is the manner in which their constitution has come to dominate the very rhetoric of constitutionalism. This is particularly the case in the United States, where the federal Constitution has the status of what might be called the "plain vanilla" brand—a standard by which we understand and judge other constitutions, as, for example, those of states and localities.[1] The federal Constitution's rhetorical dominance has extended to some degree even to other parts of the world, when foreign citizens have looked to it for guidance about their own governmental structures.[2]

What, then, might be left over for the defeated Antifederalists? This essay is an effort to reconsider the degree to which the Antifederalist road may still be trod after all, and in particular to reconstruct some elements of Antifederalism that have been incorporated into a tradition of local autonomy that continues to this day. That tradition in turn rests on a different

The original version of this essay appeared in 84 *Northwestern University Law Review*, 74–105 (1990). Reprinted by permission of *Northwestern University Law Review*.

and much older version of constitutionalism than the Federalists' plain vanilla variety.

In this sense the essay elaborates the themes of the last and explores what seems to be an antiquated constitutional mode of thought—one closely associated with the understanding of property as propriety, discussed in the previous essay. Here, of course, the older constitutional tradition was filtered through a specifically American context, where issues of "republicanism" loomed large, even though the origins of the tradition were European. The essay will proceed roughly through the following main lines: at the outset, I will try to get at the older political outlook by exploring the ways in which Federalist plans clashed with it, a task that requires me to locate Federalist constitutionalism historically and theoretically in the eighteenth-century Western political topography. Then I will pick up the Antifederalists' charge that the proposed Federalist constitution was "monarchical." This was a significant argument because, as we will see, there were a number of striking parallels between European monarchic projects and the Federalists' centralizing and commercializing plans. Neither the European monarchists nor the Federalists had much use for the "ancient constitution" so dear to the Antifederalists or to their European traditionalist counterparts, but it was on that traditional constitutional understanding that the Antifederalists tried to construct a positive program, as we shall also see.

Even the Antifederalists' defeat at the polls did not entirely settle the matter of American constitutionalism, at least as a practical matter. The Federalists' rhetoric has clearly dominated American constitutional discussions ever since their victory in 1787, but in spite of that, Antifederalist attitudes have continued to enjoy a kind of unacknowledged underground afterlife, most notably in local political practice. To be sure, these underground practices have been very much affected by the Federalist ascendency, and this essay will conclude by discussing some of the ways in which our localist tradition has been affected by its complex symbiosis with the centralizing and commercializing Federalist program.

Here, then, is the starting point: the location of the Federalist ship of state in the Atlantic world's political ocean of the day.

I. The Plain Vanilla Constitution and the Ancient Constitution

Without question, there are innumerable ambiguities in the Federalists' plain vanilla constitutional model, and there always have been.[3] Without question too, there have been quite far-ranging attacks on the original plain vanilla model and departures from it as well. Several legal scholars have argued that these departures occurred particularly during this century, as New Deal concepts were incorporated into the national governing scheme.[4] Still, that plain vanilla Federalist model has a set of elements that have always been widely understood and widely thought to structure the actions of our national government.

Our government is supposed to function in theory—if somewhat imperfectly in fact—through a series of familiar mechanics. There are divisions of branches and checks and balances among the branches; there are equal and uniform national laws operating directly on the people; there is a direct popular representation, constructed in such a way that many interests appear in the representative body and such that no one interest can dominate the others.

One underlying theme of these structural features is the protection of rights, since the mechanical operation of the whole structure works to impede incursions on individual entitlements. Historically, the right that was thought to need greatest protection was the right to acquire and hold property.[5] Today, of course, the emphasis on protecting property is subject to considerably more debate—much of it concentrated on current constitutional issues of regulatory takings of property—and some of this debate is very heated indeed.[6] But however one comes out with respect to these modern issues, it is still fair to say that the plain vanilla model of a constitution, with its attention to individual entitlements, is one that Marxists might still dub bourgeois democratic—that is, a constitution that has always had close connections with the entitlements consciousness of a capitalist economic process.

On the other hand, there are other constitutional models too, even though, in our own time, their operations are often explained or criticized by reference to the plain vanilla model. When we think back to the time of the adoption of the Constitution and to the debates over its ratification, the provincialism of our view comes into particularly sharp relief. The debates of that time show how mistaken it would be to suppose that the Federalists' constitution has always represented the basic model of a constitution, on which all others are more or less mere variants.

Years before we adopted our plain vanilla model, there was a very different vision of constitutionalism, a vision captured in the phrase of J.G.A. Pocock in his justly famous book *The Ancient Constitution and the Feudal Law.* Indeed, it is difficult to see what our plain vanilla version was all about unless we note its sharp break from this older version of constitutionalism, which, following Pocock—and indeed the rather common usage of the eighteenth century—I will call the "ancient constitution."[7]

Constitutionalism on the model of the ancient constitution was a vision of fundamental law deriving from long-standing ways of doing things, justified either by the sheer antiquity of practice or by the wisdom and suitableness that antiquity signifies.[8] Pocock himself has concentrated on the so-called civic republican tradition in the British version of the ancient constitution, and indeed his work has sparked a renewed interest in the civic republicanism in early America.[9] But in a wider understanding, the ancient constitution was not necessarily linked to republicanism; the term could be understood to apply to a great range of practices so long as they were seen as fundamental law. Indeed, in this broader sense, the ancient constitution encompassed all kinds of long-established laws, charters, practices, customs, and local privileges—not the least of which might be local economic privileges—that were thought to be constitutive of a given political realm, whether republican or not.

The elements of ancient constitutionalism were thus those ways of doing things that were so well established as to count as the "nature" of a given polity. Indeed, a constitution on this older model has close connections with the medieval and early modern vision of a "body politic." Just as one's personal physical makeup is one's constitution, so a political constitution was seen as the way that the body politic was framed and held together; the constitution was the set of established practices that gave that body politic its proper identity.[10]

We still hear an echo of this usage in the way that the British talk about the "English constitution." But in the seventeenth and eighteenth centuries, it was a commonplace throughout the European world that political life was organized about long-standing "constitutions" or "fundamental laws." These views were expounded by some able and well-known writers, such as Montesquieu and, somewhat later, Burke; but the general attitude was so widespread as to need no exposition—except of course as the "fundamental laws" came under increasing threat, particularly from the monarchs of the middle and later eighteenth century, of whom I will say more shortly.[11] The American colonists were by no means exempt from this traditionalist approach to politics, and in the early eighteenth century, for example, they argued that colonial political practices were based on the "ancient" rights declared in charters or custom—and were not to be altered at the whim of the crown.[12]

In this political tradition, it was well understood that fundamental laws and constitutions might take different names and describe quite different governmental institutions; as one eighteenth-century German jurist remarked, "England must be governed according to the English [constitution], Sweden according to the Swedish, Poland according to the Polish, Germany according to the German and also Württemberg according to Württemberg's own ancient constitution."[13] As a matter of fact, Württembergers referred to their ancient constitution as the "good old law," a somewhat vague composite in which they included their vestigial representative assembly of estates, along with the rest of their time-honored political, ecclesiastical, and legal relations.[14]

Somewhat later, Tocqueville used a different term—"aristocratic"—to describe this traditionalist and particularistic political mindset in the prerevolutionary era that he called the Old Regime. His usage of "aristocratic" was less a reference to hierarchy than a term to distinguish the undifferentiated universalism that he found in nineteenth-century American attitudes. As Tocqueville said, by way of comparing the earlier attitudes with the egalitarianism among his own contemporaries, "among an aristocratic people each caste has its own opinions, feelings, rights, customs and modes of living."[15]

In using the term "aristocratic," what Tocqueville seemed to have had in mind was a concept of privilege that is now somewhat unfamiliar to us but was much more prevalent in the eighteenth century. In this older conception, as the modern commentator C.B.A. Behrens has explained, "privilege" did indeed include hierarchy but did not end there. Privilege then did not necessarily imply, as it usually does today, an unjustifiable special favor to some groups over others. The concept was rather a larger one, denoting the way that a multiform society was organized into distinct elements, *all* of which were "constituted bodies" with *their own* privileges.[16] Hence an actual "aristocracy" or nobility was only a subset within a multiplicity of privileged corporate groups and bodies, in a society in which "privilege was an integral part of the social order."[17]

In practice, then, the ancient constitution was a dizzying array of particularistic privileges, enjoyed by localities and groups in their corporate capacity. Here is the way one Frenchman described the nature of the eighteenth-century French political scene:

> Imagine a country where there are a great many corporate bodies. The result is that ... one hears talk of nothing but rights, concessions, immunities, special agreements, privileges, prerogatives. Every town, every community, every province, every ecclesiastical or judicial body, has its interest to defend in this confusion.[18]

Even though the contents of this sort of constitutionalism varied from place to place, another historian, Robert R. Palmer, observed that in the era preceding the French Revolution, political commentators saw the Atlantic political culture as being all of a piece; they were perfectly comfortable comparing the institutions of Poland and Virginia, Venice and Geneva, Belgium and Hungary, Ireland and the provinces of France.[19]

But certainly the political culture of the ancient constitution had a sharply different set of characteristics from our plain vanilla version of a constitution. In the first place, the ancient constitution was distinctly not a political vision of impartiality or equality under uniform law. It rather recognized the special and particularized customary privileges of provinces, guilds, municipalities, families, ecclesiastical groups, nobles of varying gradations, assemblies of estates, and on and on, where all these elements enjoyed some measure of "co-governing" power with whatever purported to be the central authority.[20]

Nor, in the second place, did this version of constitutionalism have anything to do with free enterprise and the equal rights to develop property. The ancient constitution was packed with economic privileges that were treated as proprietary and sometimes inheritable rights—including exclusive rights to manufacture and sell particular goods or to conduct markets in particular places or even to hold certain offices of state, along with their accompanying annuities, fees, and perquisites.[21] Nor, finally, did the ancient constitution have any truck with a concept of unified government acting directly on the subjects. Everywhere in Europe, the partisans of the ancient constitution fought tooth and nail against any centralizing efforts of monarchs. Such efforts would have undermined the efflorescent privileges and authority of the "constituted bodies," whereas they themselves regarded both privileges and authority as their own property—their property because these matters were "properly" theirs, prerequisite to their roles as co-governing orders in the realm.

Indeed in the eighteenth century, and particularly on the Continent,[22] it was the *monarchs* who borrowed "enlightened" thinkers' ideas of economic and political reform and who wanted to oust guild privileges and market monopolies and instead open up economic enterprise and commerce; it was those same monarchs, if anyone, who wanted to abate aristocratic authority in the countryside and shift power away from local oligarchies in the towns.[23]

In a remarkable passage, James Steuart, one of the thinkers associated with the eighteenth-century Scottish Enlightenment, summed up these developments and illustrated their interrelationships: "Trade and industry owed their establishment to the ambition of princes, who supported … the plan … principally with a view to enrich themselves, and thereby to become formidable to their neighbours." But, Steuart went on, this plan also strengthened commercial enterprisers who had an interest in greater liberty, and this in turn induced princes to "introduc[e] … a more mild and more regular plan of administration," which entailed "limiting the power of the higher classes" and "restrain[ing] the great lords." Although it might appear that these centralizing efforts were designed to make all power "depend on the prince's will only," Steuart said, and "although the prerogative of some princes be increased considerably beyond the bounds of the ancient constitution, even to such a degree as perhaps justly to deserve the name of usurpation; yet the consequences cannot every where be said, upon the whole, to have impaired what I call public liberty."[24]

Arthur Young, the later-eighteenth-century British political essayist who quoted this passage at length, disagreed vehemently with Steuart's optimism, and as he quoted, he interspersed the passage with acid side comments on monarchist overreaching. As Steuart had suggested, however, the monarchs had their own reasons for liberalization and centralization, notably their effort to solve the pandemic fiscal crises that accompanied the lack of central control. It was typically the particularistic, oligarchic, and "privileged" elements—much more than the more or less liberal literati like Young—who opposed these monarchist efforts and who pounded for the "good old law," even to the point of rebellion against their kings.

Indeed, from the later sixteenth century up to the French Revolution, antiroyalist rebellions were commonplace in the Europe of the ancient constitution. Although we Americans don't pay much attention to these things, our own Revolution was in some ways just another in a long line of revolts of provincial privilege against centralizing royalist pretensions. Sometimes these rebellions were sharpened by religious differences, but at root they always rested on provincial disgruntlement, as sometimes-distant monarchs attempted to undermine local privileges or to subordinate them to centralizing and uniform administration.

We now pay little attention to the revolt of the Netherlands from their centralizing Spanish monarchs in the late sixteenth century.[25] We pay even less to the later Catalonian and Portuguese revolts against the same monarchic lines—or to the French provincial nobles' revolt after decades of Richelieu's regimentation—all at about the same time as the mid-seventeenth-century English civil war.[26] As to English civil war, we forget, if we ever knew about it, that the event that set off the calling of the Long Parliament and that led to the eventual beheading of Charles I was the rebellion of the Scots against what they thought were royal violations of their provincial privileges, notably their distinctive ecclesiastical organization.[27] We forget too that in the late eighteenth century, the French Revolution erupted only after decades of squabbles between the French monarchs and their own privileged classes.[28] We may well have heard the joke that the "enlightened" Austrian emperor Joseph II allegedly and quite characteristically said that even Mozart's music had too many notes; but we hardly notice that he also attempted to suppress fiscal and guild privileges of his many provinces, in favor of simplified and uniform imperial laws, and that his Belgian provinces and their "constituted bodies" greeted his acts with a sharp resistance—a resistance that would give an example of revolution to the neighbors in France.[29]

We may forget these things now, but our forefathers who debated the 1787 Constitution did not. They were very well aware of these historic conflicts between centralizing monarchs and long-standing local privilege and of the way in which the subversion of the ancient constitution might—and indeed arguably *ought to*—lead to revolution.[30]

Modern historians have debated whether the Antifederalists might be the American heirs to England's civic republicans or ancient constitutionalists, to the exclusion of their Federalist opponents.[31] On the one hand, in sheer conservatism and insistence on established usages, the Antifederalists undoubtedly were more closely allied with the habits of thought of ancient constitutionalism than were their Federalist opponents.[32] On the other hand, Antifederalism covered a considerable range of opinion—some of it overlapping with Federalist views. Antifederalists and Federalists alike cited similar sources and drew from the same rhetorical founts. Both sides cited Montesquieu, for example, that well-known European proponent of the ancient constitution. Both sides also seemed to eschew the institution of nobility, as Antifederalists accused the Federalists of promoting something like a nobility while Federalists more or less denied it.[33] Similarly, the Antifederalists explicitly aligned themselves with the "republicanism" and "republican virtue" that marked the Americans' chosen version of the ancient constitution—but then so did their Federalist opponents, at least in their rhetoric.[34]

But in at least one very important respect, the identification between Antifederalism and the ancient constitution did make sense: that lies in the Antifederalists' championship of local particularism. This theme ran through their remarks about all kinds of issues. Most important was a subject that I will explore more fully later: they insisted that a national, "consolidated" government would necessarily quell liberty, because a national government would be too large and its representative bodies too far removed from the people to reflect their multiform mores and natures. But in addition, when they pounded the table about "republican virtue," they were also dealing with a coded reflection of the conflict between localism and centralism: at the time, corruption was widely regarded as a tool by which centralizing monarchs and their ministers—notably in Britain—attempted to overcome the resistance of the virtuous squires of the "country."[35]

The identification between the Antifederalists and the ancient constitution, then, is most sharply presented in their charges, first, that the Federalist constitution would institute a consolidated government and, second, that this government smacked of monarchism. Given the circumstances of the contemporary Atlantic political world, these were in large measure variants on the same charge. And the Antifederalists made this charge for a very good reason: the Federalist program of a national state did indeed echo many of the eighteenth-century European monarchist projects that took aim at long-established provincial privileges.

II. The Federalist Project: Central Power and Its Monarchist Overtones

The plain vanilla constitution of the Federalists, like the centralizing efforts of European monarchs, broke with the older vision of an ancient constitution, in which the regime was composed of a multiplicity of "cogoverning" established bodies. The Federalists, like the European monarchs, saw one overwhelming problem with the ancient constitution: it kept government *weak.* Why was government weak in such a regime? It was weak because a polity riddled by special particularized rights was perpetually beset by fiscal crises—and this, of course, was also the perceived opinion about the United States under the Articles of Confederation.[36]

More generally, governance under the ancient constitution was weak because such a multiform polity, dependent as it was on those who held particularized privileges, could gather itself only with the utmost strain and effort to exercise any concentrated force or influence whatever. Alexander Hamilton drew the radical conclusion from all this and asserted that the very notion of a regime dependent on other political authorities, in their corporate or collective form, was "the bane of the old [constitution] and ... in itself evidently incompatible with the idea of GOVERNMENT."[37]

Hamilton looked to Europe in this assertion, quite as much as he looked to the United States of the Articles of Confederation. In two of the Federalist Papers that have been rather neglected in American scholarship, Numbers 19 and 20, Hamilton and Madison excoriated precisely the type of regime that appeared all over Europe before the French Revolution. One can see their viewpoint most clearly in their scathing remarks on the fragmented politics of the Dutch and Swiss republics—which were often cited by the Antifederalists as models of confederate republics[38]—and even more in their attitude to the Germans' "Holy Roman Empire," which, as Voltaire had wisecracked, was neither holy nor Roman nor an empire. Indeed, by the later eighteenth century, the old Empire had fractured into hundreds of semisovereign entities, and it undoubtedly represented the most striking efflorescence of Europe's ancient constitutional style of governance.[39]

The Federalist Number 19 treated the so-called Empire as the quintessential horrible example of the polity that exists as a "community of sovereigns," and its discussion of this "nerveless body" displays Publius' polemical style at its most savage. Upbraiding the Empire for its "general imbecility, confusion and misery," *The Federalist* followed with a litany of its subjection to external invasions, internal intrigues, overweaning strong men and oppressed weak ones, atrocious administration, and bungled enforcement.[40]

How could this weakness be overcome? The Federalists had a program, and, like the contemporary European monarchist plans, theirs entailed a sharp break from the ancient constitution altogether. The first component of their program flowed from a Hamiltonian rejection of dependence on other political bodies. The new constitution would set out a large, unified government whose laws and taxes would fall directly upon the citizenry. This government would reject the mediation of any other governmental bodies in their corporate form—all those in-between states and provinces and other local bodies, those *"pouvoirs intermédiaires"* of which Montesquieu had spoken approvingly in large-scale monarchy and that many monarchs on the Continent had at least half-heartedly attempted to supplant long before the Federalists' constitutional foray.[41]

The second component in the Federalist program also rang a familiar note of European enlightened monarchy: the new government would promote commerce. Commerce, as Publius observed, would produce wealth, and wealth would make the nation powerful.[42] And what did commerce entail? Quite apart from the enlarged markets with free exchange that would be guaranteed by the Commerce Clause, commerce itself entailed individual rights, and especially the rights of property. Security of property would encourage owners to invest time and effort in what they had, thus making their property even more valuable. And in turn, this would have positive consequences for the nation's wealth and strength.[43]

Quite a bit earlier, John Locke had pointed out the relationship between security of property and national force. As he had put it, the "wise and godlike" prince who "by established laws of liberty ... secure[s] protection and incouragement to the honest industry of Mankind against the oppression of power and narrownesse of Party *will quickly be too hard for his neighbours."*[44] Within a few years, the Physiocrats on the Continent also noted the connection between private property and national power, and they encouraged European monarchs to secure private property and remove restraints on exchange so that the fruits of individual enterprise could flow unimpeded through the nation and make the whole wealthier. Many monarchs and their advisers heard the message and attempted to liberalize commerce and promote the factory industry that undermined local privileges over labor practices and markets.[45]

The Federalists heard the message too, perhaps as translated by Adam Smith, whose *Wealth of Nations* was widely read in America.[46] In addition to the Commerce Clause that would nationalize the market, their constitution had several elements aimed at securing a commercial republic from internal threats to private property. One threat came from what Locke called "narrownesse of Party" or, in the Federalist translation, *faction*—the enthusiasms of partial interest groups that could erode individual rights and property interests and in general disrupt the "honest industry of

Mankind." To control faction, the Federalists proposed to restructure representation in a way that meshed flawlessly with their concept of a direct, unified central government. This was most explicitly stated in Madison's famous *Federalist* Number 10: in the multiparty representation of the "extended republic," parochial factions would neutralize one another's attempts to intrude on the rights of property. Moreover, the clause protecting obligations of contracts would halt local or state governments' factional encroachments on property rights—encroachments that might otherwise weaken the nation by sapping the enterprising drive of the citizenry. As to what Locke had called the "oppression of power" at a higher level, any federal encroachments would be halted before they began, through checks and balances among the various governmental institutions.

The protection of commerce and the unification of government thus aimed at the same goal: national strength. The unified commercial republic would be a more powerful political entity than the many states that were fragmented, through their ancient constitutions, into a kaleidoscope of local privileges and special laws. It would be stronger not just because it was unified politically and economically, but also because its commercially minded citizens, secure in the rights of private property, could safely hustle about their interests and enterprises in a way that would make the whole nation richer. That wealth, in turn, could be tapped by the national government.

The Federalists' plain vanilla version of constitutionalism, then, was a logical extension of some of the major European monarchical projects. It displaced ancient constitutionalism with a new constitutionalism of uniform laws operating directly on individual citizens, thus bypassing the fragmentation of local privilege. It safeguarded all in a homogeneous commercial environment of secure property and free exchange. In this environment, differences in talents could freely arrive at differences in wealth, so as to encourage the industrious in their efforts. And the resulting unified, commercial nation would be a strong and productive one, ready for any jealous threats that its own prosperity would bring forth.[47]

At bottom, of course, I am suggesting that considerations of external strength—national defense and a credible foreign policy—wagged a good part of the constitutional dog that the Federalists proposed. Their constitutional project had both political and economic dimensions, but to a considerable degree, the parts taken together came into focus on a single goal: overcoming the deplorable weakness of the early republic. By taking a leaf from Locke's Godlike Prince, they hoped to make the republic "too hard for its neighbors."[48]

I am further suggesting that some key components of the Federalists' plain vanilla constitutional scheme—uniform, large-scale central government on the one hand and the promotion of commerce on the other—were also ideas associated with monarchist projects in Europe. The European monarchs had not been particularly successful at these efforts, but as Tocqueville pointed out, the French Revolution ruthlessly carried forth the monarchist project of levelling local privileges. And as he also pointed out, the ultimate successor, the first monarch of a truly centralized state, was Napoleon.[49] What the monarchs of the Enlightenment era did was to set the direction that the French Revolution and Napoleon later followed—and that the Antifederalists so feared in the United States.

III. The Antifederalist Critique

With all this, let me turn back to the Antifederalists. The Antifederalists understood very well the Federalist goal of national strength—along with the commercialization and centralization that were designed to promote that strength. More than any other opponent to the Constitution, Patrick Henry hit upon the very nerve of the Federalist project of external strength. And he inveighed against it. "You are not to inquire how your trade may be increased," he said, "nor how you are to become a great and powerful people, but how your liberties can be secured; for liberty ought to be the direct end of your government."[50] In another passage he sneered at the Federalist aims, with a sarcasm that still drips from the page: "Some way or other we must be a great and mighty empire," he said.

> [W]e must have an army, and a navy, and a number of things. When the American spirit was in its youth, the language of America was different: liberty, sir, was then the primary object. ... But now, sir, the American spirit, assisted by the ropes and chains of consolidation, is about to convert this country into a powerful and mighty empire. ... Such a government is incompatible with the genius of republicanism.[51]

"Republican liberties" were precisely what the Antifederalists saw endangered by the plan that they termed a "consolidated" government—the liberties that guaranteed their ability to rule themselves, to choose their destiny in a way that had genuine meaning. And it was the concern for these liberties that linked the Antifederalists with the ancient constitution of Europe, particularly the republican version of the ancient constitution.

To begin with the centralizing or "consolidating" component of the Federalist project: the Antifederalists thought that an "extended republic" was an oxymoron and that any large-scale government would necessarily fall back into a system that depended on force rather than self-rule. Why was this so? First, there was the authority of Montesquieu. Montesquieu had said that even moderately extended areas could only be governed by monarchy at best (that is, when the ruler's authority was tempered by "intermediate powers," particularly the nobility) and that very large territories were necessarily despotic. Republics, on the other hand, which depended on civic participation, were necessarily small.[52]

The Federalists tried to skirt Montesquieu, arguing that representative institutions made a large republic feasible,[53] but the New York Antifederalist Melanchthon Smith countered with a theme that ran through Antifederalist arguments: even popular representation would be defective in a large territory. Electoral districts would of necessity be large, Smith said, and the constituents of those districts could not really know their so-called representatives, and vice versa. The only persons who could get elected in large districts would be the persons whose wealth and fame would enable them to publicize themselves—persons quite dissimilar from and "unrepresentative" of those for whom they purportedly spoke. The yeomen, the everyday citizens of the "middling class," would have no chance of election over against this "natural aristocracy." Thus the supposedly representative body would not be representative at all of the various elements of the constituency but would fall into the hands of a wellborn and influential upper class, which had no feel for the ordinary citizens' needs and wishes.[54] Alexander Hamilton's revealing response—that an aristocracy of wealth and talent was inevitable in any scheme of government—cannot have been reassuring.[55]

From these defects in representation, the Antifederalists concluded that the Federalists' plan necessitated force. The so-called representatives, ignorant of their constituents' needs, and both literally and psychically distant from those constituents, would pass laws that were unsuited to the different parts of the republic. As a consequence, the execution of their laws would ultimately depend on coercion rather than consent.[56] In the bleakest version of this Antifederalist view, the Federalists "extended republic" would have to depend on a standing army to enforce its laws. Nor would the states retain the ability to defend their citizens from these predators; they would lose control of their militias, which would in any event be overwhelmed by the national government's standing army.[57] Moreover, to collect the funds for such an army and for all the other misguided plans of a bloated, crypto-monarchical national government, a swarm of "bloodsucking" tax collectors would land like "harpies" on the tyrannized citizenry—at the same time emasculating the states all the more by drying up their revenue sources.[58] Better, then, and certainly more consistent with Montesquieu's description of republican principles, that the nation be a kind of league of more or less autonomous and truly republican states, in which representation was a genuine form of self-rule.[59] The preservation of local autonomy—and with it the meaningful liberty of self-rule—was thus at the center of the Antifederalist position; it was this concern that animated their objections to "consolidated government."

A more muted part of the Antifederalist argument, however, involved a critique of the Federalist approach to property rights. Although the Antifederalists supported the rights of property and even commerce and eschewed the radical levelling of the then-recent Shays' Rebellion, they may have had in mind a strand of republican thinking that saw in capitalism an escape from an inexorably hierarchical ordering of society.[60] What they rejected was the Federalist program of protecting property sheerly for the sake of encouraging individual economic efforts in the short run, and national wealth and power in the long. They had a different goal in view in protecting property: they thought that property was a basis of republican civic independence. What they had in mind was the property "proper" to the republican citizen, the property that he and his fellow citizens needed to govern himself, his household, and his community.[61]

Antifederalist speeches and writings were shot through with a kind of ideal type of citizen. The model was the yeoman, the citizen of the "middling" sort—the respectable, knowledgeable, frugal, and public-spirited individual who acts deliberately and cooperatively with other citizens of similarly modest means and independence.[62] It was important to protect this ideal citizen's property so that he could maintain the independence necessary for self-rule. But property, on this view, was only useful insofar as it aided citizens to retain a sturdy manliness, among others of like character. Some Antifederalist writings followed Montesquieu in suggesting that gross disparities of wealth could corrupt a republic.[63] The implication was that property rights should not be so zealously guarded as to reach this point, since the evil of inequality would sap a source of strength quite different from Federalists' hoped-for economic wealth. That source of strength was civic virtue.

Indeed, the real protection of liberty, the Antifederalists argued, lay not in property rights and commerce as such, but rather in those institutions that would promote the courage, independence, judgment, and selflessness of the citizenry. They maintained, as the influential *Letters from the Federal Farmer* put it, that

> if there are advantages in the equal division of our lands, and the strong and manly habits of our people, we ought to establish governments calculated to give duration to them, and not governments which never can work naturally, till that equality of property, and those free and manly habits shall be destroyed.[64]

In short, then, the Antifederalist view was that the Federalists' plain vanilla constitutional project—to become a rich and powerful nation—was a case of taking our collective eye off the main issue at stake. In order to become such a powerful state, we would have to have, at the outset, a centralized government that smacked of the worst versions of monarchism. This centralized government in turn would destroy effective liberty and self-rule, which was necessarily local. Finally, this government might so relentlessly protect a regime of property and commerce—along with the "natural aristocracy" that would dominate the regime economically and politically—as to bring about the debasement of the best citizenry.

Still another point was only hinted at by the Antifederalists, but it was to loom larger in later years: that the Federalist project of wealth and power might corrupt the polity in ways extending beyond our own citizenry and lure the nation into external conquest. As the Antifederalist "Brutus" remarked, the new United States should strive to give the world an example of "virtue and happiness among ourselves," and not follow the European governments that were "framed ... with a view to arms, and war."[65]

Though they could not know it at the time, the true culmination of Antifederalist fears—and Tocqueville's specter later—was Napoleon's empire. Here was the politically centralized regime, built up after the revolutionary levelling of local "liberties," now with a single, uniform national administration. Here was the economic regime of property rights, now established through a codified legal system that protected the citizenry's acquisitions and commercial pursuits. And here was the ruthless dictatorship, standing squarely on military force and a standing army, and capable of terrorizing the citizenry at home as well as the neighboring states.

IV. Antifederalist Echoes of Localism and Republicanism

Everyone knows that the Antifederalists lost, and they may well have lost precisely because they could not come up with an alternative to the Federalist program for national strength. Be that as it may, even in the early years of the republic, their localist position faded from view in the country's central political discussions, as a liberal, capitalist, and more or less nationalist consensus blanketed and smothered the earlier debates on the true meaning of republicanism.[66] But did they lose entirely? Or did they retain some influence on American political life—and if they did so, why did they, and where was that influence located? And is it perhaps just another version of that same question to ask, Why has the Federalist attack on the ancient constitution produced no American Napoleon?

The Echoes of a Distinctively Local Practice

Where did Antifederalist sentiments go after the Constitution was adopted? One answer might well be to states' rights, in all their various historical permutations. It is unquestionably true that later states' rights proponents mined the rhetoric of republican independence.[67] But the effort to link Antifederalism with later states' rights advocacy is really a kind of misidentification, deflecting attention from the most influential aspects of the Antifederalist legacy. It is an interesting sort of misidentification, however, because it replicates one of the Antifederalists' own unresolved problems about the states.

The Antifederalists did indeed speak fervently and often for the continuing autonomy of the states. But as Hamilton quite trenchantly pointed out, the states were themselves too large for the kind of republicanism that the Antifederalists seemed to have in mind; Montesquieu, he said, would have thought them too large for republican government.[68] Hamilton was quite right: the Antifederalist version of republicanism, with its self-rule and civic participation, is only possible at a level more localized than the states. And this is why the association of Antifederalism with states' rights arguments is a relatively sterile ground if we are looking for a lasting contribution from Antifederalist ideas. Instead, we have to look at *local* political organizations to find the continuing influence of the Antifederalist perspective and indeed the continuing influence of the ancient constitution.

Let me begin with a *first* distinctive characteristic of local governments—a characteristic that raises great chagrin among some commentators: local governments have had a quite distinctive attitude about private property rights.[69] One notices this attitude particularly in land use controls, a major area in which local governments currently exercise authority. A great number of land use decisions concern one-on-one disputes among neighbors about the appropriate level of development—one neighbor wants to build a tennis court; the other says it would be noisy and intrusive. Entitlements in these areas are notoriously fuzzy, and insofar as local governments spell them out, they lean toward the maintenance of the status quo.

Even formalized zoning restraints are often quite malleable in fact; actual decisions relate less to some formal structure of entitlements than to discussions, negotiations, and "venting" based on community understanding of appropriate behavior. As between neighbors, local institutions play less the role of the protector of entitlements and more the role of ad hoc mediators.[70] But these same local institutions are apt to make considerably higher demands on outsiders and innovators than they do on established uses and may, for example, condition a new development permit on a contribution to streets, parks, or even low income housing.[71]

In short, in these very important aspects of local government, political bodies are not much engaged as Federalist-style impartial guardians of entitlements or protectors of investment and commerce. If anything, they are more the guardians of the ancient constitution, in the sense of protecting a web of community understandings—and sometimes highly idiosyncratic ones—about the way things ought to be done.[72]

If local governments have their own views about rights, and most notably about the rights of property, what then serves as the brake on their oppressiveness? What is it that prevents local majorities from ganging up to wrest away the fruits of honest industry, particularly from out-group minorities—if anything prevents this at all? There are of course the widely discussed federal and state governments' constitutional strictures against takings of property, but I want to leave those to one side in this discussion.

An answer that could come straight from the civic republican tradition is *virtue*—and this presents a *second* difference between local governments and centralized ones. No one, of course, is naive enough to suggest that local government is necessarily more virtuous than central government; the usual suggestion is just the reverse.[73] But I would suggest that local government is the location where virtue and its opposite, corruption, are most regularly discussed as political issues, in spite of occasional spurts at higher levels of government. Our history certainly suggests this, and indeed the discussion of big-city corruption was well under way by the later nineteenth century.[74] The reason for all this concern is that at the local level, we have to rely more on the virtue of the participants, and, as a consequence, we talk more about their rectitude or corruption.

In any event (and no doubt fortunately) virtue is not the only safeguard against local oppression. Again, leaving to one side the constitutional limitations on takings of property, there are still some other restraints on local overreaching. This brings me to a *third* difference between local governments and governments on a larger scale: local governments are quite differently organized from the federal or even the state governments. Among other things, local governments have far fewer of the mechanics of checks and balances, and far less multiple-interest representation, than do larger governments. But it is at least arguable that in local governments the absence of these structural restraints is counterbalanced by the possibilities for constituent contact and civic participation—what Albert Hirschman has called the "voice" option.[75]

I think there is much territory to be explored in connection with the forms of local civic "voice." For one example, some cities themselves are rather large for the personal participation of individuals, and it may be important to consider subpolitical bodies, such as neighborhood organizations and other civic groups, as the locus for "republican" associational voice. For another and related example, some scholars may place too much weight on local participation in the form of voting and not enough on other forms of participation.[76] Indeed, voting may well be a relatively minor aspect of local civic participation, and other versions of "voice" may be much more important locally: the informal constituent contacts, the PTA meetings, the civic groups' flooding down to city hall, the cub reporters' publicistic scandalmongering, the highly issue-oriented jawboning that is the very stuff of local controversy.

Yet another and quite different safeguard on local government brings me to a *fourth* difference between local and central governments. This is the safeguard, to use Hirschman's terminology again, that we might call "exit"—the ability to abandon something when dissatisfied—and it exists most distinctively at the local level.[77] Public life at the local level is much more idiosyncratic than national public life and much less homogenized. It is primarily at the local level that we are given to wild enthusiasms about sports teams, parades, and bizarre public art; these idiosyncracies survive even what has been called the "malling of America."[78]

These local peculiarities tell us something important about the character of local government and about its relation to Antifederalist ideas of self-rule. There is a reason for the heterogeneity of local communities vis-à-vis each other: people have a *choice* about the community in which they live, in a way that they do not have so much choice about the state or especially the nation in which they are citizens. At least to some degree, people choose their localities according to compatibility with their own wishes and needs. This in turn requires local governments to be careful about the practices they adopt and the reputations they acquire, so that they will not frighten away desired citizens. This is not new; the Antifederalists themselves were accustomed to American communities in which dissatisfied persons could and did "exit" in order to form communities more to their own liking.[79]

The opportunities for local exit—perhaps even more than for voice—establish a connection between local entities and voluntary organizations. What makes a voluntary organization "voluntary" is that one can enter and leave at one's own volition. To a considerable degree, one can do the same thing with one's locality. One signal of this affinity between local governments on the one hand and voluntary organizations on the other is that we have great difficulty in sorting out the differences between "public" local governments and "private" planned communities.[80] Indeed the whole distinction between public and private becomes blurred locally, particularly when we think that people choose their localities in more or less the same ways that they choose the condominium or the retirement community in which they will live, and when we consider that in some ways localities may compete for residents in the same way that private planned communities do.[81] I will come back to this "exit" characteristic shortly, because it is this aspect of local government—related as it is to Antifederalist conceptions of local autonomy—in which modern scholarship has made some particularly interesting contributions.

We are now in a position to return to the earlier question: did the Antifederalists lose entirely? I think not, when we take political *practice* into account. We certainly see a number of the Antifederalist attitudes and concerns in our local politics: the acceptance of community definitions of the rights and responsibilities of property, the concern for virtue and corruption, the possibility for personal participation or voice, the further possibility for choice through the "exit" option.

Lest it be thought that all American government has been "consolidated" in principle through the operations of the Federalist constitution and that we are simply awaiting the eventual and inevitable demise of local self-rule, we should recall that our history reflects a tenacious and continuous countercurrent to most efforts to centralize local functions. Thus the later nineteenth century's judicial doctrine of "Dillon's Rule," which held that municipal powers should be read narrowly, was answered in the early twentieth century by *Euclid v. Ambler Realty,* which gave back under land use auspices the local authority supposedly taken away by Dillon's restrictive reading.[82] Similarly, in the 1970s, there was considerable talk of a "Quiet Revolution" in land use controls, supposedly entailing much greater state control over local land use decisions; but in the intervening years, many of the mechanisms of this Quiet Revolution have been just as quietly reoccupied by local governments.[83] In these and other instances of stubborn local particularism, one sees the working out of a kind of Antifederalist practice, almost invisible in an intellectual environment of overwhelmingly Federalist theory.

Echoes in Theory: Antifederalism and the Rethinking of Federalist Theory

The Antifederalist tradition has indeed not been a very strong strand in our political *theory,* and this seems to me a serious gap. Insofar as Antifederalist thinking is overlooked, we are overlooking an important part of our own political tradition. Happily, this neglect seems to be in the process of rectification, both from the direction of the renewed historical interest in the civic republican tradition and from the very different direction of economic analysis, which has brought into focus the ways in which local communities may compete with one another. This revived theoretical attention is particularly important, because the local governmental aspect of our tradition—as Tocqueville said of the voluntary organizations—could modify the tendencies that we otherwise may have to fall into a timorous and deadening conformity and into an obsession with getting and spending that discourages participation in public life.[84]

How, then, might the Antifederalist tradition help us to rethink our political theory? One especially fruitful way stems from the exit option at the local level and in some new reflections that this exit option might cast on the Federalists' famous discussion of faction. To state the matter succinctly, it may be that the problem of faction is an artifact of that very "extended republic" that, supposedly, was going to render factionalism harmless.

Most Americans interested in political institutions are by now aware of the oft-repeated Federalist argument for the "extended republic": that we need a large republic to safeguard our politics against faction. But because of the possibilities for exit from local government, we might question whether faction really is a serious problem at the local level. More particularly, we might consider whether the Federalists' discussion of faction is in some ways a red herring. Faction would indeed be a local problem if voice were the only safeguard against local oppression; in smaller republics, minority voices can indeed be drowned out. But where localities genuinely differ and can offer residents competing options for lifestyle choices, and where it is possible for people to learn localities' reputations and to move among them, oppression can simply be left behind or avoided before the fact. Indeed, even the local penchant for redistribution is muted under these circumstances.[85]

Let us take the argument a step further: quite contrary to the usual notion, it is at the *central* level that faction is the most serious problem. How do we see this? One way is to consult history, where we see at least two salient examples. First, the most egregious example of minority oppression in our history has been racial discrimination. There is no question but that racial discrimination existed at the local level from the very start, but racism was particularly oppressive because it spread out through an entire region. African-Americans attempted to leave that region even during the days of slavery, only to be greeted by a *national* fugitive slave law.[86] In post–Civil War days, at least some relief was available, as southern blacks exercised an "exit" option to arrive at the doubtful improvement of the northern states.[87] Racial oppression has required national solutions precisely because the pattern of racism has been so widespread and so difficult to escape by exit. The example suggests that more localized oppression, while unquestionably an intolerable evil, would have been less serious over the long run because localized oppression still would offer a genuine opportunity for escape.

The second example stems from slightly more recent times. This is the saga of the federal administrative agencies, where we see the dangers of faction under the modern name of "capture"—and it is capture at the national level. To put the matter simply, capture of an agency occurs when the agency adopts the position of a particular interest group, usually the regulated entity, to the detriment of everyone else. This is a problem that has plagued the federal administrative agencies from the start, beginning with the regulation of the railroads under the Interstate Commerce Commission and running through the agribusiness domination over water reclamation projects, to airline domination of the now-defunct Civil Aeronautics Board, and on and on.[88]

At the *local* level, those fearing oppression through factional "capture" have two lines of defense. First, they can use "voice" and complain loudly that their enemies have captured the store; this after all is a context in which limited numbers of participants at least allow minorities to be heard and to organize with fellow complainants to magnify their individual voices. Second, they can threaten to cut their losses and leave for a more favorable regulatory clime—that is, exercise the "exit" option—a threat that the locality may well fear because of the damage to its own reputation and the danger that other valuable citizens might decide ex ante to settle elsewhere.

These are not perfect solutions to local factionalism, of course. For one thing, there is a tension between the voice and exit options, insofar as the possibility for exit may undermine the community spirit represented by voice—the effort to stay and make things better. For another, some residents may indeed be "stuck" and may be unable either to exit or to be heard, and these residents may not be comforted by the knowledge that their plight warns others to settle elsewhere.

But we need to think comparatively. Despite the shortcomings, exit and voice are at least in some measure available to local residents and offer some chance to overcome factional oppression there. At the *national* level, on the other hand, the citizen whose interests are adversely affected by institutional capture has neither of these options. Despite the optimism of some recent scholars who cite the old civic republican tradition of self-government as a model for national government, individual voice is more or less useless at this level simply because the national government is too big for most people to get a hearing.[89] Even if citizens do get themselves organized at a sufficient scale to exercise influence nationally, they may not escape the capture problem, since large-scale organization may simply introduce a different version of capture, as particular members of the organized group use it for purposes of their own.[90]

What about "exit" at the national level? Here the "exit" option is useless for a different reason: there is nowhere to run and no alternatives from which to choose, save for those willing to leave the country.

Thus it is at the *national* level, not the local level, that the danger of faction is most acute, and most especially requires the trappings of checks and balances and the play of interest against interest—as is evidenced by numerous proposals for the reintroduction of something like checks and balances and interest representation into national administrative law.[91] Publius to the contrary notwithstanding, faction is far more a national problem than a local one. If we think back to the ancient constitution, where every locale and every privileged body had its own institutions and narrow interests, we can see that there is an escape from faction in such a constitutional structure. Each locale may have its foolish enthusiasms, but the person who doesn't like them can gripe or settle elsewhere—as Hirschman puts it, exercise a "voice" or "exit" option. Thus it is the large republic that presents the problem of faction, in the sense of one-sided oppression, in a particularly pointed way. We first learned this from the oppression of our minority citizenry, and in more recent years, we have learned it from the problem of capture in the administrative state.

Crosscurrents: The Federalist Contribution to a Sustained Antifederalist Tradition

I want to come now to a point that runs quite contrary to the Antifederalist critique: the Federalists' plain vanilla constitution, perversely enough, does have some important aspects that recommend it, even from the point of view of preserving a tradition of localism. I am not speaking only of the obvious point that the Federalist constitution left the states intact. There are several much more important ways in which the Federalists' victory has assured the continuation of an Antifederalist version of the ancient constitution in the United States.

For one thing, as I have tried to point out, the Federalist arguments for the "extended republic," with its size and commercial unification, were in some significant measure arguments about securing the national defense. The Antifederalists gave a devastating critique of the imperial nature of this purported republic, but on their part, they never gave a convincing account of the way the nation might be defended in the absence of a strong national government. As the Federalists repeatedly stressed, logic and historical experience belied the proposition that the states would voluntarily contribute the soldiers and money for an adequate defense. At least one Antifederalist author simply conceded the defense issue and asserted that divisions and "occasional wars" would be preferable to the "fangs of despotism" of the Federalist project.[92] It has not turned out that way. Instead, there is every reason to believe that the large republic of the Federalists has shielded the Antifederalists' smaller communities from the ravages of external enemies—not to speak of their own mutual strife.

Aside from simple defense, the Federalists' plain vanilla constitution has created a single nation of states, with minimal difficulties in bringing goods and persons across boundaries. In this way, the Federalist constitution is the guarantor of the "exit" safeguard among local communities. Once again, it is the large republic that makes it possible and safe for citizens to protect themselves, through "exit," from local oppression.

Even the commercialism implicit in the Federalist project has had an arguably salutary influence on localism. In assuring the ability of Americans to follow commercial pursuits, the plain vanilla constitution may have cooled some of the local political fervor from which individuals might wish to "exit." Commercial life, to be sure, sets up a kind of competing attraction to politics and public life.[93] But that is not altogether bad, as *The Federalist*'s authors apparently noticed, because by siphoning off partisan ambitions into money-making pursuits, commerce may moderate the temperature of local political issues.[94] In addition, insofar as commercial pursuits increase the size of the total wealth "pie," commerce can make local issues about dividing the now-more-ample pie seem less compelling. Moreover, wide commercial participation and knowledge in themselves may render local political "rent-seeking" less morally defensible to a locality's own citizens—precisely because this rent-seeking behavior can decrease total wealth.[95]

Quite aside from those matters, the Federalists' plain vanilla constitution did after all do something to prevent faction at the national level too; all those checks and balances do play a role in controlling national aggrandizement. This leaves a space for localities that was impossible in the centralized organization of Napoleon's France (not to speak of Hitler's Germany or Stalin's Russia). And American localities have known how to exploit their opportunities and have managed to entrench themselves quite firmly in the consciousness of national politicians.

There is a price to be paid for this entrenchment, just as there is a price to be paid for interest-group politics generally.[96] But it may be worth this price to prevent truly "consolidated government" and the absolute rule that might accompany it. As in Old Regime Europe, it would be unthinkable to unseat established local interests without something close to revolution. In a sense, then, the Federalists' plain vanilla constitution has incorporated a certain chocolate layering from the ancient constitution, as translated by the Antifederalist practice of localism.

Conclusion

I have been arguing that the Federalist constitution attacked the ancient constitution and replaced the older forms by commerce, uniformity, and sheer size, in large part for the sake of national defense and power. Insofar as that is true, it might be thought—as the Antifederalists said—that the Federalist constitution has corrupted the polity by lowering its aims. The choice of the plain vanilla constitution represents a decision that Big Babylon is in the long run stronger than Little Athens and probably even than Little Sparta—and that this strength is more important than civic character or other high-flown republican aspirations.

But it is well to remember that there are many people who really *like* Babylon, who prefer its coarseness to noble character, who revel in its remarkable energy and find charm in the very vulgarity of its dynamism.[97] Certainly the rhetoric of the 1987 bicentennial suggested that there is after all some moral quality to the Federalist constitution over and above mere national survival and that the plain vanilla constitution has generated a certain enthusiasm for a way of life, however gleefully crass and raw it may sometimes seem.

I would like to suggest that a continuing and countervailing Antifederalist and ancient constitutional tradition of localism—like the tradition of voluntary organizations—has enriched the cultural and political life of the Babylonian extended republic and has even enhanced the commercial vigor of that republic. The local tradition has done so, on the one hand, by keeping alive a certain cooperative initiative and a belief in the possibilities for self-help through association—all matters that are likely to be much easier at the local level, where numbers are smaller and organization is simpler. And on the other hand, the local tradition has enhanced a kind of optimistic self-confidence by reminding us that it is always possible to bail out to try something new—that is, by reminding us about the "exit" option.

With this we are back to the Antifederalists' idea that character must be nourished by institutions. Initiative and optimism are character traits that the Federalist constitution needs too, not only for political life but for commerce as well, and the national strength that commerce brings.

But if Antifederalist localist notes have sounded over time in the practical playing out of Federalist constitutionalism, the reverse is true as well. It is the Federalist constitution that has protected localities from external danger, has guaranteed the "exit" option among them, and—through the promotion of commercialism—has muted their excesses. As it has turned out, the Federalist program may have required a dose of Antifederalist character, and vice versa.

Notes

1. See, e.g., Lawrence Waggoner, "Log-Rolling and Judicial Review," 52 *U. Colo. L. Rev.* 33, 35–44 (1980); Note, "City Government in the State Courts," 78 *Harv. L. Rev.* 1596 (1965), comparing local governmental institutions unfavorably to federal ones.

2. Michael Kammen, *A Machine That Would Run of Itself* (1986) at 93. Since the collapse of Soviet dominion in Eastern Europe, American constitutional experts have flooded the fledgling reform governments; see, e.g., Jonathan M. Moses, "U.S. Lawyers Are Welcomed by Russia," *Wall St. J.*, June 12, 1992, at B-6, describing the efforts of the American Bar Association's Central and East European Law Initiative. For some prospects and pitfalls of American constitutional models, see

Bruce A. Ackerman, *The Future of Liberal Revolution* (1992), especially ch. 4, "Constitutionalizing Revolution," at 46; and ch. 6, "Judges as Founders," at 99.

3. Kammen, supra note 2, at 5–6; cf. 30–35.

4. Cass R. Sunstein, "Constitutionalism After the New Deal," 101 *Harv. L. Rev.* 421, 422–25 (1987); Bruce A. Ackerman, "The Storrs Lectures: Discovering the Constitution," 93 *Yale L. J.* 1013, 1053–56, 1069 (1984).

5. *The Federalist* No. 10 (J. Madison). On Madison's linking of constitutional structure to the protection of property, see Jennifer Nedelsky, *Private Property and the Limits of American Constitutionalism* 49–62 (1990); see also Sunstein, supra note 4, at 421, 433–40, 443; Sunstein contrasts New Deal thinking on both issues of property and constitutional structure. For the continued centrality of property as a constitutional right, see James W. Ely, *The Guardian of Every Other Right: A Constitutional History of Property Rights* (1992).

6. See, for example, the furor over Richard Epstein's book *Takings* (1985), which attempts to locate property rights as the constitutional coequals of such First Amendment rights as speech and religion. For some sharp criticisms, see Thomas C. Grey, "The Malthusian Constitution," 41 *U. Miami L. Rev.* 21 (1986); Mark Kelman, "Taking Takings Seriously," 74 *Cal. L. Rev.* 1829 (1986); Joseph L. Sax, "Takings," 53 *U. Chi. L. Rev.* 279 (1986); more sympathetic is Thomas W. Merrill, "Rent Seeking and the Compensation Issue," 80 *Nw. U. L. Rev.* 1961 (1986). For a review of the supposed political connotations of property rights and regulation, see Carol M. Rose, "The Guardian of Every Other Right" (review), 10 *Constitutional Commentary* 238 (1993).

7. J.G.A. Pocock, *The Ancient Constitution and the Feudal Law* (2d ed. 1987). For a more generalized usage of this phrase, see, for example, James Steuart, *An Enquiry into the Principles of Political Economy*, quoted in Arthur Young, *Political Essays Concerning the Present State of the British Empire* 71–72 (1970; reprint of 1772 ed.).

8. See Pocock, supra note 7, at 47–49, discussing the work of Coke on antiquity; 171–73, discussing Hale and Burke on the wisdom of ancient ways.

9. Civic republicanism has acquired the status of an academic cottage industry. See, e.g., J.G.A Pocock, *The Machiavellian Moment: Florentine Political Thought and the Atlantic Republican Tradition* (1975); Forrest McDonald, *Novus Ordo Seclorum: The Intellectural Origins of the Constitution*, at 66–77 (1985); Gordon Wood, *The Creation of the American Republic, 1776–1787*, at 46–90 (1969); for a survey, see Robert E. Shalhope, "Republicanism and Early American Historiography," 39 *Wm. & Mary Q.* 334 (1982). In the legal literature, see, for example, the symposium "The Republican Civic Tradition," 97 *Yale L. J.* 1493 (1988). All cite copious authorities.

10. Charles McIlwain, *Constitutionalism, Ancient and Modern* 25–27, (1947); see also, e.g., J. W. Allen, *A History of Political Thought in the Sixteenth Century* 196, 248 (rev. ed. 1960).

11. For Montesquieu, see generally *The Spirit of the Laws* (1984; reprint of 1751 English trans.); for Edmund Burke, *Reflections on the Revolution in France* (1790), 108–111 (1961); for Burke's similarly traditional views stated earlier, see Pocock, supra note 7 at 380. For other continental visions of "fundamental law," see C.B.A. Behrens, *The Ancien Regime* 96–98, 102 (1967) and Franklin Ford, *Robe and Sword* 232, 238–43 (1953), both on eighteenth-century France (and Ford on Montesquieu in particular).

12. See Jack Greene, *Peripheries and Center: Constitutional Development in the Extended Polities of the British Empire and the United States, 1607–1788,* at 35–42 (1986).

13. "Nach dessen ... althergebrachter Verfassung"; Letter of J. J. Moser to Duke Karl Eugen of Württemberg (1765), reprinted in Reinhard Rürup, *Johann Jacob Moser, Pietismus und Reform,* 245, 246 (1965).

14. Hartmut Lehmann, "Die württembergischen Landstände im 17. und 18. Jahrhundert," in *Ständische Vertretungen in Europa im 17. und 18. Jahrhundert* 183, 199–204 (1969).

15. Alexis de Tocqueville, 2 *Democracy in America* 173 (Bradley ed. 1945). For his view of pre-revolutionary France, see his *Old Regime and the French Revolution* 57–60 (trans. S. Gilbert 1955).

16. Behrens, supra note 11, at 46, 52–53; see also 1 Robert R. Palmer, *The Age of Democratic Revolutions* 27–30 (1959).

17. Behrens, supra note 11, at 59–60.

18. Behrens, supra note 11, at 179 (quoting Rabaut Saint-Etienne).

19. 1 Palmer, supra note 16, at 27 (citing Edmund Burke, J.-J. Rousseau, Prince Kaunitz of Austria).

20. See Dietrich Gerhard, "Problems of Representation and Delegation in the Eighteenth Century," in *Liber Memorialis Sir Maurice Powicke* 123 (1965).

21. Mack Walker, *German Home Towns: Community, State and General Estate, 1648–1871,* at 77–78 (1971) (seventeenth–eighteenth-century German guilds' local monopolies); Ford, supra note 11, at 105 (concerning "nobility of the robe," i.e., judges who purchased or inherited offices along with the claim to noble rank and saw offices as "negotiable property"); Hans Rosenberg, *Bureaucracy, Aristocracy and Autocracy: The Prussian Experience, 1660–1815,* at 80 (1958) (family monopolies over state-run Prussian industries, notably mining and metallurgy); J. H. Plumb, *The Growth of Political Stability in England, 1685–1725,* at 126 (1967) (sale of military office in seventeenth–eighteenth-century Britain).

22. In Britain centralization of authority fell increasingly to the monarchs' advisers, who could control Parliament through patronage, a practice eschewed by "republicans" as a subversion of the "ancient constitution." See J. H. Plumb, supra note 21, at 156–59, 179–80.

23. See, e.g., John G. Gagliardo, *Enlightened Despotism* 24, 37 (1967); Leonard Krieger, *Kings and Philosophers, 1689–1789* at 132, 135 (1970). Austria's Joseph II was the most extreme centralizer and rationalizer of the "enlightened despots"; the reputedly "enlightened" Frederick II of Prussia and Catherine the Great of Russia in fact made substantial concessions to the nobility. Gagliardo, at 27–29; Krieger, at 298–300; Rosenberg, supra note 21, at 156–65.

24. Quoted by Young, supra note 7, at 71–72 from 1 James Steuart, *An Enquiry into the Principles of Political Oeconomy* 248 (1767).

25. See, e.g., H. G. Koenigsberger, "Why Did the States-General of the Netherlands Become Revolutionary in the Sixteenth Century?" in 2 *Parliaments, Estates and Representation* 103, 108 (1982).

26. For a summary of these mid-seventeenth-century revolutionary disturbances, see Carl Friedrich, *The Age of the Baroque, 1610–1660* (1952), at 227–28 (Catalonia and Portugal), 236–42 (France).

27. G. M. Trevelyan, *History of England. The Tudors and the Stuart Era*, 177 (rev. ed. 1952); C. V. Wedgwood, *The King's Peace, 1637–41*, at 176–78, 196–99 (1955).

28. See Gagliardo, supra note 23, at 33–34; 1 Palmer, supra note 16, at 86–99; 448–65; for similar conflicts in Sweden and in the various provinces of the Hapsburg Empire, see id. at 99–108. For the role of the French "nobility of the robe," see generally Ford, supra note 11.

29. 1 Palmer, supra note 16, at 341–48. The Belgians planted the first tricolor flag in early 1789; id. at 348. The legendary joke about the emperor's view that Mozart's music had "too many notes" appears in the play and film *Amadeus*.

30. See, e.g., George Mason's reference (Virginia ratifying convention) to the flourishing condition of Holland after its revolt from Spain, in 3 *Debates in the Several State Conventions on the Adoption of the Federal Constitution* 268 (J. Elliot ed. 1881) (hereinafter Elliot, with state of debate in parentheses); see also remark of Randolph (Virginia), at 190, that the delegates at the convention were "harassed by quotations from Holland and Switzerland."

31. See, e.g., Isaac Kramnick, "The 'Great National Discussion': The Discourse of Politics in 1787," 45 *Wm. & Mary Q.* 3, 12 (1988).

32. See Herbert J. Storing, "What the Antifederalists Were For," in 1 Storing, *The Complete Antifederalist* 7 (1981) (hereinafter Storing).

33. See the influential Antifederalist *Letters from the Federal Farmer to the Republican* (Dec. 31, 1787) in 2 Storing, supra note 32, at 266–67; speech of George Mason (Virginia), in 3 Elliot, supra note 30, at 266–67. For the Federalist denial of "aristocracy," see *The Federalist* No. 35. Perhaps the most interesting exchange on aristocracy was that between Melanchthon Smith and Alexander Hamilton in the New York ratifying convention, described below.

34. See, e.g., the Antifederalist M. Smith (New York), in 2 Elliot, supra note 30, at 250; for the Federalists, see Kramnick, supra note 31, at 14–16, though Kramnick thinks that the Federalists were more aristocratic in favoring the rule of the best. Similar doubts on the Federalist republican rhetoric might have been raised by the revealing speech of Pendleton (Virginia), in 3 Elliot, at 295–96, who, after stressing the importance of protecting property, remarked that "the true principle of republicanism, and the greatest security of liberty, is regular government. *Perhaps I may not be a republican, but this is my idea*" (emphasis added).

35. For the "country" party's objections to patronage and corruption, see J. H. Plumb, supra note 21, at 138, 185–86; for colonial "republican" reaction, see Bernard Bailyn, *The Origins of American Politics*, 52–54 (1967); Wood, supra note 9, at 33–34. Hamilton (New York) responded to Antifederalist fears of corruption by saying that the matter related largely to royal corruption of Parliament, in 2 Elliot, supra note 30, at 264.

36. For the inability of European rulers to overcome this fiscal and administrative fragmentation, see, e.g., Behrens, supra note 11, at 116–17; for an explicit comparison, see, e.g., the remarks of Rufus King (Massachusetts), 2 Elliot, supra note 30, at 55–56; see also McDonald, supra note 9, at 170–72.

37. *The Federalist* No. 15, at 108 (Rossiter ed. 1961) (page references hereinafter to this edition).

38. For Antifederalist praise, see, e.g., Henry (Virginia), in 3 Elliot, supra note 30, at 142–43 (Switzerland), 145–47 (Holland); Mason (Virginia), id. at 268. The

Federalists complained about all these references; see Randolph (Virginia), id. at 190.

39. John G. Gagliardo, *Reich and Nation: The Holy Roman Empire as Idea and Reality, 1763–1806,* at 4–5 (1980); for Voltaire's remark, see id. at 291; see also Carol M. Rose, "Empire and Territories at the End of the Old Reich," in J. Vann and S. W. Rowan, eds., *The Old Reich: Essays on German Political Institutions, 1495–1806,* at 61, 62–63 (1974).

40. *The Federalist* No. 19, at 130–31.

41. 1 Montesquieu, supra note 11, at 18–19; for the French prerevolutionary centralization, see Tocqueville, *Old Regime,* supra note 15, at 32–41. For the Federalist program of legislation acting directly on the people, see Hamilton in *The Federalist* Nos. 15 and 16. During the ratifying period, much of the debate about direct federal authority over the citizenry concerned taxation. See, e.g., Federalist remarks of Gore (Massachusetts), in 2 Elliot, supra note 30, at 66–67; Madison (Virginia), in 3 Elliot, at 250–51; compare the opponents Lansing (New York), in 2 Elliot, at 373–74, favoring requisitions from the states.

42. *The Federalist* No. 12, at 92–93 (Hamilton).

43. See Martin Diamond, "The Federalist," in *History of Political Philosophy,* 631, 649–50 (L. Strauss and J. Cropsey eds. 2d ed. 1972).

44. John Locke, *Second Treatise,* in *Two Treatises of Government* (P. Laslett rev. ed. 1963, 1st ed. 1690), sec. 42; emphasis added.

45. See Krieger, supra note 23, at 131–35; Elizabeth Fox-Genovese, *The Origins of Physiocracy: Economic Revolution and Social Order in Eighteenth-Century France,* 7 (1976). As Krieger points out, the Physiocrats thought that all wealth flowed from agriculture, but other laissez-faire thinkers of the era extended the analysis to commerce and manufacture as well.

46. McDonald, supra note 9, at 128.

47. See Hamilton's discussion of commerce in *The Federalist* Nos. 6 and 12.

48. For some others pointing out the importance of foreign affairs for the founders, see Akhil Amar, "Some New World Lessons for the Old World," 58 *U. Chi. L. Rev.* 483, 486–94 (1991); Walter LaFeber, "The Constitution and United States Foreign Policy: An Interpretation," 74 *J. Am.. Hist.* 695–96 (1987); Gerald Stourzh, *Alexander Hamilton and the Idea of Republican Government* 127–30, 142–45, 160–61 (1970).

49. Tocqueville, *Old Regime,* supra note 15, at 19–20.

50. Henry (Virginia), in 3 Elliot, supra note 30, at 44.

51. Id. at 53–54. For a similiar view, see *Essays of Brutus to the Citizens of New York* (Jan. 3, 1788), in 2 Storing, supra note 32, at 401.

52. 1 Montesquieu, supra note 11, at 18–22, 150–53. Patrick Henry seemed to reflect this distinction between (tempered) monarchy and unrestrained tyranny, saying that Britain was a monarchy but that the Federalist plan would be a tyranny. See his remarks in 3 Elliot, supra note 30, at 44, 59.

53. *The Federalist* No. 14.

54. Smith (New York), in 2 Elliot, supra note 30, at 245–48. For similar views, see Henry, in 3 Elliot, at 64; see also *Letters from the Federal Farmer* (Oct. 10, 1787) in 2 Storing, supra note 32, at 235; *Letters of Centinel to the People of Pennsylvania,* in 2 Storing, at 142; and *Essays of Brutus* (Nov. 15, 1787), id. at 380. Hannah Pitkin has

described a "picturing" or "mirroring" theory of representation that seems to fit the Antifederalist understanding of representation. See Pitkin, *The Concept of Representation* 60–61 (1967). For an example see *Essays of Brutus,* supra.

55. Hamilton (New York), in 2 Elliot, supra note 30, at 256.

56. M. Smith (New York), id. at 246 47; *Letters from the Federal Farmer* (Oct. 19, 1787), in 2 Storing, supra note 32, at 234; *Letters of Centinel to the People of Pennsylvania,* id., at 166–67; *Essays of Brutus* (Nov. 29, 1787), id. at 385.

57. Henry (Virginia), in 3 Elliot, supra note 30, at 59–60; 384–87; see also G. Mason (Virginia), id. at 378–81 (argues for state militias instead of standing army); cf. Madison (Virginia), id. at 382 (argues for central control of militia). For the importance of the militia in traditional republican arguments, see Pocock, supra note 9, at 124, 292–93, 527–28.

58. Henry (Virginia), in 3 Elliot, supra note 30, at 51, 55–56. For the effect of direct federal taxation on the states, see, e.g., *Essays of Brutus* (Dec. 13, 1787), in 2 Storing, supra note 32, at 391. In the same way that the Antifederalists preferred to arm the nation through contributions of state-controlled militias rather than standing armies, they also argued for state financial requisitions to the national treasury rather than direct taxation; see, e.g., *Letters from the Federal Farmer* (Oct.10, 1787), in 2 Storing, at 241–42.

59. See, e.g., Smith (New York), in 2 Elliot, supra note 30, at 224 (citing Montesquieu); P. Henry (Virginia), 3 Elliot, at 44, 52–53.

60. See, e.g., *Letters from the Federal Farmer* (Dec. 25, 1787), in 2 Storing, supra note 32, at 262 (favoring property); id. (Oct. 13, 1787), in 2 Storing, at 253 (against Shays's Rebellion); see also Storing's comments, 1 Storing 45–46 (Antifederalists not primitivists with respect to commerce). For the republican, anti-hierarchical strain of pro-capitalist thinking, see Joyce Appleby, *Capitalism and a New Social Order* 31–32, 37, 94–97 (1984).

61. As was noted in the previous essay, even the republican version of property as propriety had an important element of hierarchy and contemplated that property-owning citizens would govern everybody else.

62. See, e.g., Smith (New York), in 2 Elliot, supra note 30, at 248–51.

63. 1 Montesquieu, supra note 11, at 52–57.

64. *Letters from the Federal Farmer* (Oct. 13, 1787), in 2 Storing, supra note 32, at 251.

65. *Essays of Brutus* (Jan. 3, 1788), in 2 Storing, supra note 32, at 401.

66. See John R. Nelson, *Liberty and Property: Political Economy and Policymaking in the New Nation, 1787–1812,* at 20–21 (1987); Steven Watts, *The Republic Reborn: War and the Making of Liberal America, 1790–1820,* at xvi–xvii, 310–12, 316–20 (1987).

67. See, e.g., Lacey K. Ford, Jr., *Origins of Southern Radicalism. The South Carolina Upcountry, 1800–1860,* at 49–52, 68 (1988).

68. *The Federalist* No. 9, at 73 (Hamilton); see also *The Federalist* No. 57, at 355 (Madison) (some state electoral districts as large as national ones).

69. For complaints, see Epstein, supra note 6, at 265; Douglas Kmiec, "Deregulating Land Use: An Alternative Free Enterprise Development System," 130 *U. Pa. L. Rev.* 28, at 40–43 (1981).

70. See Carol M. Rose, "New Models for Local Land Use Decisions," 79 *Nw. U. L. Rev.* 1155, 1168–70 (1984–85), and authorities cited therein.

71. See, e.g., Associated Home Builders of the Greater E. Bay, Inc. v. City of Walnut Creek, 94 Cal. Rptr. 630 (Cal. 1971); Golden v. Planning Bd. of Ramapo, 285 N.E.2d 291 (N.Y. 1972); cf. Nollan v. California Coastal Comm'n, 483 U.S. 825 (1987), requiring that development exactions be related to burdens imposed by the development.

72. For the connection between local decisionmaking and the Antifederalist tradition, see Carol M. Rose, "Planning and Dealing: Piecemeal Land Controls as a Problem of Local Legitimacy," 71 *Cal. L. Rev.* 837, 882–87 (1983).

73. See, e.g., Nat'l Inst. of Law Enforcement and Criminal Justice, *Corruption in Land Use and Building Regulation* (1979).

74. See, e.g., the collection of essays *The City Boss in America: An Interpretative Reader* (A. B. Callow ed. 1976); Ernest S. Griffith, *A History of American City Government: The Conspicuous Failure, 1870–1900,* at 97 et seq. (2d ed. 1972).

75. Hirschman, *Exit, Voice and Loyalty* (1970).

76. See, e.g., Clayton Gillette, "Plebiscites, Participation, and Collective Action in Local Government Law," 86 *Mich. L. Rev.* 930 (1988), giving short shrift to nonvoting forms of participation.

77. See Hirschman, supra note 75. For a reconsideration, see Vicki Been, "'Exit' as a Constraint on Land Use Exactions: Rethinking the Unconstitutional Conditions Doctrine," 91 *Colum. L. Rev.* 473 (1991).

78. See W. S. Kowinski, *The Malling of America* (1985).

79. Kenneth A. Lockridge, *A New England Town: The First Hundred Years: Dedham, Massachusetts, 1636–1736,* at 100–116 (1970).

80. For an early case piercing the distinction, see Marsh v. Alabama, 326 U.S. 501, 1523, 1526, 1547–63 (1946); see also the debate between Robert Ellickson, "Cities and Homeowners Associations," 130 *U. Pa. L. Rev.* 1519 (1982), and Gerald Frug, "Cities and Homeowners Associations: A Reply," 130 *U. Pa. L. Rev.* 1589 (1982).

81. Particularly important in this local-competition line is Charles Tiebout, "A Pure Theory of Local Expenditures," 64 *J. Pol. Econ.* 416 (1956). For the "major academic industry" generated by this article, see Clayton Gillette, "Equality and Variety in the Delivery of Municipal Services" (Review), 100 *Harv. L. Rev.* 946, 956, fn. 29 (1987), and sources cited therein. See also Been, supra note 77.

82. For Dillon's Rule, see Joan Williams, "The Constitutional Vulnerability of American Local Government: The Politics of City Status in American Law," 1986 *Wisc. L. Rev.* 83, 88–89. Euclid v. Ambler Realty, 272 U.S. 365 (1926) upheld the constitutionality of local zoning.

83. See U.S. Council on Envt'l. Quality, *The Quiet Revolution in Land Use Controls* (1971); for continuing local influence, see David Callies, "The Quiet Revolution Revisited," 46 *J. Am. Plan. Assn.* 135, 136, 139 (1980).

84. 1 Tocqueville, *Democracy in America,* supra note 15, at 198–202; 2 id. at 114–18, 123–28, 148–51.

85. See Ellickson, supra note 80, at 1547–48; but cf. id. at 1553.

86. See Stanley W. Campbell, *The Slave Catchers: Enforcement of the Fugitive Slave Law, 1850–1860* (1968). The author makes the point that although the statute was ineffective, federal officials did indeed try to enforce it; the impediments came

rather from northern localities' indifference or downright obstruction. Id., at 164–69.

87. See, e.g., Allan H. Spear, *Black Chicago: The Making of a Negro Ghetto, 1890–1920*, at 11 (1967).

88. For the ICC, see Gabriel Kolko, *Railroads and Regulation, 1877–1916*, at 233 (1965); compare Herbert Hovenkamp, "Regulatory Conflict in the Gilded Age: Federalism and the Railroad Problem," 97 *Yale L. J.* 1017 (1988); for water projects, C. Meyers, et al., *Water Resource Management* 874 (3d ed. 1987). For "capture" in general, see Mark J. Green, ed., *The Monopoly Makers: Ralph Nader's Study Group Report on Regulation and Competition* (1973); Robert Rabin, "Federal Regulation in Historical Perspective," 38 *Stan. L. Rev.* 1189, 1280–95 (1986).

89. For scholarly optimism, see, e.g., Frank Michelman, "Law's Republic," 97 *Yale L. J.* 1531 (1988); Cass Sunstein, "Beyond the Republican Revival," 97 *Yale L. J.* 1539, 1548 (1988); but see Kathleen Sullivan, "Rainbow Republicanism," 97 *Yale L. J.* 1713 (1988).

90. See., e.g., Russell Hardin, *Collective Action* 35–37 (1982)

91. Sunstein, supra note 4, at 483, 489–90, 505; Rabin, supra note 88, at 1298–99.

92. See *Letters of Centinel to the People of Pennsylvania,* 2 Storing, supra note 32, at 186; see generally 1 Storing, at 27–30, 42–43.

93. 2 Tocqueville, *Democracy,* supra note 15, at 165; see also Albert O. Hirschman, *Shifting Involvements* (1982) (public and private pursuits in competition).

94. Diamond, supra note 43, at 648–49.

95. For rent-seeking, see, e.g., James M. Buchanan, Robert D. Tollison, and Gordon Tullock, *Toward a Theory of the Rent Seeking Society* (1980).

96. For local lobbying, see, e.g., Carol F. Lee, "The Political Safeguards of Federalism? Congressional Responses to Supreme Court Decisions on State and Local Liability," 20 *Urb. L.* 301 (1988). For two important works on the general problem of organized interests, see Mancur Olson, *The Logic of Collective Action* (1965); James Buchanan and Gordon Tullock, *The Calculus of Consent* (1965).

97. For an example of the celebration of vulgarity, see Robert Venturi et al., *Learning from Las Vegas* (1972) (praise for Las Vegas "strip" architecture). This fondness for low life may be rather prevalent among Americans, as for example in the remark of a friend of mine: "I like country music," she said, "because it's so trashy."

PART THREE

Common Property

Like the essays of Part Two, the essays in this part are historical, but the focus is quite different. These essays concern historic property regimes for particular kinds of resources.

It is widely thought that property is best arranged and most likely to produce wealth when it is held in individual ownership. Nevertheless, there are several resilient examples of common property in our legal history. The first essay, "The Comedy of the Commons," is about certain types of property that our laws persistently hold open to the public at large—a situation normally thought to spell disaster to resources. The second essay, "Energy and Efficiency," deals with the historical development of a more limited common property regime, namely, the law of watercourses in the eastern United States.

But both essays challenge a well-known evolutionary theme in the literature of property rights: that resource-use regimes tend to evolve toward individual private property rights whenever the underlying resources grow more scarce and valuable. The essays in this part show how certain kinds of property may deviate from that evolution—and may do so in ways that are still socially wealth-enhancing, once one notices where the wealth really resides.

5

The Comedy of the Commons: Custom, Commerce, and Inherently Public Property

Introduction: The Conundrum of "Public Property"

The right to exclude others has often been cited as the most important characteristic of private property.[1] The power to exclude was a background feature in the stories explored in an earlier essay, "Property as Storytelling"; indeed, in those stories property supposedly makes everyone better off precisely because an owner can exclude others from his or her property. Because they can exclude outsiders, owners alone may capture the value of their individual investments in the things they own, and as a consequence property rights encourage them to put time, labor, and care into the development of resources.[2] Moreover, exclusive control makes it possible for owners to identify other owners and for all to exchange the things upon which they have labored until these things arrive in the hands of those who value them most highly—to the great cumulative advantage of all. For these reasons, it is said, exclusive private property fosters the well-being of the community and gives its members a medium in which resources are used, conserved, and exchanged to their greatest advantage.

As earlier essays pointed out, there is really nothing novel about the idea that exclusive property rights foster the most valuable uses of resources; Richard Posner, a modern-day proponent of neoclassical economics, has remarked that "[a]ll this has been well known for hundreds of years."[3] Posner cites Blackstone, among others, for this proposition, but he could certainly have chosen many others, both earlier and especially later. Indeed, since the advent of classical economics, it has been widely

The original version of this essay appeared in 53 *University of Chicago Law Review*, 711–781 (1986). Reprinted by permission of *University of Chicago Law Review*.

believed that the whole world of valuable things is best managed when divided among private property owners.[4]

The obverse of this coin, so to speak, is the "tragedy of the commons."[5] When things are left open to the public, it is said, they are wasted, either by overuse or underinvestment. No one wishes to care for things that may be taken away tomorrow, and no one knows whom to approach to make exchanges. All resort to snatching up what is available for "capture" today, leaving behind a wasteland—thus the tragedy. From this perspective, "public property" is an oxymoron: things left open to the public are not property at all but rather its antithesis.

Thus it is peculiar to find a long-standing notion of public property in the law of the Western world. The Romans, whose legal thinking has so much influenced later European law, were sufficiently interested in public property to separate it into at least four categories.[6] And despite the power of the classical economic argument for private property, a curious countercurrent has continually washed through our own American law. Our legal doctrine has strongly suggested that some kinds of properties should not be held exclusively in private hands but instead should be open to the public or at least subject to the *jus publicum,* to use the Roman law terminology—the "public right."[7]

Moreover, this view does not seem merely a tattered remnant of some premodern way of thought. We find in our own day an extensive academic and judicial discussion of the possibility that certain kinds of property ought to be public. In recent years the most striking version of this "inherent publicness" argument has appeared in a series of cases expanding public access to waterfront property. The land between the low and high tide has traditionally been considered public property, if nothing else subject to a public easement for navigational and fishing purposes.[8] But over the past generation, a number of modern courts have expanded the public easement to include a new use—recreation—and have expanded the area of the public's easement from the tidelands to the dry sand areas landward of the high tide mark.[9]

This emergent body of doctrine extrapolates from older precedents in which the public acquired—or allegedly *re*asserted—claims to certain types of property, most notably roadways and lands under navigable waters. Like the older precedents, the newer beach cases usually assert one of three theoretical bases. Stated most briefly, these are (1) a "public trust" theory, to the effect that the public has always had (and has never lost) rights of access to the property in question, so that any private owner's rights are now subordinate to the public's "trust" rights;[10] (2) a prescriptive or dedicatory theory, by which a period of public usage gives rise to an implied grant or gift from private owners;[11] and (3) a theory of "custom," by which the public is thought to assert ownership of property under some claim so ancient that it goes back before any memory to the contrary.[12]

These enlarged theories of public access to shores and waterways have garnered a vocal but decidedly mixed reaction. In discussing these theories, some commentators have applauded what they regard as a proper recognition of public needs.[13] The public trust idea in particular has spawned an enormous number of cases and articles, some urging an extension of a public trust beyond the beachfront and into a much wider range of property where, it is said, public access or control should be vindicated.[14]

But there have also been a number of very sharp critiques of these cases and articles and of the expansive doctrines of public control that they propound. The critics deny the notion that any rights were either "retained" by or "given" to the public in the disputed lands. They deplore what they see as an unjust and disruptive destruction of private property rights; if the public wants or needs these waterfront lands so much, these authors say, it should have to purchase them from the private owners.[15] Moreover, the critics point to the consequences of what they see as uncompensated and unpredictable transfers of property rights: frustrated private owners may overreact in trying to protect their property from any implication of "dedication." To clinch the point, one cites examples of owners who have installed guard dogs and blown up access paths to the beach in order to prevent the ripening of any purported public claims.[16]

At a more general level, the critics reiterate the basic arguments in favor of private ownership of property: uncertainty about property rights invites conflicts and squanders resources. The public access cases seem to turn the waterfront into a commons, where no one has any incentive to purchase the property or to invest in it or to care for it but only to consume as much as possible—all of which leads to deterioration and waste. Indeed one author, though not entirely unsympathetic to the new cases, sees this point as a repudiation of the view often ascribed to law-and-economics scholars, namely, that the common law is efficient. These cases, the author asserts, reverse common law doctrines that were relatively efficient and instead reinstate inefficient ones.[17]

It is hardly to be wondered that these new cases and doctrines are controversial, given the impact of expanded public rights on what were thought to be private entitlements on the waterfront. But the question whether these expanded doctrines "take" property without compensation, although exceedingly important to private owners as a practical matter, is in principle perhaps not the most radical issue about these cases. Their rhetoric suggests that no nonconsensual transfer has occurred; in theory the owner gave or granted his property to the public or only owned it subject to public rights. Even if this rhetoric sounds implausible, the cases do at least pay lip service to the principle that private property may not be taken without compensation.

The more radical feature of these cases is precisely their seeming defiance of classical economic thinking and the common law doctrines that seem so markedly to mirror classical theory: they show a preference for public access, trumping the right to exclude that is the supposed hallmark of private property. These cases instead are singular exceptions to the standard doctrines of property law. Most property is not impressed with anything like a "public trust" allowing access; why should the beaches be? It begs the question to say that the new public trust cases merely extrapolate from older doctrine about navigable waterways: why did the old cases hold submerged lands to be subject to such a trust? By the same token, no amount of general public usage will subject most property to divestment, either by "implied dedication" or by some analogy to adverse possession.[18] Why should there be an exception for the public's prescriptive acquisition of the beach? Again, to find analogies in older doctrine about prescriptive roadways is only to push the question one step back. As to custom, the same questions apply. Until the modern beach cases, "custom" was a foundation of almost no public authority in American law.[19] What can possibly now link American waterfront recreation to the rights of eighteenth-century British villagers to dig out turf and hold maypole dances on the lands of the lord of the manor?

Why, in short, are any of these types of property inherently or even presumptively withdrawn from exclusive private appropriation? What if any characteristics of some property require it to be open to the public at large and exempt from the classical economic presumption favoring exclusive private control?

Perhaps these doctrines can indeed be easily explained through classical economic thought and can be subsumed under one of the well-recognized exceptions to the general principle favoring private and exclusive property rights: "boundless" goods and "market failures." The first class of exceptions concerns things that are either so plentiful or so unbounded that it is not worth the effort to create a system of resource management with respect to them or—stated differently—things for which the difficulty of privatization outweighs the gains in careful resource management.[20] Thus the oceans and air (it used to be said) are at once so plentiful and so difficult to reduce to property that they are left open to the public at large.[21]

The plenitude or boundlessness exception, however, fails to explain the "publicness" of properties that our traditional doctrines most strenuously declared to be public property. Roadways, waterways, and submerged lands—not to speak of open squares, which have also sometimes been presumed to be public—are hardly so copious or so unbounded that they are incapable of privatization. Riverbeds and shorelands can be staked out, roadways can be obstructed, waterways diverted, squares plowed up; in short, they can easily be "reduced to possession" in the classic common law manner of creating proprietary rights out of a "common."[22] Indeed, much of the case law on these matters has arisen because some owner has succeeded in staking out some allegedly "public" area and in excluding others from it.[23] The "public" character of such lands seems to have some basis other than our incapacity to reduce them to private possession.

Perhaps the second exception to the general rule favoring private property may be more promising. Since the mid-nineteenth century, economists have told us that there are predictable instances of "market failure," where Adam Smith's invisible hand fails to guide privately owned resources to their socially optimal uses, most often because some individuals have interests that are left out of the market transactions. These instances have some conventional names—"externalities," "natural monopolies," "public goods," and so on. Where market failures occur with respect to some resource, public ownership might be superior to private ownership. This is particularly the case if we think of the public not as an unorganized assemblage of individuals but rather as a corporately organized governmental body; such "public" ownership is only a variant on private ownership, albeit on a larger scale. "Publicly" owned property, so understood, still has a single owner and speaks with a single voice; this corporate body can manage, buy, and sell its property just as any other owner does.

Such a governmental body might be the most useful manager, to take the "externalities" category, where many persons use or would like to use some portion of a given resource—air, for example—but they are too numerous and their individual stakes are too small to express their preferences completely through market transactions. A governmental management structure can broker these preferences and require individual users to take account of other users' interests.[24] Similarly, a government might be a superior manager (or regulator) of a "natural monopoly"—a property whose use involves economies of scale, like the railways, bridges, or grain elevators whose monopoly position classically justified governmental ownership or control.[25] Very closely related is governmental organization of "collective goods" or "public goods," where some management structure is required to provide a service that is unattractive to private investment because nonpaying users cannot easily be excluded from enjoying the benefits; national defense or policing services are classic examples. Indeed, in a sense we rely on governmental management and policing of our most-used system of resource management, namely, private property; we might think of the private property regime, taken as a whole, as a "public property" owned and managed by governmental bodies.

Conventional wisdom tells us that in cases of these sorts, the most productive solution might be for government to assume some or all the rights of ownership and control over the resources in question and to use its powers to prevent or correct the market's misallocations. This conventional conclusion is subject to several conventional caveats: the government must be able to identify correctly the instances of market failure; it must be clever enough to exercise its powers so as to reduce the inefficiency; it must avoid errors or political temptations to exercise its powers in ways that create new inefficiencies; and the costs of effective governmental intervention must not exceed the increase in production that it brings about.

Taken as a whole, though, this standard paradigm of neoclassical economics and modern microeconomic theory recognizes only two types of property ownership: either ownership is vested in private parties or it resides with an organized government. Thus, in the conventional lore, markets are based on private rights, or, when markets fail, property may be governmentally managed.

Yet these two options do not logically exhaust all the possible solutions. Moreover, they do not begin to describe all the arrangements that one finds in the recorded history of property in the Anglo-American legal universe. In particular, aside from various forms of private property, the common law of both Britain and America, with surprising consistency, recognized two distinguishable types of *public* property. One of these was predictable from economic theory, namely, public property owned and actively managed by a governmental body. The other, however, was property collectively "owned" by society at large, with claims independent of and indeed superior to the claims of any purported governmental manager.

Thus as we shall see, our historic doctrines sometimes held, for example, that the general public had a right of access to certain properties whether or not a governmental body had intervened. To take another example, the "trust" language of public property doctrine, in what seems a kind of echo of natural law thinking, suggested that governments had duties to preserve the property of what some cases called the "unorganized" public. Indeed the "trust" language of some of these cases suggested that governmental ownership of certain property is only a qualified, "legal" ownership, for the "use" of the public at large, which in classic trust language is the underlying beneficial owner.[26]

Thus it appears that older public property doctrine vested some form of property rights in the *un*organized public. But what could it mean for the unorganized public to have "rights" in any property at all? How could its members possibly assert their rights except through a governmental body? And even if they could do so, how could the unorganized public be thought the best property manager, or even a manager at all? Property in such a public would amount to an unlimited commons, which seems not to be property at all but at best only a mass of passive "things" awaiting reduction to private property through the rule of capture—and this, of course, is a situation that leads not to good management of resources but rather to their squandering, in the dreaded tragedy of the commons. Nevertheless, strange though it seems, precisely this unorganized version of the "public" is strongly suggested in some of the earlier public property doctrine—as it is in some modern law as well.

The modern doctrines are singularly unhelpful in explaining why and under what circumstances property rights might appear to vest in the public at large, the "unorganized public." For example, the modern public trust doctrine, in spite of its popularity, is notoriously vague as to its own subject matter; cases and academic commentaries are all too prone to say only that the content of the public trust is "flexible" in response to "changing public needs." And in general, the recent judicial expansions of public access, like the academic literature, in large part simply refer us back to traditional doctrines.[27]

Hence I turn to these older doctrines for enlightenment, and in the remainder of this essay I investigate the problem of inherently public property through a closer examination of older doctrines through which the public has acquired rights to use property. In large part, I use cases from the nineteeth century but will occasionally stray as far forward as the 1920s. I make no claim to historical completeness, and I will where appropriate use modern law-and-economics explanations, but I hope, through an admittedly impressionistic sampling, to capture the flavor of the older views about why some properties should be exceptions in the normal realm of exclusive private control.

In America the chief doctrinal support for public property came in the form of "public trust" in waterways and "prescription" for roadways. I will call these the "strong" doctrines, since they were so much more prevalent than a third, "weak" doctrine of custom. Still, this weak doctrine of custom turns out to be singularly informative. Although custom only appeared from time to time in the older cases, and then very tentatively, it nevertheless provides some powerful insights into the question of just who the public was thought to be, and into the reasons why some property seemed to be thought public by its very nature.

As will appear below, commercial travel was a central factor behind the presumption that certain property—notably roadways and waterways—were to be open to the public. When used for commerce, these properties had qualities akin to infinite returns to scale, because commerce becomes ever more valuable as it expands to larger numbers of persons. Thus here, the commons was not tragic at all but comedic, in the classical sense of a story with a happy outcome—the more people engaged, the better off we all become. What is more interesting, however, is the point that customary doctrines also suggest something else about commerce: that it might be thought a "comedy of the commons" not only by its infinite capacity to expand our wealth but also by its propensity, at least in part, to make us more sociable and better attuned to each other's needs and interests.

All this will set the stage for a return to the beach. I will conclude the essay by suggesting that in the twentieth century there may be other versions of the comedy of the commons and other practices, aside from commerce, that have the power to enhance our sociability. We might even think that properties devoted to such noncommercial uses as recreation or speech could have these qualities and thus might reach their highest value where they are accessible to the public at large—that is, where we envision the commons not as wasteful tragedy but as happy and productive comedy.

But now, back to history, and to those odd doctrines of "publicness" that begin with roads and waterways.

I. The "Publicness" of the Roads and Waterways: A Brief History of The "Strong" Doctrines

Prescription—Herein Chiefly of Roads, Highways, and Streets

If classical economic theory normally preferred individual ownership of property to limitless open access, the traditional rules for public acquisiton of streets and roads systematically overlooked that preference. Indeed, the public's acquisition of roadways by long usage seems a particularly striking illustration of the imperviousness of practice to theory. The doctrines through which the public acquired roads over private property, without voluntary purchase or even the use of eminent domain, flourished side by side with the popularization of classical economics and the burgeoning of privately organized commerce and industry.[28]

Under various "prescriptive" theories, a long period of public use was and still is said to deprive a private owner of the right to exclude the public from a travelled way. The reasoning is either that long public usage implies that the private owner has "dedicated" or granted the right of way to the public, or that long usage allows the public to take a property interest by analogy to adverse possession (a fictionalized "lost grant"), or some combination of the two. These doctrines have traditionally been narrow and quite specific, applying chiefly to roadways but not to other properties that the public happens to use.[29]

Though I shall refer to both lines of reasoning as "prescriptive," since they are both based on usage over time, "prescription" technically referred only to acquisitions based on adverse use rather than dedication.[30] In fact, "implied dedication" was the more common doctrine, and its legal deployment clearly accompanied the march of commerce and industry. Joseph Angell and Thomas Durfee, in their well-known 1857 treatise on highways, stated that the first recorded case of a landowner's "implied dedication" of a road to the public had occurred in an English case in 1735; by the middle of the nineteenth century the use of the doctrine had come into full flower.[31]

In theory, when a landowner left his land open to the public's use, a court could infer that he intended to give the land to the public—or, more technically, give the public an easement; and as with any completed gift, he and his successors could not later repudiate this "dedication." But this gift analogy raised an interesting problem in the context of nineteenth-century legal doctrine, indeed a problem bearing directly on the question whether the public can genuinely own and manage property. For a time, it was said that no one could make a gift to the public because "the public" was an insufficiently specific donee. This amounted to saying that the general public was not competent to act as a property owner: property had to be managed by particular, identifiable persons.[32]

By the later nineteenth century, American courts had found a way around this doctrinal difficulty, although their solution was something of a sidestep. Instead of addressing the issue of the public's competence to receive property, the courts focused on the "donor's" acts and asserted that however weak the public's claim to ownership might be, the landowner's was still weaker: the landowner's own acts might estop him from asserting that those to whom he had "given" a street were incompetent to receive it.[33]

The doctrine of implied dedication also raised a second much-wrangled-over problem: "dedication" required a clear manifestation of the owner's intent to give over his property to public use,[34] but this was not always easy to identify. Sometimes the owner's intent did indeed seem obvious, as when he laid out streets in a subdivision and marked them on a map, "public street." But sometimes intent was much less clear, since, as one treatise put it, intent "need not always actually exist in [the] mind of the land-owner" but was simply a matter of appearances.[35] Could the owner's "dedication" be inferred from the public's use alone? Yes, said some courts, if it went on long enough. How long? Twenty years was a common answer, but lesser periods would sometimes do if the circumstances warranted.[36]

These hagglings about length of time focused less on the manifestations of the landowner's intent than on the acts of the public, and they thus suggested an analysis based not on what the owner had wanted to dedicate but rather on the public's adverse use—or "prescription" in the technical sense. Nevertheless, particularly in the early years of the century, some courts rejected the adverse use analysis even though they would permit implied dedication. As late as 1884, the California Supreme Court shied away from the adverse use analysis, for reasons again raising the interesting issue of the public's ability to own property: adverse possession technically was based on the fiction of a "lost grant," and the general public was incapable of receiving a grant, even though it might receive property by "dedication."[37]

The distinction between a dedication and a prescriptive "lost grant" seemed as hypertechnical to some nineteenth-century courts as it does to us, and some paid no attention to it; as one New Jersey court acidly observed, the designation was "a mere difference in name."[38] Insofar as the distinction did make practical sense, the reasoning seems to have been that public prescription was doubly unfair to a landowner. A so-called lost grant (that is, prescription or adverse use) was proved by someone's long usage, inconsistent with the claims of the true owner. When the adverse usage was simply that of an isolated individual, as in private prescription, the rightful owner could prevent the usage by bringing an action to oust the interloper; but when the "user" was the public at large, he had no distinct defendant to sue and hence no way to protect his rights.[39] Another unfairness peculiar to public prescription was that substantial public claims might be based on quite thin "public" use. It unduly burdens an owner if use by perhaps only a few people can translate into a claim in the public at large; thus the public's ultimate claim may be much more intrusive than anything the private owner expected from an occasional trespass.[40] For these reasons, the general public was (and still is) usually held to be unable to claim land by prescription, based on long public usage. On the other hand, the doctrine of "dedication" looked to the *owner*'s own acts and manifestations of intent, and it was his own act (such as platting land for public use) that suggested a gift; he could rebut this suggestion by acting differently, and when he did not do so, he was presumed to make a gift.

By the end of the century, however, hardly anyone cared about the difference. The California Supreme Court distinguished away its earlier reservations about public roadway claims based on adverse use and completely mixed up adverse use and dedication theories in the 1895 case *Schwerdtle v. County of Placer*, presaging the similar blend of theories in the modern beach acquisition cases.[41] At present, courts routinely apply adverse use analyses in these road cases, or some unspecified mixture of dedication and adverse use, and they ignore the difficulties that an owner might have in bringing a trespass action against the public at large.[42]

Weary readers may well ask, Why did any of this doctrine-parsing matter? It mattered because by the end of the century, the several prescriptive doctrines for roadways, taken together, could act as a double-edged sword against the landowner. If the owner did nothing to halt the public's use, his passivity could be regarded as "dedicating" the roadway to the public. If on the other hand he attempted to halt that use but failed, he could lose his rights under a theory of the public's "adverse use." In short, aside from making the roadway physically impassable, nothing the landowner did, or refrained from doing, could prevent the implication of public ownership of any property that the public actually used as a roadway.

This is not to say that public prescriptive roadway claims always defeated private landowners; sometimes the landowners won, for some reasons that will appear later. But the prescriptive doctrines themselves generated no real tests for the ways that the public could acquire roadways through usage. Some version of prescriptive theory was—and still is—always available to give the public the road, whether the owner acquiesces in the public's use or defies it. And this in turn suggests the extraordinary strength of the view that roads should be public property, whatever the contradictions that may lurk between the concepts of "public" and "property."

Public Trust—Tidal and Submerged Lands and the Waterways over Them

Roadways seemed to enjoy a very strong presumption of "publicness" in nineteenth-century doctrine, but that presumption was trifling by comparison to the assumedly public nature of waterways and submerged lands. The idea of a "public trust," now so much discussed in modern land use and environmental literature, has its historic origins in doctrines relating to ownership of lands washed by the tides and lying beneath navigable waters.

American legal scholars have long stated that despite the general presumption in favor of exclusive individual ownership of land, submerged and tidal lands and the waters flowing over them were owned first by the king of England—more or less a metaphor for "presumptively open to the public"—and, after the American Revolution, by the duly constituted American states.[43] These lands and their waters, it was said, were held in trust for the public's rights of navigation and fishing (and possibly other uses as well); and even if alienated, these lands would continue to be part of the *jus publicum,* impressed with a trust in favor of the public. Thus the public trust seemed to be something in the nature of an inalienable easement, assuring public access for certain purposes.

Although American and English jurists confidently espoused the sovereign's "trust" ownership of the tidelands as if it dated at least from the Magna Carta, there is strong evidence that the theory was a construct of much more recent origin. A sixteenth-century royalist polemicist was apparently the first to elaborate the idea that tidal lands prima facie belonged to the crown, even though at the time English submerged and tidal lands in fact had long been held by private owners.[44] After a number of years of general disfavor, the theory reemerged in Sir Mathew Hale's treatise *De Jure Maris,* which was written in the 1660s but first published in 1786.[45] According to this widely cited work, tidal lands were "presumed" to belong to the crown unless there were evidence to the contrary, such as a charter, or a showing of long usage suggesting a "lost grant" (i.e., a prescriptive right).

In American law the presumption of "sovereign" ownership of submerged lands (lodged now with the states) was soon extended from tidelands to land beneath navigable streams generally, whether tidal or not.[46] In addition, what for Hale had been a mere presumption of publicness was transformed by American jurists into a brute assertion: not even the king himself, it was said, could alienate trust property free of its subservience to the people's trust rights.[47]

However historically contingent this idea of a "public trust" might have been, and however sharp the criticism it received both originally and in more recent scholarship, it has exerted a persistent hold on American law since the early nineteenth century.[48] Public trust doctrine has enjoyed at least three waves of popularity, traceable to particular cases or events. The first American case to apply the phrase to waterways was *Arnold v. Mundy,* an 1821 New Jersey case; despite the very doubtful authority of this case, its "public trust" language was repeated in the next decades as a foundation for public claims to submerged lands.[49] In the late nineteenth and early twentieth centuries, a second flurry occurred after the 1892 Supreme Court decision *Illinois Central Railroad v. Illinois,* as several state cases used that decision to launch their own expanded version of the public trust in waterways.[50] The most recent wave has occurred in the past generation, in the wake of Joseph Sax's 1970 article applying public trust doctrine to natural resource law more generally.[51] Since then, of course, the environmental journals have published reams of public trust literature, and a number of state courts have extended public trust doctrine to new purposes and new types of property.

A striking aspect of this historical pattern is the resonance that the public trust doctrine appears to have in our law, despite the frailties in its original authority. Equally striking is the fact that public trust doctrines in waterways, like the doctrines easing public acquisition of roadways, seemed to flourish alongside the popularization of classical economic theory—a theory that normally rejected the notion that the general public could own and manage property.

II. Who Was the Public? The Uneasy Relationship of "Governmental" and "Unorganized" Publics

One way to solve the conundrum of "publicness" is easy, of course: simply equate the "public" with governmentally organized bodies. "Publics" of this sort can act as property holders in a corporate, organized form—investing in property, managing it, exchanging it—more or less as private owners do. Indeed, this form of public ownership is little more than a variant on a corporate form of private management and could obviate the commons problems thought to accompany nonexclusive use. But some nineteenth-century doctrines rejected this neat solution and located the public's rights in what other courts sometimes disapprovingly called the "unorganized public,"[52] that is, the open and utterly nonexclusive public at large. Road and waterway cases both clearly showed this tendency—as well as its controversial character.

The Roadway "Acceptance" Controversy: Prescription and "Publicness"

Although prescriptive doctrines clearly became a powerful support for public roadway claims during the nineteenth century, some private owners nevertheless prevailed. One common reason was that the public had not "accepted" a dedicated road and thus did not own it. Just beneath the surface of this "acceptance" issue lay a thinly veiled argument about just who could count as an appropriate "public." Did an organized, governmental public have to do the accepting? Or would any old public at large do?

Among the many cases raising this question was a mid-nineteenth-century decision from Maine, *State v. Bradbury,* where a landowner was indicted for building a house on top of what was alleged to be a public road.[53] He claimed that the property was his own, and the court agreed. Although there was some evidence of his "dedication" of the roadway, the court said, the road could not count as "public" without more evidence that some organized governmental authorities had "accepted" it. *Bradbury* was particularly stringent, rejecting the normal pattern of finding "acceptance" through county grading or improvements or some such action.[54] The *Bradbury* court gave the classic reasons for insisting on official acceptance: without this, a landowner could connive to open a roadway wherever he pleased and then foist responsibility for its upkeep on local governments, thus evading the requirement that the constituted authorities assent to new duties and burdens on the public treasury.[55] A few years after *Bradbury,* the Illinois Supreme Court made the same point, adding that such acts by individual landowners could contradict "the wishes of [a local government's] proper officers and of a majority of its people" and were especially pernicious in "a state like ours," in which, because of its new and undeveloped character, roads and bridges were a cause of great expense and high taxes.[56]

The underlying theory of these "official acceptance" cases was thus government by consent. Citizens were presumed to consent to the decisions of their governing officials because they consented to the larger system of government. But it could not be assumed that the citizenry consented to be bound by acts of mere individuals, who with no authority used land as a road for their own purposes and who indeed might constitute only a minority of the citizenry.

These midcentury cases rejected a more expansive English doctrine of acceptance, which required no official adoption or acceptance and held instead that the general public could turn a passageway into a public road by its mere use. Indeed, in England there was a strong suggestion that once the public had acted in this way, local officials had no choice in the matter.[57]

Midcentury American treatise writers suggested that such informality was generally unacceptable on this side of the Atlantic,[58] but by the end of the century, things had changed even here. In the 1900 edition of their treatise on roads, Byron and William Elliott noted that the question was one on which there continued to be "much diversity of opinion" (as was still the case fifty years later) but that the "prevailing opinion" was that acceptance could be inferred from long and general use by the public as of right.[59] In this altered doctrine, the "accepting" public could be the unorganized public at large and not necessarily a public organized into a governmental body. Here too there was a "consent" theory to support the doctrine. A municipal corporation, it was said, consists of the inhabitants and not the officers, the latter being mere agents for the former; if the inhabitants by their conduct accept the dedication, this suffices as an act of the principals and needs no further intervention by the agent municipal officers.[60]

The difficulty with this theory was its insensitivity to the majority/minority problem stated in the earlier cases. A 1908 Connecticut case, *Phillips v. Town of Stamford,* illustrated the point: here a small number of individuals, who walked over a beach access road at irregular times, were held to have "accepted" the road for the larger public. According to the court, even a few members of the "unorganized public" could disclose the public's attitude by their foot traffic, at least if those who would be "naturally expected" to use the land did so at their pleasure.[61]

Perhaps this would not matter if the few "acceptors" placed no new duties on the larger community. Some cases suggested that claims for maintenance and tort liability could be distinguished from mere claims to access. In the access cases, no taxpayers' money was at stake, and the only question was whether a particular way would remain open to public usage. In such instances, the courts might not wish to give an extra "acceptance" objection to the landowner, if his own acts of "dedication" had suggested that the public could have access to his property. But that was a very different question from the liability cases, where a landowner or third party claimed that the governmental body (and, derivatively, the entire citizenry) was responsible for some road expense; here the courts might insist on formal governmental acceptance.[62]

By the end of the century, however, many courts went beyond even this bifurcated approach; in a complete turnaround of the earlier doctrine equating "acceptance" with offical acts, they held that the unorganized public's usage of a road could "accept" the road—even where the issue was governmental liability.[63] Despite its technicality, this was a quite extraordinary development. No one disputes that *governmental* authorities may decide for their constituencies to establish and maintain a roadway, but these doctrines placed the decision in the hands of an unknown set of persons, who in fact could be considerably less than a majority and whose sporadic use of a roadway foisted responsibilities on all their fellow citizens.

Why then could unorganized individuals bind their governments to "accept" roadways? The chief idea seems to have been to protect injured parties' expectations. In *Benton v. City of St. Louis*, the plaintiff's deceased had drowned in a sinkhole in a walkway that the city had never formally accepted. After repeating the usual view that the city was only an agent for its inhabitants, the court remarked that because to all appearances this was a public sidewalk, the city would be estopped from denying it—even though no official had ever done anything to suggest the public's acceptance.[64] The *appearance* of publicness, then, as much as the general public's use, fixed public "acceptance"; as in the beach road case cited earlier, even a small volume of public use would constitute "acceptance" where those were the "naturally expected" users.[65]

This leaves still another puzzle: what are the characteristics that make a sidewalk or an access "appear" public to the ordinary observer? A few cases suggested that things appear to be public if the public *needs* them. For example, an 1870 Iowa case, *Mandershid v. City of Dubuque*, concerned tort liability for a bridge that had fallen into disrepair. In holding that the general public's use counted as "acceptance," the court said (over a strong dissent) that the city has a duty to keep up those things that the public "needs."[66] But again, what is it about a bridge that suggests that the public needs it? To make such an assertion, one requires a prior conception of the things that ought by their nature to be open to the public. The waterway cases too raised this problem, and beneath their equally arcane controversies, they also suggested that some properties ought by nature to belong to the public.

Waterways and the Definition of "Public": The Issue of Legislative Power

In their observations on waterways and submerged lands, as on roadways, nineteenth-century commentators thought that the public should be in control; but here too at least some thought that "public" control meant a public organized into governmental bodies. The prolific Joseph Angell presented this standard theory in his 1826 treatise on tidelands, notably in his remarks on crown ownership of waterway "trust" lands. The king himself, said Angell, could not grant these lands free of their subordination to the public trust rights of navigation and fishing; but *Parliament* could do so, at least to the extent of the fishery, and could place fishing rights in private hands.[67]

According to Angell, the reason for distinguishing the crown from the legislature was that the legislature (unlike the crown) is the same thing as the public itself. One could not deny the legislature's authority to relinquish a right without denying that the right belonged to the public in the first place. And, the argument continued, American legislatures now had the same authority as Parliament, and while the people were sovereign, their constituted political bodies were their mouthpieces.[68] Implicit in this analysis, of course, was the denial that the "unorganized" public had any status over against its own legislatures: the people were sovereign, but they had to act through their agent legislatures. Among the states, the New York courts most emphatically followed this view of plenary legislative authority; they continued to do so until late in the century, repeatedly stating that the legislature had succeeded to the authority of both king and Parliament in navigable waterways. Subject only to the paramount federal control of commerce, the legislature's ability to act for the public was complete—up to and including alienation of public rights.[69]

But even as Angell stated this theory of legislative authority, and even as courts acted upon it, a second theory was making an appearance in the case law—a theory of an inalienable public trust in submerged lands. The case to begin all this was the New Jersey Supreme Court's 1821 decision *Arnold v. Mundy*.[70] *Arnold* involved the validity of private property rights in some submerged lands whose purported title traced back to the royal grants to the colonial New Jersey proprietors. The court restated the ordinary theory, that the crown had been unable to alienate trust lands, but then went on to assert that even the *legislature* was limited in its capacity to dispose of these lands. To be sure, the legislature could alter trust properties for the sake of improving the public's uses; but even it could not grant away trust lands in such a way as to "divest ... all the citizens of their common right." "Such a grant," said Justice Kirkpatrick, "would be contrary to the great principles of our constitution, and never could be borne by free people."[71] Apparently these lands had some inherently public character, so that even the sovereign legislature could not grant them away at will.

Within a few years, the New Jersey courts backed away from this position and even cited the New York courts to reassert the legislature's plenary control over submerged lands.[72] In the meantime, when the United

States Supreme Court decided in 1842, in *Martin v. Waddell,* that title to some submerged lands could not be derived from a royal grant, it discussed but maneuvered around *Arnold*'s public trust position.[73] But *Arnold*'s "trust" theory—through which the unorganized public had property rights that could override even the acts of its own representatives—enjoyed a spectacular revival in the United States Supreme Court's 1892 decision in *Illinois Central Railroad v. Illinois.*[74]

The backdrop to this most famous assertion of the public trust theory was a pair of acts by the Illinois legislature: first it had granted to a railroad the submerged lands all along Chicago's lakefront; then it had repented a year later and revoked the grant. The question before the U.S. Supreme Court concerned the status of the initial grant; if it were valid, the legislature could not revoke it without compensation. But according to the Supreme Court, this first grant was indeed revocable. The legislature could not permanently alienate all these submerged lands, except in the service of trust purposes for which they were held, said Justice Field. An attempted grant of this sort, he said (in a passage remarkably free of supporting authority), "would be held, if not absolutely void on its face, as subject to revocation."[75] He ignored the express safeguards to public navigation incorporated in the grant and compared a purported divestment of the public's trust rights to a government's effort to divest itself of the police power—both equally invalid and ineffectual acts.[76]

Illinois Central sparked a new line of "public trust" jurisprudence in the states. Wisconsin was particularly active in developing a public trust doctrine in the years around the turn of the century, citing *Illinois Central* to hold that waterways were necessarily subject to public rights.[77] Moreover, Wisconsin's doctrine conferred property-like interests on the general public, over against its own governmental officials and even against the elected legislature. The public's interest in navigation, it was said, could override officially sanctioned efforts to destroy navigable waters for the sake of other purposes, such as drainage for agriculture or public health.[78] Florida too had several public trust cases after the turn of the century, some of which hinted for a time that the general public's rights could act as a limitation on legislative authority.[79] Even New York appeared to be temporarily awed by the authority of *Illinois Central,* and retreated for a time from its hard-line doctrine of absolute legislative authority over submerged lands.[80]

The public trust doctrine in waterways, then, like the prescriptive doctrines for roads, has gravitated between two different versions of the public: one is the "public" that is constituted as a governmental authority, whose ability to manage and dispose of trust property is plenary. But the other is the public at large, which despite its unorganized state seems to have some property-like rights in the lands held in trust for it—rights that may be asserted against the public's own representatives. This dualism has reappeared in the modern debates over the public trust. Joseph Sax, a chief spokesman for a public trust in natural resource law, has asserted the former view of an ultimately plenary legislative authority; but other commentators suggest that his ideas implicitly go further, transforming "public trust" into a theory that confers property rights on the public at large.[81] On such a theory, even the legislature itself cannot divest the public of its rights in trust property.

This version of rights—rights vesting in an unorganized, nonexclusive public at large—departs strikingly from the ordinary view of neoclassical economics and from the ordinary depiction of what a rights holder is supposed to be. It is puzzling to see how such a body could exercise the most fundamental attributes of ownership: either investment (since no individual can capture the gain of his efforts) or management (for the same reason) or even alienation (since no potential purchaser would have a clear seller with whom to deal).

How then can we explain this very peculiar allocation of rights to the unorganized public? The notion was exceptional even in American law, and it caused obvious uneasiness even in those road and waterway cases in which it was sometimes applied. For assistance in this puzzle, I turn to an unlikely source: the weakest and least-used of the notions of public property, namely, custom.

Custom and the Concept of a Managed Commons

Unlike prescription or public trust doctrine, custom was used only very sparingly, and in only a few American states, to claim rights to use roads, pathways, and tidelands areas.[82] Joseph Angell treated customary rights as a type of prescriptive right, but he said that they differed from ordinary prescriptive rights in that they were enjoyed not by individuals as such but rather as members of a specific locality.[83] By the same token, because they benefitted only members of specific communities, customary claims also differed from public prescription or public trust claims, which benefitted the public at large. As we shall see, this was an extremely important distinction in American law, and one that underlay the general hostility of American courts to customary claims. Yet in a pattern that is significant for economic theory, customary claims did resemble the doctrines vesting property-like rights in the general public: custom too was said to bestow rights on people whose precise identity was unknown and indefinite, and thus these claims too lacked the exclusivity that normally accompanies individual property entitlements.

Customary claims derived from very old British legal doctrine, whereby residents of given localities could claim rights as "customs of the manor" overriding the common law. Thus Blackstone noted that a number of localities had their own customary rules with respect to such matters as inheritance and the time and manner of rental payments. To be held good, the custom in question must have existed without dispute for a time that supposedly ran beyond memory, and it had to be well defined and "reasonable."[84]

In British law custom had traditionally supported a community's claims to use lands in common in a variety of ways aside from roadways. Custom had historically supported manorial tenants' rights, for example, to graze animals and gather wood or cut turf on the manor commons. Though many of these commons' rights had vanished by the nineteenth century, some communities' customary claims to use land persisted. Roadway use continued, but the most notable survivals were for customary recreational uses—maypole dances, horse races, cricket matches, and so on—on what was otherwise private property.[85]

In the early nineteenth century, some American courts seemed willing—albeit reluctantly—to acknowledge at least a limited doctrine of customary claims, even though, as the New York Supreme Court put it in 1833, customary law was "prejudicial" to agriculture and "uncongenial with the genius of our government and with the spirit of independence" of our farmers.[86] By the end of the century, however, American courts appeared to have grown hostile to customary claims as a matter of principle, and they seemed to be particularly alarmed that customary claims benefitted the members of specific communities.

Graham v. Walker, for example, was a 1905 trespass action in which the defendant claimed to be using a customary right of way linking two communities. The Connecticut Supreme Court denied the claimed customary right, giving several reasons of which at least the first two seemed rather flimsy. First, said the court, in a state that had always had a recording system, it was improper to say that long usage of land demonstrated a "lost grant" (the normal theory of prescription); and, second, the purported grantee was of too "fluctuating" a character.[87] But the recording system and the "fluctuating" donee were even worse problems for purported "implied dedications" to the public at large, where the Connecticut courts were much more lenient.[88]

What was it about custom that set the court on edge? *Graham* gave a third reason, and though cryptic, it was the most interesting of all: such customary rights, said the court, would favor "forms of communities unknown in this state."[89] Certainly this remark reflected the general American hostility to the feudal and manorial basis of customary claims. But it also focused precisely on the informal character of the "community" claiming the right; the remark suggested that if a community were going to make claims in a corporate capacity, then the residents would have to organize themselves in a way legally authorized by the state.

This point was made even more forcefully in *Delaplace v. Crenshaw & Fisher*, an earlier Virginia case involving a claimed "customary" right of grain inspectors to be paid in kind from inspected goods.[90] The state constitution vested legislative authority in the legislature, said the court, whereas a claim based on custom would permit a "comparatively ... few individuals" to make a law binding on the public at large, contrary to the rights of the people to be bound only by laws passed by their own "proper representatives."[91] Indeed, if the customary acts of an unorganized community could vest some form of property rights in that community, then custom could displace orderly government.

These essentially political and constitutional anxieties give us a clue to the real character of the objection to customary rights. The fear was that customary claims might allow informal and unofficial practice to substitute for established government. But in a sense, custom does precisely this. It was a commonplace among British jurisprudes that a general custom, the "custom of the country," is none other than the common law itself.[92] Looked at from this perspective, custom is the means by which an otherwise unorganized public can order its affairs, and even do so authoritatively.

Custom thus suggests a route by which a "commons" may be managed—a means different from ownership either by individuals or by organized governments. The intriguing aspect of customary rights is that they vest property rights in groups that are indefinite and informal yet nevertheless capable of self-management. Custom can be the medium through which such an informal group acts; indeed the community claiming customary rights was in some senses not an "unorganized" public at all, even if it was not a formal government either.

From a resource-management perspective, a group capable of generating its own customs ought to be if anything a less objectionable holder of "public property" than is the unorganized public at large, because a customary public comes closer to the management capacities of a governmentally organized "public." On this reasoning, the claims for customary rights should be *stronger*, not weaker, than the claims of the general public in roads and waterways. Even though the American courts rejected customary rights on grounds of constitutional policy, one can see the logic of the English pattern, whereby customary claims encompassed a considerably broader range of property claims than mere roads and waterways.

By the nineteenth century, even in Britain, the enclosure of manorial commons had largely eradicated customary claims for such consumptive uses as pasturing and wood gathering.[93] But customary rights, whether historic or more recent, suggested that even where resources are scarce, a commons need not be a wasteland of uncertain or conflicting property claims. Customary use of the medieval commons had been hedged with restrictions that limited depletion of resources.[94] This pattern continued into the nineteenth century, insofar as the courts recognized customary claims. A customary right to take soil from a commons area, for example, would be denied unless it included limitations consistent with the tenement's ability to recover; otherwise the custom would be held to be "uncertain" or "unreasonable."[95]

Moreover, the very concept of a customarily managed commons suggests that under some circumstances property might be *more* valuable as a commons than it would be in individual hands, because the administrative costs of customary management are low relative to those of an individual property system. While early European legal and political systems were still weak, individual ownership of pasturage and woodlands might have required a prohibitively expensive policing system—certainly more expensive than communal custom.[96] In an example closer to home, during the early years of settlement in the western United States, settlers treated land, water, and other resources as a commons and managed them through their own customs. These customs were formalized into law only with the arrival of increasing numbers of claimants and conflicting claims.[97]

Given, then, that custom may be an informal technique for managing a commons, let us turn back to the roads and waterways to which the public had access, ostensibly as an "unorganized" commons. Were those road and waterway travellers really such an unorganized group? Angell and Durfee's 1857 treatise on highways suggests that they were not. It includes many pages on the "rules of the road," including travel on roads, canals, railroads, and navigable rivers. Thus travellers were to keep to a particular side and yield for one or another use and move at a moderate pace. As the authors noted, these rules derived from statutes in America, but in England from—what else?—custom.[98]

Moreover, the very confinement of roads and waterways to limited areas suggests that travel and transport on them were literally kept within bounds. Here too there was a very considerable amount of common law about what uses—if any—travellers might make of the bordering property; travellers could go around impassable spots in the road, for example, but they had to keep their detours as close as practicable to the existing road and to use alternate routes if possible.[99] Similar rules restrained the uses of waterways: navigation was said to be superior to other waterway uses such as fishing, but sailors still had to avoid disrupting fishnets unnecessarily.[100] Such rules limited impositions on others while still permitting public use of the travel lanes. They suggested that roads and waterways were "managed commons," where customary practices ameliorated problems of congestion and external harms and where alternative property regimes might not have been worth the expense, so long as the country was relatively undeveloped.

Indeed American roadway case law suggested a view of the "public" and its members that is rather at odds with that of a heedlessly self-interested and atomized mass of self-seeking individuals. The mid-nineteenth-century courts sometimes denied public claims because of a concern that such claims might "be perverting neighborhood forbearance and good nature"[101] and uprooting the generous habits and customs of the people—characteristics that the courts clearly wished to nurture, just as they wished to eschew "churlish" practices, as Angell and Durfee put it.[102] This in turn suggested that the law was a vehicle to uphold a level of civilized behavior already existing in the people.

Nineteenth-century American courts allowed claims by the general public at large, while rejecting—as a matter of political principle—the customary claims asserted by informal and unorthodox communities. The American antipathy to customary claims, however, obscured the point that small and unorthodox communities are not the only ones bound together by custom. An entire populace may have customs as well, as Blackstone and others recognized when they designated the common law as the "custom of the country." The concept of a managed but freely accessible commons presupposes just such a populace—that is, one that behaves according to customs of civic care, including a civilized regard for the resources it uses.

As we have seen from earlier essays, such a concept of the citizenry was not at all far removed from nineteenth-century American jurisprudence, given the serious discussion, during the American revolutionary and constitutional periods, of "republican virtue"—individual self-restraint and a civic regard for the greater good that was thought essential to any democratic regime. These were ideas that went back at least to Montesquieu; the Antifederalists had urged them, the Federalists had made some concessions to them, and the nineteenth-century courts showed that they still survived as concepts of republican citizenship.

The managed and organized aspect of customary rights, then, casts a somewhat different light on the public rights in roads and waterways. Like traditional communities' customary commons usages, travel and commercial transport occur where even the public at large can manage itself and prevent wasteful overuse of a resource. The "unorganized public" on roads and waterways takes on more the appearance of a civilized and self-policing assemblage; through custom, the members of this assemblage can control their relations with each other and with other claimants to adjoining property.

Custom, in short, can tame and moderate the dread rule of capture that supposedly tends to turn every common into a waste. While our normal means of staving off the tragedy of the commons is a regime of private property, even private property is frequently governed only by custom. We see this, for example, in the prosaic example of the custom that permits us to stake a claim of first possession by leaving a coat on a seat in a movie theater or a towel at a spot on the beach.[103] Indeed, an entire private property regime—whether governmental or customary—may be understood as a managed commons: a private property *regime* is itself a meta-property, held in common by those who understand and follow its precepts. In a sense, when we decide to divide up the commons into private property, we are only moving from a commons in a physical resource to a commons in the social structure that safeguards individualized resource management.

And sometimes that move takes unexpected turns. In American public property doctrine, one such turn was the saga of the lesser public trust right, that is, fishing. In spite of a wide rhetoric of "publicness," nineteenth-century jurisprudes always viewed fishing as secondary to navigation as a public trust purpose, and as subject to a considerable degree of privatization.[104] The rhetoric of publicness may well have stemmed from a perception that fish were infinitely plentiful.[105] This was clearly false, and it was seen to be false even in the nineteenth century—and even more in our own, where overfishing was our initial metaphor for the tragedy of the commons.[106] In the nineteenth century, however, privatization may also have seemed ineffective for conserving fisheries. A common—if controversial—method of privatization was allocation of fishery ownership to the shore or bank owners, who in some states owned the streambed and supposedly the wildlife resources swimming above it, subject of course to the public trust in navigation.[107] But where fish could move about and no owner could identify any particular fish as his own, the interest of every individual shore owner lay in getting as many fish as he could for himself. Thus private fishing rights for shore owners did little to solve the commons problem.

As a result, the most serious development of fishery property was the movement toward governmental management. As early as 1876, the Supreme Court held that a state could limit oyster bed planting and fishing to its own citizens.[108] In more recent years, of course, fishing rights have been very much controlled by governmental bodies, which in principle—however hesitantly in practice—should be better prepared than private owners to manage the resource in a unitary form.[109] The "public trust" that continues in fishing now quite clearly sets up governmental bodies as trustees.

Customary rights, then, teach the lesson that there may be a middle ground between regimes in which the resource is so plentiful or so difficult to privatize that it is not worth the effort and regimes in which conflicting uses are managed by privatization. This middle ground is the regime of the managed commons—a commons organized by customary practice, where common usage is not tragic but rather capable of management by orderly and civilized people. It is hardly surprising that nineteenth-century public property doctrines sometimes chose this middle ground, particularly for road and waterway travel, where such civil self-management was expected.

But the history of fishing rights adds to the lesson. Where custom failed to manage a commons adequately, the law might take one of two directions. One direction was toward ownership by individuals, as was the case with commons used for grazing, wood gathering, and other consumptive uses; all of these became private property. The other direction, however, was toward "ownership" by governments, as occurred with fishing and now of course with roads and waterways as well.

Doctrines of public trust and public prescription suggested that certain property always went in the latter direction. Such property might initially "belong" to or be acquired by the public at large as an open-access commons, but if informal or customary management of that commons should fail, governments were obliged to maintain and manage the general public's access against exclusive private claims. In answer to our first question, then, namely, who was the "public" in inherently public property, the answer was *both* the public at large *and* the governmental public, with the latter acting, when necessary, as "legal" owner to secure the general public's access.

But this brings us to the next of our three questions: what was the matter with private ownership? What were the characteristics of "inherently public properties," such that the public's access to them always had to be maintained, whether as a customary commons or if need be through governmental ownership?

III. The Dangers of Privatization: Holdouts and Monopolies

What was the worry about private control over "inherently public properties"? Governmental use of eminent domain suggests one answer. This power to force a sale of private property to the public at fair market price is typically authorized where a government-sponsored project—such as a road—requires assembly of a number of pieces of land. If these projects had to rely on voluntary sales, any individual landowner might hold out for a prohibitively high price and block the entire project. And so the power of eminent domain has been justified as permitting public bodies to acquire necessary private properties at a price reflecting fair market value rather than the holdout price or "rent" that each private owner might otherwise extract.[110]

Several nineteenth-century doctrinal controversies pointedly implied a similar anti-holdout rationale both for public prescription of roads and for public trust in waterways. But there were some anomalies as well, where properties were presumed to be public even though the danger of monopoly or holdout seemed remote. Once again, the peculiar doctrines of custom help to explain these anomalies, and, in turn, the anomalous "public" cases enrich our understanding of the more mainstream public road and waterway issues.

Roadway Prescription and the Boundedness of Location

In the nineteenth-century roadway prescription cases, a controversy of particular importance swirled about the location of purported roads. Older cases often asserted that the public could acquire prescriptive rights by passing along a narrow path but not by crossing open and uncultivated fields. On open fields, public passage was presumed to be by permission of the owner and could give rise to no inference of dedication or adverse use.[111]

Courts gave several reasons for this limitation. One long-standing rationale was the magnitude of the loss to the owner: if the public could acquire a right-of-way by going anywhere across a tract, an owner might be entirely divested of the property.[112] This reasoning acknowledged that the private owner did indeed lose something by the public's prescription and attempted to minimize the loss. Sometimes this point was stated as a wish to avoid the unneighborly acts that might follow if a landowner thought that his generosity would lead to a loss of property.[113]

But other rationales seemed to contradict the policy of preventing grievous loss. For example, it was sometimes said that passage across an open field gave the public no prescriptive rights because the public's use did not preclude any use by the owner and thus was not genuinely adverse. Here too the courts gave a neighborliness rationale: if an owner was not hurt, the law would not require him to undertake pointless, difficult, and unneighborly tasks to block public passage, such as fencing in or guarding remotely situated lands.[114] In short, public prescription doctrines would only deprive the owner of his rights if he really did stand to lose something of importance from public crossings—that is, over enclosed and cultivated fields—where one might expect an owner to defend his rights.

Taken together, these reasons seem at best inconclusive. Open spaces could not be acquired by public prescription because the owner would lose too much to be fair to him—or contrariwise, because he would lose too little to presume genuine adversity. We have to find other reasons for the narrow-passage rule, and the anti-holdout rationale is a very strong contender.

Insofar as the rule applied to areas where much land was open and unused, the public had no need for any particular plot as a passageway and hence was scarcely threatened if one owner or another enclosed his land and blocked public crossing. Conversely, insofar as the rule did permit public prescription of a relatively narrow and defined path, it suggested that the public had settled upon a particular passage that might be especially appropriate. Without a doctrine of public prescription, each successive owner along the way might act as a little monopolist, threatening to cut off the public passage and siphoning off the public value of the passageway, thus capturing the "rents" from that public usage. It was precisely this that the public prescription rule prevented.

As a general pattern, then, the public could not acquire most property by prescription at all; the exception for roadways applied only to narrow passageways and not to open spaces. This exception prevented private owners from exploiting public passage but came into play only with a genuine threat of such behavior. Public meanderings anywhere across an open field suggested that the public had no focused need for a particular tract, and thus private owners had no pronounced temptation for holdout and exploitation; consequently these meanderings would raise no presumptions of "dedication."

The anti-holdout rationale is even more persuasive in the light of other American roadway doctrines with similar objectives. Roadways were of course the classic subject for the use of eminent domain by the "organized" public; prescriptive doctrines assured that the "unorganized" public—which was unable to exercise eminent domain—would also be protected from private holdout. Similarly, private owners could sometimes own toll roads, but only with assurances against private capture of the rents from public use. These private roads were treated as public utilities; they were open to all members of the public, while the roadway proprietor could charge not what the market would bear but only what would suffice to reimburse the proprietor's investment at a reasonable rate.[115]

There was one nagging problem with the anti-holdout explanation, though, because the specific-path exception had a notable exception of its own: public squares. These spaces, wide open though they were, could indeed be acquired by the public through "implied dedication."[116] To be sure, the public may have used squares a good deal for strolling, meetings, or soapbox speeches, but these spaces hardly seemed to present the potential holdout problems of roadways, where the public had to travel over long stretches of land held by many potentially exploitative owners. Squares were more concentrated, and if one property owner refused to let the public use his property as a square, the public or its agents could move elsewhere, with no reason to fear rent capture through holdout or monopoly.

On the other hand, *President of Cincinnati v. Lessee of White,* a Supreme Court case involving implied dedication of a square, did raise an extortion point, though rather obliquely. One may infer that the public has "accepted" a square's dedication, the court said, if the public had used the square a sufficiently long time to be "materially affected by an interruption of its enjoyment."[117] But why should long use raise the possibility of extortion, if other spaces were available? Why should interruption in any given place really matter much at all?

Some waterway cases throw light on the issue raised by the public squares exception, since recreational uses loom large in both areas. Indeed, despite the obvious anti-holdout reasoning behind the many waterway cases involving travel, recreational waterway use challenged that rationale.

Navigable Waterways and the Recreation Controversy

Waterway doctrine, like roadway doctrine, reflected an antipathy to the possibility of private monopolization of public passage. This was hardly surprising, since it was a commonplace of nineteenth-century jurisprudence that waterways were a type of "highway" for travel and commerce.[118] What is more, their location was more or less fixed by nature, so that their use was even more vulnerable to holdout than roadways. The potential for holdout can explain several cases that elevated the public right of water passage above all other uses, even bridges for land roads, unless specifically authorized by legislatures.[119] Land traffic might find some other route, whereas vessels had no alternative to the waterway and thus were especially susceptible to exploitation.

But the most interesting holdout questions emerged from controversies about recreation and, specifically, whether recreation was a public trust purpose that might support public rights of access to waterways and their shores. This issue in turn was curiously related to fishing as a public trust purpose. Fishing of course is not necessarily or even primarily a recreational use. But as it became assimilated to sporting and recreation in the later nineteenth century, fishing—as well as hunting—seemed to acquire more and more the attribution of a public trust purpose, supporting free public access to navigable waters.[120]

Putting to one side other arguments for (or against) public fishing rights, the holdout argument seems thin indeed. Even in those states where riparian owners controlled fishing rights, they could always sell the right of access; and unless one or a few owners held the entire shore or riverbank, no particular owner could monopolize fishing. And where special circumstances permitted private monopolization of fishing, as at the mouth of a spawning stream for anadromous fish, early-nineteenth-century law did grant private property rights but obviated the monopoly problem by treating the private fishery as a public utility—with obvious analogies to the public utility treatment of private toll roads.[121] The potential for holdout against the public is even more dubious in the case of hunting, since wild animals may roam over wide spaces; nevertheless, some later cases began to designate hunting a public trust right.[122]

All this may help explain why fishing historically has been weaker than commerce as a "public right" on navigable waterways, and why riparian owners often received private fishing rights—as well as why hunting was often not mentioned at all as a public trust purpose: there was no real danger that the public would be excluded from hunting and fishing or would be charged monopoly prices for those activities. But why, then, was fishing so often described as *jus publicum,* and why were fishing and hunting increasingly treated as public rights as they acquired greater recreational connotations?

The question is equally puzzling for other and more general recreational uses. Early-nineteenth-century doctrine denied that recreation was a public trust purpose, but by the later part of the century several American jurisdictions recanted, holding that recreational purposes would support a public right to use navigable waterways. Here too questions of monopoly and holdout were thought relevant, and contemporary courts dealing with recreation claims occasionally glanced on such issues.

A leading precedent against public rights to waterfront recreation was an 1821 British case, *Blundell v. Catterall,* which presented one of the more peculiar fact situations in land use law. The case concerned a claim that the public had the right not only to use shorelands for swimming but also to bring horse-drawn "bathing machines" across the beach and into the water for that purpose.[123] *Blundell*'s majority opinions distinguished shoreland recreational uses from the historic public rights of navigation and fishing and focused chiefly on the excessive limitations and irritations that would burden waterfront owners if such intrusive public access were upheld. Having fishermen and commercial vessels pass by was one thing, but having one's waterfront improvements curtailed or having to put up with naked youths splashing about—or even modest ladies and gentlemen in and around their rather sizeable "bathing machines," with what must have been attendant horse droppings and wheel ruts in the sand—was quite another.[124] The public right to use the seashore was thus held to exclude these recreational purposes.

Justice Best dissented. Although he has been described as an "old-fashioned judge,"[125] his opinion has a curiously up-to-date flavor, and indeed it strikingly presages the modern arguments for recreation as a trust purpose. He argued that the shore has always been impressed with a public trust for the people's use; that "universal custom" also supports the people's recreational use of the beach; that bathing is important and indeed a necessity for the public health; that bathing is not really different from navigation. Best even argued that bathing is an *aid* to navigation: swimmers learn to feel at home in the water and thus can assist sailors in distress.[126]

One of Best's arguments obliquely raised the holdout issue: if private owners had exclusive control of the beach, he said, they could thwart the public's use for no good reason of their own, excepting only "the hateful privilege of vexing their neighbors."[127] This of course presumed monopoly—that is, that the would-be swimmers could find no other shore owners with whom they could bargain for permission to swim. Perhaps other early-nineteenth-century judges simply disbelieved this; Justice Best's colleagues seemed unconvinced. Beach recreation had only come into its own in the later eighteenth century and may not have seemed to be a matter of great demand or urgency; and in any event, it hardly seemed that private shore owners could monopolize waterfront recreational uses in the same way that they might threaten or obstruct navigation lanes. Indeed, as one of Justice Best's colleagues pointed out, shore owners were quite willing to enter into commercial arrangements for other people's recreational use.[128] After *Blundell,* which was much cited in American courts, the standard position until late in the century was that recreation was not a trust purpose that would support public use of waterways or adjacent riparian tidelands.

This rejection of recreation as a public trust purpose, taken together with the very strong protection of commercial travel on waterways, suggests that the fear of private holdout was central to nineteenth-century thinking about public access to waterways. Later on, courts came to favor recreational uses, but they still attempted to rely on the holdout rationales implicit in commercial travel. One early-twentieth-century case recognizing recreation as a trust use was Oregon's *Guilliams v. Beaver Lake Club;* it was by no means the first in this trend, but it defended recreation in an interesting way. The court likened recreational uses to commerce and travel over a roadway, saying the waterways had become "valuable highways" and that a vessel using the waterway to carry picnickers to a beach was just as much engaged in commerce as a boat carrying grain or merchandise.[129]

This rationale, however, hardly applied to the swimmers who stayed roughly in one place and who could pick and choose about where that place would be. The waterway uses most subject to monopolization or holdout were clearly transportation and commerce, because these uses involved movement over a relatively narrow "path" between potentially distant places. As a British court said in 1899, the beach is "not to be regarded as in the full sense of the word a highway"; no matter how ungenerous the act, beach owners are entitled to treat as trespassers "every bather, every nursemaid with a perambulator, every boy riding a donkey, and every preacher on the shore."[130]

It is difficult, then, to find a convincing holdout rationale for such public trust uses as swimming, fishing, and hunting. These recreational uses might occur in numerous locations, without requiring any great stretch of waterway. If enough members of the public wished to engage in them, one might well expect that a variety of riparian owners would compete to accommodate them and provide swimming or other recreational facilities. Recreational uses thus replicate the problem we saw in implied dedication of squares: why should the law guarantee public access to waterways for recreational purposes when there seemed to be no threat of private holdout?

Customary Claims: Was There a Holdout Problem?

It was pointed out earlier that in nineteenth-century English law, custom supported a wide variety of claims to use land, and among the most striking of these were recreational uses, where the holdout problem was far less evident than it was for roads and waterways. Residents of some British communities claimed customary rights to use otherwise private property for such purposes as horse races, dances, and cricket matches. Even the hapless "bathing machine" users in *Blundell* might have had a better chance if they had been able to plead a local customary right.[131] Thus customary claims in England presented the same puzzle that appeared in the American cases upholding implied dedications of public squares or permitting recreation as a public trust purpose. What need was there to guard the public against private holdout when to all appearances there ought to be many locations for such activities? Custom, however, gives us more to go on and suggests why squares and recreational uses might have presented holdout problems after all.

Let us reconsider, for a moment, the point that custom is a medium through which a seemingly "unorganized" public may organize itself and act, and in a sense even "speak" with the force of law. Did customary recreational uses require particular spaces, in the way that roads or paths did? One might well think that people could hold their maypole dance anywhere or could rent a neighboring field if a particular owner would not permit the annual horse race. This reasoning, however, is insufficiently attentive to precisely the *customary* nature of the practices in question. Over time, communities may develop strong emotional attachments to particular places and to staging particular events in those very places.[132] As one who will always regard Chicago as home, I need only ask rhetorically, Does it matter that the Cubs play in Wrigley Field? To Detroit residents, just why might Tiger Stadium be described as "Detroit's anchor"?[133] No one could miss the point: over time, a community may develop the firm view that there are particular and proper places for its public activities.

Thus the location of customary public activities may matter a great deal after all, not because it would be physically impossible to conduct these activities elsewhere but because to do so would rupture the continuity of the community's experience and diminish the significance of the activity itself. The community's custom signals its emotional investment in a place and indeed communicates this information to all—including the owner of the property on which the customary claim is made, an owner who, according to British customary law, acquiesced in that investment.

If one pursues this metaphor and thinks of a custom as a kind of community investment, then the danger of holdout comes into focus. An idea of that sort may have motivated the Supreme Court's remark, in the public square case *President of Cincinnati v. Lessee of White,* that land "dedicated" to the public could be regarded as "accepted" by sheer public usage if that use had continued so long that the public's "accommodation" would be substantially affected by interruption.[134] It was the public's habit of use, rather than anything unique about the property ab initio, that made the property singularly valuable and thus subject to private rent-seeking.

Thus habit, expectation, and custom, perhaps tied to a whole variety of community practices, may make a property hostage to private holdout power—even where there was nothing unique about the property at the outset. The public's custom of dancing and carousing in a particular place, like its habit of travelling on certain paths, makes these various lands essential. Returning to the recreational uses of waters, perhaps the customary recreational use of particular places eventually made American courts realize that those uses were uniquely valuable to the public—and hence the old swimming hole or fishing spot might be especially vulnerable to private rent-seeking behavior.

But are roads and waterways really different from these customary recreational uses? In a sense, the answer must be no. Any given travelled way, like any given maypole field, is only unique because the public has singled it out and used it over a period of time. In an even deeper sense, these travel and transport spaces are valuable because we are in the *custom* of trading and in general have the customs of a commercial people, for whom ever-expanding markets are particularly important. By its commercial habits, the general public communicates to everyone the high value that it places on roads and waterways, just as the smaller locality signals its value on the maypole field. Where this signalling goes on over time without interruption, the public's "investment" grows ever higher and may tempt an owner to hold out and siphon off the public value; to prevent this, the law shifts the presumption to favor the public's use over the private owner's right to exclude.

Custom thus suggests how holdout problems might affect recreational properties. Indeed it goes further and deepens our understanding about the holdout problem for roads and waterways as well: for a society with the habits of commerce, like our own, the routes of transport are especially important places—and they are places where our commercial proclivities make us especially vulnerable to private holdout and rent-seeking.

And so the threat of holdout against the public goes some distance to explain why privatization seemed so unacceptable for some kinds of properties. But even if the holdout danger was *necessary* for a presumption of "publicness," that danger cannot have been *sufficient*. Surely there should also be some reason to suppose that a property will be more valuable if open to public access than it would be under exclusive private control. We know from eminent domain law that many properties are unique and that holdout may be a problem, yet some of these are nevertheless unsuited for public appropriation simply because the public body is not willing to pay for them. Unlike eminent domain, public prescription and public trust doctrines require no payment to the owner, and thus they never make even this simple test of comparative value of public and private uses. How, then, can we know whether such property will be more valuable in public hands?

IV. What Was the Value of Public Use? Open-endedness, Negotiations, Interactions

There is at least one place to look for answers to the relative public/private value problem: the police power exercised by the "organized" public. The analogy comes to mind because the police power also entails uncompensated public controls over otherwise private property. Frank Michelman's well-known formulation of the Benthamite "felicific calculus" explains these uncompensated controls on efficiency grounds. No compensation is paid when the costs of arranging payment are too high or, more specifically, when the "demoralization costs" of nonpayment to the owner are outweighed by the "settlement costs" of administering and paying compensation.[135]

Some echoes of this formulation can be found in public prescription and public trust doctrines. We have already seen some doctrines that attempted to minimize private owners' "demoralization costs," either by restricting public access in order to preserve the owner's property, as in the narrow-passage limitation on roadway prescription, or in the common law prohibitions against public abuse of roads or waterways. In addition, the public's use was normally limited to an easement rather than a fee interest, so that the public use only partially divested private ownership and could be compatible with a private owner's continued title to roadway land or land submerged beneath waterways.[136] Customary doctrines showed the same concern, by limiting or denying consumptive rights as "unreasonable" or "uncertain"—that is, as too damaging to the underlying property.

Public prescription and trust doctrines fit the other side of Michelman's equation as well—that is, the high cost of negotiating a compensated settlement—although the settlement cost rationale does not completely solve the relative value question, as we shall see.

Settlement Costs and Open-ended Access: The Roadway Cases

Traditional roadway doctrines drew several distinctions that effectively limited public prescription to properties that were subject to high settlement or negotiation costs. According to one important doctrine, a given property could be claimed as "public" only if its users made up an indefinite and open-ended class of persons; as one Pennsylvania case said, it had to be open to "strangers."[137] Indeed, a routine ground for denying that long usage had made a street or road "public" was that the users had really been only specific persons rather than anyone who simply happened along. This is still true; the idea seems to be that if the users are the same few persons, then the road is not really "public," and its usage will give rise at most to private prescription benefitting only the actual users.[138]

This issue arose chiefly in cases about cul-de-sacs or roadways ending in particular locations. Cul-de-sacs are used chiefly by small and identifiable groups, but those persons may be visited by anyone at all; not surprisingly, they caused considerable ponderings among the nineteenth-century roadway jurisprudes. Some experts viewed them as genuine roadways, but others, particularly in Britain, thought that cul-de-sacs did not count. They urged that the public could acquire a roadway through usage only if the road in question were a throughway; that is, a road would not count as *public* if it just stopped somewhere. Some American courts added another refinement to this delicate matter: roads could be acquired by public prescription if they ended at some other transportation terminal, such as a ferry.[139]

All this dithering about open-endedness makes some sense from a modern law-and-economics perspective. If a few specific persons use a roadway, they can locate each other relatively easily and negotiate together and with the owner to transfer a right of passage. If they do not enter these negotiations, they presumably value the right of passage less than the owner values the right to exclude them. But the more users, and the less specific their identities, the less likely it becomes that they can overcome the costs of a consensual bargain—even though they might value the right of passage very highly.[140] Moreover, the larger the number of road users involved, the greater the likelihood that they collectively will value the right of passage more highly than the owner values his right to exclude—but the greater the difficulty of making those respective valuations manifest.

On the other hand, the number of users was not the only factor in roadway cases or necessarily the crucial one. As noted earlier, nineteenth-century doctrines sometimes awarded roadways to the public even though users were few and their use unintensive—so long as their identity was indefinite. This too could be consistent with a law-and-economics analysis. A landowner and an indefinite "public" are rather differently situated; an indefinite collection of persons, even though few in number, might be unable to demonstrate a collective interest in a pathway, since all would have to find one another and arrange a bargain. The owner, on the other hand, could demonstrate and protect his interest relatively easily and could rebut any presumption of "dedication" by a variety of acts. He could put up a fence or plow up the passageway or do any one of a number of acts inconsistent with passage by others. Hence when he failed to perform these relatively simple acts, the legal doctrines perhaps appropriately presumed that he did not value his property very highly, and that in effect he wished to "give" it to the unidentified persons who used it.

But this only complicates the puzzle of relative value. Even supposing that it is difficult for indefinite "strangers" to find each other and negotiate if their overall numbers are small and their usage merely casual, those facts would weaken any presumption that their use was more valuable than the private owner's. Why then did indefiniteness of use—abstracted from numbers or intensity of use—count as the essential measure of "publicness"?

Waterways and the Definition of "Navigable"

When we turn to waterways, we find the same insistence on indefiniteness of users—in their numbers and identity—but unlike the roadway cases, the waterway and submerged lands cases seldom stated this indefiniteness requirement explicitly. The criterion is implicit, however, in the limitation of the public trust to "navigable" waters and lands underlying them.

"Navigability" has been defined in a variety of ways and for a variety of purposes.[141] For example, "navigable waters" have sometimes been said to include only waters capable of carrying commercial vessels;[142]

more generous definitions have included turbulent waters, so long as they could float logs to market,[143] or—somewhat later—waters that permit use by recreational vessels even as insubstantial as canoes.[144] But the classic measure of navigability has been suitability for commerce, however defined, and commercial use in turn suggests an indefinite and open-ended set of individuals who use the waterway. All these definitions require that the navigable waterbody have a considerable extent; none would define as "navigable" a waterbody that is confined within the ownership of one or a few landowners. Like a cul-de-sac, a small body of water is generally confined to a few identifiable users (who presumably can adjust their respective rights by negotiation) and is quite different from a "long thin roadway of water joining regions and communities," as one more modern Pennsylvania case put it.[145]

Thus only those waters that are potentially open to indefinite numbers of "strangers" count as navigable and hence subject to a "public trust." With waterways as with roads, the traditional doctrines required that the users of the "public" space be indefinite; and as with roadways, modern law-and-economics analysis would suggest that the reason behind this requirement was that an indefinite set of users would be the group least able to negotiate a transfer to themselves, no matter how highly they valued the resource collectively.

But again as in the roadway cases, the waterway definitions hinged on the "public" as an open-ended class and not on the "public" as a group with large numbers or particularly intense use. This was most obvious when the courts upheld navigation over all other waterway uses, no matter how intensive or valuable by comparison. When an early-nineteenth-century Massachusetts court ruled that the public's right to use an inlet was superior to an obstructing bridge, the court specifically stated that it was of no consequence that few boats used the inlet or that there was little settlement along its banks or that the bridge was of greater public utility.[146] When a Wisconsin court one hundred years later halted an agricultural drainage project because it would impede boaters from reaching their accustomed fishing sloughs, the court paid little heed to the respective values of the competing uses.[147]

Open-ended classes of users face negotiating problems, together with the possibility of holdout by private owners, and as such seem to present the classic case for governmental acquisition through purchase or eminent domain.[148] But the analogy to purchase or eminent domain once again raises doubts about public prescription or public trust in roads and waterways. The "organized public" has to pay at least fair market value when it exercises eminent domain and thus signals its greater valuation on the property it acquires. True, the "unorganized public" has negotiating difficulties, but that only begs the question: the unorganized public is *never* capable of negotiating, precisely because it is unorganized. How can we surmise that this public's use is more valuable than that of private owners, when no exchange is bargained for, no payment made?

There are, after all, strong reasons for *not* favoring publicness. Unlimited access, by unidentified users, creates precisely the problem that theorists regard as the bane of publicness: no one minds the property because no one has a specific interest in doing so. If negotiation costs are too high for a purchase to be arranged, then they may well also be too high for the users to allocate among themselves responsibilities for upkeep or even to establish rules for avoiding congestion. To be sure, customary practice may "govern" even an unorganized public, so as to manage common property in a rudimentary way; indeed, the doctrines of inherently public property tended to attach to properties that were capable of such customary self-management. But these doctrines never required the public—organized or unorganized—to purchase its rights of access; and it is precisely for this reason that we might doubt that the public's use is more valuable than a competing private one. To push the point, even where the public is organized and purchases the property at fair market value through eminent domain, we might still wonder why the public use should be presumed more valuable, given that the private owner is unwilling to sell at that very price.

Nineteenth-century police power doctrines, and once again the doctrines of custom, suggested a rationale for this presumption. These doctrines suggested that an expansive, open-ended public use might enhance, rather than detract from, the value of certain kinds of property.

Scale Returns, Custom, Interaction

At the turn of the century, police powers were commonly linked to the powers of eminent domain. Certain private enterprises, like the railways, could be given eminent domain powers to serve the public interest, but this same factor was thought to subject them to regulation under the police power.[149] Moreover, rate regulation itself seemed analogous to eminent domain: the public, purchasing at regulated rates, could acquire goods or services at fair market value rather than at the higher rates the producers would otherwise charge.[150] The enterprises so linked to eminent domain and regulation, according to nineteenth-century theory, were the "natural monopolies": those with increasing returns to scale, where greater production led to proportionally lower costs per unit of product. According to Henry Carter Adams, such industries could not be "governed" by market competition, since they could temporarily lower their charges and drive out competitors. In a sense, Adams implied that these enterprises were naturally public. Either they could be publicly owned or they could be privately owned and subject to a public regulation of their rates; in the latter case the entrepreneurs should receive a fair return, but the benefits of scale economies would redound to the consumers.[151]

Analogies to scale returns appear in various doctrines of public property in roads and waterways, but the analogy is most easily illustrated through the customary doctrines—particularly in the British customary claims for recreational uses. An example was the right of some communities to hold periodic dances, a custom that was among those held good even against a landowner's objections.[152]

Consider this for a moment in the light of scale returns: at least within the limits of the community, the more who join the dance, the greater the enjoyment of each participant. Each new dancer adds opportunities to vary partners and share the excitement; and as with festive activities generally, the more members of the community who participate, the more they come to feel as one. Indeed such festivities can be part of a community's self-definition. The British writer Thomas Blount recounted, among his countrymen's many "jocular customs," celebrations stemming from fabled incidents in particular communities' histories; similarly, the British cases reveal sporting and festive events that appeared to be part of regular, repeated community gatherings.[153] Activities of this sort may have value precisely because they reinforce the solidarity and fellow-feeling of the community as a whole; thus the more members of the community who participate, even only as observers, the better for all.

In a sense, this type of practice is the reverse of the tragedy of the commons. It is rather a comedy of the commons, as is so felicitously expressed in the phrase "the more the merrier." Indeed, the real danger is that individuals may "underinvest" in such activities, particularly at the outset. Few of us, after all, want to be the first on the dance floor, and in general, individuals engaging in such activities cannot capture for themselves the full value that their participation brings to the entire group. Here indefinite numbers and expandability take on a special flavor, relating not to negotiation costs but to what may be called "interactive" activities, where increasing participation *enhances* the value of the activity rather than diminishing it.[154] This quality in turn is akin to scale economies in industrial production: crudely stated, the larger the investment, the higher the rate of return per unit invested.

To be sure, increasing returns to scale were by no means an obvious feature of all customary rights. Pre-eighteenth-century customary rights included such matters as cutting peat and grazing on commons areas, where one might well think that each participant's use diminishes opportunities for the others. Recent economic history suggests, however, that even these traditional commons usages were related to economies of scale; the commons were an integral part of a mixed economic pattern where (due to limited markets) labor-intensive individual cultivation and scale-economy common livestock management were necessarily practiced together.[155]

"Interactiveness" or scale return—greater value with greater participation—was thus a dominant feature in customary commons usages and offered a potent reason for their protection. If we were to suppose that a private individual completely controlled a traditional festival ground, and if we supposed in addition that, at least for the festival day, the local residents placed a higher value on this festival use than could be reaped from any alternative uses, then we could easily see how exclusive private ownership of this uniquely valued property could give the owner a classic opportunity for "rent capture" from the community at large.

But what created the "rent"? The answer, of course, is the very publicness of the festive use. Here nonexclusivity adds value, because this sort of activity is enhanced by greater participation: "the more the merrier." Here too the usual rationing function of prices would be counterproductive; participants need encouragement to join these activities, where their participation produces beneficial "externalities" for other participants.[156] It was precisely these sorts of activities—where value is enhanced exponentially by increasing use—that customary doctrine refused to permit private owners to thwart or exploit.

Now we can take this juxtaposition of elements in customary doctrine—scale economies and the possibility of private holdout—and see in a new light the American doctrines of public property in roads and waterways. Let us ask, once again: how different were the customary doctrines from the doctrines concerning roads and waterways? One difference was that customary recreational uses quite clearly had an upper boundary on "interactively" enhanced returns to scale. Recreation and festivals have meaning and special social value for the members of a given community, but not for the world at large. Indeed, outsiders to a community might make a mockery of the local festivals; they might not know the rules and would not be part of the group whose behavior could be kept in line by habits, gossip, and social interaction with neighbors about whom one cares.[157] Perhaps in recognition of this point, the old cases accorded customary rights to dance and play at sports only to residents of a community and not to outsiders who chanced to be there[158]—a limitation that undoubtedly also helped to preserve the underlying resource.

But there was no such upper boundary on the expansiveness of commerce, that quintessential favorite of public road and waterway doctrine. According to classical economists, commerce is an interactive practice with exponential returns to increasing participation, returns that run on without limit. The more people who engage in trade, the greater the opportunities for all to make valuable exchanges; and the more exchanges, the greater the opportunities for division of labor and for all the attendant increase in wealth and productivity that Adam Smith told us about.[159] The great Commerce Clause cases of the Marshall court reflect the same view: even a state cannot "privatize" commerce for the benefit of its own citizens to the exclusion of others but must leave commerce open to the entire nation.[160] Through ever-expanding commerce, the nation becomes ever wealthier, and hence trade and commerce routes must be held open to the public, even if this is contrary to private interest. Instead of worrying that too many people will engage in commerce, we worry that too few will undertake the effort.

It is now clear why doctrines of the "inherent publicness" of roads and waterways accompanied the very ascendency of classical economics, which otherwise places so much store on exclusive ownership. As Adam Smith well knew, commerce itself requires that people interact with one another, even over long distances, and this in turn requires that they have access to certain physical locations, namely, those "long, thin" waterways and roads.[161] The individuals involved in commerce help themselves, but they help others as well, and they need encouragement to do so; thus the cost of the locations necessary for commerce—particularly transport and communication facilities—should be kept at a minimum and is sometimes borne by the organized community at common expense.

Nineteenth-century doctrine attempted to maintain public access to the locations so essential as avenues of commerce, even at the expense of exclusive ownership rights. It was, after all, the publicness of commerce—the increasing returns from greater and greater participation—that created the value of any roadway or waterway; and private owners were not to be permitted to capture the rents of commerce itself. In an odd Lockeanism, the public *deserved* access to these properties, because publicness, nonexclusive open access, created their highest value.

The doctrines of custom, then, tell us why certain kinds of property—particularly those necessary to commerce—were presumed to be most valuable if access were open to all. Holdout may have been a *necessary* prerequisite to asserting public rights in property, but the public's own contribution added a *sufficient* reason to do so. The publicly created rent established a public entitlement to access.

These attitudes about public entitlement also underlay the nineteenth-century jurisprudence of two other chief components of public law: the police powers and the power of eminent domain.

Inherently Public Property, Eminent Domain, Police Power

The public's right to its rents could assume several guises. An organized public could use eminent domain powers to capture the rents of publicness, paying for the underlying land at fair market value but appropriating to itself any additional rent created by the nonexclusiveness and expandability of public use. The "unorganized" public, of course, had to fall back on the doctrines of public prescription and public trust, thereby acquiring easements for public access over what otherwise remained in private hands. But eminent domain and the public property cases were only variant assertions of the same public entitlement—to the rents that public use created.

The police power had very similar characteristics, sometimes explicitly. Nineteenth-century theorists thought that a major police power function was to regulate enterprises with economies of scale—that is, the so-called natural monopolies like the railroads, the grain elevators, and so on—where greater consumption lowered the average costs per unit of production.[162] Though the police power had larger concerns than the physical locations so important in road and waterway doctrines, the basic elements were the same that triggered those doctrines: increasing returns to scale, together with the possibility of holdout or monopoly. To take the example of railroad regulation: more railroad tickets meant that everyone should be able to pay less per ticket, and private monopoly prices would only discourage what should instead be encouraged—that is, additional participation in a market where more participation enhanced values for everyone. Moreover, viewed as a property matter, any "rents" above opportunity costs were due to the increasing scale returns of public use, and they arguably belonged to the public that created them. Thus police power regulation, like the public property doctrines, only safeguarded publicly created rents, here by holding would-be monopolistic appropriators to "reasonable" rates.[163]

Even more fundamental was the central role of commerce, for the police power as for the public property doctrines. Just as commerce dominated the definitions of "public" roads and "navigable" waters, commerce was at the core of what some regarded as the most important task of the police power: the protection of private property.[164] If we envision a property-rights system as a common "meta-property," then it was through the police power that the organized public managed this meta-property. Like any other common property, a property rights regime has obvious returns to scale for a commercial people, and becomes more valuable as more participate and as all rights holders can enter into commercial transactions with one another. In this sense, a property rights regime is in itself as much "inherently public property" as the roads and waterways that carry public commerce, and the public protects its meta-property through the police power.

Nineteenth-century jurists had a propensity to slide easily between police power and public property terminology. The 1847 *License Cases*, for example, used a formulation that the historian Harry Scheiber once described as a "blunt instrument": the police power, said Chief Justice Taney, is the authority of "every sovereign to the extent of its dominions."[165] This definition is considerably more precise, however, when we take into account the connections between publicly created rents and public rights—between the values created by publicness and the things that the public inherently "owns." Taney's formulation is entirely in keeping with the view of the police power as the realm of things that in some senses *belonged* to the public, because publicness created their value.

It was no accident that when the classic police power case, *Munn v. Illinois*, established the regulability of enterprises "affected with a public interest," it quoted at length from Sir Mathew Hale's treatises on waterways and seaports.[166] Police power regulation thus mirrored public property doctrine (and eminent domain as well), which claimed for the public the rent created through the openness of travel and routes. By the same token, Justice Field in *Illinois Central* made perfect sense when he equated the inalienability of the public trust with the inalienability of the police power:[167] each concerned a kind of "easement" over things otherwise thought private—an easement to which the public is entitled and that cannot be bargained away to private individuals by governments or anyone else. Finally, the suggestion of some modern critics of public trust doctrine—that the public trust doctrine does nothing that cannot be done by the police power—now hardly seems so surprising.[168] According to nineteenth-century doctrine, public trust and police powers concepts shared the same concern: the prevention of private rents on scale economy uses, where value in a sense is created by the very publicness of the practice in question. That value belongs to the public, and the police power—like the doctrines of inherently public property—allows the public to claim what it has created.

The activity that was most clearly public, in the sense of bringing forth infinite returns to expanding participation, was commerce. Commerce itself necessitated a regime of private property and a police power to preserve it for all; but commerce also necessitated a limited and complementary regime of public property in the avenues of transport and communication, along with a jurisprudence of public trust and public prescription to hold that public property open to all.

V. Implications and Conclusions: Commerce, Sociability, and Historic Change in Public Property Doctrine

We have now worked through the major features of "inherently public property," the *jus publicum*, of nineteenth-century doctrine. The "public" in question was the "public at large"; sometimes it acted through organized governments, but it was also capable of acting without those governments, through the medium of the customs and habits presumed of a civilized citizenry. For this public to claim property, two elements were essential. First, the property in question had to be physically susceptible to monopolization by private persons—or would have been without doctrines that secured public access against such threats. Second, the public's claim had to be superior to that of the private owner because the property itself was most valuable when used by indefinite and unlimited numbers of persons—that is, by the public at large. Publicness created the "rent" of such a property, and the doctrines of public property, like doctrines of the police power, protected that publicly created rent from capture through private holdout.

The protection of commerce was clearly the central object of earlier "inherently public property" doctrines. In some ways, the reason seems obvious. Commerce, of all practices, is ever more valuable as more participate: markets expand and create opportunities for specialization, and we all become exponentially richer as more of us "truck, barter, and exchange," as Adam Smith said.[169] Given the centrality of commerce, public property becomes perfectly logical and falls into place with the very classical economic thinking that, for the most part, requires that property be separately held.

But now we need to explore commerce more deeply, to see whether its characteristics are shared with other purposes that might also support a presumption of publicness.

Commerce and Sociability

Commerce is an interactive practice because it has the capacity to expand wealth. But that is not the only reason. Eighteenth- and nineteenth-century commentators thought that commerce had other interactive virtues as well, most notably that it was an educative and socializing institution. This has all been made stunningly clear by the economic historian Albert Hirschman, who reminds us that eighteenth-century economic thinkers hoped to harness human avarice and turn it from a vice into the very basis for sociability.[170] By contrast to the often violent aristocratic pursuit of honor and glory, commerce, it was said, sprang from calmer passions. A nation of merchants would scarcely reach to its arms at slight provocations; even Madison—not to speak of more recent political economists—seemed to think that commerce would lessen social frictions by making everyone richer, and that the wider world of trade would distract citizens from their private grievances.[171]

Even more important is a quality that goes beyond mere conflict avoidance: eighteenth-century thinkers argued that "doux commerce" would make manners more gentle and stable and would focus people's attention on the wants of others.[172] This now seems a rather strange notion, given the many years of intervening clichés about "cutthroat" business practice; yet on reflection, commerce may indeed be our quintessential mode of sociability. Despite its appeal to self-interest, commerce also carries a culture: it inculcates rules, understandings, and standards of behavior enforced by reciprocity of advantage. To do business, one must learn the ways and practices of others; and arguably, doing business can make even the hard-bargaining trader more accustomed to dealing with strangers and more ready to sympathize with them and feel responsibility for their needs. Indeed with just these considerations in mind, recent historians have shown some interest in the possible links between the development of eighteenth-century commerce and the simultaneous emergence of philanthropy.[173]

Seen in this light, the "unorganized public" of commerce is no more a mob than the community that uses the village green to dance; it too is a community organized by custom, albeit a community capable of infinite expansion. And like the dancers on the green, the more members of the community that are engaged in commerce, the better—not only for the sake of greater productivity but also for the sake of socialization and the inculcation of habits of considering others. Thus commerce tends to *create* customs—the customs that in turn keep a "public" from turning into an unruly mob.

This perhaps overly roseate Enlightenment view of commerce places in a different perspective the "returns to scale" protected by our public property doctrines. Perhaps the most important scale returns arise from activities that are somehow sociable or socializing—activities that allow us to get along with each other. When one begins to think of scale returns in this sense, other practices and activities besides commerce come easily to mind. Education is one important example: the value of one's liberal education is enhanced when others are also educated, so that one can share and exchange ideas.[174] Good manners are another example: one person's considerateness is valuable when reciprocated (even though distinctly disadvantageous when not reciprocated).[175] Commemorative practices may have this quality as well; one values one's own honoring of some great event all the more because others do so as well; as *United States v. Gettysburg Electric Railway* so eloquently reminded us at the end of the nineteenth century, the commemoration of a great battle would not have been so valuable had it not been shared by all at common expense—nor would a memorial have been so poignant anywhere other than the battlefield itself.[176] And generally speaking, practices that enhance the sociability of the practitioners have greater returns with greater scale: one cannot get too much of them.

To be sure, not all these socializing activities—politeness, for example—need to be carried out in particular locations. But insofar as they do need specific places, and insofar as the doctrines of inherently public property go beyond commerce to embrace other socializing activities, we should expect to find that other practices too give rise to the thought that their locations are simply and inherently public—parts of the public trust.

Sociability and Historical Change in Inherently Public Property

The example of commerce should remind us that our high regard for any particular interactive practice is an historical phenomenon. Prior to the seventeenth century, political thinkers would not have dreamed that commerce could be a socializing activity with infinitely increasing returns of sociability. Quite the contrary, commerce was thought an activity that tended to avarice and mean-spiritedness: trade might be necessary for the body politic, but its practice definitely was to be confined to a particular class—and a somewhat despised one at that.[177] Indeed, even Adam Smith seems to have had doubts about the effects of commerce on character and, derivatively, on the body politic.[178]

Given the possibility of historical change in our attitudes about what are and what are not valuable socializing institutions, we might expect that our views of inherently public property would also change over time. Indeed, we should recall that the Romans had a category of public property for religious structures and places; this makes sense in a society that regards religion as a form of the "social glue" that holds the whole together.[179]

Leaving commerce to one side, perhaps a more important social glue of our own society is free speech rather than religion. Speech, it is said, helps us rule ourselves. On this view—though it is not entirely uncontested—the more ideas we have through free speech, the more refined will be our understanding and the better our capacities for self-governance.[180] Thus it is perhaps not surprising to find hints that property used for political speech may be viewed as inherently public, to be held in trust for the speaking and listening public. In *City Council of Los Angeles v. Taxpayers for Vincent,* for example, Justice Brennan suggested in dissent that certain publicly owned properties—utility poles in this case—are uniquely suitable for the dissemination of certain kinds of speech and should be held open to the "time-honored" practice of posting signs.[181] This could be stated as a kind of public trust notion: these properties are needed for the public's political communication, and thus even governments hold them only in trust and with only limited abilities to divest the public of its trust rights.[182]

And so, free speech might take a place alongside commerce as a socializing practice for our society—a practice with infinite returns to scale, whose necessary locations might be subject to a public trust. Certainly Holmes drew the analogy in his famous and much-repeated reference to the "marketplace of ideas."

But what about recreation, and, specifically, what about the beach cases with which we began? Certainly recreation has undergone a striking role transformation in public property doctrine, a transformation that began in the nineteenth century and that continues today. If recreation now seems to support the publicness of some property, this undoubtedly relates to a change in our attitudes toward recreation. In turn, from what we know about public property doctrine, we might suspect that this changed attitude relates to an increasing perception of recreation as a scale-return activity, and specifically as a socializing institution.

Recreation is often carried on in a social setting, and as such it clearly improves with scale at least to a some degree: One must have a partner for chess, two teams for baseball, and so on. But Frederick Law Olmsted argued in the middle of the 19th century that recreation had scale returns in a much more expansive sense: recreation, he said, can be a socializing influence and an education in democratic values. Thus, according to Olmsted, rich and poor would mingle in park settings and learn to treat each other as neighbors. Parks would enhance public mental health, with ultimate benefits to sociability; everyone could be soothed by the refining influence of parks and revive from the antisocial characteristics of urban life.[183] Later recreation and park advocates, though they departed from Olmsted's more contemplative ethic, continued to stress the democratic education that comes with sports and team play.[184]

Insofar as recreation educates and socializes, it acts as a "social glue" for everyone, not just those immediately engaged. And of course, the more people involved in any socializing activity, the better. From this vantage, recreation, like commerce, has political overtones: the contemplation of nature elevates our minds above the workaday world and helps us to cope with that very world; recreational play trains us in the democratic give-and-take that enables our regime to function. Not everyone takes so sanguine a view,[185] but insofar as these arguments have any merit, we ought not worry that people engage in too much recreation, but rather too little. This again argues that recreation should be open to all at minimal costs or at costs borne by the general public, since all of us benefit from the greater sociability of our fellow citizens.

If we accept these arguments, it should follow that unique recreational sites ought not be purely private property, subject to the usual price rationing through which access might be granted. Their greatest value lies in civilizing and socializing all members of the public, and this value should not be "held up" or siphoned off by private individuals, which would only discourage what ought to be encouraged instead.[186] Indeed, the same could be said of the uniquely scientific and educational areas of our national parks or the uniquely commemorative areas of our national monuments. All this might go some distance to defend the latter-day decisions to secure public access to the beach. The public's recreational use is arguably the most valuable use of this property and requires an entire expanse of beach (for unobstructed walking, viewing, contemplation) that could otherwise be blocked and "held up" by private owners.

But are these beach recreation areas really comparable to Olmsted's parks or to the Gettysburg monument—not to speak of commercial transportation routes? Do they serve a democratizing and socializing function that can be compared to commerce or speech, that becomes ever more valuable as more people are involved? Do people using the beach really become more civil and acquire the mental habits of democracy? And even if they do, is there really a danger of holdout that necessitates inalienable public access?

Attractive as this Olmstedian perspective may seem, these are not always arguments with conclusive proofs. With respect to the holdout question, one might object that where waterfront owners are numerous, they cannot really siphon off the value of expansive public uses; a reply from modern environmental thinking might counter that beaches are unique resources and that they need to be managed as unified, large-scale ecosystems of interacting parts. As to the issue of scale returns, there is a long pedigree to the argument that recreation or the contemplation of nature makes us more civilized and sociable;[187] moreover, it may seem particularly attractive insofar as our confidence has waned (perhaps somewhat unjustifiably) in the socializing qualities of commerce.[188] Nevertheless, antiquity and aesthetic appeal are not demonstrative evidence.

But whether or not one accepts these arguments in the modern beach debate, older doctrine suggests that the scale returns of sociability, taken together with the possibility of private holdout, will underlie any arguments for the inherent publicness of property. Perhaps the chief conclusion we can draw from the nineteenth-century public property doctrines, then, is that while we may change our minds about which activities are socializing, we do think that the public requires access to some physical locations for at least some socializing activities. Our law consistently allocates that access to the public, because public access to those properties is as important as the general privatization of property in other spheres of our law. In the absence of the socializing and sociable activities that are performed on "inherently public property," the public is a shapeless mob whose members neither trade nor converse nor play but only fight, in a setting where life is, in Hobbes' all-too-famous phrase, nasty, brutish, and short.

Notes

1. See, e.g., Loretto v. Teleprompter, 458 U.S. 419, 435 (1982).

2. Perhaps most venerably, 2 William Blackstone, *Commentaries on the Laws of England* (1979; reproduction of 1766 ed.) at 7.

3. Richard Posner, *Economic Analysis of Law* 30 (3d ed. 1986).

4. See, e.g., Jeremy Bentham, *Principles of the Civil Code,* in *Theory of Legislation,* 109–14 (1987; reprint of C. K. Ogden ed. 1931); Adam Smith, *The Wealth of Nations* at 669–70 (1776; Modern Library 1937 ed.); for a modern version, Bruce Yandle, "Resource Economics: A Property Rights Perspective," 5 *J. Energy L. & Pol.* 1–2, 8 (1983); for a challenge, Duncan Kennedy & Frank Michelman, "Are Private Property and Freedom of Contract Efficient?" 8 *Hofstra L. Rev.* 711 (1979–80).

5. Named, of course, for Garrett Hardin, "The Tragedy of the Commons," 162 *Science* 1243 (1968).

6. For Roman law categories of public property, see Daniel R. Coquillette, "Mosses from an Old Manse: Another Look at Some Historic Property Cases About the Environment," 64 *Cornell L. Rev.* 761, 802–803 (1979). For applications, see, e.g., Patrick Deveney, "Jus Publicum and the Public Trust: An Historical Analysis," 1 *Sea Grant L. J.* 13, 29–36 (1976); Glenn J. MacGrady, "The Navigability Concept in the Civil and Common Law," 3 *Fla. St. L. Rev.* 511, 518 (1975); Samuel C. Wiel, "Natural Communism: Air, Water, Oil, Sea and Seashore" 46 *Harv. L. Rev.* 425 (1934).

7. See Harry N. Scheiber, "Public Rights and the Rule of Law in American Legal History," 72 *Cal. L. Rev.* 217 (1984); Molly Selwin, "The Public Trust Doctrine in American Law and Policy 1789–1920," 1980 *Wisc. L. Rev.* 1403.

8. See, e.g., Martin v. Waddell, 41 U.S. (16 Pet.) 367, 412–14 (1842); cf. MacGrady, supra note 6, at 566–67.

9. See, e.g., City of Berkeley v. Superior Court, 606 P.2d 362 (Cal.), cert. denied 449 U.S. 840 (1980); Gion v. Santa Cruz 465 P.2d 50 (Cal. 1970); City of Daytona Beach v. Tona-Rama, Inc., 294 So.2d 73 (Fla. 1974); Van Ness v. Borough of Deal, 393 A.2d 571 (N.J. 1978); Borough of Neptune City v. Borough of Avon–by-the-Sea, 294 A.2d 47 (N.J. 1972); State ex rel. Thornton v. Hay, 462 P.2d 671 (Or. 1969); Seaway Co. v. Attorney-General, 375 S.W.2d 923 (Tex. Civ. App. 1964).

10. *Berkeley,* 606 P.2d 362; *Van Ness,* 393 A.2d 571; *Neptune City,* 294 A.2d 47; Matthews v. Bay Head Improvement Ass'n., 471 A.2d 355, 365 (N.J.), cert. denied 105 S.Ct. 93 (1984); Just v. Marinette County, 201 N.W.2d 761, 768–69 (Wis. 1972). For commentary, see, e.g., Deveney, supra note 6; Note, "The Public Trust in Tidal Areas: A Sometimes Submerged Traditional Doctrine," 79 *Yale L. J.* 762 (1970); Note, "Public Beach Access Exactions: Extending the Public Trust Doctrine to Vindicate Public Rights," 28 *UCLA L. Rev.* 1049, 1069–86 (1981).

11. *Gion,* 465 P.2d 50; *Seaway Co.,* 375 S.W.2d 923; and (somewhat reluctantly) Gewirtz v. City of Long Beach, 330 N.Y.S.2d 495 (N.Y. Sup. Ct. 1972), aff'd 45 A.D.2d 841 (1974). Cf. Department of Natural Resources v. Mayor of Ocean City, 332 A.2d 630 (Md. 1975) (doctrine not apply because no clear intent to dedicate); State v. Beach Co., 248 S.E. 115 (S.C. 1978) (no intent to dedicate).

12. For this approach, see *Daytona Beach*, 294 So.2d 73 (Fla.); County of Hawaii v. Sotomura, 517 P.2d 57 (1973), cert. denied 419 U.S. 872 (1974); In re Ashford, 440 P.2d 76 (Hawaii 1968); *Thornton*, 462 P.2d 671 (Or.).

13. See, e.g., Daniel A. Degnan, "Public Rights in Ocean Beaches: A Theory of Prescription," 24 *Syracuse L. Rev.* 935, 960–65 (1973); Jan S. Stevens, "The Public Trust: A Sovereign's Ancient Prerogative Becomes the People's Environmental Right," 14 *U. C. Davis L. Rev.* 195, 221–23 (1980); Note, "Public Access to Beaches," 22 *Stan. L. Rev.* 564, 580 (1970), all favorable to beach and recreation uses.

14. The modern opening salvo was the much-cited article by Joseph Sax, "The Public Trust Doctrine in Natural Resource Law: Effective Judicial Intervention," 68 *Mich. L. Rev.* 471 (1970). For an extensive bibliography, see Richard Lazarus, "Changing Conceptions of Property and Sovereignty in Natural Resources: Questioning the Public Trust Doctrine," 71 *Iowa L. Rev.* 631, 643–44, nn. 75–77 (1986), listing many articles and approximately one hundred cases in half the states concerning public trust doctrine; see also the extensive annotation in Michael C. Blumm, "Public Property and the Democratization of Western Water Law: A Modern View of the Public Trust Doctrine," 19 *Envt'l L.* 573 (1989). For efforts to extend the trust doctrine, see, e.g., Ralph N. Johnson, "Public Trust Protection for Stream Flows and Lake Levels," 14 *U. C. Davis L. Rev.* 233 (1980); Alison Rieser, "Ecological Preservation as a Public Property Right: An Emerging Doctrine in Search of a Theory," 15 *Harv. Envt'l L. Rev.* 393 (1991); Note, "Protecting the Public Interest in Art," 91 *Yale L. J.* 121 (1981).

15. See, e.g., James L. Huffman, "Avoiding the Takings Clause Through the Myth of Public Rights: The Public Trust and Reserved Rights Doctrines at Work," 3 *J. Land Use & Envt'l L.* 171 (1987); Note, "Assault on the Beaches: 'Taking' Public Recreational Rights to Private Property," 60 *B.U. L. Rev.* 933 (1980).

16. Note, "This Land Is My Land: The Doctrine of Implied Dedication and Its Application to California Beaches," 44 *S. Cal. L. Rev.* 1092, 1096 (1971).

17. Neal A. Roberts, "The Efficiency of the Common Law and Other Fairy Tales," 28 *UCLA L. Rev.* 169, 175–80 (1980).

18. See, e.g., State ex rel. Shorett v. Blue Ridge Club, 156 P.2d 667, 671 (Wash. 1945).

19. See, e.g., Graham v. Walker, 61 Atl. 98 (Conn. 1905); Note, "Easements, Customs and Usages," 21 *Minn. L. Rev.* 107 (1936) (New Hampshire the only state allowing public easements by custom).

20. See, e.g., Yandle, supra note 4, at 5.

21. See, e.g., 2 Hugo Grotius, *De Jure Belli ac Pacis* 190 (Kelsey trans. 1925). Now of course even the air has been privatized to a degree, insofar as the law provides for limited pollution "allowances" that may in turn be traded. See the acid rain provisions of the Clean Air Act (as amended 1990), 42 U.S.C.A. sec. 7651b.

22. See the earlier essay on "Possession as the Origin of Property."

23. See, e.g., Martin v. Waddell, 41 U.S. 367 (1842) (tidelands appropriation); Attorney Gen. v. Woods, 108 Mass. 436 (1871) (tidal creek obstruction); Corvallis Sand & Gravel Co. v. State Land Board, 439 P.2d 575 (Or. 1968) (streambed obstruction); Carson v. Blazer, 2 Binn. 475 (Pa. 1810) (navigable river alteration).

24. For some of the control strategies, see Carol M. Rose, "Rethinking Environmental Controls: Management Strategies for Common Resources," 1991 *Duke L. J.*

1. For efforts to mimic the market in such regulation, see, e.g., Robert W. Hahn and Robert N. Stavins, "Incentive-Based Environmental Regulation: A New Era from an Old Idea?" 18 *Ecology L. Q.* 1 (1991), and literature cited therein.

25. See Henry Carter Adams, "Relation of the State to Industrial Action," in *Two Essays by Henry Carter Adams* 57, 109–14 (Dorfman ed. 1954); Arthur T. Hadley, "Legal Theories of Price Regulation," 1 *Yale Rev.* 56, 60 (1892). The earlier essay "Property as Propriety" notes this rationale for regulation in the context of "takings" cases.

26. See, e.g., Rung v. Schoneberger, 2 Watts 23, 25–26 (Pa. 1833) (government's ownership of square is "qualified"; city is "trustee" for the public's "use"). The word "use" itself is a traditional way to designate beneficial ownership in property held in trust.

27. See, e.g., Sax, supra note 14, at 556–57; Matthews v. Bay Head Improvement Assn. 471 A.2d 355, 365 (N.J. 1954). Rieser, supra note 14, at 399, also notes the general dearth of theory in public trust writing.

28. Aside from the informal prescriptive doctrines discussed here, officially sanctioned acquisitions of roadways could also quite drastically curtail private property rights; see, e.g., M'Clenachan v. Curwin, 3 Yeates 362 (Pa. 1802) (taking property for turnpike without compensation). On these limited compensations, see generally Morton Horwitz, *The Transformation of American Law,* 74–77 (1977); Harry Scheiber, "The Road to *Munn:* Eminent Domain and the Concept of Public Purpose in the State Courts," 5 *Perspectives in Am. Hist.* 329, 362–65 (1971); but cf. Tony Freyer, "Reassessing the Impact of Eminent Domain in Early American Economic Development," 1981 *Wisc. L. Rev.* 1263, challenging the thesis of undercompensation.

29. See, e.g., Starr v. People, 30 P. 64, 65 (Colo. 1892).

30. See, e.g., State v. Kansas City, St. L. & C.B. Ry., 45 Iowa 139, 142 (1876); Virgil Childress, "Does Public User Give Rise to a Prescriptive Easement or Is It Merely Evidence of Dedication?" 6 *Tex. L. Rev.* 365, 367–68 (1928), drawing distinctions between these doctrines.

31. Joseph Angell and Thomas Durfee, *A Treatise on the Law of Highways,* secs. 131, 133 (1857).

32. Id. at sec. 135. For some variants on this theme, see President of Cincinnati v. Lessee of White, 31 U.S. (6 Pet.) 431, 435 (1832); Bolger v. Foss, 3 P. 871, 871–72 (Cal. 1884).

33. See, e.g., Smith v. City of San Luis Obispo, 30 P. 591, 593 (Cal. 1892); Wood v. Hurd 34 N.J.L. 87 (1869); see also Byron Elliott and William Elliott, *A Treatise on the Law of Roads and Streets,* sec. 132 (2d ed. 1900).

34. Angell and Durfee, supra note 31, at sec. 147; see also, e.g., Kyle v. Town of Logan, 87 Ill. 64, 66–67 (1877).

35. Elliott and Elliott, supra note 33, sec. 126.

36. See, e.g., Odiorne v. Wade 22 Mass. 421 (1828); Angell and Durfee, supra note 31, at secs. 143–45; Elliott and Elliott, supra note 33, at secs. 159–61.

37. Bolger v. Foss, 3 P. 871, 871–72 (Cal. 1884); see also Childress, supra note 30, criticizing adverse use doctrine and favoring dedication.

38. Wood v. Hurd, 34 N.J.L. 87, 92 (1869).

39. See the discussion in State ex rel. Thornton v. Hay, 462 P.2d 671, 676 (Or. 1969).

40. See Margit Livingston, "Public Access to Virginia's Tidelands: A Framework For Analysis of Implied Dedications and Public Prescriptive Rights," 24 *Wm. & Mary L. Rev.* 669, 690 (1983), and authorities cited therein.

41. *Schwerdtle,* 41 P. 448, 449 (Cal. 1895). The modern leading case, Gion v. Santa Cruz, 465 P.2d 50 (Cal. 1970), similarly mixes theories of dedication and adverse use.

42. For one of many examples, see, e.g., State ex rel. Game, Forestation & Parks Comm'n v. Hull, 97 N.W.2d 535, 541 (Neb. 1959) (adverse use and prescriptive theories called "substantially identical").

43. See Martin v. Waddell, 41 U.S. 367, at 410–16 (1842); Joseph Angell, *A Treatise on the Right of Property in Tide Waters and in the Soil and Shores Thereof* 17–20, 38–39, 50–51, 106–107 (1826); see also Deveney, supra note 6, at 14; MacGrady, supra note 6, at 546; Note, "Tidal Areas," supra note 10, at 763–64.

44. MacGrady, supra note 6, at 554, 559–62; see also Deveney, supra note 6, at 41–42; Wiel, supra note 6, at 451.

45. Hale, *De Jure Maris,* reprinted in Stuart A. Moore, *A History of the Foreshore and the Law Relating Thereto* 370, 374 (3d ed. 1888). For the publication history, see Moore, at 317–18. 1 Robert Clark, *Waters and Water Rights,* at sec. 36.3A (1967 & Supp. 1978) and Scheiber, supra note 28, at 336, 339–44, both describe Hale's book as having great influence.

46. The leading early case is Carson v. Blazer, 2 Binney 475 (Pa. 1810); see also Barney v. Keokuk, 94 U.S. 324, 338 (1876). For several different functional definitions of "navigable," see text at note 141, infra.

47. Angell, supra note 43, at 21.

48. For early criticism, see Justice Catron's dissent in Pollard's Lessee v. Hagen, 44 U.S. (3 How.) 212, 232 (1845), along with the very able arguments of losing counsel in *Martin,* 41 U.S. at 398, 400–404; for modern legal historians' criticism, see, e.g., MacGrady, supra note 6, at 549; Deveney, supra note 6, at 51–56.

49. Arnold v. Mundy, 6 N.J.L. 1, 71–78 (1821); for wider use of the doctrine, see Selwin, supra note 7, at 1410–18; for a critical view see also MacGrady, supra note 6, at 590–91.

50. *Illinois Central,* 146 U.S. 387 (1892); for expansive readings, see, e.g., Lamprey v. State, 53 N.W. 1139, 1143 (Minn. 1893); Diana Shooting Club v. Husting, 145 N.W. 816 (Wis. 1914); see also Sax, supra note 14, at 509.

51. Sax, supra note 14.

52. See Phillips v. City of Stamford, 71 361, 363 (Conn. 1908); Guthrie v. Town of New Haven, 31 Conn. 308, 320–21 (1863); Sage v. Mayor of New York, 47 N.E. 1096, 1101 (N.Y. 1897).

53. 40 Me. 154 (1855).

54. See Elliott and Elliott, supra note 33, at secs. 152–53.

55. 40 Me. at 157–58.

56. People ex rel. Shurtz v. Commissioners of Highways, 52 Ill. 498, 502 (1869).

57. Rex v. Leake, 110 Eng. Rep. 863 (K.B. 1833).

58. Angell and Durfee, supra note 31, at secs. 159–60; but compare Reed v. Northfield, 30 Mass. (13 Pick.) 94, 97 (1832), where Shaw, C. J., remarked that if

forty years' public use was insufficient, some of the oldest and most important highways would not be public.

59. Elliott and Elliott, supra note 33, sec. 154. For more recent cases, see, e.g., Bain v. Fry, 89 N.W.2d 485, 488–89 (Mich. 1958) (requiring an official act to accept a road), to Union Transportation Co. v. Sacramento County, 267 P.2d 10, 15 (Cal. 1954) (discussing contrary rule while requiring at least informal acceptance by officials).

60. See Green v. Canaan, 29 Conn. 157, 164 (1860); for some variations, see Reed v. Inhabitants of Northfield, 30 Mass. (13 Pick.) 94, 98 (1832); Devenpeck v. Lambert, 44 Barb. 596 (N.Y. 1865).

61. 71 A. 361, 363–64 (Conn. 1908).

62. See Livingston, supra note 40, at 693; compare, e.g., Way v. Fellows, 100 A. 682, 684 (Vt. 1917) (cites maintenance case requiring acceptance) with, e.g., Smith v. City of San Luis Obispo, 30 P. 591, 593 (Cal. 1892) (owner estopped from raising acceptance issue in access case); see also Tolliver v. Louisville & N.R.R., 10 S.W.2d 623, 624–25 (Ky. 1928) (distinguishing public access from public duty to repair).

63. Elliott and Elliott, supra note 33, at sec. 154.

64. 118 S.W. 418, 423 (Mo. 1909).

65. Phillips v. City of Stamford, 71 A. 361, 364 (Conn. 1908).

66. 29 Iowa 73, 85.

67. Angell, supra note 43, at 106–107.

68. Id.

69. Lansing v. Smith, 4 Wend. 9, 21–22 (N.Y. 1829); see also People v. New York & Staten Island Ferry Co. 68 N.Y. 71, 77–78 (1877) (citing Angell's *Tide Waters*); Langdon v. Mayor of New York, 93 N.Y. 129, 155–56 (1883). New York may have been particularly sensitive because of New York City's traditional (and politically important) sale of submerged "water lot" property; see Hendrik Hartog, *Public Property and Private Power: The Corporation of the City of New York in American Law, 1730–1870,* at 48–52, 206–207, 223–24 (1983).

70. 6 N.J.L. 1; MacGrady, supra note 6, at 590–91.

71. 6 N.J.L. at 12–13; for a slightly different formulation, see id. at 77–78.

72. Gough v. Bell, 22 N.J.L. 441, 457, 467, 473 (1850), aff'd 23 N.J.L. 624 (1852); Stevens v. Paterson & N.R.R., 34 N.J.L. 532, 549–52 (1870). In the more recent past the New Jersey courts revived their internal debate over privatization of the waterfront; in Matthews v. Bay Head Improvement Ass'n, 471 A.2d 355, 360–61 (N.J. 1984), Arnold v. Mundy once again received favorable treatment.

73. Martin v. Waddell, 41 U.S. 367, 417; *Arnold* was the apparent authority for Chief Justice Taney's discussion of a "public trust" in tidelands; compare the dissenting Justice Thompson's more extensive (and unfavorable) discussion of *Arnold* at 419–21.

74. 146 U.S. 387.

75. 146 U.S. at 453. Field cited New York's People v. New York & Staten Island Ferry Co., 68 N.Y. 71 (1877), which in dictum explicitly denied the inalienable trust theory; his strongest authority was Kirkpatrick's opinion in the much-battered *Arnold.*

76. 146 U.S. at 453; the leading authority for the inalienability of the police power is Stone v. Mississippi, 101 U.S. 814, 817 (1880).

77. Priewe v. Wisconsin State Land & Improvement Co. N.W. 67, 918, 922 (Wis. 1896); McLennan v. Prentice, 55 N.W. 764, 770 (Wis. 1893).

78. *Priewe,* 67 N.W. at 922; In re Darcy Drainage District, 108 N.W. 202, 205 (Wis. 1906); In re Crawford County Levee & Drainage Dist. No. 1, 196 N.W. 874, 875–77 (Wis.) cert. denied 264 U.S. 598 (1924); compare In re Trempealeau Drainage District, 131 N.W. 838, 840 (Wis. 1911); City of Milwaukee v. State, 214 N.W. 820, 830–32 (1927) (both permitting alterations that improved navigability).

79. For this history, see Michael L. Rosen, "Public and Private Ownership Rights in Lands Under Navigable Waters: The Government/Proprietary Distinction," 34 *U. Fla L. Rev.* 561, 588–610 (1982).

80. See Coxe v. State, 39 N.E. 400, 402 (N.Y. 1895); Long Sault Devel. Co. v. Kennedy, 105 N.E.2d 849, 852 (N.Y. 1914) (both citing *Illinois Central* despite contrary New York doctrine of alienability); compare People v. Steeplechase Park Co., 113 N.E. 521 (N.Y. 1916) (distinguishing *Illinois Central* in a case of small grant of tidelands).

81. See Sax, supra note 14, at 478–84, denying that the doctrine rests on property rights in the general public. For those who say that it does, see, e.g., Coquillette, supra note 6, at 811–13; Julian C. Juergensmeyer and James B. Wadley, "The Common Lands Concept: A 'Commons' Solution to a Common Environmental Problem," 14 *Nat. Resources J.* 361, 377–79 (1974); Rieser, supra note 14, at 397.

82. New Hampshire was the chief state to recognize customary claims. See, e.g., Nudd v. Hobbs, 17 N.H. 524 (1825) (customary right of passage); see also Knowles v. Dow, 22 N.H. 387 (1851) (customary right to deposit seaweed); cf. Van Rensselaer v. Radcliff, 10 Wend. 639 (N.Y. Sup. Ct. 1833) (customary rights generally contrary to American law but recognized on specific older manors). For a review of major customary doctrine, see Gillies v. Orienta Beach Club 289 N.Y.S. 733 (N.Y. Sup. Ct. 1935); discussed in Note, 21 *Minn. L. Rev.* 91, 107 (1936).

83. Angell, supra note 43, at 87–88; see also 2 Blackstone, supra note 2, at 263.

84. 1 Blackstone, supra note 2, at 74–75; 2 id. at 90–91, 95–97; see also 8 *Halsbury's Laws of England* secs. 476–77 (3d ed. 1954); see also Donald R. Denman, *Tenant Right Valuation in History and Modern Practice* 18 (1942).

85. For traditional customary land rights, see 2 Blackstone, supra note 2, at 32–35. For loss of rights, see, e.g., Dean and Chapter of Ely v. Warren, 26 Eng. Rep. 518 (Ch. 1741) (statutory enclosure ends customary right to take turf). For continuing customary claims, see, e.g., Abbot v. Weekly, 83 Eng. Rep. 357 (K.B. 1665) (upheld customary right to dance on plaintiff's land); Fitch v. Rawling, 126 Eng. Rep. 614 (K.B. 1795) (same to play cricket); Mounsey v. Ismay, 158 Eng. Rep. 1077 (Q.B. 1863) (same for annual horse race); Hull v. Nottinghan, 33 L.T.R. 697 (Ex.D. 1876) (same for maypole dance, other recreation).

86. *Van Rensselaer* 10 Wend. at 649. Some courts also questioned customary claims because they thought there was no such thing as "immemorial usage" in the United States. See, e.g., Ackerman v. Shelp, 8 N.J.L. 125, 130 (1825). "Time immemorial" was obviously a fiction even in England, however, since some relatively modern usages were upheld as good customs there, such as the cricket match upheld in *Fitch* (1795).

87. 61 A. 98, 99 (1905).

88. See, e.g., Phillips v. City of Stamford, 71 A. 361 (Conn., 1908).

89. 61 A. at 99.

90. 56 Va. (15 Gratt.) 457 (1860).

91. Id. at 475.

92. 1 Blackstone supra 2, at 67 ("General customs; which are the universal rule of the whole kingdom ... form the common law").

93. 8 *Halsbury's Laws of England,* supra note 84, at sec. 498; see also the 1741 *Dean of Ely* case, 26 Eng. Rep. 518. For enclosure generally, see G. E. Mingay, *English Landed Society in the Eighteenth Century* 179–88 (1963).

94. Carl Dahlman, *The Open Field System and Beyond: A Property Rights Analysis of an Economic Institution* 23, 101 (1980); Jerome Blum, "The Internal Structure and Polity of the European Village Community from the Fifteenth to the Nineteenth Centuries," 43 *J. Mod. Hist.* 541, 542 (1971); S. V. Ciriacy-Wantrup and Richard C. Bishop, "'Common Property' as a Concept in Natural Resources Policy," 15 *Nat. Resources J.* 713, 719 (1975); Susan Jane Buck Cox, "No Tragedy of the Commons," 7 *Envt'l Ethics* 49, 53–59 (1985).

95. See Wilson v. Willes, 103 Eng. Rep. 46, 49 (K.B. 1806); Clayton v. Corby, 114 Eng. Rep. 1306, 1307–08 (Q.B. 1843) (both denying customary claims to remove soil as incompatible with sustained use, respectively as "uncertain" and "unreasonable"); see also Bland v. Lipscombe, reported in Race v. Ward, 99 Rev. Rep. 702, 710 n.(2) (Q.B. 1855) (distinguishing unintrusive right to dance from potentially damaging fishing right).

96. Dahlman, supra note 94, at 116–17; for a very useful analysis of costs, see Steven N. S. Cheung, "The Structure of a Contract and the Theory of a Non-Exclusive Resource," 13 *J. L. & Econ.* 49, 64 (1970). For a leading example of the revived interest in customary regimes and their costs and benefits, see Elinor Ostrom, *Governing the Commons* (1990).

97. See, e.g., Terry L. Anderson and P. J. Hill, "The Evolution of Property Rights: A Study of the American West," 18 *J. L. & Econ.* 163 (1975); see also Charles W. McCurdy, "Stephen J. Field and Public Land Law Development in California, 1850–1866: A Case Study of Judicial Resource Allocation in Nineteenth Century America," 10 *Law & Soc'y Rev.* 235, 240–46 (1976); John Umbeck, "A Theory of Contract Choice and the California Gold Rush," 20 *J. L. & Econ.* 421, 434–37 (1977).

98. Angell and Durfee, supra note 31, at secs. 327–449; for usages and customs, id. at secs. 327–33.

99. Elliott and Elliott, supra note 33, at secs. 12–14; see also Campbell v. Race, 61 Mass (6 Cush.) 408, 412–13 (1851), describing these matters as an "incidental" burden on property that was expected in a "civilized community"; Morey v. Fitzgerald, 56 Vt. 487, 490 (1884).

100. See, e.g., Post v. Munn, 4 N.J.L. 68, 70, 72 (1818).

101. 100 Pearsall v. Post, 20 Wend. 111, 135 (N.Y. Sup. Ct. 1838).

102. For references to generous customs, see, e.g., Warren v. President of Jacksonville, 15 Ill. 236, 241–42 (1853); Starr v. People, 30 P. 64, 66 (Colo. 1892); see also Angell and Durfee, supra note 31, at sec. 151.

103. See the earlier essay "Possession as the Origin of Property."

104. For the fishery's secondary status, see, e.g., Post v. Munn, 4 N.J.L. 68 (1818).

105. In England public fishing rights historically were confined to tidal waters, that is, to ocean fish, which must have seemed limitless. See MacGrady, supra note

6, at 581–82, 589. American definitions of "navigation" in some states extended fishing rights inland, but fish, like American wildlife generally, must have seemed inexhaustible. James A. Tober, *Who Owns the Wildlife? The Political Economy of Conservation in Nineteenth-Century America* 17 (1981), describes Americans' belief in the limitless nature of a number of species that in fact soon succumbed to overhunting.

106. H. Scott Gordon, "The Economic Theory of a Common-Property Resource: The Fishery," 62 *J. Pol. Econ.* 124 (1954) is generally seen as the article that set the stage for much of the "commons" literature.

107. See, e.g., Schulte v. Warren, 75 N.E. 783 (Ill. 1905) (public rights not include fishing), but cf. Collins v. Gerhardt, 211 N.W. 115 (Mich. 1926) (public rights included fishing). Early nineteenth-century legislatures granted private fishing rights in shad and other anadromous fish; see, e.g., Nickerson v. Brockett, 10 Mass. 212 (1813). English law permitted private fishing rights either by grant or by prescription. See Angell, supra note 43, at 106–108.

108. McCready v. Virginia, 94 U.S. 391 (1876); see also Geer v. Connecticut, 161 U.S. 519 (1896); but see Hughes v. Oklahoma, 441 U.S. 322 (1979) (state prohibition on export of minnows violates interstate commerce clause).

109. For the development of state regulation in the nineteenth century, see Tober, supra note 105, at 139 et seq.; for an exhaustive history of what is now an advanced state regulatory system, that of California, see Arthur McEvoy, *The Fisherman's Problem: Ecology and Law in the California Fisheries, 1850–1980* (1986).

110. For this standard rationale, see, e.g., Thomas Merrill, "The Economics of Public Use," 72 *Cornell L. Rev.* 61 (1986); Guido Calabresi and A. Douglas Melamed, "Property Rules, Liability Rules, and Inalienability: One View of the Cathedral," 85 *Harv. L. Rev.* 1089, 1106–07 (1972).

111. See Elliott and Elliott, supra note 33, at secs. 164, 176; see also, e.g., Kyle v. Town of Logan, 87 Ill. 64 (1877).

112. See, e.g., Pearsall v. Post, 20 Wend. 111, 135 (N.Y. Sup. Ct. 1838).; F. A. Hihn v. City of Santa Cruz, 150 P. 62 (Cal. 1915) (overruled sub silentio by O'Banion v. Borba, 195 P.2d 10 [Cal. 1948]).

113. See *Pearsall,* 20 Wend. at 135.

114. See, e.g., *Kyle,* 87 Ill. at 67; Warren v. President of Jacksonville, 15 Ill. 236, 241 (1853), remarking that it was "neither the temper, disposition, fashion or habit of the people, or custom of the country" to prevent public use.

115. See, e.g., Commonwealth v. Wilkinson, 33 Mass. (16 Pick.) 175, 177 (1834); Elliott and Elliott, supra note 33, at sec. 88.

116. See, e.g., *Pearsall,* 20 Wend. at 117–19; Trustees of Methodist Episcopal Church v. Mayor of Hoboken, 33 N.J.L. 13, 22 (1868); Commonwealth v. Alburger, 1 Whart. 469 (Pa. 1836).

117. 31 U.S. (6 Pet.) 431, 439 (1832).

118. See, for example, the well-known case of Carson v. Blazer, 2 Binn. 475, 485 (Pa. 1810), where the state legislature had declared the Susquehanna River a "highway"; for this general usage, see R. Timothy Westonk, "Public Rights in Pennsylvania Waters," 49 *Temp. L. Q.* 515, 531 (1976).

119. Commonwealth v. Inhabitants of Charleston, 18 Mass. (1 Pick.) 180, 187–88 (1822); Inhabitants of Arundel v. M'Colluch, 10 Mass. 70 (1813) (both bridge/waterway conflicts, waterway viewed as superior).

120. 1 Clark, supra note 45, at sec. 36.4(B); State ex rel. Thompson v. Parker, 200 S.W. 1014 (Ark. 1917); Ainsworth v. Munoskong Hunting and Fishing Club, 116 N.W. 992, 993 (Mich. 1908); Diana Shooting Club v. Husting, 145 N.W. 816, 820 (Wis. 1914).

121. See Thomas A. Lund, "Early American Wildlife Law," 51 *N.Y.U. L. Rev.* 703, 718 (1976).

122. See, e.g., *Ainsworth,* 116 N.W. 992; *Diana Shooting Club,* 145 N.W. 816.

123. 106 Eng. Rep. 1190 (K.B. 1821). When I first wrote the article on which this essay is based, I searched in vain for a picture of a bathing machine, learning only secondhand that they looked like horse-drawn outhouses (this from Richard Helmholz of the University of Chicago and Mark Grady at Northwestern University) and that one had appeared in the 1939 movie *The Ghost and Mrs. Muir* (this from my law review editor). I am happy to say that I have been inundated with information and pictures since then, the most accessible (with wonderful pictures) being Peggy Heinrich and Ray J. Worssam, "Bathing Machines Brought Elegance to Skinny Dipping," *Smithsonian Mag.,* July 1974, at 57. Special thanks go to Professors Richard Cunningham of Hastings and Kenneth Salzberg of Hamline.

124. *Blundell,* 106 Eng. Rep. at 1199–1204. The machines were generally one-horse box structures on wagon wheels, but grew over the course of their history to 6 feet by 41/2 feet, with wheels growing from 4 to 6 feet in diameter; one late eighteenth-century British beach experimented with huge machines 20 feet by 30 feet. The fashion for swimming included bathing machines from the mid-eighteenth century well into the twentieth; Heinrich and Worssam, supra note 123, at 58–61; see also "The Public and the Foreshore," 139 *The Times* (London) 381, 383 (1915).

125. P. S. Atiyah, *The Rise and Fall of Freedom of Contract* 169 (1979).

126. *Blundell,* 106 Eng. Rep. at 1194–95, 1197 (Best, J., dissenting). In 1984 Best's comments were quoted approvingly by the New Jersey Supreme Court in Matthews v. Bay Head Improvement Ass'n, 471 A.2d 335, 364–65 (1984).

127. *Blundell,* at 1197.

128. Id. at 1207 (Abbott, C. J.).

129. *Guilliams,* 175 P. 437 (Or. 1918); for similar reasoning, see Attorney Gen. v. Woods, 108 Mass. 436, 439–40 (1871).

130. Llandudno Urban Dist. Council v. Woods, 81 L.T.R. 170, 171 (Ch. 1899).

131. 106 Eng. Rep. at 1198 (opinion of Holroyd, J.).

132. See Kevin Lynch, *The Image of the City* 125–28 (1960), noting the individual sense of orientation to memories of activities in specific physical locations.

133. See Bob Logan, "A Timeless City Beauty: Wrigley Field's Tradition Spans Generations," *Chicago Tribune,* June 28, 1985, sec. 4, at 1; Bob Logan, "Tiger Stadium: Detroit's Anchor," *Chicago Tribune,* June 27, 1985, sec. 4, at 1.

134. 31 U.S. (6 Pet.) 431, 439 (1832).

135. Frank Michelman, "Property, Utility and Fairness: Comments on the Ethical Foundations of 'Just Compensation' Law," 80 *Harv. L. Rev.* 1165, 1214–15 (1967).

136. See generally Livingston, supra note 40, at 688–98.

137. Rung v. Shoneberger, 2 Watts 23, 25–26 (Pa. 1833). Though this case was about a square, the court likened the land to a street.

138. See, e.g., Simmons v. Mumford, 2 R.I. 172, 183–84 (1852); for more modern cases, see, e.g., Batchelder Co. v. Gustafson, 335 N.E.2d 565 (Ill. App. 1975); Rominger v. City Realty Co., 324 S.W.2d 806 (Ky. 1959).

139. Angell and Durfee, supra note 31, at secs. 136–38.

140. For an excellent and succinct statement of this point, see Thomas Merrill, "Trespass, Nuisance, and the Costs of Determining Property Rights," 14 *J. Legal Stud.* 13, 21–22, 26–35 (1985). See similar considerations in the next essay, "Energy and Efficiency."

141. For an exhaustive discussion, see MacGrady, supra note 6, at 587–605. The major American differences relate to purposes of federal admiralty jurisdiction, federal regulatory authority, and state and federal definitions of subsoil ownership.

142. E.g., The Daniel Ball, 77 U.S. 557, 563 (1870).

143. E.g., Moore v. Sanborne, 2 Mich. 520 (1853).

144. E.g., Lamprey v. State, 53 N.W. 1139 (Minn. 1893).

145. Lakeside Park Co. v. Forsmark, 153 A.2d 486, 487 (Pa. 1959); see also Conneaut Lake Ice Co. v. Quigley, 74 A. 648, 650 (Pa. 1909), distinguishing navigable streams from small waterbodies of little interest to the public.

146. Commonwealth v. Inhabitants of Charlestown, 18 Mass. (1 Pick.) 180, 187–88 (1822).

147. In re Crawford County Levee & Drainage Dist. No. 1, 196 N.W. 874, 878 (Wis.), cert. denied, 264 U.S. 598 (1924).

148. See Calabresi and Melamed, supra note 110, at 1106–1107.

149. Scheiber, supra note 28, at 366–68.

150. For an elegant statement of this argument, see excerpts from John W. Davis' brief cited in Mahon v. Pennsylvania Coal Co., 260 U.S. 393, 401–402 (1922) (analogizing railroad and rent regulation to eminent domain).

151. Adams, supra note 25, at 98–114.

152. Abbot v. Weekly, 83 Eng. Rep. 357 (K.B. 1665), Hull v. Nottinghan, 33 L.T.R. 697 (Ex.D. 1876).

153. Thomas Blount, *Fragmenta Antiquitatis; or, Antient Tenures of Land and Jocular Customs of Some Mannors* 154 (1674) (customary commemoration of a battle fought in 750; residents of Burford community made a dragon, carried it around on Midsummer Eve "in great jollilty"). For cases, see *Hull*, 33 L.T.R. 697 (maypole dance); Tyson v. Smith, 112 Eng. Rep. 1265 (Ex.Ch. 1838) (annual fair); Mounsey v. Ismay, 158 Eng. Rep. 1077 (Q.B. 1863) (horse race every Ascension Day); Fitch v. Rawling, 126 Eng. Rep. 614 (K.B. 1795) (cricket match).

154. Some alternative terms from economic literature are "network" or "system scale economies"; see Paul A. David, "Clio and the Economics of QWERTY," 75 *Am. Econ. Rev.* (Papers and Proceedings) 322, 335 (1985) (concerning common typewriter keyboard); or "interdependent demand," Jeffrey Rohlfs, "A Theory of Interdependent Demand for a Communications Service," 5 *Bell J. Econ. & Mgmt. Sci.* 16 (1974).

155. Dahlman, supra note 94, at 6–8, 124–25.

156. For a similar problem of encouraging a "critical mass" of initial subscribers to a communications network, see Rohlfs, supra note 154, at 28–30, 32–37.

157. For the importance of custom and gossip in a contemporary California community, see Robert C. Ellickson, *Order Without Law: How Neighbors Settle Disputes* 57–58, 79–80, 213–15 (1991).

158. See, e.g., Fitch v. Rawling, 126 Eng. Rep. 614, 615 (K.B. 1795).

159. Smith, supra note 4, at 7–16.

160. Gibbons v. Ogden, 22 U.S. (9 Wheat.) 1 (1824).

161. Smith, supra note 4, at 7–16; Lakeside Park Co. v. Forsmark, 153 A.2d 486, 487 (Pa. 1959).

162. Adams, supra note 25, at 109–14; see also Munn v. Illinois, 94 U.S. 113 (1877), and the discussion in Scheiber, supra note 28, at 356.

163. Nineteenth-century jurists also recognized a police power right to abate (or permit) public nuisances, such as widespread health hazards. This power essentially concerned scale aspects of harms: an individual health hazard might cause personal hardship (without scale effects), but the harms of a widespread or public nuisance might expand exponentially to epidemic, panic, workforce shutdown, etc. For some other distinctions between public and private nuisances, see, e.g., Richards v. Washington Terminal Co., 233 U.S. 546, 551 (1914) (legislature could authorize public but not private nuisances).

164. See Bentham, supra note 4, at chs. 6–7.

165. License Cases, 46 U.S. (5 How.) 504, 583 (1847); Scheiber, supra note 7, at 221–22.

166. Munn v. Illinois, 94 U.S. 113, 126–27 (1877) (quoting from Hale's *De Jure Maris* and *De Portibus Maris*).

167. 146 U.S. 387 (1892).

168. See, e.g., Lazarus, supra note 14, at 674; see also Steven M. Jawetz, "The Public Trust Totem in Public Land Law: Ineffective—and Undesirable—Judicial Intervention," 10 *Ecology L. Q.* 455, 473 (1982).

169. Smith, supra note 4, at 13.

170. Albert O. Hirschman, *The Passions and the Interests* 49–66 (1977).

171. Martin Diamond, "The Federalist," in Leo Strauss and Joseph Cropsey, eds., *History of Political Philosophy* 573, 590–92 (1963); see also the earlier essay on Antifederalists for the Federalist hopes for commerce.

172. Hirschman, supra note 170, at 58–63. Some eighteenth-century thinkers were more skeptical, however; see J.G.A. Pocock, *The Machiavellian Moment: Florentine Political Thought and the Atlantic Republican Tradition* 497–98, 502 (1975).

173. See Thomas Haskell, "Capitalism and the Origins of the Humanitarian Sensibility" (part 2) 90 *Am. Hist. Rev.* 547, 555–63 (1985); see also Joyce Appleby, *Capitalism and a New Social Order: The Republican Vision of the 1790's* 87 (1984) (concerning the republican view of commerce as expanding horizons). See also the essay "Crystals and Mud" later in this volume.

174. This is probably the chief difference between liberal education and education for marketable skills; in the latter, the educated person has an advantage when others remain ignorant.

175. See, e.g., Robert Axelrod, *The Evolution of Cooperation* 35 (1984); see also the essay on women and property later in this volume.

176. 160 U.S. 668, 681–83 (1896). See also Joseph Sax, "Some Thoughts on the Decline of Private Property," 58 *Wash. L. Rev.* 481, 486–87 (1983) on the bandwagon effect in matters as trivial as fashion, where people value things more because others value them as well.

177. See R. H. Tawney, *Religion and the Rise of Capitalism* 31–35 (1926); Lester K. Little, "Pride Goes Before Avarice: Social Change and the Vices in Latin Christendom," 76 *Am. Hist. Rev.* 16 (1971).

178. Pocock, supra note 172, at 502; Hirschman, supra note 170, at 104–108.

179. For Roman *res sacrae,* see Coquillette, supra note 6, at 802 n. 194.

180. See, e.g., New York Times v. Sullivan, 376 U.S. 254, 270 (1964). Dissenting views point to coercive aspects of speech and its First Amendment protections; see, e.g., Catherine MacKinnon, *Feminism Unmodified* 206–13 (1987).

181. 466 U.S. 789, 818–19 (1984) (Brennan, J., dissenting).

182. For the idea of a protected "public forum," see United States v. Grace, 461 U.S. 171, 177–78 (1983); explicit trust language is used in Hague v. CIO, 307 U.S. 496, 515–16 (1939).

183. Olmsted, *Civilizing American Cities: A Selection of Frederick Law Olmsted's Writings on City Landscapes* 65–66, 74–81, 96 (ed. S. Sutton 1971); see also Geoffrey Blodgett, "Frederick Law Olmsted: Landscape Architecture as Conservative Reform," 62 *J. Am. Hist.* 869, 878 (1976); Galen Cranz, "The Changing Role of Urban Parks," *Landscape,* Summer 1978, at 9, 11. For these ideas in the courts, see, e.g., Higginson v. Treasury, 99 N.E. 523, 527 (1912), asserting that parks are a public good because they are "civilizing" amidst urban congestion (Mass. 1912).

184. See Cranz, supra note 183, at 12–15. For a modern-day echo of the sports/contemplation conflict, see J. William Futrell, "Parks to the People: New Directions for the National Park System," 25 *Emory L. J.* 255, 269–72, 277–78 (1976).

185. Blodgett, supra note 183, at 877, and Cranz, supra note 183, at 9, see the park movement as a social-control effort aimed at blunting lower-class discontent.

186. This does not mean that everyone must be allowed to use the same facilities concurrently—on the contrary, recreational resources clearly need some management and rationing. But *some* recreation should be available to all, and without substantial cost.

187. See Roderick Nash, *Wilderness and the American Mind,* at 17–20 (1973).

188. See Appleby, supra note 173, at 104–105.

6

Energy and Efficiency in the Realignment of Common Law Water Rights

Introduction: The Property Story and the Water Law Story

The previous essay was about public property and what it has meant in our law. This essay is about private property, but more particularly, it is about two stories. The first is a theoretical story about the evolution of private property rights generally. The second is an historical story about private property rights specifically in water, and particularly about the evolution of riparian law during the period of early Anglo-American industrialization. These two stories have been told separately a number of times, but they diverge substantially on several important matters. If they are told together, each needs to be modified in some interesting ways, and that is what I will attempt to do in this essay.

The Theoretical Story: The "Natural History" of Property Rights

The older and more persistent of these stories is the theoretical one, and readers of these essays have already seen a gross version of it several times. It amounts to a kind of natural history of private property rights generally, and it is the stuff of those standard narratives of property told and retold by classical and neoclassical economic property theorists over the past three centuries.[1] According to this story, when there is plenty of everything, there is no need for articulated property rights, because everyone can take what she wants without competing against anyone else. But as some resources become scarce, people get into disputes over them. They race to grab the most resources they can before others do, but in so

The original version of this essay appeared in 19 *Journal of Legal Studies*, 261–295 (1990).

doing, they may decimate the resources themselves. On the other hand, the story goes, human beings are at least sometimes clever enough to avoid this problem by devising some kind of property scheme to allocate rights among themselves.[2]

Property rights, the story goes, reassure the various owners that no one can just grab up things at will from others; thus assured, all owners can put time and effort into developing their respective resources and making them still more valuable. Just as important, by specifying who has control over resources, property rights allow the whole group of owners to trade resources instead of fighting over them.[3] Thus this "natural history" presents property rights as an emergent response to scarcity, inducing individuals to invest and trade resources instead of dissipating their time and effort—and the resources themselves—in unproductive disputes and wasteful attempts to be the first to grab the most.

A number of commentators have suggested a refinement of the story: that one or more intermediate steps may come between the unpropertied commons that is characteristic of plentiful resources and the fully specified individual property rights that are more prevalent when resources are scarce.[4] For example, a group or tribe may jointly take over the resource—such as a hunting area or a set of common fields—and reserve access to its own members, perhaps allocating in-group access according to a set of informal customary arrangements. At such an intermediate stage the group excludes outsiders but treats the resource as common property among the particular group of users. This intermediate solution allows the group to preserve a given resource, even though the diffuse rights of group members may retard individual investment and exchange. Nevertheless, a system of group/customary property may be fairly cheap to manage and police and may prove especially useful where things are not so scarce as to induce people to move all the way to the more effective, but more expensive, resource management regime of individualized property rights.[5]

Taken together, all this adds up to a "natural history" of property rights when resources are growing scarcer: a stage 1 of plenty, where some given resource is unowned, unmanaged, and open to all; a stage 2 where the resource is less plentiful and is appropriated by a group and subjected to somewhat diffuse common property arrangements, often customary; and a final stage 3 in which the resource is scarce enough to be subject to full-blown individualized property rights.[6]

The moves between the stages of this evolutionary story present some interesting problems. In a way, property rights really begin at the move to stage 2, when a group takes over a resource for itself; but how do people talk about that move? What kind of rhetoric incorporates the group's control over a resource that was previously open to all? As to the next move, from stage 2 to stage 3, do people really always make this move? Is stage 2 really an intermediate stage, a stepping stone to fully individualized stage 3 rights, or might it sometimes represent the final or ideal system of resource management?

This essay will try to answer those questions. What should help is an actual history of the development of property rights in a particular resource. But the historical treatments of property rights in one resource—water—only raise more questions, because the historical story has some dramatic differences from the theoretical story.

A Conflicting Story: Water Rights and How They Grew

The law of water use bears a larger significance than might be immediately apparent. Not only did waterpower play a significant role in the industrialization of the Atlantic world,[7] but in addition, the concurrently created riparian law exemplifies a distinct class of legal entitlements. Riparian law centers on the "reasonable" rights to water enjoyed correlatively by all the riverbank owners; this regime is a kind of model for the more general property law doctrine of nuisance and arguably also for the general tort law doctrine of negligence.[8] Indeed, the current historical treatment of riparian rights really took shape in the middle 1970s, when Morton Horwitz used a water rights story as a prototype for the evolution of modern American civil law.

Horwitz's argument, in brief, was that until the early nineteenth century, American water rights were governed by a very traditional doctrine: every owner along the stream was entitled to the undiminished and unaltered "natural flow" of the stream. With the proliferation of water-powered manufacturing plants and the attendant increased demand for water, however, the "natural flow" doctrine was gradually supplanted by a doctrine of "reasonable use," which in effect allowed each riparian owner to use up a roughly equal portion of the stream, at least insofar as the owner's use conformed to other owners' normal practice and to the perceived needs of the community. Horwitz's larger argument linked this development to the civil law of torts, and particularly to the supplanting of the traditional tort doctrine of strict liability by the more relaxed doctrine of negligence. On his argument, these parallel legal developments—water law and tort—gave a kind of common law subsidy to capitalist developers, allowing them to inflict some injury upon weaker and less enterprising folk without having to pay for the consequences.[9]

Horwitz's larger subsidy thesis has attracted a considerable body of commentary and criticism.[10] But his specific story about riparian rights is quite striking for another reason: it seems to contradict the more general evolutionary property rights story, in which property rights become more clearly demarcated as demand for resources intensifies. Indeed, Horwitz describes a kind of reverse evolution—a move from a sharply defined set of property rights ("natural flow") when water resources were relatively plentiful, followed by a much mushier set of rights ("reasonable use") precisely when demand for water surged during the early stages of industrialization. If Horwitz's historical account is correct, the scarcity wrought by industrial uses seems to have made property rights *less* clear and distinct rather than more so.

Reinforcing this perception is Robert Bone's somewhat later and very extensive discussion of later-nineteenth-century nuisance law, in which water law played an important role.[11] Bone's analysis stresses the internal doctrinal developments within the states whose riparian and nuisance law he examines—developments that, he thinks, sprang from the play of inconsistent legal theories.[12] But his analysis also confirms a progression from absolute rights at the outset to equally shared but vaguely defined group property rights thereafter.[13] Thus in Bone's work too one can glimpse behind the doctrinal complications a move that would not be predicted at all from the theoretical story of property: the courts seemed to define the sharpest "absolute" water rights when water was relatively plentiful, only to shift to vague "reasonable" correlative rights when water resources became scarcer.

Notwithstanding this marked divergence from the theoretical natural history of property rights, these historical water rights stories do track the theoretical story in some spots. Most notably, the riparian rights of reasonable use do look like the theoretical stage 2—that is, limited group rights, based more or less on equal access according to customary practice. Moreover, a later doctrinal shift neatly tracks the theoretical transition from stage 2 to stage 3, that is, the transition from riparian rights in the humid East to an appropriative system in the arid West. Thus as settlers moved West, according to a number of authors, scarcity and the need for careful husbanding of water resources drove water law beyond riparianism's vague correlative rights and into the more expensive but also more effective appropriation regime, which accords individualized and tradeable property rights in water.[14] Similarly, Mark Ramseyer's interesting analysis of water law in imperial Japan suggests that there too, as competition for water increased in the late nineteenth and early twentieth century, a set of customary use doctrines shifted toward a system akin to the prior appropriation system of the American West.[15]

Given the widely held view that western water rights historically evolved by tracking the theoretical story, moving from vague stage 2 rights to more precisely defined and individualized stage 3 rights, the earlier history of water rights seems almost an embarrassing anomaly. In that earlier period, increasing scarcity seemed to drive property rights in exactly the opposite direction, away from sharp definition and toward mushy "reasonableness."

In this essay I hope at least in part to close the gap between the theoretical and historical accounts of the evolution of private property rights. On closer analysis, it will appear that the early common law's regime of "natural flow" (or "ancient use") was well suited to its era because it offered a workable system for allocating entitlements, at a time in which a stable and relatively low demand for water resources was only sporadically threatened by extreme individual behaviors. In contrast, the reasonable use doctrine was better suited for the industrial era that followed; it permitted more intensive private utilization of flowing water, in part because the system of correlative reasonable rights obviated the need for agreements among all the owners along the stream.

But the reasonable use doctrine is not necessarily a primitive way-station or mere transitional stage, as the orthodox theory of property rights suggests. On the contrary, a water rights doctrine quite similar to the later western appropriative system was extensively discussed in the earliest period of industrialization. The courts in Britain and the eastern states knew of this doctrinal approach, but they nevertheless ultimately found riparianism more suited to their environment and rejected the opportunity to jump immediately to stage 3.

In order to explain why the stage 2 system of correlative rights worked well in its historical setting, it is important to pay close attention to the actual uses that might be made of water. When we do so, we can see that the decisive reason that eastern water law evolved as it did was that water there was used primarily for *power*. When water is used for power rather than consumption, it has striking characteristics of a common pool or public good, in which the value to riparians is increased by allowing only a slight modicum of water loss from each riparian's use, while the bulk of the river flow is retained for all. When we take all this into account, we can locate the reasonable use doctrine as a way to manage a partial public good, similar to many other environmental resources.

The larger moral is that there is no universal presumption that systems of private individual rights must necessarily dominate systems of collective ownership, as the standard property story seems to suggest. Much depends on the underlying nature of the resource and the uses to which it can be put under existing and evolving technology.

To develop these arguments, the essay considers riparian owners' private conflicts as they appear in three jurisdictions up to about 1850: England, Massachusetts, and New York. I leave to one side the conflicts that erupted over recognized public uses of water, such as navigation; I have said a great deal about those in the previous essay and wish to concentrate here only on the private sphere, where the theoretical property story should not be blurred by public trust questions.[16] As to the jurisdictions chosen, English law is appropriate for two reasons: first, it served as the backdrop for the American states' law, and, second, England itself was the earliest of the industrializing nations, and its law should have been among the first to show the effects of increasing demand for waterpower. Similarly Massachusetts, as an early and dominating industrializing state, also should illustrate the legal response to an increasing scarcity of waterpower resources. I include New York for a different reason: citations from Britain and Massachusetts suggested to me that New York played a central role in creating the reasonable use doctrine adopted generally in the East—and indeed it did, as we shall see.

I. Rivalry Denied: English Water Law in (What Should Be) Stage 1

The Ancient Use Doctrine, and Its Expected and Unexpected Elements

If the theoretical story of property rights is correct, England in the period before industrialization ought to have had a relatively relaxed legal regime for managing conflicts over flowing surface waters. The country had plentiful rainwater, so that irrigation was not a major issue in the competition for water. As far back as the Middle Ages, England had had numerous water mills—gristmills for grain, fulling mills for wool, other mills for mining, pumping, silversmithing, glassmaking, and so on—but these placed far lower demands on the available streams than did the many mills built after the great eighteenth-century expansion of textile-producing technology. Prior to that expansion, the more easily developed upstream millsites had long been occupied, but the larger and more difficult streams were still available to mill developers, particularly as these entrepreneurs acquired more sophisticated mill- and dam-building technology.[17] Thus the pre-eighteenth-century water environment was much closer to "plenty" than the later situation, and one's intuition might be that the law of flowing waters would come considerably closer to saying, "Anything goes."

This intuition, however, is sharply contradicted by at least one aspect of the old cases—that is, the *substance* of 17th- and 18th-century doctrine on watercourses. There are rather few reported cases, largely centering on conflicts about mills;[18] but far from the relaxed "anything goes" style that one might expect where there were numerous watercourses and potential millsites, these early cases reflected a sharp determination to maintain a well-established status quo.

In this preindustrial era, riparian owners could successfully contest any disturbance in the way a stream "was accustomed to flow and ought to flow" ("*qui currere consuevisset et debuisset*").[19] This meant that established uses could resist complaint. Note, however, that the doctrine did not shield "first occupancy" as such but only "*ancient*" occupancy; new disturbances could be halted so long as they had not yet existed for "time out of memory," which conventionally meant a prescriptive period of twenty years.[20] Moreover, the concern for "ancient" or accustomed uses clearly outweighed any worry about the "natural" course of a stream. Although a riparian owner could challenge the diversion of an "ancient stream" from its accustomed course, he could also claim that his own diversion was itself unassailably ancient if challenged by someone else. And in conflicts between two diversions, he could defend his own as the more ancient of the two.[21] The pattern, then, was quite emphatically that whatever had been in place for a generation or so was entitled to stay as it was, free from novel disruptions.

This hardly seems to be an "anything goes" attitude about plentiful resources. But another aspect of this body of water law does confirm the intuitive expectation of a relaxed legal regime: all this doctrine seemed quite marginal to the actual uses of streams. Over the seventeenth and eighteenth centuries, the reported watercourse cases came in fits and starts, and they appeared to be only sketchily understood by the parties.[22] Their marginality is underscored by Blackstone's attitude in the 1760s. As we shall see shortly, he simply ignored them all in his *Commentaries* and proceeded on the idea—quite antithetical to the existing case law—that water rights were governed by the more general principle of first occupancy, applicable to, say, wild animals as well.[23]

Practical businessmen must have ignored the older doctrines as well or must have at least found them inconsequential. According to the economic historian T. S. Ashton, "much of the capital investment of the eighteenth century went into mill ponds, conduits, and water-wheels,"[24] but any of these could have been actionable disturbances under the prevailing doctrines that protected "ancient" uses. Extensive investment in these improvements in itself suggested that legal doctrines placed few practical impediments in the path of private conduct.

Why Were the Rules So Rigid?

This history leaves a puzzle: why did British legal doctrine adopt such a rigid substantive law for waterpower resources when those resources were at least relatively freely available and when the legal restraints had little practical significance? The historiography of the past few decades suggests one possibility that we have seen in earlier essays, traceable to the character of the political *mentalité* of the preindustrial Atlantic world. Recitations of "ancient" water rights, like recitations of the "ancient constitution," must have seemed attractive in an intellectual climate in which the rightness of things seemed linked to their long usage.[25]

A quite different possibility is suggested by Steven Shavell's analysis of strict liability in tort and by his distinction between levels of *care* and levels of *activity*.[26] Under a regime of negligence, an actor is liable only for harms due to careless behavior. Under a regime of strict liability, however, an actor is liable for all harms that he causes, whether he acts carefully or not, and thus this regime may induce the actor to regulate the frequency of his acts in addition to his level of care. A strict liability rule is particularly attractive where there is little possibility that victims might have assumed a risk or might have taken countermeasures of their own to avoid harm—for example, in the case of new technology, whose harms may catch victims by surprise.[27]

This appears to have been the situation for established watercourse users during a time when water use was fairly stable; precisely because things did not normally change much, they had no reason to know about or take precautions against new and conflicting mill development. By analogy to strict liability, then, one might see "ancient use" doctrines as a device not just to protect old and established watercourse uses against new ones but rather to induce new waterpower industries to regulate their level of activity, requiring them to buy out or to pay for damage to conflicting older uses. That is to say, early in the eighteenth-century industrial revolution, while the new manufacturing mills' ultimate social value was generally unknown, their owners had to pay the full cost of avoiding damage to other, established riparian uses.

Moreover, when viewed from this perspective, what seem to be rigid doctrines may not have been so static and antidevelopmental as Horwitz and other authors have suggested.[28] The old cases all involved quarrels between neighbors over adjacent diversions or water backups. Under normal circumstances, economists would identify these as situations of low transaction costs. If bargaining was simple, the doctrines favoring "ancient uses" meant only that a new mill developer had to buy out or reach agreement with a known neighbor who would otherwise have preferred to enjoy the "ancient" situation. In that light, the older doctrines hardly seem to be such an impediment to development. From the perspective of Ronald Coase's famous theorem, the older doctrines simply look like a way of specifying rights between neighbors, so that negotiations could take place and so that the resources could flow through the bargaining process to the one who most valued them.[29]

To be sure, even in one-on-one dealings between neighbors, there are opportunities for extortion and recalcitrance, so that efficient voluntary transfers of rights may fail.[30] This was certainly the case with millsites; some spots were obviously better than others to capture the fall of the water, and these localized scarcities clearly did lend themselves to occasional standoffs. In fact, the old cases seem to center on figurative shootouts between adjoining owners. They are full of instances where neighbors haul down each other's millworks by main force, and in one case, a certain Lord Byron apparently tried to use his upstream advantage to extort cold cash from a downstream cotton mill.[31] These all-too-human instances of trading breakdown, of course, were undoubtedly magnified in a culture in which landownership carried considerable symbolic freight and in which commercial dealings for land must have seemed considerably less acceptable than they do today.

To the modern eye, however, any such negotiating impediments suggest that older legal institutions may have allocated property interests to the parties deemed most likely to place the highest value on the resource.[32] Indeed, there are at least two reasons to suppose that preindustrial legal institutions might have regarded established uses as generally more valuable than new ones, so that older uses should prevail over new ones in cases of irreconcilable conflict.

First, a presumption favoring older uses made some sense where the resource use was relatively stable or at most was changing only gradually; under those circumstances, it was more likely that someone had figured out the best uses of a stream a long time ago and had put that use in place. Prior to the sharply increased demands of industrialization, this logic might have been at work in fixing the right on "ancient" uses of streams.

A second reason has to do with the relatively plentiful supply of water and waterpower. Where alternative water resources were available, it must have seemed reasonable to send a signal to the new user that he had to bargain to get his preferred location; if he could not make a deal there, he could go somewhere else and bargain with other existing users or perhaps establish his new mill where it would not disturb any of them.[33] If water was generally available elsewhere, any dispute over its use must have seemed to be the fault of newcomers, and the law treated as such.

On reflection, it is a familiar cultural phenomenon to give preference to older uses in a period of relative stability. Consider, for example, the reaction of established neighborhoods when developers begin to build high rises and to use up the previously plentiful light and air. The reaction is very far from "anything goes"; rather it is a rejection of the new use and a recitation of the antiquity (and therefore presumed rightfulness) of the existing situation.[34] The current users claim that the "plenty" they enjoy is *their* plenty; the new use is illegitimate precisely because it may create scarcity *for them.*

A rigid "no-change" rhetoric, then, is an entirely recognizable response to a threat to plenty. This response already moves a first step away from stage 1 and toward stage 2. It is an assertion that while the particular "plenty" may be a commons, it is a commons limited to one group, namely, the group that already enjoys it. Indeed one economist, Steven Cheung, has identified a similar move—the exclusion of outsiders while leaving insiders' uses intact—as a first step in imposing a property regime on a given resource.[35] In the English water rights story, newcomers were the "outsiders" who were excluded, while established users were the privileged "insiders" who could continue to enjoy the streams as they had anciently run. No-change doctrine was a kind of denial that scarcity was a problem, a rhetoric to tell newcomers that there would be no unpleasant rivalries if the newcomers would just go away.

An evolutionary view of property rights would suggest that this no-change approach occurs only in a zone between a perceived plenty and an increased demand that threatens to make a given resource scarce. Accordingly, no-change doctrines may crumple when the resource comes under more serious pressure. But the seventeenth- and eighteenth-century watercourse law tells us that the no-change approach may also be fairly stable, at least under certain conditions.

Those conditions are, first, that rivalries are relatively infrequent; second, that they involve one-on-one conflicts, so that in the normal case it is fairly easy to negotiate reallocations from the baseline of no-change property allocation; third, that it is relatively easy to go elsewhere if negotiation fails; and, finally, that the actual use of the resource is fairly stable over time, so that one can reasonably presume that an established use is the most valuable one. All those conditions combined to maintain a certain stability in the doctrinally rigid water law of preindustrial Britain. It was stable in large measure because the legal arrangements did not matter very much and were marginal to most ordinary behavior.

But these conditions collapsed in the later eighteenth and early nineteenth centuries. With the vastly intensified competition for waterpower sources and with the application of waterpower to novel and thriving industrial uses, it became more difficult to defend the presumption that established uses were more valuable than new ones. A changed attitude is visible with Blackstone, who ignored the law favoring established "ancient" uses and instead argued that the law endorsed "occupancy," which meant that the right would go to the first one to *alter* a resource from its natural state. His position implicitly shifted the balance to favor the rapidly developing new mills, which clearly altered the millsites along the water—as against "ancient uses," which were often simply passive enjoyments of the water's flow with no special marks of occupancy.

Early-nineteenth-century British water law came to reflect at least some of Blackstone's view, favoring "occupancy" doctrine over "ancientness." The pattern was echoed as well in the law of Massachusetts, at least until the middle of the nineteenth century; it is doubtless more than coincidental that Massachusetts law, considerably more overtly than Blackstone's *Commentaries*, aimed at mill development of water sites.

II. Rivalry Recognized: The Detour Through the Rule of Capture

The Blackstonian Paradigm of "Occupancy"

Blackstone's *Commentaries* devoted only scattered attention to water rights, but they give the reader an immediate sense that something important had changed, even as early as the 1760s. In stating that rights to flowing water should follow "occupancy," the *Commentaries* diverged dramatically from traditional views.[36] The notion that the right should go to the first occupant presumes that there is no prior occupant—that is, that the resource is up for grabs and that there are no existing rights in the resource at all. The contrast from traditional water law could hardly have been sharper: the older law saw the "right" in whatever condition was anciently in place; there was no category of "no rights" with respect to water and hence no rightful room for any new occupancy except by grant, real or presumed. By contrast, "occupancy" treated the resource as basically empty of property rights and welcomed those who would stake a claim.

Occupancy doctrine was fundamentally a rule of capture, which gives to the individual first possessor those things that are taken out of a "wild," unowned state. As such, "occupancy," far more than "ancient use," is a rhetoric keyed to a rapid transition from a stage 1 condition of unrivalrous and unpropertied plenty directly into a stage 3 regime, where rivalrous claims are organized around individual ownership. Moreover, Blackstone's views on water rights were quite influential for a time, in Britain as elsewhere.[37] Given this substantial influence, it seems odd that British and eastern American jurisdictions should first take up Blackstone's occupancy rule only to abandon it later in favor of a less precisely defined doctrine of reasonable use. And it seems particularly odd that they should turn to this uncertain reasonable use when, if they had continued to follow Blackstone, they would have embraced a regime very like the appropriation system that later evolved in the western United States. Why was Blackstone put aside? Why wasn't the stage 2 rule of reasonable use simply leapfrogged in favor of an immediate regime of individualized property rights? The British cases raise all these questions.

Blackstonian Occupancy in British Water Law

The 1805 case of *Bealey v. Shaw* was a straightforward example of the influence of Blackstone's occupancy principle in early-nineteenth-century British water law. *Bealey* involved competing mills on the heavily developed

Irwell River.[38] The upstream party had diverted water for a mill in the early and mid-eighteenth century but had added a new sluice after a downstream neighbor had established his own waterworks in 1785. The new upstream sluice had not existed long enough to count as "ancient"; thus older law would have unambiguously disapproved it, as this case did. But Judge LeBlanc, in an opinion that was frequently cited in the next decades, thought that occupancy rather than ancient use should govern the issue. The new-sluice builder could have diverted even more water, LeBlanc said, but not after the downstream owner had claimed the waterpower for himself by constructing his own works on the waterway. On LeBlanc's reasoning, a rule of capture, as proved by "occupancy" and prior capital expenditure, was the way to establish one's right to the fall of the river.

In one development the British courts even outdid Blackstone; this was a rather subtle shift in their handling of "prescriptive" water rights. In the older water law, prescriptive use meant only a use that ran beyond the memory of man, as the conventional phrase had it—that is, a fairly old use and one that everyone was accustomed to having in place. For legal purposes such a use was presumed to rest on a "lost grant." But in the newer cases, the judges began to look more pointedly for rivalry in this fictional "lost grant." Just who had had a right that could be granted in the first place? And what counted as the acquiescing behavior that would give rise to the presumption of a lost grant? The older cases had asked only for lengthy practice to establish prescription, but after 1800, one finds much more conscious insistence that no adverse right could ripen without a period of "*actual injury*" to someone's interests.[39]

With this move the courts seemed to abandon the view of prescription as the mere passage of time and instead required something akin to the underlying rivalry of "adverse possession": prescription would give you nothing against one who had never had reason to complain of your usage. The closer judicial inquiries about prescription mirrored the new occupancy doctrine, since in both instances the courts implicitly contended that water rights arose only where uses were rivalrous. The occupancy doctrine dealt with *potential* rivalry and protected one who faced rivals only after he had made initial expenditures. The new prescriptive doctrines concerned *actual* rival claims; here, even though a new user was generally expected to seek the consent of those with prior claims,[40] prescriptive doctrine would protect the later claimant whose rivals had slept on their rights for a protracted period.

Although these Blackstonian ideas of "occupancy" and rivalrous use made notable inroads on British water law, they certainly did not sweep the field. The early-nineteenth-century British cases rather give the impression of vacillation and disagreement about the basis of watercourse rights. In the 1810s and 1820s, some judges continued to decide water conflicts on the basis of ancient use principles, while others adopted Judge LeBlanc's (and Blackstone's) occupancy.[41] By the 1833 case of *Mason v. Hill*,[42] the judges seemed to be completely at a loss to identify the governing rule. This case's facts suggested a nasty vendetta between nearby mill owners; among other things, the downstream owner destroyed the upstream dam, whereupon the upstream owner diverted a stream to circumvent the downstream rival entirely. To resolve the matter the court used both ancient use and occupancy doctrines but gave "occupancy" an odd twist to favor only downstream occupants.[43] And in general, the *Mason* judges seemed unable to put forth a coherent idea of prior occupancy or of its relationship to the older idea of protecting the "ancient" character of the stream.

Indeed, the British cases suggested an increasingly unhappy impasse. From the 1820s to the 1840s, as the waterways became ever more congested with complex waterworks and diversions,[44] the British courts floundered for a doctrinal basis to settle the ever more frequent disputes over waterpower; they were unable to settle either on ancient usage or on prior occupancy or on some combined doctrine. It was not until the middle of the century that they located a stable doctrinal basis in the correlative rights doctrine of "reasonable use."[45] For this the British courts explicitly cited the American cases and treatises, notably those of Justice Story and Chancellor Kent. Before reaching those authorities, however, we need to turn back the clock to another American jurisdiction, Massachusetts, whose commitment to a watercourse law of prior occupancy for a time seemed even more firm than England's.

Massachusetts and the Idea of Occupancy

In the early nineteenth century, the Massachusetts courts quite determinedly pursued the idea that rights in flowing water should be acquired through a doctrine of occupancy. In developing this law, they seldom referred to Blackstone's authority, and they appear to have arrived at an occupancy rule on their own, without borrowing from treatises. But like the British courts, the Massachusetts courts eventually veered away from the individually defined rights of occupancy and instead adopted the looser, group-oriented correlative rights and reasonable use doctrine of the riparian system. This doctrinal evolution in Massachusetts, even more than in Britain, poses a challenge to the theoretical "natural history" of property rights and raises even more sharply the question why a regime of firmly individuated property rights should give way to a much more blurred one.

Massachusetts' early occupancy doctrine grew in part in response to another concern, that is, the legislative encouragement of millsite development. In Massachusetts, as in several other American colonies (and later states), the legislature had enacted a "mill act" in the early-eighteenth century, amending and reenacting it periodically in later decades.[46] This Mill Act permitted owners of millsites to build dams that overflowed the lands of upstream neighbors, subject to the duty to pay damages to the overflowed owners. Enactments of this type initially aimed at promoting traditional gristmills and sawmills, but by the first decades of the nineteenth century, some of these acts—especially the Massachusetts statute—came to be used more aggressively for private industry, most notably in the rapidly expanding new lumber and textile industries.[47]

Massachusetts' Mill Act in effect recognized that waterpower developers might come into conflict with other users of land and water, and it gave mill developers what amounted to a right of eminent domain over conflicting non-mill land uses. As Chief Judge Shaw put it, the Mill Act provided that "as the mill owner and the owner of lands to be flowed cannot both enjoy their full rights, without some interference, the latter shall yield to the former" so long as damages were paid.[48]

But the Mill Act may also have influenced the evolution of Massachusetts water law in a more subtle way. By routinizing the numerous mill-against-farmer problems that arose when milldams flooded the farms behind them, the Mill Act may have permitted the Massachusetts courts to construct the state's early-nineteenth-century water law around a different kind of controversy: conflicts in which mill owners were pitted not against farmers or foresters but against other mill owners. In this context, the statute had no clear application, but it was precisely here that the Massachusetts courts developed a very strong doctrine of occupancy or first possession as a basis for water rights claims. Moreover, they developed this doctrine during the 1820s and early 1830s, the very years in which industrial uses of Massachusetts' waters began to boom.

An important step toward an occupancy doctrine came in an early-nineteenth-century case, *Weston v. Alden* (1811),[49] which was not about mills at all but which had to be distinguished in later mill cases. Here an upstream owner was permitted to keep his irrigation sluices even though they diverted a certain amount of water from a downstream neighbor. The case was soon to be cited in a controversy involving a mill: in *Colburn v. Richards* (1816) an upstream irrigator claimed that *Weston* had established his right to divert water, even to the detriment of a downstream neighbor's dam and mill.[50] Chief Judge Parker disagreed and held for the downstream owner, but the reasons were ambiguous, since the victorious downstream owner, covering all doctrinal possibilities, had claimed both the prior occupancy and the "ancientness" of his dam.

More interesting were Judge Parker's comments distinguishing the earlier *Weston* case. In *Weston,* he said, the downstream owner had "merely enjoyed the natural benefit of the stream, without any labor or expense of his own"—whereas here, the mill owner had installed actual waterworks prior to the offending diversion. Older law would not have treated an established passive use any differently from an established mill; as "ancient uses," both would have been protected from change. But Parker implied that a riparian owner could lay claim to the stream when he had made capital improvements—and otherwise not.[51] With his remarks, the Massachusetts court began to move toward a doctrine favoring the first party who undertook active investment—who went to the "labor and expense" of improvements on the watercourse.

That, of course, was the idea behind a doctrine of first occupancy, and in 1821 the Massachusetts court decisively adopted it. *Hatch v. Dwight* presented a scenario that would become very familiar in Massachusetts, as it already was in the British cases: the downstream millworks that backed up waters and flooded an upstream owner's previously installed mill wheel. This time Judge Parker stated flatly that the owner of a millsite "who first occupies it by erecting a dam and mill" had a right to water sufficient to work the waterwheels, "notwithstanding he may, by occupation, render useless the privilege of the [owner] above or below him on the same stream."[52]

For the next few years, particularly in the years just after 1827—roughly corresponding to the expansion of the great millworks and canals at Lowell[53]—the principle of occupancy resolved the increasing volume of mill cases. In the typical case an upstream mill, even though it might have been fairly new itself, complained of backflow and swamping from a still newer milldam just downstream.[54] The Massachusetts courts were not unaware of other ways to manage these conflicts between upstream and downstream neighbors; one way was of course the venerable rule of ancient use. But an additional doctrinal candidate appeared after the late 1820s. Several Massachusetts mill developers, when accused of swamping adjacent upstream mills, cited the reasonable use doctrine that had been developed in New York and that had recently been used in the United States courts. This rule would have given the new downstream dam a "reasonable" water claim equal to the earlier upstream neighbor's. But the notion had little immediate impact on the Massachusetts courts.[55] Things were to change later, particularly under Chief Judge Shaw, who led the state's adoption of reasonable use. But even the sympathetic Shaw used prior occupancy as the basic mode of settling these backflow cases between nearby millworks.[56]

The Massachusetts courts, then, were well on the way to an occupancy regime similar to that which later would emerge in the American West. The first person to install actual waterworks for utilizing the power of the fall would be entitled to keep that power, against either a prior unimproving user—however "ancient" his use—or against a subsequent improver along the same watercourse. For the Massachusetts courts, this occupancy regime had at least two powerful attractions relative to the older regime of ancient usage. As this state's courts were well aware, an occupancy rule dovetailed well with the legislative judgment behind the Mill Act, which also favored mill improvements over alternative uses of the streams.[57] Perhaps more importantly, in an early period of rapid industrialization and change, the great value of capital-intensive uses must have seemed obvious over against less-intensive uses—if for no reason other than the common tendency, sometimes evident in our own era as well, to overvalue the contributions of new technologies while underestimating their dislocations.[58] Thus as between ancient use and occupancy doctrines, a major difference lay in the implicit assessment they made of the relative value of water uses. Ancient use assumed that the water use in place for many years was superior, whereas occupancy assumed that the first capital expenditure marked the more valuable use.

But what was *not* different was that the occupancy cases, like the older ancient use cases, took place in a micro-context of one-on-one conflicts between owners of relatively nearby sites, who had every reason to know of each other's existence and actions. Until the middle of the nineteenth century, the leading Massachusetts occupancy cases were backflow-and-flooding cases, and these almost certainly involved relatively few parties, easily knowable to one another—usually a downstream neighbor with a new dam and an upstream neighbor whose earlier waterwheel was flooded by the new dam. Whether these two-party site-use conflicts were to be governed by ancient use or by occupancy, it should have been relatively easy for most parties to organize a bargain, particularly before a new mill was constructed.[59] Indeed, the cases themselves show that in both Britain and America, fall-line riparian owners entered quite complex contractual arrangements for the distribution of given sites' waterpower.[60]

First occupancy and ancient use doctrines, then, were alike in two senses: both surfaced in cases where some rule had to resolve the occasional unresolvable conflict between nearby owners; and both doctrines established baseline points for future bargains. These doctrines differed dramatically on the allocation of that initial baseline entitlement, clearly reflecting very different attitudes about the most valuable use. But given the opportunity for trades (or even alternative site development), the Coase theorem suggests that this initial entitlement may have made little practical difference to the ultimate patterns of resource utilization.

Considerations of trading opportunities, however, also explain why the eastern states could not long adhere to the occupancy doctrine. The key element was transactions costs: as waterpower came to be developed more vigorously, the condition of low bargaining costs no longer held. In

Massachusetts, first possession doctrine was no doubt adequate for the typical case of mill wheel swamping, where the damage stemmed from backflow at an easily ascertainable dam downstream. But a new kind of case, involving large numbers of unknown potential claimants, began to appear by midcentury in Massachusetts and in England as well. The new cases concerned interruption of the flow and pollution from upstream sources. These upstream problems potentially affected not just a few known adjoining millsites but many unknown downstream riparian users, and hence they dramatically raised the costs of bargaining. When the courts confronted these new large-number cases, they turned away from first appropriation doctrine toward reasonable use.

New York led the way.

III. Rivalry Mediated: Large-Number Problems and the Emergence Of Reasonable Use Doctrine

The New York Experience

The circumstances of *Palmer v. Mulligan* (1805),[61] one of New York's most important early-nineteenth-century mill cases, perhaps fortuitously reversed the typical Massachusetts fact pattern. The *Palmer* complaint came not from the swamped upstream mill wheel owner so familiar in Massachusetts law but rather from a downstream owner, whose grievance arose from both pollution and interruption of the flow from above on the stream. The upstream owner had built a mill and extended a dam far out into the Hudson—far enough to divert logs out into the stream past the complaining sawmill operator downstream; moreover, debris from the new mill clogged the downstream millworks.

The *Palmer* plaintiff used all the available streamflow arguments; he argued ancient use (roughly, "My mill is forty years old") as well as a version of first occupancy ("He cannot build a dam that injures mine"). But the court's majority rejected both arguments and set the groundwork for a quite different doctrine, that of reasonable correlative rights. Judge Livingston gave the most elaborate statement: every owner had a right to do the same things as every other, he said, so long as the damage was relatively slight. As for what had come to be the "familiar maxim" of first possession, he said, it should not be read so as to give the first dam builder "an exclusive right" to the river flow for some indefinite distance beyond his own property lines.[62]

Thus the *Palmer* court clearly considered waterflow conflict as a larger matter than two disputing neighboring sites, and in this larger context depicted the river's flow as a commonly owned resource of all the riverfront owners. The court's correlative rights doctrine set out the main principles governing consumption of that resource: first, riparian owners enjoyed limited but more or less equal rights to use the stream; second, their various uses could cause some inconvenience to other owners; and, third, those inconveniences were not actionable if they were merely minor. Even the dissenters in *Palmer* agreed with this general picture, although they thought that the damage in the case was more serious and unreasonable than was acknowledged by the majority.[63]

The facts of *Palmer* lent themselves to this common-resource depiction. *Palmer's* upstream pollution and diversion, unlike the site-specific backflow-and-swamping cases, raised the possibility of some injury to large numbers of unascertainable riparian owners below on the stream. To grant the whole right to one party or another—that is, to hold either that the downstream owner be free of all diversion/pollution from upstream or that the upstream owner be entitled to pollute/divert at will against all downstream owners—could freeze the river's uses at one pole or the other, because there was no easy way to bargain for a reallocation of a right once granted or decreed. The doctrine of reasonable correlative rights avoided these larger pitfalls of ancient use or occupancy and instead allowed every riverbank owner some equal use of the riverflow, without the need to undertake arduous multiple bargains with all the others along the stream.

As the New York courts followed and developed *Palmer*, the riparian doctrine ripened into a full-fledged legal regime for water use. It is striking that these cases all concerned instances where downstream owners complained of upstream activities affecting the flow—that is, situations that called attention to the real or potential harms that might be suffered by multiple riverfront owners all the way down the stream.

In this pattern, we see a downstream sawmill's complaint about an upstream mill's flow interruption in *Platt v. Johnson* (1818), where the court rejected a Blackstonian occupancy defense as "dangerous and pernicious" to the interests of others who had equal rights to the river's flow.[64] Similarly, we see in *Merrit v. Brinkerhoff* (1820) another complaint about alternating interruptions and torrents from an upstream dam; the court upheld a jury finding of "unreasonable" use and noted that the lower owners were entitled to a "fair participation" in the water's flow.[65] And in *Reed v. Gifford* (1825), another stream interruption case, the court commented that the flow of a stream "becomes the property of each of the complainants successively, ... [and this gives them] a community of interest" in it.[66] Subsequent important waterflow cases in New York had the same fact pattern, and by the late 1820s, the courts could cite Chancellor Kent's *Commentaries* for a version of reasonable use doctrine[67]—a doctrine that Kent had indirectly borrowed from New York's own cases on upstream disturbances.[68]

As if to draw a contrast to the factual background for reasonable use doctrine, in 1828 the New York Chancery Court dealt with a backflow case. In this one-on-one dispute between owners who could easily locate and bargain with each other, the chancellor made no reference to "reasonable use"; instead, he reverted to an all-or-nothing position that made a nod to ancient use but was more akin to simple trespass. That is, if the downstream dam's backflow exceeded the natural level of the stream at the lot line, the owner would have to lower the dam or pay damages.[69]

Problems that began upstream, then, forcefully presented a picture in which users might potentially be hurt from the point of the problem's origin all the way to the sea. Because of their large numbers and diverse water needs, vulnerable downstream users might be difficult to identify and organize for bargaining. This context, then—potentially high transaction costs and multiple interests—gave the occasion for New York courts' development of what we now consider the riparian doctrine. It is a doctrine that substitutes for multiple transactions and instead gives more or less equal, correlative rights to reasonable use among a group of riparian owners, who are treated as the common owners of the stream's waterpower.

The factual background of these cases also helps to place the whole of riparian doctrine in a larger context. According to Thomas Merrill, the common law has frequently responded to high-transaction-cost situations with what Merrill calls discretionary or "judgmental" doctrines—as opposed to the all-or-nothing "mechanical" doctrines that Merrill finds dominant in low-transaction-cost situations.[70] This would suggest that in our theoretical natural history of property, stage 2 property rights—that is, correlative rights based on something like reasonable ordinary practice—might emerge where transaction costs are high and where the parties cannot easily bargain around an initial allocation of rights. And indeed, when we observe the historical story elsewhere and the adoption of New York's riparian doctrine in other jurisdictions, we once again see a background context of high transaction costs and multiple interests.

The Adoption of the New York Approach

Joseph Story's opinion in a federal case, *Tyler v. Wilkinson*,[71] marked one of the most important doctrinal turning points in the general adoption of New York's riparianism. The case involved a dispute among several mill owners on a river near Providence, a river fall area that had been among the first developed in the burgeoning New England textile industry; perhaps for that reason, Story opened the case with a brief comment on its great importance.[72]

In *Tyler*, to simplify a quite complex situation, certain long-established mill owners complained of an upstream diversion trench that circumvented their establishments. Because of the increased use of this diversion trench, the several mills along it were leaving less and less water for the plaintiffs' mills. The *Tyler* plaintiffs argued from ancient use principles that, except insofar as the upstream trench's use was an "ancient" one, the diverters could take only so much water as the plaintiffs themselves did not and would not use for any purposes whatever. In defense, the diverters too claimed ancient use, though they also seemed to imply a right by occupancy to all waters that had not been previously occupied.[73]

Thus both upstream and downstream mill owners effectively claimed a plenary right to control the entire current of the river—the upstream owners by their occupancy of the current and the downstream owners by ancient usage of that same current, whether or not they had been using it previously. Unlike the numerous backflow cases involving only issues of priority between adjacent millworks, these claims to control the current could affect rights of many other owners up and down the stream, because each claim tacitly assumed legal priority to any inconsistent use of the river's flow, whether upstream or down. Thus to adopt either of these positions, in the large-number context of controlling the entire river current, might well freeze the use of the river for all users, since no reallocation could be negotiated easily among all these affected riparians.

Story's response (though mixed with some ambiguities favoring ancient use) was to state that the streamflow was owned "in a perfect equality of right" by all riparian owners; there was no right to diminish the water itself save "that, which is common to all, a reasonable use."[74] For these propositions, he cited three British cases, one case apiece from Connecticut and New Jersey—and three recent New York cases.

Tyler propelled the doctrine of reasonable use into the American standard for water law, particularly after Chancellor Kent picked it up in his *Commentaries.* Britain in turn followed the United States' lead by midcentury in *Embry v. Owen*[75] and did so in a context that we should now be able to predict: an upstream diversion that potentially affected large numbers of downstream owners. The court cited Kent and Story extensively in rejecting the argument that any slight diminution of the natural flow was actionable. Some consumptive use of the flow had to be allowed, the court said, or all valuable use would be denied to riparians; hence only unreasonable (or unequal) uses would be actionable. With this case, Britain joined the Americans in adopting a riparian doctrine of equal correlative rights—a doctrine that stabilized British water law after decades of waverings.

But what of Massachusetts, that firm adherent to prior appropriation? Soon after *Tyler* was handed down, some parties cited it along with New York's reasonable use cases, but they made no immediate headway. From the perspective of transactions costs, this was quite predictable, since their cases involved one-on-one backflow issues, which even New York treated in an all-or-nothing fashion. Until the middle of the century, these low-transaction-cost backflow cases dominated the water cases before the Massachusetts higher courts, and, predictably, Massachusetts continued to apply what was essentially an all-or-nothing law of first occupancy. Even then, however, the Massachusetts judges showed that they might be interested in reasonable use in the appropriate circumstances; Shaw's opinion for the court in *Cory v. Daniels* (1844) pronounced a long dictum to the effect that owners generally may use a stream in a manner "reasonable [and] conformable to the usages and wants of the community, ... and not inconsistent with a like reasonable use" by other owners; but that where one owner's use of the fall excluded other dams there, as in the backflow case at hand, the first one to raise a dam would prevail.[76]

At midcentury the state's high court finally confronted some complaints about upstream diversions and flow interruptions. In this context of potential large numbers and high transaction costs, Massachusetts turned with remarkable alacrity to the reasonable use approach. In *Elliot v. Fitchburg Railroad,* a case involving upstream diversion, Justice Shaw announced that riparian owners have a common and equal right to a just and reasonable use of flowing water; upstream owners cannot entirely divert a stream to the detriment of downstream owners, but neither can downstream owners complain of some reasonable diversion upstream.[77]

Punctuating the shift to riparian law in this high-transaction-cost context, the Massachusetts court slightly later upheld, per curiam, a trial court's instructions based on correlative water rights and reasonable use according to the ordinary practice of the community.[78] And in several more cases over the next few years—all in cases implicating potential large-numbers problems from upstream flow interruption or pollution—the Massachusetts court consistently relied on reasonable use doctrine and downplayed the prior occupancy rule suggested by the Mill Act and by the court's own earlier cases about one-on-one backflow issues.[79]

IV. Stage 2 Reassessed: Correlative Rights and Public Goods

Transaction Costs and Their Explanatory Limits

Massachusetts completes our historical tale of the move from stage 1 (plenitude) to stage 2 (correlative rights). It should be clear that this move was not a matter of doctrinal confusion or even entirely of an attempt to assist industrialization. It is undoubtedly true that the evolving riparian law of the eastern states had an eye cocked on industrialization, since the courts at least implicitly deemed power generation the most valuable private use of streams, and they adapted water law to that use.[80] But if we suspend judgment and take this view as a given—that is, that power was the most valuable use of flowing water—then these doctrinal shifts look like entirely logical responses to the increasing scarcity of waterpower and to the increasing number of claimants for its use.

The temporary adoption of "occupancy" doctrine falls into place as an early response to the increasing rivalry for water power. Like the older ancient use doctrines, occupancy could allocate rights easily enough where transaction costs were low; but unlike ancient use, occupancy doctrine reflected a new attitude, namely, that a use coupled with capital improvement was likely to be superior to a use that was merely "ancient."

But neither ancient use nor prior occupancy could cope with the high-transaction-cost scenarios so forcefully presented by the diversion, flow interruption, and pollution problems originating upstream in the eastern rivers. Large numbers of mill owners were potentially involved in these issues, with uses that were not easily ascertained in advance, particularly as the numbers and complexity of industrial river uses increased. They clearly could not easily contract around all-or-nothing rules, whether ancient usage or prior appropriation. The courts in industrializing states quite sensibly looked for different doctrines that would make the total river usage most valuable even under these circumstances of bargaining difficulty.

One sees the logic of this judicial response only when one breaks down the riparian cases by subject matter. If one lumps downstream-origin backflow cases together with the upstream-origin current alterations, one misses a crucial aspect of the courts' quite subtle response to the increasing demand for waterpower. Indeed, what is striking is the rapidity with which the courts adopted a system of correlative rights when faced with the high-transaction-cost scenarios. The British courts floundered briefly in responding to the transition from low- to high-transaction-cost doctrines, but Massachusetts did not. Quite the contrary, when faced with high-transaction-cost scenarios, the Massachusetts courts adopted riparian doctrine with what seemed almost effortless ease.

But if we look at transaction costs alone, the eastern water rights story suggests a next step, namely, the step taken in the West. Just at the time that riparianism took hold in the eastern states and in Britain, the miners and settlers of the West were busily developing an informal water rights regime of occupancy or "prior appropriation" not just for particular sites but for the waters of entire streams.

This new water regime now seems far more modern than riparianism, and if seen in a somewhat euphoric light, it appears almost to approximate an ideal type of stage 3's individualized property rights.[81] To the western settlers, it hardly seemed to matter that their acts of appropriation implied rejection of the East's governing riparianism; the courts seemed equally indifferent, powerfully assisting the settlers' informal practices and making explicit their deviation from riparianism.[82] Thereafter, western legislatures formalized appropriation even further, through state administrative structures that coordinated the allocation and trading of individualized appropriative water rights.

Why did this further move toward property/contract never really ripple back to influence the eastern water regimes?[83] Transaction costs alone cannot be the whole story; western rivers also had many persons claiming their waters. Why did not the East, like the West, retrieve the occupancy doctrine and extend it from the adjoining-site context all the way to a completely individualized property rights scheme for water, dividing up the entire stream volume? The western states did this, even in the face of large numbers of claimants and high transactions costs among them; despite these costs, the most arid states simply jettisoned reasonable use and correlative rights doctrine and instead organized systems for individualized, tradeable rights, through which individuals could decide for themselves how much water to acquire. Was the East merely "stuck" at stage 2 for reasons of cultural lag, while the newer western states could adopt a modern private property regime in water, before the full baggage of riparianism weighted them down? Or did the answer lie again in the theoretical natural history of property rights?

That theoretical story would suggest that water was only a little bit scarce in the East—scarce enough to install occupancy rules for specific locational conflicts but not scarce enough to move past stage 2's correlative rights in dealing with the waters of a whole stream. But in the West, the story goes, water was *really* scarce;[84] hence the westerners undertook the effort to privatize the streams more or less completely, so that claimants could bid against each other not just for the rights to develop specific locations but for the rights to the water itself. Indeed, the western experience suggests that when a resource is very scarce indeed, stage 2's regime of equal, group-based correlative rights may be bypassed altogether.

I am going to suggest that the East's retention of stage 2 may not be so antediluvian after all and that stage 2's common property in some ways offers an alternative to the individualized rights of stage 3. Moreover, common property may be a fairly stable alternative and not just a way-station or transition phase in an ever more individualized definition of entitlements. Again, the crucial point is to pay attention to distinctions of subject matter.

Western Consumption, Eastern Public Goods

Western water rights evolved from uses of water that were essentially consumptive. Some of these were power uses, such as the forced-water hosing of offstream mining slopes, while other uses included such partial consumption as irrigation. The point about western water uses was that they *consumed* the water in question because they took the water away from the stream and did not return it, or at least not much of it.[85] Thus from the start, westerners used water in ways that vastly expanded the potential claimants and did so in the manner of a zero-sum game: the miner who transports water from the stream in the foothills does so at the expense of the farmer who wants to irrigate his land in the valley, and vice versa.

But eastern riparian rights did not grow up around these consumptive uses of water, even though consumptive uses were sometimes at issue. Eastern riparian rights grew up around the use of water for *power*—that is, instream power—which is not necessarily a zero-sum game. The difference is this: if you and I both want water to irrigate our respective farms, the water I take is unavailable to you (except for a possible leftover return flow); that is, our uses are a zero-sum game. But if I have a mill on the river, and you do too, we can both use the water as it flows by—provided that we do so carefully and do not, for example, alternately interrupt and pour out the water in such a way as to disrupt the millworks downstream. Thus waterpower is in a sense a *renewable* resource—in a way that consumed water cannot be—and the maximum development of water for power requires not consumption but rather use and relinquishment among the group of riparian owners, so that the volume of the water may be used again and again on its way downstream.

To take a different analogy, the use of water for power may be likened to the use of a dictionary in a town library: reference usage does not consume the pages and one person's use does not preclude later reference users—even though we could think of uses for the dictionary (such as scratch paper) that do indeed consume the pages, and in which one person's use would be incompatible with use by another. But if we want to make maximum use of the dictionary as a reference work for all the townspeople, we ask that patrons use the book unintrusively and leave it for others—not that they use it and tear out the pages that they want.

These considerations suggest something more than a simple transaction-costs account of riparian law. Transaction costs are undoubtedly at stake among the large numbers of owners along a river; it is hard for them to get together and bargain over things they want to do. But this was true of western rivers with consumptive uses as well as for eastern rivers with power uses; in the West, however, the states developed appropriative schemes to overcome those transaction costs, whereas in the East, generally speaking, they did not.

Why did they not? Again, the library's dictionary is a helpful analogy. Take page 498 of the dictionary: no one is really concerned about transaction costs among the readers who want page 498 for themselves, and no one even thinks of allocating page 498 to the person who really values it most; what concerns us is to have the book stay intact as a whole, so that *all* the readers can use *all* its pages. We want this because we think the value of the book is at its highest when available for use as a unified entity. Similarly, if a river is used for instream power, as eastern rivers were, the transaction-costs account misses something important about it, particularly if that account narrows water law problems to those of organizing exclusive rights for individual consumption. If a river is used for power, it is most effectively used only if its bulk is *not* consumed exclusively, by *any* individual owner along the banks, but rather flows in its entire volume downward over the fall of its whole course.

To be sure, there were some consumptive, zero-sum aspects to the use of water even for power; for example, millponds and sluices lost somewhat more water to seepage and evaporation than would the stream itself. These consumptive aspects of waterpower usage could be compared to wear and tear on our library dictionary. In riparian law such consumptive aspects were the subject of reasonable use, through which individual owners could indeed consume some modicum of water—so long as they did not disturb the bulk that went to other power uses downstream. But the point of riparian law was to place boundaries on these necessarily consumptive aspects of waterflow use, holding them within "reasonable" and commonly accepted bounds so that the bulk of the waterflow would be left intact.

What I am suggesting, of course, is that eastern riparian law evolved from an aspect of water use, namely, power, that has the aspects of a public good, quite unlike the individually consumptive uses of water that are characteristic of the West.[86] In a sense, the successor to riparian law is not individualized appropriative water rights on the western states' model at all, but rather such modern environmental statutes as the Clean Air Act, in which some modicum of "consumption" (such as a small amount of pollution) is permitted at the periphery, but the bulk of the resource remains un-"consumed," for the sake of the public's common health and enjoyment.[87]

Riparianism Reclaimed

The shift from riparian law to appropriative systems, then, was not just the next step in the theoretical natural history of property rights, the next ratcheting of scarcity that makes it worth the price to install a full-fledged individualized property system. The western states' adoption of an appropriation system followed a shift not only in scarcity but even more in *subject matter,* because the westerners valued different aspects of the water resource. The eastern states in the nineteenth century organized their water law around the water's use for instream power, a public good among riparian owners. The West, on the other hand, organized its water law around offstream consumption—an aggregate of private goods, where one person's use was incompatible with another's, where my irrigation leaves less for you. Indeed, insofar as the eastern states in recent years have tentatively moved to adopt the semiprivate entitlements of permitting systems, they seem to have done so particularly in times and locations (like Florida and Iowa) where zero-sum issues of irrigation and groundwater depletion have become more serious. In a sense, the subject matter of eastern water law is now changing too, from the public good of power to the aggregate private goods of consumption.[88]

But the historical tenacity of riparian water law suggests that stage 2 property management—group access to a resource that the group maintains as a common property—may be more than a mere way-station on the route to stage 3's individualized rights. Stage 2's common property instead may be an independent management style, and one that is particularly useful with respect to public goods. If some eastern states are now beginning to adopt systems related to zero-sum uses, the reverse is happening in the West, where in recent years we have seen a reversion to something like stage 2. This has accompanied a view that some important uses of the western rivers are instream uses and require the river volume to remain intact, just as nineteenth-century eastern power uses did. Fishing is such a use, since the fish require a certain volume of water; scenery is another—at least if the scenery is going to have water in it.[89] With the emergence of these instream goals for water, it should hardly surprise us that some western courts and legislatures have pulled back from the individualized property of stage 3 and are once again looking at water as something more akin to a stage 2 common resource.

V. Conclusion

When we tell the theoretical property rights story together with the historical water rights story, we see some reasons for modifying both. In looking at the historical water rights story, we have to note that water has many different uses; and when we pay close attention to the particular uses at stake, we may see legal developments as quite sensible responses to the problems presented by those specific uses. The theoretical story can help us to identify those responses. In order to observe some theoretical logic in the historical evolution of water regimes, we particularly need to segregate instream uses (such as power or recreation) from zero-sum or consumptive uses (such as irrigation or uses of certain situses). When we segregate those uses, we can identify either "no-change" (prescriptive) or "first-come-first-served" (occupancy) doctrines as rules that were likely to develop for zero-sum games, particularly in relations between competing neighbors; but on the other hand, we can see that reasonable use and correlative rights law accompanied water uses involving multiple indefinite users and public goods.

What about the other side of the coin? How does the historical story suggest modifications in the theoretical story of the evolution of property rights? The history of water rights suggests first of all that stage 1—that is, a resource regime in a state of relative plenty—may develop an oddly rigid rhetoric. Rather than a rule of "anything goes," stage 1 may acquire a rhetoric of "no change," especially in the face of a perceived threat to plenty. In essence, this rigid response seems to be a way of saying, "Newcomers keep out," and it may last only as long as there is a good deal of the resource around and as long as rival users can either cut deals easily or find more of the resource somewhere else. That is to say, the rigid legal rhetoric of stage 1 continues only so long as the resource is not under inordinate pressure and the law is more or less marginal to most people's actual dealings with the resource in question.

Second, we need to reassess stage 2, the regime of more or less informal group control over resources. Sometimes this common control may only represent individual property rights manqué—that is, the resource in question is generally used in a mutually exclusive way, and only transaction costs stand in the way of fully realized private rights. But in such cases, stage 2 is likely to have a short lifetime whenever a resource continues to grow scarcer and more valuable: at some point it will be worth the cost to move from the group's customary regime to the stage 3 of individualized property rights. This was the case, roughly speaking, in the evolution of appropriative water rights in the most arid parts of the West, where riparian systems were quickly bypassed.

But the historical water law story also suggests that stage 2's group control may have a much more lasting pattern and much greater stability if the resource in question has the characteristics of a public good. Eastern riparian law revolved around such a resource use, that is, waterpower, which had these public-good characteristics. For this reason, riparian law may be usefully studied not just as a temporary stop-off on the march to the individualized property rights but rather as an example of the ways we might manage those resources that are most useful when they are treated as nonconsumptive common property. For this reason too, no doubt, we are currently seeing an encroachment of common-property thinking even in those western states that have generally gone quite far to turn water rights into private commodities. This development almost certainly reflects a heightened concern with some public-good aspects of water, such as fishing and recreational uses.

Perhaps what the theoretical property story really needs is a reconceptualization of stages 2 and 3. Perhaps we should think of stage 2 as an informal group management that generates *two different* stage 3s, in a kind of a Y shape instead of a straight line. One branch would be the familiar stage 3-A, dealing with formalized property regimes for the zero-sum resources—that is, regimes for resources that can be managed in individual chunks, which can be traded about among individuals with exclusive rights to them. Branch 3-A is the standard individualized property regime.

But the other branch would be a stage 3-B, to encompass the formalizaton of management schemes for non-zero-sum, public-good resources. Here careful common management permits some individual consumption at an appropriately low level but aims primarily at conserving the bulk of the resource as a whole, for the common benefit of the entire collectivity of users. Our modern air and water pollution control legislation takes this 3-B form: here some consumption (i.e., pollution) is allowed, but the main object is to preserve an unconsumed (that is, unpolluted) bulk for the sake of the public's health and enjoyment.

Eastern riparian law was an early but extensive model of this kind of common resource regime, and it was managed by custom and common law decision-making for users all along the riverways. In this light, historical eastern water law once again takes the role of an exemplar of regimes of entitlements. But if we think the matter through, we see that riparian water law illustrates not just a subsidy to industrial development, as in some conventional historical stories, and not just a stepping-stone to fully individualized rights, as in the theoretical story. It rather exemplifies a way of managing those resources that are most valuable when they are retained, in unitary form, by the whole community that uses them.

Notes

1. See the essay "Property as Storytelling" earlier in this volume and authorities cited therein.

2. Sometimes, of course, they aren't so clever. The well-known description of what happens then is Garrett Hardin, "The Tragedy of the Commons," 162 *Science* 1243 (1968). For motives and problems in creating property rights, see Gary Libecap, *Contracting for Property Rights* 11–28 (1989).

3. See Richard A. Posner, *Economic Analysis of Law* 30 (3d ed. 1986); for specifying ownership, see Clifford Holderness, "A Legal Foundation for Exchange," 14 *J. Legal Stud.* 321 (1985).

4. See, e.g., S. V. Ciriacy-Wantrup and Richard C. Bishop, "'Common Property' as a Concept in Natural Resources Policy," 15 *Nat. Res. J.* 713, 714–15, 717–19 (1975); Steven N. S. Cheung, "The Structure of a Contract and the Theory of a Non-Exclusive Resource," 1 *J. L. & Econ.* 49, 64 (1970); Robert Nelson, "Private Rights to

Government Actions: How Modern Property Rights Evolve," 1986 *U. Ill. L. Rev.* 361, 374 (1986).

5. See, for example, Cheung, supra note 4, at 64; see also Bruce Yandle, "Resource Economics: A Property Rights Perspective," 5 *J. Energy L. & Pol'y* 1, 16–17 (1983); Carol M. Rose, "Rethinking Environmental Controls: Management Strategies for Common Resources," 1991 *Duke L. J.* 1.

6. Obviously these stages are more a spectrum than single steps. Cheung, supra note 4, identifies several intermediate steps, and though I am collapsing them for now, I will return to a modified version of one of Cheung's in-between stages.

7. See Delores Greenberg, "Reassessing the Power Patterns of the Industrial Revolution: An Anglo-American Comparison," 87 *Amer. Hist. Rev.* 1237, 1248–54 (1982); Terry S. Reynolds, *Stronger Than a Hundred Men: A History of the Vertical Water Wheel,* 95–96 (1983). For New England, see generally Theodore Steinberg, *Nature Incorporated: Industrialization and the Waters of New England* (1991).

8. See Morton J. Horwitz, *The Transformation of American Law* 102 (1977).

9. Horwitz, supra note 8, at 32–42, 101, 102.

10. See, e.g., Richard A. Epstein, "The Social Consequences of Common Law Rules," 95 *Harv. L. Rev.* 1717, 1729–36 (1982); Gary T. Schwartz, "Tort Law and the Economy in Nineteenth-Century America: A Reinterpretation," 90 *Yale L. J.* 1717 (1981); Stephen F. Williams, "Transforming American Law: Doubtful Economics Makes Doubtful History," 25 *UCLA L. Rev.* 1187 (1977).

11. Robert G. Bone, "Normative Theory and Legal Doctrine in American Nuisance Law: 1850 to 1920," 59 *So. Cal. L. Rev.* 1101, 1202 (1986).

12. Id. at 1224.

13. For example, Bone describes the New Hampshire courts as rejecting absolute water rights in favor of "reasonable use." Id. at 1203–1206.

14. See, e.g., Terry Anderson and P. J. Hill, "The Evolution of Property Rights: A Study of the American West," 18 *J. L. & Econ.* 176–78 (1975); see also Williams, supra note 10, at 1203–1204.

15. J. Mark Ramseyer, "Water Law in Imperial Japan: Public Goods, Private Claims, and Legal Convergence," 18 *J. Legal Stud.* 51, 68 (1989).

16. Public claims were somewhat limited since navigation, the most important public use of the era, did not normally conflict with water mills; millsites usually occupied fall lines that were a natural impediment to vessels; see Lewis C. Hunter, *Waterpower in the Age of the Steam Engine* 142 (1979; vol. 1 of *A History of Industrial Power in the United States,* 1780–1930). There were exceptions, however, particularly where milldams disrupted American waters "navigable" for log floating or anadromous fish runs; see Steinberg, supra note 7, at 120–21, 166–76. I am also not considering groundwater controversies, which had rather different features in this era.

17. Reynolds, supra note 7, at 55, 69–70, 96–97, 113–14, 136–51, 267–71.

18. T. E. Lauer, "The Common Law Background of the Riparian Doctrine," 28 *Mo. L. Rev.* 60, 83 (1963).

19. Anon. case, 79 Eng. Rep. 1031 (1638).

20. Although there were other conventional meanings of "time out of memory" (or "mind"), by the late eighteenth century, British usage had generally settled at twenty years. See, for example, Robinson v. Lord Byron, 18 Eng. Rep. 1315 (1785); Bealey v. Shaw, 102 Eng. Rep. 1266 (1805). "Ancient" in this context may not have

meant age-old but rather something more akin to "former" or "earlier," as in the French usage of *ancien régime,* or indeed the "ancient constitution."

21. For uses of "ancient" language to claim rights to diversions, see Russell v. Handford, 74 Eng. Rep. 248 (1583); Luttrel's Case, 4 Coke 85a, 86b (K.B. 1600); Richards v. Hill, 87 Eng. Rep. 611 (1695); Cox v. Matthews, 86 Eng. Rep. 159, 160 (1673) (Hale, in dictum); Brown v. Best, 2 Wils. K.B. 174 (1747) (dictum). Some cases did refer to a river's natural course, e.g., Shury v. Piggot, 81 Eng. Rep. 280, 281 (K.B. 1625), but a pure "natural flow" doctrine would have been awkward for British law, since among other things watercourse users were required to scour out the rivers rather than leaving them to nature. See Lauer, supra note 18, at 90–91. "Natural flow" language did appear more extensively in early-nineteenth-century cases, including American ones. See, for example, Tyler v. Wilkinson, 24 F. Cas. 472, 474 (C.C.D. R.I. 1827); Hammond v. Fuller, 1 Paige R. 197 (N.Y. Ch. 1828).

22. See Lauer, supra note 18, at 80 (few cases). As to parties' mistakes, defendants regularly overstated what plaintiffs had to allege in diversion cases, as was observed by Chancellor Kent in Palmer v. Mulligan, 3 Caines R. 307, 320 (1805) (Kent, dissenting); for similar errors earlier, see Countess of Rutland v. Bowler, 81 Eng. Rep. 1087 (1622); Anon. case, 79 Eng. Rep. 1031 (1638); Sands v. Trefuses, 79 Eng. Rep. 1094 (1639); Keblethwait v. Palmess, 90 Eng. Rep. 311 (1686).

23. See 2 William Blackstone, *Commentaries on the Laws of England* 14, 17, 403 (1979; reproduction of 1766 ed.).

24. Ashton, *An Economic History of England: The Eighteenth Century* 94, 109 (1966).

25. See J.G.A. Pocock, *The Ancient Constitution and the Feudal Law. A Study of English Historical Thought in the Seventeenth Century* 17, 19 (1957); and see two earlier essays in this book, "Property as Propriety" as well as "Ancient Constitution."

26. Steven Shavell, *An Economic Analysis of Accident Law* (1987).

27. Cf. id., at 21–32, 57–58.

28. See Horwitz, supra note 8, at 32, 36; Lauer, supra note 18, at 84.

29. Ronald Coase, "The Problem of Social Cost," 3 *J. L. & Econ.* 1 (1960).

30. See Robert D. Cooter, "The Cost of Coase," 11 *J. Legal Stud.* 1 (1982), commenting on the problem of strategic bargaining.

31. For Lord Byron (evidently not *the* Lord Byron, given the date of the case), Robinson v. Lord Byron, 28 Eng. Rep. 1315 (1785). For cases where downstream owners pull down upstream dams, see, e.g., Luttrel's Case, 4 Coke 85a, 4 Coke 86b (K.B. 1600); Sands v. Trefuses, 79 Eng. Rep. 1094 (1639); Cooper v. Barber, 128 Eng. Rep. 40 (C.P. 1810); Mason v. Hill, 110 Eng. Rep. 692 (1833).

32. See, for example, Posner, supra note 3, at 14 (where voluntary exchange is not possible, efficient allocation may place right with one who *would* have bought it).

33. See Reynolds, supra note 7, at 55, 135–36, on the gradual mill expansion into larger and more difficult streams prior to eighteenth century; nineteenth-century Americans particularly developed larger rivers, as in Massachusetts; see generally Steinberg, supra note 7.

34. See, e.g., T. Egan, "New Fight in Old West: Farmers vs. Condo City," *N.Y. Times,* Oct. 3, 1989, at A10. For a certain parallel, see the Wintu Indians' property assertions in traditional fishing grounds when under threat from white settlers;

Arthur McEvoy, *The Fisherman's Problem: Ecology and Law in the California Fisheries, 1850–1980* 48 (1986).

35. Cheung, supra note 4, at 64.

36. See 2 Blackstone, supra note 23, at 14, 17, 403; Lauer, supra note 18 at 96–99.

37. Lauer, supra note 18, at 99, states that by 1825, "it was as though Blackstone had been literally adopted as declaratory of English water law." This overstates the case, since, as will appear later, British case law of the era was quite mixed; but Blackstonian views were certainly cited both there and in the United States. Lauer also notes elsewhere that prior appropriation was short-lived in British water law; see his "Reflections on Riparianism," 35 *Mo. L. Rev.* 1, 8 (1970).

38. 102 Eng. Rep. 1266 (1805). For the Irwell, see Reynolds, supra note 7, at 276.

39. Wright v. Howard, 57 Eng. Rep. 76, 82 (1823); see similar questioning of terms of prescription in William v. Nelson, 40 Mass. 141 (1839).

40. The judges made this point in *Bealey,* 102 Eng. Rep. at 1269 (Ellenborough), 1270 (Grose).

41. See, e.g., Cooper v. Barber, 128 Eng. Rep. 40 (C.P. 1810), where Lawrence decided on basis of absence of "ancient use" while Mansfield argued prior occupancy; Saunders v. Newman, 106 Eng. Rep. 95 (K.B. 1818), where all but one judge cited ancient use and one judge cited prior appropriation.

42. 110 Eng. Rep. 692.

43. 110 Eng. Rep. at 698. Both before and after this case, some American courts criticized the idea that occupancy should only favor downstream owners, since this would enable the extreme downstream user, at the mouth of the river, to control all upstream uses. See, for example, Platt v. Johnson, 15 Johns 213, 217–18 (N.Y. 1818); Elliot v. Fitchburg RR., 64 Mass. (10 Cush.) 191, 195 (1852).

44. See Reynolds, supra note 7, at 273–76.

45. Wood v. Waud, 154 Eng. Rep. 1047 (1849); Embry v. Owen, 155 Eng. Rep. 579 (1851); see also the section below describing the adoption of New York's approach.

46. For a description of the several states' mill acts as of 1833, see Joseph Angell, *A Treatise on the Common Law of Watercourses* 118 (2d ed. 1833); Angell dated the original Massachusetts statute at 1713. The Supreme Court later described the Mill Act in Head v. Amoskeag, 113 U.S. 9, 16–20 (1885). For more recent historians' descriptions, see Denis J. Brion, "The Common Law of Waterpower in New England," 5 *Vt. L. Rev.* 201, 224–25 (1980); Hunter, supra note 16, at 33–34; Harry N. Scheiber, "Property Law, Expropriation, and Resource Allocation," 23 *J. Econ. Hist.* 232, 239–40 (1973); Steinberg, supra note 7, at 30–32.

47. For early mills, see Hunter, supra note 16, at 2–4, 8–28. For Massachusetts' leadership in new manufacturing mills, see 1 J.D.B. DeBow, *The Industrial Resources, Statistics &c of the United States* 208–219 (1854); Reynolds, supra note 7, at 276–77; see generally Steinberg, supra note 7.

48. Fiske v. Framingham Mfg. Co., 29 Mass. 67 (1832); see also Boston & Roxbury Mill Dam Corp. v. Newman, 29 Mass 467, 477, 480 (1832). New York courts, however, were very critical of Massachusetts' permissiveness, especially toward manufacturers' mills (see, e.g., Hay v. The Cohoes Co., 3 Barb. [N.Y.] 42, 47 [1848]), as was the treatise writer Joseph Angell, supra note 46, at 132. Manufacturing use of a mill act was ultimately challenged, unsuccessfully, in Head v.

Amoskeag, 113 U.S. 9 (1885), as a grant of eminent domain powers without a public purpose. Mill acts for traditional gristmill purposes were less problematic, since they were open to the public, arguably for public purposes along the lines of a public utility.

49. 8 Mass. 136 (1811).

50. 13 Mass. 420 (1816).

51. 13 Mass. at 422. Parker again distinguished *Weston* in a similar case, Cook v. Hull, 20 Mass. 269, 271 (1825), stating that the *Weston* downstream owner never "created any works of art upon the stream, or ... appropriated the water ... by any artificial means." Readers may note a similarity to the relatively intrusive acts required for common law "possession"; see the essay "Possession as the Origin of Property" in this volume.

52. 17 Mass. 289, 296–97 (1821).

53. See Patrick M. Malone, *Canals and Industry: Engineering in Lowell, 1821–1880,* at 5–9 (1983) (first major mill canal completed 1825, others in original complex constructed 1825–1836); Steinberg, supra note 7, at 59–69.

54. See, for example, Sumner v. Tileston, 24 Mass. 198 (1828); Thompson v. Crocket, 26 Mass. 59 (1829); Bigelow v. Newell, 27 Mass. 348 (1830) (all backflow/swamping cases).

55. See below, section on New York approach. For unsuccessful attempts to put forward the New York "reasonable use" doctrine, see the defendants' arguments in *Sumner* 24 Mass. at 200; *Thompson* 26 Mass. at 59–60. One exception, in which the Massachusetts court required an equitable adjustment between two dams on the Charles, was Bemis v. Upham, 30 Mass. 169 (1832); the case may have been influenced by the fact that the two dams were completed within just three months of each other, and thus neither presented a compelling claim of priority.

56. See Shaw's opinion in Cary v. Daniels, 49 Mass. 468, 476–77 (1844).

57. See Shaw's comments on the effect of the Mill Act on Massachusetts common law in Gould v. Boston Duck Co., 79 Mass. (13 Gray) 442, 450–51 (1859).

58. See, for example, the high praise for manufactures and millworks in Boston & Roxbury Mill Dam Corp. v. Newman, 29 Mass. 467, 477, 483 (1832); Hazen v. Essex Co., 66 Mass. 475, 478 (1853); for a more general tendency to overvalue technological developments and discount their problems, see James Krier and Clayton Gillette, "The Un-Easy Case for Technological Optimism," 85 *Mich. L. Rev.* 405 (1985).

59. Large industrial milldams, such as the works along the Merrimack, could create substantial ponds, affecting streamflows and waterfront properties for long distances; see, e.g., Steinberg, supra note 7, at 89; but a swamped mill even several miles upstream should have had no difficulty in locating the source of the problem. Farmers' claims were effectively sidetracked by the Mill Acts of course, and even in states without a mill act, such as New Hampshire, mill developers knew where the backed-up water was going and could buy up land or flooding easements from riparian landowners. Id. at 133. The more numerous agricultural claims meant more possible holdouts and other bargaining problems, of course.

60. For Britain, see, e.g., the contractual arrangements in Wright v. Howard, 57 Eng. Rep. 76 (1823); Mason v. Hill, 110 Eng. Rep. 692 (1833); for similar contracts in American cases, see, for example, Hurd v. Curtis, 48 Mass. 94 (1843); Pratt. v.

Lamson, 84 Mass. 12 (1861). For the effective metering and sale of waterpower by the Lowell mill developers, see Steinberg, supra note 7, at 85–88.

61. 3 Caines R. 307.

62. Id. at 313–14. See also Spencer's opinion, at 313.

63. See Thompson's opinion, id., at 317–18; see also Kent's opinion, id. at 320.

64. 15 Johns 213, at 215–16, 218 (N.Y., 1818) (citing Livingston in *Palmer*).

65. 17 Johns 306, at 320–21 (1820).

66. 1 Hopkins R. 416, 418–19 (1825).

67. See, e.g., Arnold v. Foot, 12 Wend. at 331 (1834) (upstream diversion held as "unreasonable," citing 3 James Kent, *Commentaries on American Law* 439 et seq. (2d ed. 1832; in the first [1828] edition, at 353 et seq.); compare Horwitz, supra note 8, at 39 and 276, fn. 27.

68. 3 Kent, *Commentaries* 353–59 (1st ed. 1828). Kent also cited the brand-new federal case Tyler v. Wilkinson, but *Tyler* had also cited New York cases prominently. For *Tyler*, see below.

69. Hammond v. Fuller, 1 Paige R. 197 (Ch. 1828). A similar federal case is Whipple v. Cumberland Mfg. Co., 29 Fed. Cas. 934 (C.C.D. Me. 1843). Compare Horwitz, supra note 8, at 275–76, n. 25, citing *Hammond* as a repudiation of Story's adherence to correlative water rights doctrine; my own view is that the all-or-nothing approach here is explained by facts of the case—a simple backflow case whose parties knew of each other's actions, rather than an issue with potentially large numbers of claimants whose damage could not be known in advance.

70. Thomas Merrill, "Trespass, Nuisance and the Costs of Determining Property Rights," 14 *J. Legal Stud.* 13 (1985).

71. 24 Fed. Cas. 472 (C.C.D. R.I. 1827).

72. Id. at 473. For the early mill development around Providence, see David J. Jeremy, *Transatlantic Industrial Revolution: The Diffusion of Textile Technologies Between Britain and America, 1790–1830s,* at 82–91 (1981).

73. 24 Fed. Cas. at 473, 475. Story appeared to attribute an occupancy argument to the upstream defendants, though he also noted that they claimed that their practice conformed to "ancient" usage. Id. at 476.

74. Id. at 474. Story rejected the occupancy claim, saying that diverted water—apparently meaning diversions above and beyond those allowed by a common reasonable use—could be claimed only through a twenty-year period (as in ancient use). Horwitz, supra note 8, at 39, emphasizes Story's ambiguity but correctly notes that the case was particularly cited for reasonable use.

75. 155 Eng. Rep. 579 (1851).

76. 49 Mass. (8 Met.) 468, 476–77 (1844).

77. 64 Mass. (10 Cush.) 191, 193–95 (1852). Shaw cited *Embry* from Great Britain, *Tyler,* Kent's *Commentaries,* and a New York case.

78. Barrett v. Parsons, 64 Mass. (10 Cush.) 367, 372 (1852).

79. See Thurber v. Martin, 68 Mass (2 Gray) 394 (1854); Haskins v. Haskins, 75 Mass. (9 Gray) 390 (1857); Gould v. Boston Duck Co., 79 Mass. (13 Gray) 442, 450–51 (1859).

80. American courts consistently ruled, however, that in instances of conflict, public uses of waterways—notably navigation—"trumped" private uses; see the earlier essay "Comedy of the Commons."

81. See Anderson and Hill, supra note 14, at 176–78. For some persistent impediments to a complete property/contract system in western water rights, see George A. Gould, "Water Rights Transfers and Third-Party Effects," 23 *Land & Water L. Rev.* 1 (1988).

82. Perhaps most famous is Coffin v. The Left Hand Ditch Co., 6 Colo. 443 (1882); for California's more mixed system, see Charles W. McCurdy, "Stephen J. Field and Public Land Law Development in California, 1850–1866: A Case Study of Judicial Resource Allocation in Nineteenth-Century America," 10 *Law & Soc'y Rev.* 235, 253–63 (1976).

83. In recent years some riparian states have instituted permit systems; for a critical assessment, see Robert Abrams, "Water Allocation by Comprehensive Permit Systems in the East: Considering a Move away from Orthodoxy," 9 *Va. Envt'l L. J.* 255 (1990). But these systems continue a number of riparian elements; see Peter N. Davis, "Eastern Water Diversion Permit Statutes: Precedents for Missouri?" 47 *Mo. L. Rev.* 429, 445–56 (1982).

84. See, e.g., Williams, supra note 10, at 1203–04.

85. See, e.g., the description of mining appropriation in Jennison v. Kirk, 98 U.S. 453, 457–58 (1878).

86. The public-good aspects of waterpower appear perhaps most clearly from the perspective of the owner at the mouth of the stream. This owner might pay an upstream owner to let the river flow downstream but cannot exclude other intermediate owners from enjoyment of the flow.

87. For the public-good aspects of health (particularly positive externalities), see Carol Rose, "Environmental Faust Succumbs to Temptations of Economic Mephistopheles" (Review), 87 *Mich. L. Rev.* 1631, 1638–39 (1989).

88. For modern eastern permitting systems, see Davis, supra note 83, at 445–56; for their problems, see Abrams, supra note 83. Compare also Ramseyer, supra note 15, at 76, who states that the differences between eastern and western water law argue against any "convergence" of legal principles on efficient solutions; one may see more convergence if one notes that eastern and western water law developed around quite different aspects of water use.

89. For these and other public goods in western streams, see, for example, Robert G. Dunbar, *Forging New Rights in Western Waters* 216–17 (1983); David H. Getches, "Water Planning: Untapped Opportunity for the Western States," 9 *J. Energy L. & Pol'y* 1, 3 (1988); Lori Potter, "The Public's Role in the Acquisition and Enforcement of Instream Flows," 23 *Land & Water L. Rev.* 419 (1988); A. Dan Tarlock, "Discovering the Virtues of Riparianism," 9 *Va. Envt'l L. J.* 248, 251–52 (1990). Concern for instream and public uses is particularly notable in California; see Eric T. Freyfogle, "The Evolution of Property Rights: California Water Law as a Case Study," in *Property Law and Legal Education. Essays in Honor of John Cribbet* 73, 95–97 (P. Hay and M. H. Hoeflich eds. 1988).

PART FOUR

Bargaining and Entitlement

This part takes up some of the interactions between bargaining processes and property—particularly the ways that individual bargains, when they are added together, can influence the rules and patterns of ownership. In "Crystals and Mud" I begin with the evolutionary theme explored in Part 3 and even more radically challenge the idea that a given resource's scarcity tends to drive its property regime toward ever more sharply defined individual entitlements. Instead, I describe a cyclical pattern that often emerges over time in the legal treatment of bargains: property definitions do indeed move from fuzzy social accounts toward more sharply bounded individual entitlements—but then they move back again, in an oscillation that relates once again to questions of rhetoric and persuasion.

"Women and Property" may be the most offbeat essay of the book, though it too is about bargaining patterns. In this essay I take men and women as hypothetically illustrating different styles of "dealing" and then explore how those different bargaining strategies might interact to yield unequal distributions of entitlements—and unless we are careful, might subtly or not so subtly punish some of the very traits of "niceness" upon which bargaining depends.

7

Crystals and Mud in Property Law

Introduction

Property law, and especially the common law understanding of private property, has always been heavily laden with hard-edged doctrines that tell people exactly where they are. Default on paying your loan installments? Too bad, you lose the thing you bought and your past payments as well. Forget to record your deed? Sorry, the next buyer can purchase free of your claim, and you are out on the street. Sell that house with the leak in the basement? Lucky you, you can unload the place without having to tell the buyer about such things at all.

In a sense, hard-edged rules like these—rules that I call "crystals"—are what property is all about. If, as Jeremy Bentham said long ago, property is "nothing but a basis of expectation,"[1] then crystal rules are the very stuff of property. Their great advantage, or so it is commonly thought, is that they signal to all of us, in a clear and distinct language, just precisely what our obligations are and how we may take care of our interests. Thus I should record my deed and make my payments if I don't want to lose my home; and if I sell it to someone else who wants to be sure about its condition, he can inspect it or hire an engineer to do so or even buy insurance to cover potential problems. We all know where we stand, and we can all strike bargains if we want to stand somewhere else.

Indeed, as the earlier essays in this book have pointed out, economic thinkers for several centuries have been telling us that the more important a given kind of thing becomes for us, the more likely we are to work toward hard-edged rules to manage it.[2] We draw ever sharper lines around our entitlements so that we can identify the relevant players and so that

---

The original version of this essay appeared in 40 *Stanford Law Review* 577–610 (1988).

we can trade instead of getting into confusions and disputes—confusions and disputes that would otherwise only escalate as the goods in question became scarcer and more highly valued.[3]

At the root of these economic analyses lies the perception that it costs something to establish clear rules about things, and we won't bother to undertake the task unless it is worth it to us to do so.[4] What makes it worth it? Increasing scarcity of the resource and the conflicts attendant on scarcity. In the example given by Harold Demsetz, one of the best known of the modern economists telling this story, when the European demand for fur hats increased demand for (and scarcity of) fur-bearing animals among Indian hunters, the Indians developed a system of property entitlements to the animal habitat.[5] As I tried to point out in the essay on water law, economic historians of the American West tell a similar "natural history" about the development of property rights in water—as well as in land, timber, grasses and minerals, and natural resources of all kinds; on those accounts, easygoing, anything-goes patterns of use at the outset came under pressure as competition for resources increased, and they were finally superseded by much more sharply defined systems of entitlement.[6] In effect, as competition for a resource raises the costs of conflict over it, the conflict itself comes to seem costlier than the effort of setting up a property regime. We then try to establish a system of clear entitlements in the resource so that we can barter and trade for what we want instead of fighting.

The trouble with this analysis (which I will here call the "scarcity story") is that things don't seem to work this way, or at least not all the time. The previous two essays described some notable divergences for properties that have been historically recognized as "inherently public," like avenues of commerce, or that may be most efficiently managed in the form of common or shared property, like the old mill-driving watercourses. Those configurations, diverging markedly from hard-edged individual rights, tend to occur where a resource is not easily divisible into individual property and where joint management is more profitable for all the participants.

What is still more striking, however, is a pattern that we sometimes see with the most divisible and seemingly private and unshared types of individual property. Even with respect to these divisible and exclusive properties, we sometimes seem to start out with perfectly clear, open-and-shut demarcations of entitlements—and then shift to fuzzy, ambiguous rules of decision. I call this the substitution of "mud" rules for "crystal" ones. Thus, to go back to the examples with which I began this essay, the straightforward common law crystalline rules have been muddied repeatedly by exceptions and equitable second-guessing, to the point that the various claimants under real estate contracts, mortgages, or recorded deeds don't quite know what their rights and obligations really are.

And the same pattern has occurred in other areas too. For example, sunlight: Wisconsin, like other states, used to have what seemed to be a workable crystalline rule about sunlight rights; that is, your neighbor has no right to the sunlight that crosses your yard unless the neighbor acquires an easement from you. But Wisconsin's courts have transformed this clear rule into a mud doctrine; these days, if you block the light to your neighbor's lot, the neighbor may have a nuisance action against you—at least according to Wisconsin's *Prah v. Maretti.*[7]

Now, nuisance is one of those shapeless areas of "reasonableness" in the law of property, and it is often compared to the riparian rights discussed in the previous essay on water law. In *Prah,* the nuisance question hinged on a typically vague formulation: "all the underlying facts and circumstances." Does it matter that you built before your neighbor did? Could you or your neighbor have adjusted your respective buildings to avoid the problem? How valuable was the sunlight to you and how valuable to your neighbor?[8] You don't know how to answer these questions in advance or how to weigh the answers against one another. That is to say, you don't know in advance whether a building will be found a nuisance or not, and you won't really find out until you go through the pain and trouble of getting a court to decide the issue, after you have built the structure or have at least had your plans drawn up. Before doing all that, you might try to purchase a release from your neighbor, but since you don't know whether your use will be adjudged to be a nuisance, you don't know how much you should let the neighbor charge you. Indeed, since the sunlight might cross your front yard on its way to several other neighbors' lots as well, it is not altogether clear how many clearances you need before you can build your ten-story dream house.

As Wisconsin's sunlight saga suggests, quite aside from any wealth transfer issues that may accompany a change in the rules, the change may sharply alter the *clarity* of the relationships among interested parties. Indeed, moves toward the uncertainty of mud seem disruptive to the very practices of private ordering through private property and contractual exchange. It is hardly surprising, then, that we individually and collectively attempt to clear up the mud with new crystal rules—as when private parties bargain to opt out of ambiguous warranties or when legislatures pass new versions of crystalline recording systems—only to be overruled later, when courts once again reinstate mud in a different form.

These odd permutations on the scarcity story must give us pause. Why, in ordering our bargaining for scarce resources, should our legal patterns shift back and forth between crystal and mud, instead of relying on crystal? Is there some advantage in the mud rules that the courts are paying attention to? And if so, why do we not opt for mud rules instead?

This essay is about the blurring of clear and distinct rules of property and contract with the muddy doctrines of "maybe or maybe not," and about the reverse tendency to try to clear up the blur with new crystalline rules. It poses the question, Why can't we seem to get it right? Why don't we choose one side or the other or find some satisfactory intermediate position?

I. A Closer Look at the Examples

From all appearances, and despite the obvious advantages of crystalline property rules for the smooth flow of bargains and and commerce, we seemed at least until recently to be caught in an era of intractable and perhaps even increasing muddiness.[9] One could chose any number of areas to see this, and I will briefly discuss only a few, namely, the examples with which I began. The first is the example of the law of caveat emptor in real estate transactions; in recent years caveat emptor has shown a strikingly generalized slide toward mud.

The Demise of Caveat Emptor

For several hundred years, and indeed right up to the past few decades, caveat emptor was the staple fare of the law of real estate purchases, at least for already constructed buildings.[10] The purchaser was thought to be perfectly capable of inspecting the property and deciding for himself whether he wanted it, and if anyone were foolish enough to buy a pig in a poke, he deserved what he got. Short of outright fraud that would mislead the buyer, the seller had no duties to disclose anything at all.

One chink in this otherwise smooth wall, however, was the doctrine of "latent defects"; like the exception for fraud, this suggested that perhaps the buyer can't really figure things out entirely. For some time now in a number of states, a seller has had to tell a buyer about material problems known to the seller but undiscoverable by the purchaser even upon reasonable inspection.[11] Naturally, this soon raised a few muddinesses. What defects are "material"? What does the seller "know"? How much should the buyer "reasonably" have to inspect for herself?[12]

Within the past few decades, the movement to mud has become even more pronounced, particularly with respect to the sellers who were also the builders of the houses they sold: it has come to be thought that such builder/vendors implicitly warrant that a new house is "habitable."[13] But what does that mean? Is the house's habitability coterminous with the local housing code, or does "habitability" connote some less definite standard?[14] What if the defects were obvious to any prospective purchaser, and just what does "obvious" mean, anyway? We don't know until we litigate the issue.

Even if builder/vendor warranties do muddy up property rights, there are certainly some plausible reasons for them. After all, the builders are supposed to be professionals, and they certainly ought to be better informed about the houses they contruct than the purchasers are. Besides, one might well think that they could have avoided the problems in the first place by building more carefully.[15] It is somewhat more difficult to extend those arguments to sellers who are themselves merely homeowners rather than builders, yet we find that even these nonprofessional sellers too have increasing obligations to anticipate the buyers' desires and to inform buyers about any unpleasantnesses that might make the buyers think twice. A California court, for example, ruled that the sellers should have informed the buyer that a mass murder had taken place in the house a decade before.[16] The courts now seem to presume that a buyer can't figure much out for herself at all, and to protect that buyer they have adopted a mud standard. Like a good neighbor, a seller must tell buyers about any "material" defects—whatever those may be.

The increasingly mushy relationship between real estate buyers and sellers has parallels in the law of consumer sales generally, and indeed the cases about houses borrow much of their language from other cases about such items as cars, hairdryers, and water heaters.[17] All this might suggest that the scarcity story is exactly backward, and that the normal movement of property law is not toward ever harder-edged rules at all but toward the fluidity and imprecision of mud—in this case, uncertain duties of disclosure or warranty.

But there is a set of countermoves in the caveat emptor saga as well. Even if the legal rules have moved toward mud, private bargainers often try to reinstate their own little crystalline systems through contractual waivers of warranties or disclosure duties—for example in the "as is" sale or the "no warranty" clause. In effect these private deals move things into a circular pattern, from crystal to mud and then back to crystal. And the circle turns once again when the courts ban such waivers, as they sometimes do,[18] and firmly reestablish a rule of mud—only to be followed by even more artful waivers.

The back-and-forth pattern of crystal and mud is even more evident in the next example, the loan secured by landed property—a type of real estate transaction whose history has been described as something resembling a seesaw.[19]

Of Mortgages and Mud

Early common law mortgages were very crystalline indeed. They had the look of a pawnshop transaction and were at least sometimes structured as conveyances: I borrow money from you, and at the same time I convey my land to you as security for my loan.[20] If all goes well, I pay back my debt on the agreed "law day," and you reconvey my land back to me. But if all does not go well and I cannot pay on the appointed day, then no matter how heartrending my excuse, I lose my land to you, and presumably also any of the previous payments I might have made.[21] As the fifteenth-century commentator Thomas Littleton airily explained, the name "mortgage" derived from the rule that, if the debtor "doth not pay, then the land which he puts in pledge ... is gone from him for ever, and so dead."[22]

This system had the advantage of great clarity, but it sometimes seemed very harsh on mortgage debtors, sometimes to the advantage of scoundrelly creditors. Littleton's detailed warnings about specifying a precise place and time for repayment, for example, conjure up the image of a wily creditor hiding in the woods on the repayment day; without such specification a creditor needed only to be "in England," and if unfound he might keep the property.[23] But by the seventeenth century the intervention of courts of equity had changed things. In 1628 we find a creditor coming to an equity court to *ask* for the property when the debtor had not repaid;[24] and by the next century, the equity courts were regularly giving debtors "enlargements" of the time in which they might pay the debt and redeem the property before the final "foreclosure," even where the excuse was lame.[25] As one later-nineteenth-century judge explained, an equity court might well grant more time even after the "final" order of "foreclosure absolute"—it all depended on the particular circumstances.[26]

The muddiness of this emerging judicial remedy argued against its attractiveness. As early as 1672 Chief Justice Hale fumed that "[b]y the growth of Equity on Equity, the Heart of the Common Law is eaten out, and legal Settlements are destroyed; ... as far as the Line is given, Man will go; and if an hundred Years are given, Man will go so far, and we know not whither we shall go."[27] Instead of a precise and clear allocation of entitlements between the parties, the "equity of redemption" and its elusive foreclosure opened up vexing questions and uncertainties. How much time should the debtor have for repayment before the equitable arguments shifted to the creditor? What sort of excuses did the debtor need? Did it matter that the property, instead of dropping in the lap of the creditor automatically, was sold at a foreclosure sale? In the nineteenth century, a luxuriant efflorescence of foreclosure law developed around these and other issues.[28]

But as the courts mired down in muddiness, private parties attempted to bargain their way out of these costly uncertainties, and to reinstate a crystalline pattern whereby lenders could get the property immediately upon default, without the costs of foreclosure. How about a separate side deal with the borrower, for example, whereby he agrees to convey any equitable interest to the lender in case of default?[29] Nothing doing, said the courts, including the United States Supreme Court, which in 1878 stated flatly that a borrower could not bargain away his "equity of redemption."[30] Well, then, how about an arrangement whereby it looks as if the lender already owns the land, and the "borrower" only gets title if he lives up to his agreement to pay for it by a certain time? In the 1890s California courts thought it perfectly just to hold the buyer to his word under such an agreement and to give him neither an extension nor a refund of past payments.[31] But by the 1960s they were changing their minds about these "installment land contracts." After all, these deals really had exactly the same effect as the old-style mortgages: the defaulting buyer can lose everything if he misses a payment, even if it is the very last payment. And as usual, human vice and error put the crystal clear rule in jeopardy. In a series of cases culminating with a default by a "willful but repentant" elderly woman who had stopped paying when she mistakenly thought that she was being cheated, the California Supreme Court decided to treat these land contracts as mortgages in disguise. It gave borrowers like this "relief from forfeiture"—a time to reinstate the installment contract or get back her past payments.[32]

With mortgages and mortgage substitutes, then, we see a back-and-forth pattern: crisp definition of entitlements made fuzzy by accretions of judicial decisions, once again crisped up by the parties' contractual arrangements, and once again made fuzzy by the courts. Here we see private parties apparently following the scarcity story in their private law arrangements: when things matter, they define their respective entitlements with ever sharper precision. Yet the courts seem at some times unwilling to follow this story—most particularly when one party might be hurt badly by them—and simply do not permit these crystalline definitions. And so the cycle alternates between crystals and mud.

But the subject matter that has truly defied the scarcity story has not been mortgages and mortgage substitutes. It has been the recording system, to which I now turn.

Broken Records

In establishing recording systems, legislatures have stepped behind private parties' efforts to sharpen the definitions of their entitlements. The very raison d'être of such a system is to clarify and specify landed property rights exactly, for the sake of easy and smooth transfers.

But the Anglo-American recording system in fact has been a saga of frustrated efforts to make clear who has what in land transfers. Common law transfers of land required a certain set of formalities between the parties, but thereafter, conflicting claims were settled by the age-old principle "First in time, first in right."[33] Thus on Tuesday, I might sell my farm to you and on Wednesday might wrongfully purport to sell it once again to innocent Farmer Brown; poor Farmer Brown remained landless even though he knew nothing about the prior sale to you and indeed had no way of knowing about it.[34] This was scarcely a satisfactory situation from a property rights perspective. "First in time, first in right" may work well enough in a community where everyone knows all about everyone else's transactions, but outside that context, the doctrine does little to put people on notice of who owns what, and the opportunities for conflicting claims are endless.

But the efforts to find a remedy have gone through new cycles of certainty and uncertainty. Henry VIII attempted to establish public registration of land claims through the Statute of Enrollments in 1536, but the statute only applied to certain types of land transfer, and common lawyers, with their customary aplomb, figured out ways to restructure their deals and avoid registration.[35] Versions of the statute resurfaced in Massachusetts' 1640 recording act, as well as in other seventeenth- and eighteenth-century colonial recording acts, all of which were applied more widely (though still somewhat irregularly) than their Henrician model.[36]

Henry's statute and its original American counterparts reflected an emphatically crystalline view of the world of property. Their literal language suggested that these were versions of what has come to be called a "race" statute: the first purchaser to record his claim (the winner of the "race" to the registry) can hold his title against all other claimants, whether or not he was the first to purchase.[37] What this means is that the record system is treated as the only source of relevant information about land title: information in the records may give good title; information outside the records is simply irrelevant.

In a race system, then, the official records become an unimpeachable source of information about the status of land ownership; the law counts the record owner and only the record owner as the true owner. Thus a purchaser can buy in reliance on the records without fear of divestment by some unknown interloper and without the need to make some cumbersome extra-record search for such potential interlopers.

It was a system too crystalline to last. The characters to muck it up by now should be sounding familiar: ninnies, hard-luck cases, and the occasional scoundrels who take advantage of them. What is to be done, for example, with the silly fellow who buys some interest in property but simply forgets to record? Or with the more conscientious one who does attempt to record his interest but whose records wind up in the wrong book? Or with the lost soul whose unimpeachably correct filing is dropped behind the radiator by the neglectful clerk?[38] Some courts take a hard line, perhaps on the view that the first owner was in a better position than our innocent outsider to detect and correct the flaws in the records.[39] But our sympathies for the luckless unrecorded owner indeed put pressure on the recording system that would divest him in favor of the later-arriving outsider.[40]

Our sympathies are all the greater when the outsider is not so innocent after all. What shall we do, for example, when the unrecorded first buyer is snookered out of his claim by a later purchaser who knows perfectly well that the land had already been sold? Shall we allow this nasty (or at best coldly indifferent) second buyer to perfect a claim, simply because he carefully follows the official recording rules?[41] This thought was too much for the courts of equity and too much for American legislatures as well. By the early nineteenth century in Britain, the equity courts had imported an element of nonrecord "notice" into what had initially been a "race" system. Under these doctrines, the later purchaser could take the property free of the prior claims only if he did not know about those prior claims, either from the records or from nonrecord facts that should put him on "notice."[42] American legislatures followed this move to such a degree that, at present, only Louisiana and North Carolina carry out a race system with any rigor. All the rest deny a subsequent claim made by someone who went ahead and bought in spite of notice of an earlier claim.[43]

This means mud: what "should" a purchaser know about, anyway? To be sure, if someone is living on the land, perhaps the potential purchaser should make a few inquiries about the occupant's status. But what if the "occupant's" acts are more ambiguous, consisting of, say, shoveling some manure onto the contested land? Well, said one court, a buyer should ask about the source of all that manure—and since the later buyer did not ask, and thus did not find out about the manure shoveler's prior but unrecorded claim, the later buyer did not count as an innocent purchaser after all. His title was a nullity.[44]

With the emergence of this judicial outlook, the crystalline idea of the recording system has truly come a full cycle back to mud. To be sure, the recording system can give one a fair guess about the legal status of the property that one is thinking of buying, but by the end of the last century, as one Massachusetts court put it, "it would seldom be that a case could occur where some state of facts might not be imagined which, if it existed, would defeat a title."[45] Thus the test of a title's "marketability" became a question not of its perfection but whether the title was subject to "reasonable" doubt—a matter, of course, for the discretion of the court. In the meantime, in order to calm the fears of would-be purchasers who wanted to avoid questions about which doubts were reasonable and which were not, a whole industry built itself up around title insurance and title-searching lawyers, each with his own "plant" of title abstracts, amounting to a kind of private shadow record system. It is this industry, in a sense, that once again makes crystals out of the recording system's mud; and according to some reformers, it is this industry that now stands in the way of some more rational way of cleaning up the mess once and for all.[46]

Yet one must wonder whether cleaning up the mess might not just repeat the round of mud/crystal/mud. One of the most popular suggestions for reform is the so-called Torrens system, named for the someone who thought that shipping registry methods might well be applied to real estate.[47] In this system, all claims on a given property—sales, liens, easements, etc.—are first registered and then incorporated in a certificate. Torrens registration recreates the colonial "race" statutes: no unregistered claim counts, and the certificate for a given property acts as the complete record of everything that anyone might claim.

Well, perhaps not everything. Government liens, fraudulent transactions, and, according to some courts, even simple errors or neglect in registration can produce unregistered claims that count after all.[48] Hence this neo-race system provides no complete relief from the recording system's mud after all. Even after we look at the Torrens certificate, we still have to be on the lookout for the G-men, the forgers, and the ninnies who neglected to register their claims properly. Not a lot of mud, to be sure, but just wait. In some jurisdictions with a long history of Torrens registration, courts have in effect reestablished a "notice" system, defeating the title of anyone who registered a claim when he knew about a prior unregistered one—or merely when he *should* have known about the prior claim, from his knowledge of facts outside the registry. And this, of course, means that the registry and certificate no longer count as a complete source of information about a property's title status.[49]

The most striking aspect of these developments is that title recording acts, and later the registration systems, represented deliberate choices to establish crystalline rules for the sake of simplicity and ease of land sales and purchases. People who failed to use the records or registries were to lose their claims, no matter how innocent they might have been, and no matter how nastily their opponents might have behaved. Yet these very crystalline systems have at least sometimes drifted back into mud, through the importation of equitable ideas of notice—only to be replaced by new crystalline systems in the form of private contract or public legislation.

All these examples put the scarcity story to the test. What has happened to that story, according to which our rules should become more crystalline as resources become scarcer and more valuable? Why instead do we shift back and forth between hard-edged, yes-or-no crystalline rules, and discretion-laden, post hoc muddy rules? Why do we have, over time, both mud and crystal rules with respect to the very same things, with no noticeable relationship to their scarcity or plenty? The following section runs through a few theories that might help to sort out this mystery.

II. Some Tentative Explanations

Taking Sides

One way to cope with the mud/crystal dilemma is to choose one type of rule over the other and to attribute the choice of the nonpreferred rule to some perversity like muddleheadedness or hardheartedness. Perhaps in keeping with the market-conscious spirit of the times, the preferred mode among legal academics currently seems to favor crystals. In a recent example, Clifford Holderness put forth the argument that precise and complete specifications of entitlements are to be preferred to nonexclusive, tentative, open-ended entitlements.[50] Why? Because precise entitlements facilitate the efficient allocation of goods. Precision allow us to identify rightholders and to organize trades with them, until all goods arrive in the hands of those who value them most. On the other hand, open-ended (or, as I would call them, muddy) entitlements generate one of two unfavorable outcomes: either they do not allow a complete identification of the parties with whom we need to trade, or they give some sort of entitlement to so many people that it becomes virtually impossible to cut a deal. In short, under muddy rules, trading is so difficult that Pareto-superior moves remain unmade, and goods languish in inefficient uses, even when someone would pay a great deal to use them more efficiently.

A similar argument appeared in an article that preceded Holderness's by one year. Douglas Baird and Thomas Jackson also argued that where crystalline specifications of rights are possible, they are preferable to mud, because muddy doctrines unduly obfuscate commercial transactions.[51] In discussing a filing system for commercial transactions (somewhat akin to a recording system for land), they strongly urged that nonusers be penalized with the loss of their unfiled claims. If the filing system is easy to use, they argued, it is just too bad about the careless or foolish people who fail to use it.

Crystalline rules have a related advantage that also has been much discussed of late: they discourage what is called "rent-seeking" behavior in decisionmakers, particularly when those decisionmakers are legislators.[52] Take the situation of a legislature that has the authority to decide, say, the incidence of taxation or the location of a new convention center. How will the decision be made, on the supposition that legislators are rational utility maximizers? The rent-seeking analysis suggests that the decision will be sold to the highest bidder, that is, to the interest group whose cohesiveness, tenacity, and resources allow it to bring the greatest temptations and the greatest pressure to bear on the legislators.[53] And of course, the greater the authority of the decisionmaker to change its mind—in other words, the muddier the rules—the greater the likelihood that interest groups will bid for whatever "asset" is the object of the decisionmaker's discretionary choice, frittering away resources in the bidding process.

In the world of private transactions, the analog to this frittering-away process is the very story that the economists tell about scarcity. In the absence of clear definitions of property rights, the story goes, individuals dissipate resources in conflicts and bullying or, as the case may be, in taking precautions against being bullied. What can halt this frittering away, be it public or private? Why, crystalline rules, of course. Hard-edged rules define assets and their ownership in such a way that what is bought stays bought and can be traded to others safely, instead of repeatedly being put up for grabs.

Placing a kind of temporal overlay on these market-oriented preferences for crystal over mud, Frank Easterbrook has applauded what he describes as the "ex ante" perspective of some court decisions. Instead of trying to adjudge situations "ex post," doing fairness to the parties from the perspective of what we know about their positions after things fall apart, the courts should try to consider matters from the perspective of persons similar to the parties at the outset of their relationship, and figure out how we want them to think and act *before* all contingencies become actualized.[54] And how do we want them to act? Well, we want them to be careful planners, so that things *don't* fall apart so easily.

To put it baldly, the ex ante perspective generally means sticking it to those who fail to protect themselves in advance against contingencies that, as it happens, work out badly for them, though perhaps advantageously for others. No muddiness here: all parties are presumed to be clearsighted overseers of their own best interests. It is up to them to tie up all the loose ends that they can, and the courts should let the advantages and disadvantages fall where they may. Why? Because this will encourage people to plan and to act carefully, knowing that no judicial cavalry will ride to their rescue later.[55] It will also allow the people that John Locke once called "the Industrious and Rational" to reap the fruits of their industry and rationality, and thus encourage productivity generally.[56]

But this approach means that the legal consequences of rules ought to be clear in advance, in other words, crystals rather than mud. The industrious and rational need to know that the consequences of their dealings are fixed, at least legally, with no shifts of responsibility after the fact. Judicial punctiliousness about establishing and following clear rules, one would suppose, can influence behavior in the direction of greater carefulness, planning, and productivity.

Things would be easier if one could say that crystals are the uniform choice among the modern scholars knowledgeable about these matters. But that is not the case. Several scholars, particularly those associated with the Critical Legal Studies movement, have decried what we might call the excessively crystalline character of our legal system, which they associate with a kind of alienated individualism. Instead, they plump for more attention to mud or, as the phrase has it, to "standards" instead of "rules."[57] Duncan Kennedy, who coined the distinction between rules and standards, argues that hard-edged, crystal rules systematically abandon people to the wiles of the bad and the mean-spirited. As Kennedy reminds us, Holmes even framed these doctrines in terms of the "bad man." They are designed to tell the bad man the limits within which he can get away with his badness. Standards, on the other hand, are aimed at protecting goodness and altruism—whatever internal contradictions may lurk in the notion of enforcing goodness by a legal order.[58]

But if people are to be guided by standards rather than hard-edged rules, then the rules of decision must necessarily be muddy ones, like "fairness" or "reasonableness," under which no one can entirely specify entitlements until faced with the consequences. As Frank Easterbrook quite bluntly states it, fairness is an ex post consideration, and he apparently puts it second to the greater productivity he associates with the ex ante position.[59] Lawrence Tribe entangled himself in a debate with Easterbrook on this very point, rejecting Easterbrook's preference for the ex ante perspective, particularly in the context of constitutional decision-making. According to Tribe, when judges make decisions, they are not only trying to facilitate the rational calculations of the actors and people situated similarly to the actors; they are also telling a story about the kind of society we live in. These decisions, as he puts it, are *constitutive,* and it would corrode our moral understanding of ourselves as a society if we were to permit gross unfairness to reign, simply for the sake of retaining clear rules and rational ex ante planning—particularly if those rules covertly serve the wealthy and powerful.[60]

Thus a business deal that might seem fair ex ante may turn out to be grossly unfair ex post, once we see how the facts actually play out—particularly when the Holmesian "bad man" exploits his superior knowledge of the rules over against the innocent but well-meaning fool. When a court rules, ex post, that unfairness will not be allowed to reap the reward that might have been expected ex ante, it adds to our moral education and tells us that our society is one in which the good person (in Kennedy's phrase) may feel secure.[61]

The difficulty with adopting either position is that to do so suggests that we in some way have a whole-hog choice between crystal and mud, whereas the history of property law tells us that we seem to be stuck with both, at least over time. Even when we choose one (such as a hard-and-fast recording system), the choice seems to dissolve, and instead of really choosing, we seem to rotate between them. Because this pattern recurs so often in so many areas, it is difficult to believe that it is due to abnormal foolishness or turpitude or that it can be permanently overcome by a more thoughtful or more virtuous choice of one side or the other.

Can we, then, look to other theories that will take into account the point that we have *both* crystals *and* mud?

Refinements on the Economic Perspective

Some economic theory relates the crystal/mud problem to the different characteristics of the objects we consider to be "property." One theory looks to what are called "transaction costs" to explain why we sometimes have crystals and sometimes mud. Thomas Merrill has argued that where transaction costs are low—where it is easy to make a deal—we tend to have clear, hard-edged yes-or-no rules. Thus in trespass law, your invasion of my property, no matter how trivial, is an actionable wrong. Only two parties are involved; if you want to come onto my property, it is relatively easy for you to find me and to bargain with me for the right. The hard-edged rule requires you to enter into those negotiations with me, and presumably if you want the right to enter more than I want to keep you out, you can offer me enough so that I will agree. Thus the clear, crystalline rule punishes those who could easily bargain for an entitlement but who instead bypass that opportunity and act unilaterally, in the process (perhaps) transferring a resource from one who values it more (me) to one who values it less (you).[62]

On the other hand, Merrill's argument goes on, we find "discretionary" (or muddy) rules where the costs of transacting are high, as, for example, in the area of nuisance doctrine or the closely related riparian law discussed in the previous essay. Here the conflicts typically involve numerous parties, such as the victims of noxious odors that spread through a neighborhood, or the downstream owners affected by water pollution. It is not easy for all the affected parties to find each other, to agree on a common strategy, and to negotiate a deal whereby the sufferers pay to have the fumes stopped or, alternatively, where the fume-producing plant pays some agreed-upon price to make up for the sufferings it causes.[63] Since the parties cannot easily arrive at a negotiated agreement, a court must solve the mess itself, deciding whether the costs of the fumes or pollutants outweigh the benefits. In the absence of any chance at a nice clear market transaction to put a price on costs and benefits, the court has to muddle through with conjectures. In short, in these scenarios of high transaction costs, we have to fall back on judicial discretion—as well as the ambiguous, muddy doctrines that give the judges some room for guesswork.

The difficulty with this explanation is that we sometimes fall back on muddy doctrines even where transaction costs are low. Consider some of the examples discussed earlier: for one, Wisconsin's new "nuisance" treatment of sunlight rights flys in the face of what would seem to be a relatively easy negotiation between neighbors. Similarly, the all but universal abandonment of the caveat emptor rule for house purchases appears to have occurred against a bargaining backdrop of low transaction costs (one buyer, one seller); so does the movement to introduce equitable mushiness into the hard-edged contractual relations of mortgages and installment land contracts. By the same token, land record systems seem to become periodically muddy even when a given system is relatively easy to use. Something in the crystals/mud back-and-forth pattern, then, eludes straight application of the transaction-cost analysis.

Historians' Stories

At least one historian, P. S. Atiyah, has noticed the back-and-forth between mud and crystal in our legal rules and has written a long book on British contract law to illustrate the point that we have had both kinds of rules over time.[64] Atiyah has argued, in effect, that our preference for mud over crystal (or vice versa) takes place in long historical cycles. Roughly speaking, he regards the eighteenth century as largely a mud era, full of ambiguity and judicial discretion, but he sees the period between 1770 and 1870 as an era in which crystal rules, or "principles," as he calls them, came to seem particularly important. His explanation (again in very gross terms) is that Parliament and the courts acted on a perceived need to discipline an unruly population during the later period and used sharply enforced legal rules to instill in the people generally the habits of foresightful, productive activity necessary to a market economy.[65] The preference for crystal, under this analysis, seems to be one of education or rhetoric: you will be held to the very terms of your bargain, so that in the future you will not be so foolish as to get yourself into such a mess but will rather plan your affairs more carefully. Atiyah seems to think—with a certain regret—that we have abandoned this age of principle and are now back to a muddier ethos of "individualized justice" that he dubs "pragmatism."[66]

This analysis, interesting though it is, does leave a residue of puzzlements. Aside from quibbles about dates with respect to Europe, we do observe other societies adopting some extremely rigid rules (Islamic codes, perhaps, or kosher rules) that do not seem to have much connection with economic discipline.[67] Moreover, even if we suppose that Western societies did adopt crystalline legal rules for the sake of labor discipline, the explanation must make us wonder why we no longer think we need those rules. Are our populaces less inclined to unruliness today than we were in the nineteenth century? If we still have unruly tendencies, why do we no longer think we need the discipline of those crystalline rules? Or alternatively, if we no longer think we need those rules, why did people think so earlier?

If we look to the work of another economic historian, Albert O. Hirschman, we might start to think that these swings result not from some external economic patterns or social history but rather result from *each other.* In other words, mud and crystal are not so much alternatives but a matched pair, like + 1 and –1 in a sine curve. In his book, *Shifting Involvements,*[68] Hirschman is not discussing legal rules but rather the periodic swing in social moods between public involvement and private self-gratification. He argues, in effect, that people desire both these ends, but both cannot be satisfied simultaneously. Suppose one begins with private self-gratification: one's activities in behalf of one's self have certain rewards, but they also leave certain regrets, particularly about the absence of one's participation in public affairs. At some marginal point where the rewards of privately focused activity are declining (or even becoming negative), the actor turns to public participation—where a similar process of satisfaction/satiation/disappointment begins.[69]

Might this process parallel the shift between mud and crystal in property law? Hirschman's book suggests that where we see recurring patterns, we might look for some internal—or, as they say, endogenous—factors that lead to these cyclical patterns. Does such an account apply to the oscillation between crystal and mud in our definitions of entitlements? One can see the outlines in at least one legal domain: the recording system, where we have so often resolved unclarities with a crystalline system, only to muddy it so thoroughly over time that we have to start all over again with a newly minted set of clear rules.

Let us suppose that we initiate a system for the clarification of property titles. Might we have a tendency to overuse the system, so that in the end it becomes so hopelessly bogged down in detail that the purpose of clarity is defeated? Certainly our traditional land records have this quality. For example, some early cases permitted only fee interests to be recorded, but the system's very attractiveness created pressure to allow the recordation of other claims as well—liens, for example, or easements.[70] Indeed, some claims may be placed in the records even though they are not legally recordable. Then too, many claims are recorded and just stay put over time, and sometimes they turn out to conflict with still other recorded claims.[71] These layers of recorded but unextinguished claims can grow so thick that it hardly seems worth the time to go back and check everything. In a sense, then, we treat our clarifying systems—in this case the recording mechanisms—as a kind of a "commons," a more or less free good whose overload over time is entirely predictable.[72] The resulting overuse of the system, in turn, diminishes its clarifying function and creates a certain disgust with the lush proliferation of records; that is the origin of the numerous proposals for reform, some of which would dramatically pare down the instruments that count as valid.

Thus the very attractiveness of a clarifying system defeats the purpose of the system, in this instance, to clarify all claims against a given property. The same pattern is evident in the excessively long contracts that attempt to specify all possible contingencies and that no one actually reads. However comforting it may be to "have it in writing," it really isn't worth the effort to nail down everything, and the overly precise contract may wind up being just as opaque as—and perhaps even more arbitrary than—the one that leaves adjustments to the contingencies of future relations.[73]

The trouble, then, is that an attractively simple legal device draws in too many users or too complex a set of uses. And that, of course, is where the simple rule becomes a booby trap. It is this booby-trap aspect of what seem to be clear, simple rules—the scenario of disproportionate loss by some party—that seems to drive us to muddy up crystal rules with all the exceptions and post hoc discretionary judgments. Hence I turn now to that subject of disproportionate loss, the subject to which some courts apply the shorthand label of "forfeiture."

III. Forfeiture as Overload: The Problem and the Players

A strong element of moral judgment runs through the cases in which mud supersedes crystal. These cases are often rife with human failings—sloth and forgetfulness on the one hand, greed and self-dealing on the other. These vices put pressure on our efforts to elaborate clear and distinct property specifications, and they make judges and others second-guess the deals that call for a pound of flesh.

Perhaps we can get at this by thinking not about the moral qualities as such that are at issue but rather about the pound of flesh. We have already seen that in the decisions about mortgages and installment land contracts, the judges exhibit a deep antipathy to what is explicitly called the debtor's "forfeiture." The same antipathy to "forfeiture"—a loss disproportionate to the lapse—also appears in our other examples and many others as well.[74] Thus without some relief, the nonrecording (or improperly or negligently recording) owner would lose the very property itself; thus the noninspecting (or imperfectly or negligently inspecting) buyer would be stuck with a house that may be flooded twice a week with the neighbor's sewage.

Our law seems to find these dramatic losses abhorrent. James Gordley has written convincingly that unequal exchanges have been overwhelmingly disfavored in the Western legal tradition, and his work suggests that rules leading to forfeitures and penalties generally are unstable in our law. Why is this so? Gordley argues that exchanges centering more or less on a market price traditionally counted as "equal." Taken collectively, such market-based exchanges tended to restore the sellers' costs; beyond that, Gordley argues, the law has had no reason to enforce what he calls random redistributions.[75]

Mark Grady has suggested something comparable to this aversion to forfeiture in another context, namely, the "last clear chance" doctrine in older tort law. The usual rule was that one whose own negligence had contributed to his injury could not recover against the injurer, even if the injurer were negligent too; if either person could have avoided the accident, the loss was left where it lay. But as Grady has pointed out, judges used the doctrine of "last clear chance" to fine-tune the respective responsibilities of the parties, so as to adjust those responsibilities as the time of the accident drew closer and as potential foresight about it grew greater. If an injurer failed to take a last-minute precaution that might have helped, he might still be held liable, even against a contributorily negligent victim.[76] Put another way, the "last clear chance" doctrine relieved an injured party from the forfeiture that would otherwise have accompanied his own careless behavior.

But the judicial double-clutching entailed in this doctrine complicated the relation between the parties and introduced whole new layers of facts and litigative possibilities, for the sake of avoiding a disproportionate loss to the injured party. Whether for efficiency reasons or not, it illustrates a way of thinking that eschews forfeitures or penalties and that is willing to undertake an elaborate ex post analysis in order to allocate precise responsibility.[77]

Unexpected redistribution in the tort context is one thing, but why should we find a distaste for forfeiture in people's *contractual* agreements about their property, as Gordley suggests we do? After all, contracting parties presumably know about the potential for forfeiture and agree to it anyway. Why complicate their relations by asking elaborate ex post questions comparable to "last clear chance"—that is, asking who could have avoided the redistributive event, when both apparently contemplated it as a possibility? Are there reasons to make this after-the-fact inquiry, regardless of how firmly the parties seem to have agreed to possible forfeitures before the fact?

Perhaps forfeiture might be seen as a symptom of the overloading of crystal rules in bargaining. Crystalline doctrines yield fixed consequences for defaults because they ignore reasons and excuses; predictability makes these doctrines attractive. But for the very reason that they are attractive, these doctrines may be overused or overloaded, in contexts that make them *un*predictable and counterproductive.

Consider the way that the enforcement of a penalty affects the incentives of persons on either side of a property entitlement. If we were to enforce penalties against defaulters or violators, it is no doubt true that the persons involved would be especially careful to avoid violations. But perhaps they would be *too* careful and would try to live up to their obligations even when circumstances changed radically, when everyone would really be better off if they defaulted and paid normal damages for whatever harm their default caused another.[78]

Furthermore, penalties might affect the behavior of the nondefaulting parties. Because they would gain much more than their damages if penalties were enforced, unscrupulous dealers might expend efforts to find trading partners who would *fail* rather than succeed; sharp dealers might even take measures to make their partners trip up, in order to take the penalty proceeds and run—as, for example, the mortgage lender who might have hidden in the bushes to prevent the borrower from repaying and getting his land back.[79] These are the people that petty con artists in my former hometown of Chicago might call "mopes,"[80] a term that undoubtedly could include the unsuspecting house purchasers who overestimate their own ability to live up to the loan payments or who never suspect that there might be rats in the basement or who don't have a clue that they have to record their titles.

Fools on the one hand and sharp dealers on the other, then, are central players in the crystal-to-mud story, because they are the characters most likely to have leading roles in the systematic overloading of crystalline rules. From this perspective, as indeed the more sophisticated economic analyses tell us, crystalline rules seem less the king of the efficiency mountain than we might normally suppose. One could argue that elaborate ex post allocations of responsibilities might be efficient too, even if they make people's entitlements obligations fuzzier ex ante. The very knowledge that one cannot gull someone else and get away with it makes it less likely that anyone will dissipate time and effort in trying to find the gullible. This knowledge will also reassure those of us who fear we may be made fools: we can go about our business and take part in the world of trade without cowering at home because we think we need to hire a lawyer and an accountant every time we leave the car at a commercial parking lot.

How can we fit all this together with the scarcity story about property rights? According to that story, the driving force toward crystalline rules is the overuse of a "commons" in a given resource. The conflicts and waste from commons overuse induce us to define boundaries around entitlements, so that we can trade our entitlements instead of fighting over them.

But the driving force toward mud rules seems to be an overuse in the "commons" of the crystal rules themselves. We are tempted to take rules that are simple and informative in one context—as, for example, "First in time, first in right" may be in small communities—and extend them to different or more complex situations, where the consequences may be unexpected and confusing. It is in these "overload" situations that crystal rules ultimately may be ruinous for trade. Not only might sharp dealers seek out situations in which trade will fail (allowing them to collect a forfeiture from the mopes), but the mopes themselves, as well as other people, may be frightened out of dealing altogether.[81]

Simple boundaries and simple remedies, it turns out, may yield radically unexpected results and may destroy the confidence we need for trade rather than fostering it. It is forfeiture, the prospect of dramatic or disproportionate loss, that brings this home. But forfeiture—and the detailed ways in which it might have been avoided—can only be known to us ex post.

IV. The Context of Forfeiture: Crystals and Mud as Institutional Responses to Estrangement

What can be said to generalize the context of forfeiture, where crystal rules are overloaded? Where in our commercial life, for example, do we tend to find the invocation of those crystalline rules, causing great forfeiture to others? Stewart Macaulay's work on contracts suggests that forfeitures and penalties emerge in one context in particular: where the parties have no long-term relationship with each other.[82]

This is also precisely the context for the fool/scoundrel relationship. Scoundrels, of course, hope never to see their dupes again, at least after the dupes figure out that something is amiss. Contrast this ultimate form of the one-shot deal to normal business relations: businesspeople who work together routinely relax the letter of their respective obligations and readjust the terms of their relationships in the face of unexpected hardships.[83] To be sure, hard-edged rules might make business partners plan more carefully in advance; but is it worth it to do all that planning, when they can write adjustment clauses into their deals? After all, they can trust each other, since they have to live together over the long haul. According to Macaulay, they show their hard edges, demanding forfeitures and penalties and the hard crystalline features of their entitlements, only against customers whose business they are willing to forgo.[84]

Macaulay's work, as well as that of Ian Macneil,[85] suggests that crystalline rules (and their attendant forfeitures) are only designed for people who see one another on a onetime basis and whose temptations to dupe one another, or simply to play commercial hardball, might be strongest. By way of contrast, where two persons are members of the same community or religion or family or ongoing business deal, there are inducements to cooperation and trust that are entirely independent of the enforcement of crystalline rules.

Modern game theorists buttress this point, telling us that if we can arrange things in such a manner that we have repeated contact with our opposite numbers, then we can enforce cooperation through the game of "tit for tat."[86] Recent historical work supports the point from another direction, telling us that prior to the eighteenth century, much European commerce was dominated by Jewish and Quaker merchants, whose family and religious connections could assure their mutual reliability.[87] Recent historical literature also suggests that as modern property and contract law developed, it became possible for people to do business with one another simply on the basis of their mutual promises, even though they had none of these familial or other long-term relationships.[88] The legal categories of contract acted as an artificial, officially sponsored re-creation of a kind of confidence and trust that would otherwise come only through the mutual constraints of community, religion, and family.

In an important sense, then, the enforceability of clear rules enables us to deal with the world of strangers, apart from any pattern of dealing or mutual membership in close-knit communities, and to arrange our affairs with persons whom we never expect to see again. We can do so, we think, because rules are rules are rules—we all know them and know what to expect. Crystalline rules thus seem to perform the service of creating a context in which strangers can deal with one another in confidence: the rules define expectations and allow people to rely on each other, even people who have no familial or coreligious or ongoing commercial leverage with each other.

But what is easily overlooked is that mud rules too attempt to re-create an underlying nonlegal trading community in which confidence is possible. In those communities, the members tend to readjust in the face of unforeseen complications rather than to drive hard bargains when the opportunity arises. By analogy, mud rules mimic a pattern of post hoc readjustments that people *would* make if they were in an ongoing relationship with each other. People in such relationships would scarcely dupe their trading partners out of their titles, sell them defective goods, or fail to make minor readjustments on debts. If they did such things, they would lose trading partners (or suffer denunciation in church or become black sheep), and everyone would know it.

Now we can see why crystal and mud are a matched pair. Both are distilled from a kind of nonlegal commercial context where people already in some relationship arrive at more or less imperfect understandings at the outset and expect post hoc readjustments in their bargains when circumstances require. Just as the parties call on courts to enforce contractual promises and protect entitlements that would otherwise be enforced by the threat of informal sanctions, so too do they call on the courts to figure out the post hoc bargaining readjustments that, in more close-knit circumstances, would have been made by the parties themselves.

It is in our onetime dealings with strangers that a wedge splits a trading relationship into ex ante and ex post, crystals and mud. One-shot dealings are the situations in which it seems most important to have clear definitions of obligations, but in which it is also most important to have some substitute for the pattern of ongoing cooperation that would protect us against sudden and unexpected loss.

The split between crystals and mud has an institutional reflection as well—that is, in our political and legal institutions. We call for crystals, those precise specifications of entitlements, when we are in what Mel Eisenberg has called our "rulemaking" mode, that is, when private parties make contracts with strangers or legislatures make prospective law for an unknown future.[89] We call for mud and exceptions only later, after things have gone awry, but at that point we stand before judges.

But these two perspectives may be ineluctably different. It is obvious that "rulemakers" cannot see into the future in any very precise way when they are laying down crystal rules; thus we know that those who are in an ex ante position cannot see things ex post. Much less obviously, however, it may be equally true that judges cannot think their way back into an ex ante frame of mind in any way except metaphorically.

Borrowing a leaf from Hans-Georg Gadamer, some scholars of historical interpretation have treated our efforts to understand the past as a kind of *translation* in which we cannot help but use our own experience to understand prior experience.[90] This does not mean that the past's perspective is incomprehensible to us but only that our understanding of it is inevitably filtered through our subsequent experience; what we know post hoc about those fools and scoundrels necessarily transforms the way we *now* think about what we *used to* think.

If this is so, then judges, who see everything ex post, really cannot help but be influenced by their ex post perspectives. They are likely to lean ever so slightly to mud, every so often, in order to save the fools from forfeiture at the hands of scoundrels. Indeed, if judges have even an occasional preference for the post hoc readjustments that avoid forfeiture, this preference will gradually place an accretion of mud rules over people's crystalline arrangements. By the way, all this suggests something of a modification of claims about the efficiency of common law adjudication. That is, contrary to some of the claims made for the judiciary, we may be more likely to find that judicial solutions veer toward ex post mud rules, while it is legislatures that are more apt to join with private parties as "rulemakers" with a tilt toward the ex ante approach of crystal.[91]

Hence a circular pattern: if things *matter* to us, we try in our rulemaking, contractual mode to place clear bounds around them in our bargains with strangers, so that we know who has what and can profitably invest in the things or trade them. But the use of clear bounds may lead to forfeitures—dramatic losses that we can see only post hoc and whose post hoc avoidance makes us ask judges to muddy the boundaries we have drawn. Then at some point we may become so stymied by those muddinesses that as rulemakers we will start over with new boundaries—followed by new muddinesses, and so it goes.[92]

V. Does It Matter? "Mere" Rhetoric in the Opposition of Crystals and Mud

The crystal/mud cycle occurs most strikingly in a context of dealings with strangers. But it is wise to keep in mind the limited extent of dealings of this type. Macaulay and Macneil have reminded us, as Robert Gordon notes, that the one-shot context for the enforcement of crystal rules is really quite marginal to ordinary business activity.[93] Robert Ellickson's wonderful study of Shasta County suggests that property "rights" too are normally defined and readjusted by community understandings and are subject to community pressures along a number of interactive "fronts" among neighbors.[94] And if the context for crystal rules is marginal, then the same must perforce be true for mud rules, insofar as these attempt to inject a kind of substitute for negotiation or continuing dialog into what would otherwise be a crystalline, open-and-shut situation. No doubt there is a difference in "administrative costs" between these jurisprudential modes.[95] But if most transactions actually take place in some kind of community or some kind of ongoing relationship, even the administrative costs should not matter very much.

All this suggests that the crystal/mud dichotomy carries little practical weight in ordinary commerce and property relations. Why, then, do we find so much heat in the discussions of these matters, when relatively little in our economic life seems to hinge on them? If their opposition makes little practical difference, then perhaps the answer lies in the rhetorical characteristics of crystals and mud.

Crystals and mud each are ways of talking about the character of our dealings with the world at large—with people that we do not necessarily know and do not necessarily expect to see again. Crystal rhetoric and mud rhetoric, however, hark back to features of our dealings with people in a very different context, that is, the context of an ongoing community or relationship: the rhetoric of crystals focuses on the sense of predictability and security embodied in long-term dealings; the rhetoric of mud focuses on the flexibility, forgiveness, and willingness to make adjustments that long-term dealings normally offer.

Of the two, the legal rhetoric of crystals is more clearly associated with a larger Enlightenment project, in principle as well as historically.[96] Indeed, insofar as crystal rules may give us confidence and security in our dealings with strangers, it seems no coincidence that the doctrines of fixed promise-keeping and fixed property entitlements developed more or less contemporaneously with an Enlightenment-era social theory that envisioned a radical separateness among human beings.[97] When the world is populated by strangers, one needs fixed entitlements to secure what is one's own.

A dominating strand of our social theory posits a world of individuals whose relationships with one another are fundamentally those of strangers; thus it matters how we talk about our dealings with strangers, because that is the way that we deal with *everyone.* I am going to suggest, however, that neither crystal rhetoric nor mud rhetoric can sustain the image of a world of strangers.

The rhetoric of crystals suggests that our safety with strangers derives from an ability to define and bound off every entitlement with a kind of perfect language, a language that reflects in the present all future contingencies. This rhetoric suggests that regardless of context, background, or culture, everyone understands the content of each entitlement. Thus in bargains and trade, each understands what she is giving up and what she is gaining—or can at least "discount" any risks into a present value.[98] And because of this perfect language, this perfect present understanding of the future and its contingencies, it is only just to enforce promises and property entitlements to the limit.[99] And indeed, there is a meaning of "justice" implicit in the rhetoric of crystal: Adam Smith once lectured that "justice" means (in his note-taker's idiosyncratic spelling) "prevent[ing] the members of a society from incroaching on one anothers property, or siezing what is not their own," and he later interpolated the comment that "[t]he end proposed by justice is the maintaining [of] men in what are called their perfect rights."[100]

What is wrong with this idea? The chief accusation levied at crystal rhetoric, mainly by scholars associated with Critical Legal Studies, is that crystalline rules are hardhearted and mean-spirited, that they glorify an attitude of self-seeking and "me first," and that they act as a kind of cover-up for the domination of the weak by the strong through the vehicle of unbridled capitalism.[101]

A related and in some ways more profound objection is that the notion of fixed entitlements, known or "discounted" perfectly in the present and traded about in their discounted form, is a kind of false understanding of the importance of *time* in human affairs. It is a notion that—like the "covering law" theory of historical explanation—equates knowledge of human action with knowledge about the objects of nature; it supposes that human beings have no memories or new ideas that influence later choices, no ability to persuade one another—in short, no changes of consciousness over time that will cause them to redefine their views about "entitlements," just as they redefine other aspects of their thought.[102]

But if time, memory, and consciousness do matter in human affairs, then the paths we take and the things we become persuaded we are "entitled to" may be explored fully only by ex post hoc narrative; they cannot be foreseen in advance or predicted from what falsely appears to be a set of identical conditions in the past.[103] To adopt the rhetoric of crystal rules, then, seems to be a way of denying the necessarily dialogic character of human interactions and to act as if we can compel human behavior by a perfect specification of unchanging rights and obligations.

But it is often forgotten that there is a much softer, more sociable and dialogic side to crystal rules and to the commerce that accompanied their development. At least some Enlightenment thinkers discussed commerce in a way that now seems novel but that we have already seen in connection with the "comedy of the commons" and the enormous public importance of commerce described there. The great hope for commerce was that it would enlarge sociability and would in a sense be a constitutive force in ever larger communities of "interest." Enlightenment thinkers argued that "gentle commerce"—and presumably also the fixed entitlements that commerce seems to require—would not harden manners but rather soften them and make its practitioners more attentive to the needs of others, precisely because everyone could count on a reliable return in meeting those needs.[104] Thus commerce and fixed entitlements would *create* communities—at the very least, communities of interest—and would also create the ongoing dialog that is a part of such communities.

Lest this view be too rapidly written off as Enlightenment Panglossianism, we should note that some more recent historians have attributed the development of eighteenth- and early-nineteenth-century philanthropy to the legal rhetoric of fixed entitlements and promise-keeping. It seems that confidence in firm rules did indeed instill a sense that one could deal with strangers; and when commercial traders dealt with strangers, they came to feel sympathy for the plight of those strangers, as well as confidence in their own ability to help. Indeed, it is hard to imagine the historical development of anything like altruism—in the sense of selfless attention to the needs of strangers—in the absence of the far-flung commercial ties that seemed to overcome the casual savagery toward outsiders so characteristic of earlier times.[105]

Moreover, the language of crystal rules sometimes conveys a kind of sturdiness that, at least in our culture, suggests a very important social virtue, namely, courage. The rhetoric of firmly delineated entitlements supports that courage. One can envision in almost romantic terms the pioneer woman who, armed and ready, turns away the intruders at the threshold of her homestead cottage, or the tavern owners who refuse all offers to give up their little establishment and instead force the giant office building to be built around them and their happy customers.[106] Even the child psychologists tell us that uncertainty about rules is not always good for us and that it does not improve our temperaments, our character, or our ability to get along with others.[107] Thus crystal rules not only depend upon shared social understandings, they at least arguably enhance sociability and facilitate ongoing social interactions—that is to say, crystal rules in some ways turn out to mirror mud rules.

It is indeed the element of ongoing social interactions that mud rules focus upon. Mud rules follow a rhetoric that takes place in time; they attempt to introduce an element of continuing dialog among persons who have initially ordered their affairs more or less as one-shot strangers. When a court introduces ambiguity into the fixed rules that the parties adopted at the outset, it in effect is reinstating the kind of weighing, balancing, and reconsidering that the parties might have undertaken if they had been in some longer-term relationship with each other. Thus if the mortgage cannot be paid on time, the lender's expectation of prompt payment has to be weighed against the borrower's loss of the deal; if the house buyer discovers a leaky sewage line, perhaps he should get some break from the seller to make up for this unexpected damage. These judicial interventions are a crude substitute for dialog—for talking things over and adjusting entitlements, as one would be likely to do in an ongoing trading relationship or as one would in a family or religious community.

The chief critique levied against mud—particularly by scholars associated with law and economics—is that all other things being equal, mud is inefficient: mud rules make entitlements uncertain and thus increase the costs of trading and of resolving disputes at the same time that they discourage careful planning.[108] But this too overstates the case: at least in some instances, there is a great deal more clarity and certainty about a mud rule than a crystal one. This view is reflected in the Uniform Commercial Code, where a muddy term like "commercial reasonableness" is regarded as a more predictable standard for businesspeople than such precise arcana as the mailbox rule of offer and acceptance.[109] Perhaps we could dream up some formulation that would more clearly express our understanding than "commercial reasonableness" does, and commercial traders indeed often do so. But language is always imperfect, and much of the time, it is not worth the effort to specify everything. It is easier and cheaper to rely on a set of socially understood conventions. Mud rules, then, can take on a greater clarity than crystal in a social setting among persons with some common understanding—who know, for example, that a "baker's dozen" numbers thirteen.

Just as there is a version of sociability and dialog in crystal rules, then, there is a version of certainty and predictability in mud rules. Where do these reversals occur? They occur just where crystals or mud move into a genuine social context. No wonder: crystals and mud themselves are rhetorical extractions from the practices of ongoing trading relationships, where the participants are likely to enjoy both upstream security as well as downstream readjustment. In our dealings with strangers, it seems as if we can only have the one or the other—hence crystals on the one hand, for upstream security, and mud on the other, for downstream readjustment. But in fact, most of our interactions are much more sociable than the one-shot deal. We are repeat customers; we care about our reputations; we hope that our clients will come back. And at these junctures, where we establish some long-term tie, crystals and mud dissolve into each other.

To be sure, from time to time we do deal with strangers, on a one-shot basis, so that they stay strangers. And that is where we are faced with a choice of crystals and mud and where we seem to zigzag back and forth over time between these two jurisprudential modes. But it is an illusion to think that either of these rhetorical modes is a paradigm for normal living or even normal commercial dealings. They are only our metaphors for the lapses of community—lapses that may be much more occasional than our dominating political theory would suggest.

But it is precisely as metaphor or rhetoric that the choice between crystal and mud matters. The lapse of community may occur only infrequently in our everyday lives, but this world of estrangement has had a robust life in our highly individualistic *talk* about politics and economics since the seventeenth century.[110] In the context of that talk of universal individualism, the metaphoric or rhetorical character of crystals and mud has a certain independent significance. However much crystal rules may have a dialogic side like mud and however much mud rules may lend the certainty of crystal, as *rhetoric* crystals and mud bear sharply divergent didactic messages.[111] They suggest quite different ways that each self-contained individual should behave and converse with all those other self-contained individuals. Thus crystal rhetoric suggests that we view friends, family, and fellow citizens from the same cool distance as those we do not know at all; while mud rhetoric suggests that we treat even those to whom we have no real connection with the kind of engagement that we normally reserve for friends and partners. And for this reason—for the sake of the different social didactics, the different modes of conversation and interaction implicit in the two rhetorical styles—we debate endlessly the respective merits of crystals and mud.

Notes

1. Jeremy Bentham, *Principles of the Civil Code,* in *Theory of Legislation* 111 (1987; reprint of C. K. Ogden ed. 1931).

2. See especially the essay "Energy and Efficiency" on the theoretical evolution of property regimes toward clearly defined rights; see also "Possession as the Origin of Property" and "Comedy of the Commons."

3. Clifford Holderness, "A Legal Foundation for Exchange," 14 *J. Legal Stud.* 321, 322–26 (1985); 2 William Blackstone, *Commentaries on the Laws of England* 4 (1979; reproduction of 1766 ed.) (property rights necessary to avoid "innumerable tumults" of many persons striving for same thing); see also Harold Demsetz, "Professor Michelman's Unnecessary and Futile Search for the Philosopher's Touchstone," 24 *Nomos* 41, 46 (1982).

4. Steven N. S. Cheung, "The Structure of a Contract and the Theory of a Non-Exclusive Resource," 1 *J. L. & Econ.* 49, 64 (1970); see generally Gary Libecap, *Contracting for Property Rights* (1989), on the gains and impediments to clarifying property regimes.

5. Harold Demsetz, "Toward a Theory of Property Rights," 57 *Am. Econ. Rev.* (Papers & Proceedings) 935 (1981).

6. See, e.g., Terry L. Anderson and P. J. Hill, "The Evolution of Property Rights: A Study of the American West," 18 *J. L. & Econ.* 163 (1975); J. Willard Hurst, *Law and Economic Growth: The Legal History of the Lumber Industry* 298 (1964); Libecap, supra note 4, also takes this approach and gives many examples from the settlement of the West.

7. Prah v. Maretti, 321 N.W.2d 182 (Wis. 1982). Some other jurisdictions have rejected *Prah,* however; see Sher v. Leiderman, 226 Cal. Rptr. 698 (Cal. App. 1986).

8. *Prah,* 321 N.W.2d at 192.

9. Cf. John Edward Cribbet, "Concepts in Transition: The Search for a New Definition of Property," 1986 *U. of Ill. L. Rev.* 1 (describing the proliferation of exceptions, special cases and so on as a recognition of "social side" of property).

10. See, e.g., Swinton v. Whitsonville Sav. Bank, 42 N.E.2d 808 (Mass. 1942); Tudor v. Heugel, 178 N.E.2d 442 (Ind. App. 1961); William D. Grand, "Implied and Statutory Warranties in the Sale of Real Estate: The Demise of Caveat Emptor," 15 *Real Estate L. J.* 44 (1986).

11. See Paul G. Haskell, "The Case for an Implied Warranty of Quality in Sales of Real Property," 53 *Geo. L. J.* 633, 642–43 (1965).

12. See, e.g., Lingsch v. Savage, 29 Cal. Rptr. 201, 209 (Cal. App. 1963).

13. See, e.g., Theis v. Heuer, 280 N.E.2d 300 (Ind. 1972); McDonald v. Mianecki, 398 A.2d 1283 (N.J. 1979) and authorities cited therein.

14. See Oates v. JAG, Inc., 333 S.E.2d 222, 225 (N.C. 1985). For a similar problem in residential lease warranties, see Javins v. First National Realty Corp, 428 F.2d 1071, 1082, nn. 62–63 (D.C. Cir.) cert. denied, 400 U.S. 925 (1970).

15. See, e.g., Humber v. Morton, 426 S.W.2d 554, 562 (Tex. 1968), criticizing the older caveat emptor rule as "lending encouragement to the unscrupulous, fly-by-night operator and purveyor of shoddy work." However, if warranty work costs the builder more than expected damages, builders may not build better but may rather simply accept losses from occasional damage suits.

16. Reed v. King, 193 Cal. Rptr. 130 (Cal. App. 1983).

17. *McDonald,* 398 A.2d at 1291, using the analogy of a water heater warranty; Wawak v. Stewart, 449 S.W.2d 922, 923 (Ark. 1970), making a similar analogy to a walking stick or kitchen mop. One obvious difference between a mop and a house, of course, is that the cost of an engineer's report is entirely disproportionate to the price paid for a mop.

18. See Lingsch v. Savage, 29 Cal. Rptr. 201, 209 (1963), stating that an "as is" clause does not necessarily immunize a seller from disclosure obligations.

19. Steven Wechsler, "Through the Looking Glass: Foreclosure by Sale as De Facto Strict Foreclosure—An Empirical Study of Mortgage Foreclosure and Subsequent Resale," 70 *Cornell L. Rev.* 850, 855, n. 25 (1985), quoting Madwoy, "A Mortgage Foreclosure Primer," 8 *Clearinghouse Rev.* 146, 148 (1974).

20. See *The Treatise on the Laws and Customs of the Realm of England Commonly Called Glanvill* 121 (G.D.G. Hall trans. and ed. 1965), a twelfth-century treatise stating that the borrower may immediately give seizin to the creditor. See also 3 Richard Powell, *The Law of Real Property* sec. 438 (P. J. Rohan ed. 1984).

21. 3 Powell, supra note 20, sec. 438, at 547; Wechsler, supra note 19, at 856.

22. Thomas Littleton, Tenures (E. Wambaugh ed. 1903), at sec. 332. For Littleton's life and work, see id. introduction.

23. Id. at secs. 340–43. See also Wechsler, supra note 19, at 856.

24. How v. Vigures, 21 Eng. Rep. 499 (1628–29).

25. See, e.g., Anonymus [sic] Case, 27 Eng. Rep. 621 (1740) (debtor given additional six-month extension after three previous extensions and in spite of promise to ask for no more); Nanny v. Edwards, 38 Eng. Rep. 752 (1827) (three or four extensions claimed to be usual; some excuse needed for extension though "not ... a very strong one").

26. Campbell v. Holyland, 7 Ch.D. 166, 172 (1876). See also Sheldon Tefft, "The Myth of Strict Foreclosure," 4 *U. Chi. L. Rev.* 575, 578 (1937).

27. Roscarrick v. Barton, 22 Eng. Rep. 769, 770 (1672).

28. See, e.g., Novosielski v. Wakefield, 418 34 Eng. Rep. 161, 162 (1811); Holford v. Yate, 69 Eng. Rep. 631, 632 (1855); Campbell v. Holyland, 7 Ch.D. 166, 173 (1876); Perine v. Dunn, Johns. Ch. 140, 141 (N.Y. 1819).

29. For a discussion of the permutations, see Comment, "Mortgages—Deed in Lieu of Foreclosure—Validity," 36 *Mich. L. Rev.* 111 (1937).

30. Peugh v. Davis, 96 U.S. 332, 337 (1878).

31. Glock v. Howard and Wilson Colony Co., 123 Cal. 1 (1898).

32. McFadden v. Walker, 488 P.2d 1353 (Cal. 1971). For the evolving case law, see John R. Hetlund, "The California Land Contract," 48 *Cal. L. Rev.* 729 (1960); for related developments in other jurisdictions, see Annotation, "Specific Performance of Land Contract Notwithstanding Failure of Vendee to Make Required Payments on Time," 55 A.L.R.3d 10 (1974).

33. 6A Powell, supra note 20, at secs. 880, 904.

34. He might, however, have an action against the seller for breach of a warranty of "seizin," i.e., a covenant that I really own what I purport to sell. See 6A Powell sec. 896.

35. R. G. Patton, "Evolution of Legislation on Proof of Title to Land," 30 *Wash. L. Rev.* 224, 225–26 (1955); 6A Powell, supra note 20, at sec. 880. The lease transfer was one type of circumvention.

36. See Francis S. Philbrick, "Limits of Record Search and Therefore of Notice," 93 *U. Pa. L. Rev.* 125, 140 (1944); 6A Powell, supra note 20, at sec. 904[1]; but see David Thomas Konig, "Community Custom and the Common Law: Social Change and the Development of Land Law in Seventeenth-Century Massachusetts," 18 *Am. J. Legal Hist.* 137, 143–44 (1974), pointing out the seventeenth-century laxity about deed recordation in Massachusetts.

37. Patton, supra note 35, at 226.

38. See, e.g., Farabee v. McKerrihan, 33 A. 583 (Pa. 1896) (wrong book); Bamberg v. Harrison, 71 S.E. 1086 (S.C. 1911) (instrument misplaced; the case involved an interest in a horse).

39. See, e.g., In re 250 Bell Road, Etc., 388 A.2d 297, 300, n. 3 (Pa. 1978).

40. See, e.g., *Farabee*, 33 A. at 583 (if holder of interest has done all he can, it would be a "hard rule that would deprive him" of interest; citing Glading v. Frick, 88 Pa.St. 460, 464 [1879].

41. See, e.g., Hurst, supra note 6, at 305, discussing the later nineteenth-century Wisconsin "land cruisers" who searched records for unrecorded timberland claims and then purchased them from record owners at nominal prices; Wisconsin courts held that prior unrecorded deeds prevailed over noninnocent record purchaser.

42. For a historical review of equitable intervention, see Doe d. Robinson v. Allsop, 106 Eng. Rep. 1145, 1147 (1821). This case was at law and granted no relief to the nonrecording interest-holder, though it noted the availability of equitable relief. Many British land claims, of course, were not recorded at all.

43. 6A Powell, supra note 20, sec. 905 [1][a].

44. Miller v. Green, 58 N.W.2d 704 (Wis. 1953).

45. First African M. E. Church v. Brown, 17 N.E. 549, 550 (Mass. 1888). A particularly sharp critic of an earlier generation was Francis Philbrick, supra note 36, at 140, who commented that the Massachusetts courts' importation of "notice" into early recording statutes was "the notion by which the Massachusetts judges began the ruin of their own recording system, and that of this country generally." For other problems and reform proposals, see, e.g., Martin Lobel, "A Proposal for a Title Registration System for Realty," 11 *U. Rich. L. Rev.* 501, 505 (1977); John L. McCormack, "Torrens and Recording: Land Title Assurance in the Computer Age," 18 *Wm. Mitchell L. Rev.* 61 (1992).

46. Lobel, supra note 45, at 501–502, 514.

47. For a brief history of Torrens registration, see McCormack, supra note 45, at 70–73; Comment, "Yes, Virginia—There Is a Torrens Statute," 9 *U. Rich. L. Rev.* 301, 302–304 (1975).

48. See, e.g., Baart v. Martin, 108 N.W. 945, 950 (Minn. 1906); Echols v. Olsen, 347 N.E.2d 720 (Ill. 1976). More exceptions, both statutory and judicial, are described in McCormack, supra note 45, at 89–99.

49. See J. G. Davies, "Equity, Notice and Fraud in the Torrens System," 10 *Alberta L. Rev.* 106, 110–16 (1971). There is a comparable blurring phenomenon in another recording reform effort, the marketable title statutes, which attempt to abbreviate the title search by extinguishing long-unasserted claims. See Walter E. Barnett, "Marketable Title Acts—Panacea or Pandemonium?" 53 *Cornell L. Rev.* 45, 53, 67–91 (1967).

50. Holderness, supra note 3, at 322, 324.

51. Douglas G. Baird and Thomas H. Jackson, "Information, Uncertainty and the Transfer of Property," 13 *J. Legal Stud.* 299, 312–18 (1984).

52. See, e.g., James M. Buchanan, "Rent Seeking and Profit Seeking," in James M. Buchanan, Robert D. Tollison, and Gordon Tullock, *Toward a Theory of the Rent-Seeking Society* 8–11 (1980). See also Richard A. Epstein, *Takings* 203 (1985).

53. See Mancur Olson, *The Rise and Decline of Nations* 17–35 (1983).

54. Frank H. Easterbrook, "The Supreme Court 1983 Term—Forward: The Court and the Economic System," 98 *Harv. L. Rev.* 4, 10–11, 19–21 (1984).

55. Id. at 11–12.

56. John Locke, *Second Treatise of Government* sec. 34, at 333, in *Two Treatises of Government* (P. Laslett rev. ed. 1963; 1st ed. 1690).

57. See Duncan Kennedy, "Form and Substance in Private Law Adjudication," 89 *Harv. L. Rev.* 1685, 1710, 1745, 1774 (1976).

58. Id. at 1722, 1742, 1772–74.

59. Easterbrook, supra note 54, at 11–12; he adds that the ex ante judge will "pay less attention to today's unfortunates and more attention to the effects of the rules."

60. Lawrence H. Tribe, "Constitutional Calculus: Equal Justice or Economic Efficiency?" 98 *Harv. L. Rev.* 592–98 (1985); see also Easterbrook's reply, "Method, Result and Authority; A Reply," 98 *Harv. L. Rev.* 622, 627–29 (1985).

61. Kennedy, supra note 57, at 1773.

62. Thomas W. Merrill, "Trespass, Nuisance, and the Costs of Determining Property Rights," 14 *J. Legal Stud.* 13–14, 25–26 (1985).

63. Id. at 25–26, 32–34.

64. P. S. Atiyah, *The Rise and Fall of Freedom of Contract* (1979).

65. Id. at 146–49, 252–53, 272, 281–82, 394–96.

66. P. S. Atiyah, "From Principles to Pragmatism: Changes in the Function of the Judicial Process and the Law" (Oxford Inaugural Lecture), 65 *Iowa L. Rev.* 1249, 1270–71 (1980).

67. Cf. Phillip Roth, *Portnoy's Complaint* 87–88 (Bantam ed. 1970), describing a childhood revelation that the whole point of kosher rules was to establish habits of discipline, precisely so that each child would grow up to be a "tight-ass human being."

68. Hirschman, *Shifting Involvements: Private Interest and Public Action* (1982).

69. Id. at 11, 21, 62, 120.

70. See 6A Powell, supra note 20, at sec. 904[4].

71. See Philbrick, supra note 36, at 171–76, 305–306.

72. Other clarifying devices, such as particularly expressive phrases, can also be treated as a "commons"; for example, the pithiest phrase is the one most likely to become trite through overuse. George Orwell took a rather disaffected view of the trivialization of expressive terms in "Politics and the English Language," in *Collected Essays* 353, 356 (1961), but one must wonder whether the tendency to trivialize might be inevitable.

73. See, e.g., Arthur Allan Leff, "Unconscionability and the Code—The Emperor's New Clause," 115 *U. Pa. L. Rev.* 485, 504 (1967); Ian R. Macneil, "The Many Futures of Contract," 47 *S. Cal. L. Rev.* 691, 783–85, 804–805 (1974).

74. See, e.g., Borgerding Inv. Co. v. Larson, 170 N.W. 2d 322, 327 (Minn. 1969) ("forfeiture" not favored in Minnesota law); Barkis v. Scott, 208 P.2d 367 (Cal.

1949) (statute provides relief against forfeiture); see also Campbell v. Holyland, 7 Ch. D. 166, 173 (1876) (loss of something of special value a factor in mortgage payment extensions); Maxey v. Redevelopment Authority of Racine, 288 N.W.2d 794 (Wis. 1980) (lease provision to be construed so as to avoid forfeiture in eminent domain context).

75. Gordley, "Equality in Exchange," 69 *Cal. L. Rev.* 1587, 1609–12, 1625 (1981).

76. Grady, "Common Law Control of Strategic Behavior: Railroad Sparks and the Farmer," 17 *J. Legal Stud.* 15 (1988).

77. See also Robert Rabin's analysis of the tort law's denial of recovery for negligently inflicted economic loss: potentially huge costs could be levied on relatively minor wrongs, evidently evoking the law's "deep abhorrence to the notion of disproportionate penalties for wrongful behavior." Rabin, "Tort Recovery for Negligently Inflicted Economic Loss: A Reassessment," 37 *Stan. L. Rev.* 1513, 1532–34 (1985).

78. For such "efficient breach," see Richard Posner, *Economic Analysis of Law* 114–15 (3d ed. 1986).

79. See Samuel A. Rea, Jr., "Efficiency Implications of Penalties and Liquidated Damages," 13 *J. Legal Stud.* 147, 160–63 (1984); see also Melvin Aron Eisenberg, "The Bargain Principle and Its Limits," 95 *Harv. L. Rev.* 741, 782–84 (1982), discussing door-to-door sales practices as an effort to find price-ignorant customers and intercept their market search; cf. Ian Ayres and Robert Gertner, "Filling Gaps in Incomplete Contracts: An Economic Theory of Damage Rules," 99 *Yale L. J.* 87, 98–99 (1989), arguing that contract doctrine can induce a better-informed party to reveal information.

80. "Home Repair Fraud Rages," *Chi. Trib.*, Jan. 26, 1986, at 1 (fraudulent home repair contractors fight to get lists naming potential victims, or "mopes").

81. See also Carol M. Rose, "Giving Some Back—A Reprise," in Symposium on Giving, Trading, Thieving, and Trusting, 44 *U. Fla. L. Rev.* 365, 373–75 (1992), discussing the way that the "market for lemons" may undermine confidence in markets generally. The term is from George Ackerlof, "The Market for 'Lemons': Quality, Uncertainty, and the Market Mechanism," 84 *Q. J. Econ.* 488 (1970).

82. Macaulay, "Elegant Models, Empirical Pictures, and the Complexities of Contract," 11 *Law & Soc'y Rev.* 507, 509 (1977).

83. Id. at 509; Stewart Macaulay, "An Empirical View of Contract," 1985 *Wisc. L. Rev.* 467–68. See also Macneil, supra note 73, at 756–57, 804–805.

84. Macaulay, supra note 82, at 514 (giving the example of debt collection).

85. For Macneil, see supra note 73.

86. See Robert Axelrod, *The Evolution of Cooperation* (1984).

87. Thomas Haskell, "Capitalism and the Origins of the Humanitarian Sensibility," 90 *Am. Hist. Rev.* 547, 556 (1984).

88. Id. at 554–55; see also Atiyah, supra note 64, at 139–42, 212–16.

89. Melvin Aron Eisenberg, "Private Ordering Through Negotiation: Dispute-Settlement and Rulemaking," 89 *Harv. L. Rev.* 637, 665 (1976).

90. Jürgen Habermas, "A Review of Gadamer's *Truth and Method*," in *Understanding and Social Inquiry* 335, 336–39, 345–47 (F. R. Dallmayr and T. A. McCarthy eds. 1977).

91. For the efficiency of the common law, see Paul Rubin, "Why Is the Common Law Efficient?" 6 *J. Legal Stud.* 51 (1977); George Priest, "The Common Law Process and the Selection of Efficient Rules," 6 *J. Legal Stud.* 65 (1977).

92. Cf. Jason Scott Johnston, "Uncertainty, Chaos and the Torts Process: An Economic Analysis of Legal Form," 76 *Cornell L. Rev.* 341 (1991). Johnston is one of the few other legal scholars who has examined cyclic patterns; he argues, however, that in tort law, judicial decisions have a cyclic pattern even without legislative action. See id. at 373. Bargain patterns may differ, though, since torts generally deal with accidents rather than conscious structurings.

93. Robert W. Gordon, "Macaulay, Macneil and the Discovery of Solidarity and Power in Contract Law," 1985 *Wis L. Rev.* 565, at 569, 571.

94. Robert Ellickson, "Of Coase and Cattle: Dispute Resolution Among Neighbors in Shasta County," 38 *Stan. L. Rev.* 623, 675–76 (1986). Ellickson draws extensively on this material in *Order Without Law: How Neighbors Settle Disputes* (1991).

95. See Richard A. Epstein, "The Social Consequences of Common Law Rules," 95 *Harv. L. Rev.* 1717, 1742 (1982), arguing that mud rules are apt to have high social costs.

96. For the history, see Atiyah, supra note 64, at 345–50, arguing that legal rhetoric of crystal or "principle" in legal rhetoric began in the Enlightenment period.

97. Among the best known is Locke's argument that the state of nature becomes a dangerous and uncertain state of war, which civil society is formed to avoid. Locke, supra note 56, secs. 21, 123.

98. See the critical view of Macneil, supra note 73, at 801.

99. It is probably not coincidental that Richard Epstein, a well-known proponent of the crystal position, argues that the meaning of language and legal doctrine is stable over time. See Margaret Radin's comment in "Proceedings of the Conference on Takings of Property and the Constitution," 41 *U. Miami L. Rev.* 1, 73 (1986). See also Radin, "The Consequences of Conceptualism," 41 *U. Miami L. Rev.* 239 (1986).

100. Adam Smith, *Lectures on Jurisprudence* 5 (R. L. Meek, D. D. Raphael, and P. G. Stein eds. 1978; originally delivered 1762). Readers might compare this understanding of justice to the idea of justice as equality, discussed earlier in this volume in the essay "'Takings' and the Practices of Property."

101. Kennedy, supra note 57, at 1773; Betty Mensch, "Freedom of Contract as Ideology" (Book Review), 33 *Stan. L. Rev.* 753, 766–67 (1981).

102. James Boyd White, "Thinking About Our Language," 96 *Yale L.J.* 1960–66 (1987); for a critique of the covering law theory of historical interpretation, see 1 Paul Ricoeur, *Time and Narrative* 111–20 (1984).

103. Charles Taylor, "Interpretation and the Sciences of Man," in *Understanding and Social Inquiry* 101, 129 (F. R. Dallmayr and T. A. McCarthy eds. 1977); 1 Ricoeur, supra note 102, at 156–57; see also the essay "Property as Storytelling" earlier in this volume.

104. Albert O. Hirschman, *The Passions and the Interests: Political Arguments for Capitalism Before Its Triumph* 59–63 (1977); cf. Albert O. Hirschman, "Rival Interpretations of Market Society: Civilizing, Destructive, or Feeble?" *J. Econ. Lit.* 20 (1982): 1463, 1464–66. Alexander Hamilton, however, was among the skeptical; see *The Federalist* No. 6, at 56–57 (C. Rossiter ed. 1961).

105. Haskell, supra note 87, at 549–59; cf. David Brion Davis, "Reflections on Abolitionism and Ideological Hegemony," 92 *Am. Hist. Rev.* 797 (1987).

106. See Joanna L. Stratton, *Pioneer Women: Voices from the Kansas Frontier* 116–17 (1981), relating a story about a pioneer woman defending some Indians who had taken refuge in her home, by threatening to shoot the soldiers at the door; Joanne Lipman, "The Holdouts: Owners Who Stay Put Play a Part in Shaping the American Skyline," *Wall St. J.*, May 22, 1984, at 1, concerning one Duffy's Shamrock Pub in Denver, whose owners cheerfully concede that their building is an "eyesore" to the nearby Republic Plaza Tower, meanwhile doing a land-office business.

107. See, e.g., Benjamin Spock, *Raising Children in a Difficult Time* 116–17 (1974).

108. See, e.g., Baird and Jackson, supra note 51, at 314; Easterbrook, supra note 54, at 10–12; Holderness, supra note 3, at 324.

109. See, e.g., U.C.C. secs. 2–206, where an offer is construed to invite acceptance in any reasonable manner.

110. A well-known twentieth-century example is John Rawls, *A Theory of Justice* 11 (1971), constructing a political theory on the choices that would be made by "free and rational persons concerned to further their own interests."

111. Cf. Margaret Jane Radin, "Market-Inalienability," 100 *Harv. L. Rev.* 1849, 1877–81 (1987), on the significance of the rhetoric of "commodification."

8

Women and Property: Gaining and Losing Ground

Introduction

Readers will have noticed how often "we" and "us" and "our" appear in several of the preceding essays, as if "our" society made up its property regimes to serve persons and groups with fundamentally similar goals and convergent interests. Such a cozy scenario! What a pity when it fractures—not all the time, to be sure, but certainly sometimes. In this essay I explore how such fractures may become visible in the ways that different groups of people relate to one another within a given property regime. I concentrate on the ways that differences, or purported differences, among these groups may affect the ways that they bargain, and those bargaining differences in turn may give rise to systematic inequalities in their assets. The focus is on gender relations and their repercussions in property.

A quite common perception about women and property is that women do not have much, at least by comparison to men. Virginia Woolf certainly had this view. Her famous book *A Room of One's Own* repeatedly posed the question, Why are women so poor?[1] Even when women do have formal title to property, men seem to be the ones who initially acquired it and actually control it; and though there are exceptions—even whole societies that are exceptional—they seem to have a rather exotic air, like Amazons or other relatively unfamiliar folk.[2]

In the ordinary course of things, it is a bit surprising to find women of great wealth, just as it is surprising to find women who lead Fortune 500 companies.[3] In contrast, it is hardly news that women are disproportionately represented as heads of household among the poor.[4] Between those extremes of wealth and poverty, women just don't seem to be as "propertied"

The original version of this essay appeared in 78 *Virginia Law Review*, 421–459 (1992). Reprinted by permission of *Virginia Law Review* and Fred B. Rothman & Co.

as men, except insofar as they happen to be located in families that are headed by men. Indeed, even within the household, the serious money has often seemed to be at the disposal of the husband and not the wife.[5]

Why might this be? Why might women be systematically worse off than men when it comes to acquiring and owning property? There are many possible explanations, ranging through theories of exploitation, sociobiology, and historical circumstances, among others. I take an approach somewhat different from those, although some of the ideas from those other approaches will appear here, too.

My plan is to take a few simple ideas from game theory and to explore how women might do systematically worse than men with respect to property, if one makes either of two related assumptions. The first assumption is that women have a greater "taste for cooperation" than men. The second and considerably weaker assumption is that women are merely *perceived* to have a greater taste for cooperation than men, even though that perception may be erroneous. Following the lead of much modern law-and-economics literature, I use examples from both market and nonmarket "economies," and although these examples are largely hypothetical, I expect some will seem quite familiar. Indeed, that is precisely the goal: to see if a small number of assumptions can generate a wide range of familiar examples.

At the outset, I want to stress that I am not arguing that women would be better off in a world without property or without entitlements generally. I think that is wrong. On the contrary, as a general matter, women are better off in a regime in which they and others can acquire property. But I do mean to suggest that in a world of property and entitlements, there may be systematic reasons why women may tend to acquire less property and fewer of those entitlements than men do. Moreover, there may even be some cases in which dealings with entitlements make women worse off in an absolute sense—that is, not just worse off relative to men but worse off than they themselves would have been if such dealings had never taken place. Again, I do not think that this is generally true, but I think that such more or less exceptional cases are nonetheless important enough to explore, and I try to do so in the later sections of the essay. Needless to say, I do not think either of these situations is a desirable state of affairs, either for women in particular or for the larger society of women and men. I hope the reasons are clear by the end of the essay.

I. The Game-Theory Approach

To set the stage, I will discuss two kinds of "games," both of which are now familiar in legal academic circles. The first is the prisoners' dilemma, familiarly known as PD, named for its most famous illustrative story in which two prisoners are induced to rat on each other even though jointly they would be better off if both remained silent. The second has no conventional name, except perhaps the descriptive one of "zero-sum game"; this is a noncooperative game in which the parties vie to win the most of a fixed total payoff.

PD Games

PD games ought to be positive-sum games—that is, games that result in gains from working together—but they have an unfortunate propensity to fail. In such games, two (or more) parties are collectively better off if they cooperate than if each of them "cheats" or "defects," but both (or all) have an incentive to cheat rather than to cooperate.[6] I will not run through the "prisoners' dilemma" story here because it is so familiar but instead use an agrarian version.

Suppose two people, Sam and Louise (and perhaps a number of others) graze cattle on common grounds: they would be better off collectively if each would cooperate and restrain the numbers of their cattle or the intensity of their grazing, so that the field's grasses could replenish themselves. But Sam fears that Louise will cheat if he restrains his cows, so that he will be a patsy while she gets most of the benefit of his self-restraint. On the other hand, even if he thinks she will cooperate, it may occur to him that he himself can gain by cheating while she goes along with the program and restrains her cows. Thus either way—whether Sam thinks that Louise is going to cooperate or to cheat—his own immediate maximizing strategy is to cheat. And by parallel reasoning, so is hers. As a result of these calculations, neither restrains the cows, and they wind up with an overgrazed desert. That is, they reenact the dilemma, or the "tragedy of the commons," as multiple-person PD games are often called.[7]

Overcoming PD Problems—Watching and Mimicking. Luckily, there are some ways around the dilemma or tragedy. One escape route opens up when Sam can see what Louise is doing and vice versa. Sam may start by restraining his own cows, but he will keep an eye on Louise. If Louise does not restrain her cows too, he will just go ahead and let his own munch, which of course gives Louise a good reason to cooperate. Meanwhile, of course, she is keeping an eye on Sam's cows. Their cooperative arrangement is thus enforced by the threat of retaliation—by his threat to do the same thing that she does and by her counterthreat to match his actions.[8] Each keeps the other in line by playing on the fear of losing the gains that they jointly make from cooperation.

It has been noted in game-theory literature—and indeed in the essay "Property and Storytelling" earlier in this volume—that there are some major roadblocks to this escape from the PD. One such roadblock appears because somebody has to start by cooperating, presumably at a point when the players have no history of dealing and no reason to trust each other.[9] Beyond that roadblock is another: the escape only works where there is a sequence of moves or turns, and where each iterated move raises the threat of retaliation if one player cheats. But then the iterated game has a problem at the so-called endgame stage.[10] That is, unless Sam and Louise anticipate an infinite sequence of cooperative steps, there is going to be a last move in their little minuet. As they approach that point they realize that there are no further opportunities for retaliation, so that each has an incentive to cheat just before the last move. Unfortunately, this endgame incentive then infects the second-to-last move, too, where each thinks, "Hmm, I will cheat before he (or she) does." Then the cheating infects the third-to-last move, and so on all the way back to the first move.

With all these problems, one might suppose that cooperative acts would be quite unusual. That is, even where cooperation could make all players collectively better off, the tendency to act as self-interested utility maximizers runs counter to the collective best interest and makes the players more likely to cheat and lose the advantages of cooperation. Prudence dictates that each player let others take the first step—but if all are prudent, none will take that step.

Attitudinal Solutions—A Taste for Cooperation. If we shift gears and move to the real world, as the "Storytelling" essay pointed out, we realize that cooperation is not rare at all. In fact, there is an enormous amount of cooperative behavior in everyday life, in spite of all these supposed theoretical difficulties. In that earlier essay I dubbed the cooperative character "Mom" and noted that according to a feminist psychologist like Carol Gilligan, such characters abound and seem to be willing to put the common good ahead of their own self-interest.[11] There I pointed out too that legal institutions take account of this kind of behavior and to some degree try to encourage it.

But, be it noted once again, from a certain perspective this kind of behavior is not rational. At the very least, the willingness to take that trusting, risky first move—the move that makes further cooperative gains possible—depends on one or both parties' behaving imprudently, acting on something like a taste for cooperation; whatever the story may be behind such a taste, it is not explained by the pure logic of self-interest.[12] By a "taste for cooperation" I mean one or another of those nonrational attitudinal factors—wherever they came from—that enable cooperation to get under way. By using the word "taste," of course, I do not mean to suggest only mild preferences; I also include the deeply felt emotions or convictions. For example, the "taste" may derive from an enjoyment of the process of working with others. Alternatively, the taste might stem from a personal identification with a team or other group that shares a common goal. It is quite common to find the taste in the form of an altruistic enjoyment of, or sense of responsibility for, the well-being of other individuals. An overlapping feature may be simply a matter of scope or intensity: that is, supposing that lots of people have *some* cooperative attitudes, the taste would signify a relatively broad or deep attitude of sociality and/or responsibility for others. As I suggested in "Storytelling," any of these motivations might make up an important part of one's life history, and any of them might lead one to recognize and act in the furtherance of a shared "good" or the good of another, even at some risk to one's purely personal interest.[13]

Conversely, noncooperative attitudes may also take several different forms. Most common, no doubt, is mere "rational" indifference to others or to common interests, or the merely prudent unwillingness to risk personal loss in taking first steps toward forming or maintaining associations. This is the behavior of the "homo oeconomicus," whom I described in "Storytelling" as John Doe. An intermediate form of noncooperation involves a limited range or scope for cooperation. For example, the noncooperator may be willing to cooperate only on a limited basis, or with some classes of persons but not with others.[14] The most extreme form of noncooperation is malice or hostility—a willingness to take actions that alienate or hurt others, such as punishment or cruelty. This type of noncooperator is the reverse altruist: he does indeed care about the well-being of others, but negatively.[15]

In real life we do find considerable taste for cooperation—and we also see some noncooperative attitudinal factors. Although the former facilitates utility-maximizing cooperation, the latter may hinder such cooperation, particularly at the outset of dealings, when some trusting move has to be made. On the conventional supposition that rationality means indifference to others, however, the helpful attitudes are irrational (nonindifferent/helping), whereas the unhelpful ones may be either rational (indifferent) or irrational (nonindifferent/hostile).

The Zero-Sum Game

All this discussion about cooperative moves and their difficulties and solutions brings me to a brief mention of the second game—the zero-sum game. This game is not about gaining through cooperation but rather about parcelling out a fixed sum. In spite of the difference, though, this game does have a bearing on potentially positive-sum games like the PD, in which there could be gains from acting in concert.

Suppose that our two parties, Sam and Louise, do agree in principle to cooperate on restraining their cows' use of the grazing field. Collectively, the two of them will be better off by some amount, which I will call X.

They now have a self-renewing grassy field that is worth X dollars more than it would have been if they rushed in to fatten up Bossy and Sadie to the maximum and left a wasteland behind.

But how are Sam and Louise going to split that gain of X dollars? The point here is that even if Sam and Louise do see the advantage of a cooperative deal, they still have to decide how to split those X proceeds, and every part of X that Sam gets is at Louise's expense, and vice versa. They are faced, in short, with a little zero-sum game inside the bigger positive-sum game. Indeed, unless someone gives on the zero-sum game, they may be unable to solve the larger positive-sum game.

II. The Two Games Applied—Gaining and Losing Relatively

How can we apply these two games—the potentially positive-sum and the zero-sum game—to explain the relative property acquisitions of Sam and Louise? One way to think about this is to focus on the taste for cooperation. In the discussion that follows, I am going to suppose that the taste for cooperation is unevenly distributed between the genders and that women have this taste more strongly than men do.

I will not try to prove that such a gender difference actually exists, although there are a variety of anecdotal materials to suggest that this may be the case—for example, the reports that daughters rather than sons normally take care of aging parents;[16] or that sisters are the ones who establish and maintain stronger sibling ties;[17] or that under experimental conditions, women may overcome bargaining problems more readily than men;[18] or, looking at the matter from the angle of the scope of cooperative tastes, that little girls are interested in all kinds of television celebrities, whereas little boys will only watch boys or men.[19] The idea, of course, is also stated—and vigorously debated—in feminist literature, where some argue that women are more concerned with relationships than men are.[20]

My own assumption on the matter is only hypothetical and indeed heuristic, but I also want to note that even in this hypothetical form, the assumption is *not* that all women are cooperators and no men are. Although I will continue to talk about Sam and Louise in a generic sense, the assumption can coexist with lots of wonderfully cooperative Sams and stubbornly recalcitrant Louises. The only assumption is that women, taken as a group, are more likely to make cooperative moves than men are, taken as a group. It is only a matter of degree between groups and says nothing about individuals.

Nevertheless, even this generic mode is quite a strong assumption, and at certain points of the essay I will relax it substantially. At those points I will instead ask how things would look if women were merely *thought* to have a more highly developed taste for cooperation. But I will ask the readers to go along with the stronger assumption at the outset—that Louise really is more cooperative than Sam—because an initial run-through on that basis makes it considerably easier to clarify the alternative story, the one in which assumptions of difference are very much relaxed.

Louise Loses Ground Relatively

Sam and Louise Strike a Deal. If we suppose that Louise has a greater taste for cooperation than Sam does, we can predict some things about their dealings. We can predict, for one thing, that it will be easier for Sam and Louise to arrive at a cooperative use of the grazing field than it would have been for, say, Sam and Tom. This means that Louise's taste for cooperation aids in the creation of the agreement that produces collective gains. In addition, we can predict that Louise will be better off than she used to be before she and Sam decided to cooperate. But alas, we can also predict that she will not be *as much* better off as Sam. She will wind up with the short side of the split of the proceeds.

Why is this so?

Well, at the outset, Louise has to offer Sam more to get him to cooperate. He may not even notice that cooperative arrangements are beneficial, and he certainly won't take any first steps to get them started—he puts his own safety before a cooperative deal. And since a cooperative deal does not rank as high in Sam's priorities as in Louise's, he can insist that he take a disproportionate amount of the proceeds, so that, in the now familiar example, he gets to run more cows than Louise does.

Louise, of course, is just the reverse. She is quicker to see the mutual benefits of cooperation, she likes such cooperative relationships more than he, or she is at least more willing to take responsibility for getting such arrangements off the ground. Those traits, however, mean that she may accept a deal even though she pays a higher price for it. Sam thus gains a bargaining advantage, just as he would with anyone who was more anxious than he is for the deal or had a "higher discount rate" about it.[21] When Sam knows that Louise is the more eager player, he can offer her less favorable terms right from the start. That is, when the two of them successfully play the larger cooperative game, Sam has an advantage in the smaller zero-sum game of splitting the proceeds.

This asymmetry continues into the course of the deal. Indeed, it may not even begin until later, when the pattern of dealings has got under way. At those later points when, for example, some contribution has to be made to the upkeep of the field, Sam may have an advantage as well, and he may get Louise to pay for more of the field's routine maintenance. This is because he can make a more credible threat than Louise can to scotch the whole arrangement.[22] And in general, he is the better enforcer of the ongoing arrangement—he can be quite demanding about making her stick to the letter of the deal, while she may put up with more shirking on his part and wind up doing part of what she initially thought would be his chores. All this happens because she is more committed to maintaining deals than he is or because she may feel a greater responsibility to him than he does to her.

Notice that Louise is not losing absolutely here; she too is getting some portion of the X amount that they jointly gain from their arrangement. She is only losing ground relatively to Sam, because she contributes more to the deal. Sam on the other hand can contribute less to the deal and walk away with the larger portion of the gains from dealing.

Now, let us leave the arena of cow-field bargaining and see how the larger world of entitlements spins out the negotiating patterns between Sam and Louise.

The Nonmarket "Economy" of Domestic Relations. Insofar as material goods are concerned, it is probably reasonably safe to assume that Sam and Louise are better off married (or at least living together) than they would be if each maintained a separate residence. The theory here is that two may live more cheaply than one or, more accurately, than two "ones," so that there are gains to be made from living in a common household.

But from Sam and Louise's bargaining pattern, we can predict that Louise is going to have to do more to keep the household together. In particular, she (like wives generally) will be stuck doing the bulk of the housework.[23] She is the one with the taste for commonality, whereas he can bide his time until he gets a favorable offer on the household work front. Moreover, he can make a more credible threat of withdrawing from the household unless she keeps his shirts ironed. We may think he is a lout for doing so—indeed he probably is a lout—but that is not the point. The point is that if her desire or sense of responsibility for cooperative arrangements is stronger than his, he can cut a deal in which he gets the lion's share of their joint gains.[24]

One might well think that Louise would rather share the household with someone other than Sam or find some more cooperative Sam, and no doubt many Louises do feel this way. Can Louise do anything about it—say, find a different domestic partner or organize her domestic affairs differently? Well, yes; but it is tricky to do so within conventional notions about sexuality and family.[25] Quite aside from any difficulties associated with single-sex relationships, monogamous marriage itself has a bearing on Louise's problem. Whatever the attractions of monogamy (and they are no doubt many), the institution does mean that each monogamous domestic unit places an individual Louise with an individual Sam; if enough such units are formed, and if the taste for cooperation is indeed unevenly distributed between the genders, then some cooperative Louises are going to get stuck with loutish Sams. Indeed, even though they phrased it somewhat differently, some nineteenth-century Mormons thought that the Sams' greater propensity for loutishness was a pretty good reason for plural marriage, where the more cooperative Sams got lots of wives and the less cooperative ones presumably got none.[26]

Short of divorce, then—that is, giving up on a common household—there is little Louise can do to extricate herself from this regrettable state of affairs, at least within traditional notions of domestic relations. Besides, divorce negotiations themselves may only replicate the bargaining disadvantage that Louise has in marriage.[27]

The Employment World. Employment relationships are another positive-sum game, rather like domestic relations—perhaps too much like domestic relations, in fact. In any event, the employer presumably values labor more than the wages he or she has to pay to get it, whereas the employee puts a higher value on the wage dollars than on the leisure that he or she would otherwise enjoy. And so both employer and employee benefit from the exchange of dollars for labor.

The next question is, How do they split the gains they jointly make from the positive-sum game? Well, in general, the employer might offer a man a greater portion of those gains. Sam has less taste for cooperation than Louise does and more tolerance for confrontation. Sam can thus make a more credible threat that he will walk away from a potential job or quit an actual one.

On the other hand, the employer might offer a woman a relatively smaller share of the collective gains made from their labor-wage trade. The employer can rely on her taste for cooperation—that is, that she will "give" something to be assured that a cooperative relationship will take place or (perhaps a more likely scenario) to be sure that she can take care of others for whom she feels responsible.[28] Indeed, if Louise is skittish, the employer might offer her the same wage he offers Sam at the outset, in order to bring her into a relationship; but then he might give her relatively few promotions and raises as time goes by. He can rely on the attachments she makes to weaken her bargaining power over time.[29]

Now, one would think that the rational employer would hire a great number of Louises instead of Sams, since Louises cost less, and that if enough employers took this rational course, their bids would raise the price for Louise's labor until it equalled Sam's.[30] And indeed, sometimes employers do hire a lot of Louises, when there are a lot of Louises around, as in the famous example of Lowell, Massachusetts, where great numbers of young women were hired to work in the mills for low wages in the 1820s and 1830s.[31] Similarly, immigrant laborers sometimes have been hired in large numbers at low wages, raising the point that a taste for cooperation sometimes has a more than incidental likeness to a dearth of alternatives.[32] I will return to that subject, but for now the point to note is that both conditions—the taste for cooperation and the lack of alternatives—make the potential employee desire the job more urgently, and this means that the employer can do relatively well in wage bargains with such persons.

But by the same token, one would expect these laborers both to crowd out other laborers and eventually to rise in cost, as employers bid for their services. Why, then, do employers hire so many Sams instead, at relatively high costs? One reason is that the employer may need to hire some persons with characteristics conventionally associated with Sam instead of Louise—perhaps physical strength or perhaps the image of toughness and willingness to punish. This may make the employer think he needs to hire Sams, even though he knows the Sams are going to demand more of the gains from trade. Note that other employees' skills may be worth just as much to the employer, but the employer doesn't have to pay as much for them because they can be bought from Louise, who is not so demanding.

In any event, if the employer does try to hire more Louises, and if their asking price does increase as a result, he may then start to bid for the relatively higher-priced Sams too. Another factor then enters, that is, the Sams themselves. Sams who get hired are not without *some* taste for cooperation, and they may be able to hold together and credibly threaten to quit if they have to compete for jobs against Louises. Some of the Sams may be of the more or less hostile variety, and they may happily punish interloping Louises.[33] One might expect similar retaliatory measures against any other "undesirables" whose urgent needs lead them to accept low wages, and even against the more cooperative Sams who agree to work with the Louises and the others. Insofar as the employer needs Sams, a pattern of retaliation among them may encourage the employer to segregate the Sams and Louises into the high-paying and low-paying jobs, respectively. Why should an employer pay Louise as much as he pays Sam to operate a forklift when she can be hired as a secretary so much more cheaply and with so many fewer hassles? Note that the employer may need secretaries as much as forklift operators, but he cannot hire Sam as a secretary at all, at least not at the wages he is paying secretaries; and he cannot hire Louise as a forklift operator either, because the Sams may either hound her out or quit en masse.

This pattern of segregation does not always happen, but it does happen rather often.[34] Note that the pattern touches on issues of "comparable worth," that is, the attempt to classify and pay sex-segregated jobs according to skill levels rather than the levels arrived at through bargaining. This is of course a large and difficult area with many complicated subissues—not the least of which is whether comparable worth payments might lessen actual job opportunities for women.[35] And there are real questions of "comparability," too. For example, insofar as Sam is perceived as "tough" and Louise is not, an employer may think that personnel struggles may be avoided if he promotes Sam instead of Louise to the foreman's job, particularly if there are a lot of working-stiff Sams who would not cooperate with a Louise-foreman or who would challenge any foreman perceived to be a softie. Nevertheless, one way to approach the subject might be to consider whether the comparable worth problem might have something to do with Louise's taste for cooperation and the possibility that it exceeds Sam's—and whether it is that taste, rather than some lesser value of her employment to the employer, that results in her lower levels of pay and slower rates of promotion.

Could Louise look for another employer, for example, another Louise? Well, as with domestic arrangements, again the answer is a qualified yes. The fact is, some Louises do become employers. Why not more? Well, if a Louise is generally likely to have experiences that lower her earning power, this pattern will typically undercut her ability to raise capital and become an employer herself. Louise's capital-raising potential is a subject to which I will return, but preliminarily, if it is true that she runs behind in this area, there will not be very many Louise-employers to offer jobs to Louise-employees.[36]

Tastes and Deals in the Bigger Picture. It is important to notice that Louise's taste for cooperation is not a *bad* taste, from the point of view of the world at large. In fact, everyone is much better off if people have such a taste, because otherwise it would be much harder to start and sustain cooperative arrangements, and everyone would find it harder to work together and enjoy the added benefits that joint efforts bring.

Moreover, the taste for cooperation is not a bad taste even for the individuals who have it, so long as they are dealing with other individuals who share the taste. Business news of the last generation has given us what is no doubt an unrealistically rosy example of the Japanese, where the men all seem to act like Louises, at least with respect to each other.[37] According to the somewhat anxious stereotypes of the remaining industrialized world, the Japanese seem to have a marked taste for cooperation and for putting the interests of the collectivity first—a taste that appears to have resulted in an enormous increase in their collective wealth.

Nor, finally, is a taste for cooperation simply a bad thing among those who have it, even if they are dealing with others who do not share it equally. The cooperators do get something out of the deals they make, even if they do not get as much as others who are less eager to work collectively.

So in short, a taste for cooperation isn't at all a bad thing. It just happens to lead to a relative losing strategy in a world where one's trading partners do not share the taste. Louise's situation thus suggests a very important point: that successful cooperative ventures, taken over a broad range of partners, require both cooperative and noncooperative traits or tastes. The success of the "tit-for-tat" strategy has become almost a cliché in the game-theory literature,[38] and this strategy entails *both* a willingness to cooperate, in order to get things under way, *and* a willingness to exit or even retaliate to protect against noncooperation.

The characteristic flaw of those with a taste for cooperating, but not for retaliating, may be vulnerability to exploitation by noncooperators; and this may explain some of Louise's travails. But the noncooperators, even the merely prudent and indifferent noncooperators, have a characteristic flaw too, and in a way it is a good deal more serious: they may be unable to get things going in the first place, or perhaps even to imagine how a cooperative solution might occur.[39] This is not a trivial matter, since a systematic failure of this sort could dramatically constrict the social gains available through cooperative ventures.[40]

I will return to the importance of making cooperation safe for cooperators, but before doing so I want to move to a somewhat different question: what happens when we weaken the assumption that women actually have a greater taste for cooperation? The answer is that we may arrive at very much the same relationship between Sam and Louise—if we assume, instead of an actual taste difference, a certain set of cultural beliefs about men and women.

Losing Ground Relatively, Reconsidered—The Culture Version

It may not matter very much that any difference actually exists between Sam and Louise's taste for cooperation. What may matter is that people *think* it exists. Indeed, widespread belief patterns about her "taste" may matter more than her actually having it. An earlier passage, for example, described the employer who capitalizes on Louise's taste for cooperation by offering her a low percentage of their mutual gains from their employment relationship. But attentive readers may have noted that the employer believed in advance that Louise was likely to take such an offer, perhaps thinking that she likes or feels responsible for cooperating.

Suppose that she has no such taste and she refuses to take such a low cut. Given a sufficiently widespread cultural presumption that women have a greater taste for cooperation than men, the employer will continue to make low bids for women for some time before he changes his mind. And he may not get around to changing his mind, because at least some Louises will take his low offer, making him think he was right about Louises all along.[41]

Indeed, in a sense, he may be right. Louise herself knows about this set of beliefs and cannot easily challenge them. If she thinks that she is only going to face another low bid from Employer B, she may well just go ahead and accept Employer A's offer. The Louise who insists on something better might well not get a job at all, given a widespread set of beliefs about what her wage demands should be. It will cost her something to try to break the stereotype. So why should she be the one to stick her neck out, particularly when it looks hopeless anyway? This set of beliefs, in short, presents Louise with a collective action problem, and her failure to solve that problem only reinforces the belief system.[42]

The employer's offer to Sam, on the other hand, will be higher, on the assumption that Sam will demand a higher percentage of the gains from the employment relationship. Note that this assumption can be quite false for any given Sam. A particular Sam might well have accepted a job for lower pay, but given the employer's beliefs and given that dickering over wages takes time and money, Sam won't even be challenged with a low offer. Hence here too, the actions the employer takes, on the basis of even weakly held beliefs, may wind up reinforcing those very beliefs.[43]

A similar tale can be told of physical threats to women. Suppose people generally think that women are weaker than men, and suppose some people pick on weaker persons. A particular woman may in fact be very strong, but she will have to prove it constantly if she goes to places where others think that the weak are fair game. A man in the same place actually may be weaker than she, but he will not be challenged, or not challenged so often, because it is assumed that he can retaliate even if he cannot. The upshot is that a man may be more likely to think he can roam where he chooses, whenever he wishes; while a woman, even a strong one, may grow weary of the constant challenges and simply stay at home. By doing so, of course, she reinforces the very stereotype that disadvantages her.

One can also think of domestic examples of this kind of belief-reinforcing phenomenon. Husband Sam may assume that wife Louise is going to cook and do the dishes as well, but when he is out with his hunting buddies, he will split the campground chores. Louise faces the prospect of a scene if she refuses, whereas Sam's hunting buddies do not even encounter a request. Sam assumes that they will only "play the game" on even terms. Between Louise, who has to face the scene of Sam's yelling at her, and Sam's friends, who face no such scene, Louise is doubtless more likely to give in and do a major chunk of the housekeeping. This of course reinforces Sam's belief that he can shirk with Louise but not with his hunting pals.

Cumulative Effects

The effect of all this is that Louise falls relatively behind Sam, whether she actually has a taste for cooperation or is just *thought* to have it. We should note the snowball effect of this pattern, too, because this is where things can get really serious.

Let us now make a quick move to the world of finance. Once again, recall that Louise does get something from her various cooperative relationships with Sam, but not as much as Sam does. This means that by comparison to Sam, Louise acquires relatively few assets, and this means that she is a riskier investment prospect. As a consequence, she has to pay higher interest or otherwise bear relatively unfavorable terms.[44] Not only might the bank look to Louise's relatively low assets in setting these terms, but it also might assume that she will be insufficiently quick to retaliate against the uncooperative Sams of the business world and hence may risk business losses that Sam would not. From the bank's point of view, she is a riskier proposition than Sam, and so she is going to have to pay more to get capital. This means that it is more difficult for Louise to be financially independent.

Business loans, of course, are not the only investments that might be made in Sam or Louise. Though the turn of phrase may sometimes seem odd, it is now fairly widely recognized that one can see certain kinds of expenditures as investments in "human capital."[45] Education and training are the most notable items under this rubric, and nutrition and health-related expenditures might be candidates as well. Quite aside from the pleasure that such investments may bring, both to giver and receiver, they can also be cast in quite hard-nosed business terms, just like any other investments. That is, they are expected to enhance future income by some amount greater than the investment expenditures themselves.

With respect to these "human capital" investments too, Louise may fall behind. Potential investors (such as parents) may be less willing to pay for her education, on the ground that she is going to get suckered too often in dealing with the Sams and the investment in her just won't pay off. Better to put their money in Sam's education, they think: he will protect himself (and their investment) by ready retaliation. In fact, the general belief in Sam's readiness to retaliate means that he may never even be faced with the unpleasant prospect of having to do so. By contrast, Louise will be challenged at every step, and she is bound to slip sometimes. And so at every turn, the better bet seems to be to invest in Sam—in his business, in his education, in his health and nutrition too, and in whatever other projects for which he needs capital, whether financial or "human."[46]

In these investment decisions, Louise's second-fiddle status starts to hurt her exponentially. This is where her taste for cooperation—or the mere belief in her cooperative taste—really begins to limit her possibilities. And this is where we especially notice that her apparent taste for cooperation is really the same thing as her relative lack of alternatives—she gives in because there is not much else she can do. Investment could have made her more independent, but she is competing for investment resources against Sam, who looks like a better bet. Hence Louise is looking more and more stuck: her willingness to take the short end of the stick—or, more accurately, the belief in her willingness to do so—ultimately puts up a barrier to her independence and limits her alternatives. That is, the belief that she will stand back and make sacrifices for others finally may mean that she has little choice but to do so, whatever her real taste may be.

Now, this is a rather bleak place to shift to a new story, but things are going to get bleaker, at least for a time.

III. Disinvesting, or Losing Ground Absolutely

The problem of falling behind *absolutely*—that is, not just a tale of Louise getting fewer of the gains from trade than Sam but rather of losing the assets she had before the "game" started—initially made me think that game theory might have some application in the analysis of Louise's cooperative moves. In particular, the problem that set me thinking was that of battered women and of their battered or murdered children. Their plight presents itself all too often in horrifying stories about women who seem to have bargained away all assets, literal and figurative.[47] It hardly seems plausible that such ghastly scenarios could happen all of a sudden. Rather, they seem much more likely to unfold over time in a dreadful sequence, where the woman adopts some losing strategy vis-à-vis her partner's "game" and where each move leaves her worse off than she was before.

Do women get into such scenarios in disproportionate numbers? And if they do, can one analyze these scenarios on the assumption of an unevenly distributed taste for cooperation? I think one can, but once again, there is a version with a strong assumption and a second version with a weaker assumption. The strong version postulates that women do indeed have a greater taste for cooperation than men. The weaker version is cultural—that they are *thought* to have such a taste—but though "weaker," this version is, if anything, even more devastating to Louise's prospects and aspirations.

Disinvesting in Assets, Literally and Figuratively

Let us begin by picking up the subject just left, namely, investment. With conventional assets, such as actual income-producing property, if you do not continue to invest you may find the asset losing ground, compared to the assets of others—your manufacturing plant may decline, relatively speaking, if owners of other plants are plowing more funds back into retooling. But there is more to the story than that. In the case of a farm or a factory, you may need to make continuing investments just to keep the asset in good working condition; if you never reinvest at all, your asset will eventually become less productive than it once was, and you are simply treating it as a wasting asset. This can be a sensible decision, of course, when repair and revamping costs are too high relative to expected future gains. But sensible or not, if you decide in effect to consume your assets now by simply failing to keep them in repair, you may have a higher current income from them, but the cost will be paid later, in the form of lower future income. Over time your farm or factory will decline in value, relative not just to other farms or factories but also to what your own farm or factory itself used to earn. This is one result from having a high "discount rate"—you consume lots now, but you have less to work with later.

One can say much the same about "human capital." Suppose your only assets are your body and mind and their ability to labor. Even here you need to "invest" over a very short run, for example, in food, so that you can work later on in the day. Over a longer period you need to invest in your health so that you can continue to work, and in your education and training so that you can keep up with changing needs for labor. If you do not make these investments—if your discount rate is too high and you spend too much on other things right now—you are effectively disinvesting, albeit gradually. You are treating your abilities as if they are wasting assets, and your greater consumption today comes at the cost of lesser wealth tomorrow.

Now, how does a taste for cooperation relate to this sort of disinvestment? To start with something already discussed, we know that *non*cooperation can bring about disinvestment, especially in a jointly held asset. This disinvestment, of course, is what the "tragedy of the commons" is all about. The "tragedy" revolves about assets that are available to a number of persons who need to cooperate by investing positively (e.g., by buying fertilizer) or by restraining practices that disinvest through overuse (e.g., overgrazing). If the partners can't cooperate on investing or restraining disinvestment, the common asset effectively wastes away.

In the case of the "tragedy," the disinvestment is in a common good. Too *much* cooperation might also waste common goods, as in the adage about "too many cooks."[48] But Louise's problem is the disinvestment that comes with *asymmetrical* cooperation—either she cooperates too much or he too little—and here the disinvestment is likely to be in the assets of only *one* of the partners, namely, the more cooperative one. That is, if Louise cooperates too much, she might get into a pattern of decisions whereby, step by step, she loses the assets that she had at the outset.[49]

Louise Disinvests

One important reason why our friend Louise may get into such seemingly self-destructive patterns is that her cooperative tastes create "hostages"—persons or things that Sam can use as leverage in bargaining with Louise, because he has some control over them even though she values them more than he does. These hostages put her at risk. One type of hostage is a relationship itself, which may matter more to Louise than it does to Sam. Perhaps this is because Louise is one of those "women who love too much" and becomes "overinvested" (as we sometimes say) in sticking to some nogoodnik; or perhaps it is because Louise, trusting soul that she is, has given up more for the relationship at the outset than Sam has and hence has more to lose from its collapse.[50] For Louise, either circumstance means that something that matters very much to her is controlled by another.

Then too, the hostages in question may be children or other people that Louise is worried about—elderly parents or other relatives or an ailing spouse or friend. Louise is disproportionately burdened by such hostages if she does have a greater taste than Sam for commonality and the responsibilities entailed by commonality; since she cares about these persons or at least feels responsible for them, she cannot make as credible a threat as Sam's that she will abandon existing relationships. She believes the feckless Sam when he says he won't take care of Mom or the kids, and so she is the only one left to take on the necessary efforts.[51]

Thus children (or other hostages for whom Louise feels responsible) are a negative factor in Louise's ability to make rational investment choices. The needs of hostages make her even more anxious to have current income, even if this means a job with low wages and killing hours; or those needs may induce her to bargain away personal relationships or her own aspirations just so that she can continue to persuade a higher-wage spouse to help her support the children. In these ways, Louise's sense of responsibility to others translates into a higher discount rate: she requires *more now* to take care of others, even if the cost is disinvestment in her own abilities, her personal well-being, or even respect in the community.[52] For her, the price tag of losing the kids or seeing them suffer is even greater than the price she will pay later in life for being poor, ill-trained, and perhaps sick and friendless.

Louise might be a better bargainer and make better investment decisions if she didn't have the kids, but she can't stand the thought of losing them, and everyone knows it. She cannot make a credible threat to give them up or stop caring for them. Her high discount rate is obvious to all, and her bargaining position is thereby weakened vis-à-vis those who might wish to take advantage of her.[53] And so she gives in, takes the job, and maybe moonlights too, and she may even "spend" more of her assets than she takes in. That is, she spends the assets she has in her bodily health and social contacts, and she does nothing to retool her skills. She is treating what she has as a wasting asset. She is losing ground.

It is in this sense that Louise's hostages can do her in: they make her vulnerable to third parties. In the larger bargaining world of commerce and employment, the relevant third parties have no direct control over any hostages that Louise gives up; hostages are simply a factor that others can use, more or less abstractly, for greater bargaining leverage with Louise. Although such parties may exploit this bargaining advantage as they would any other, they may not know or care that Louise is treating herself as a wasting asset.

Domestically, the story may be very different. At home, the hostages Louise gives up may be in the direct control of another, and they make her an object of purposeful abuse—a steady assault on the assets that could enable her to act independently. Threats to her children and to her own body may lead her, over time, to bargain away her own sources of income, her contacts with friends and family, and ultimately the independent judgment that such contacts would provide her. This is how one may read a book like Linda Gordon's *Heroes of Their Own Lives,* which describes battered women of the turn of the century; they regarded themselves as taking abuse to protect their children.[54] This may be what is happening as well in the particularly poignant modern example of immigrant women whose residency status depends on their husbands: some appear to accept battering in order to avoid the breakup of their families and the threatened loss of contact with their children.[55]

And so, since hostages may subject Louise to the control of a third party, they eventually may make her lose control of whatever assets she had at the outset of "bargaining." Through threats to these hostages, most notably to her children, she can be punished radically for noncooperation; but though she may cooperate to stave off the threats to hostages, she herself loses ground each time she does so. She may still bargain, but now she is no longer bargaining to get some part—even a relatively small part—of a positive joint good; she is bargaining at each step to keep from losing even more of what she has, and losing that even faster.

It is not clear what Sam gains by a steadily increasing domination over her, and for the record Sam certainly seems like the crazy person in the duo. The prevalence of spousal abuse suggests that for some, the domination over others carries some perverse payoffs and may satisfy a kind of anticooperative or malicious taste like spite or envy—in itself suggesting a kind of dependency on the part of the abuser, even if lethal for its victims.[56] It is not surprising that our law often disfavors motives of this sort when they are discernible and, for example, enjoins the "spite fences" sometimes built by feuding neighbors.[57] On the whole, actions taken from motives of jealousy and spite make us collectively worse off and waste resources in the doubly wasteful end of destroying other people's resources. But in domestic relations, the law's slow pace has left Louise pretty much on her own to deal with an abusive Sam.[58]

And so Louise may deal with Sam by cooperating, which under the circumstances may not be an irrational thing to do. In cooperating with an abuser—say, in agreeing to give up a job or stop seeing family and friends—she is retreating and losing ground, in the sense of losing the assets that might make her independent in the future. But she is also cutting her short-term losses. At each step she deflects some drastic punishment in the present by cooperating and "spending" some further portion of her assets, whether those assets are financial or social, physical or psychological. With each loss of assets, of course, she weakens her bargaining position for the next move, where she begins from a more isolated and more desperately needy position. Given a sufficiently demanding partner, we can predict that ultimately Louise faces the prospect of complete disinvestment, losing even the figurative assets of social alliances with others or perhaps (more controversially) psychological independence[59] or the hostages she was attempting to protect or ultimately even her own life. Perhaps not surprisingly, our law recently has had to deal with some women's turn to violence to stave off that final retreat.[60]

Now, this is an extremely grim scenario. It presumes not only that Louise is burdened by her concern for some form of hostage but also that Sam has a taste for domination that is not frequently encountered—or at least not noticed—in everyday experience. All the same, it is not an entirely unrecognizable scenario. Quite the contrary, it is all too recognizable, not only in the worst and most extortionist relationships between men and women but in the worst and most extortionist relationships between anybody and anybody else, relationships that we think of as occurring in conditions of kidnap, enslavement, and the most lawless forms of imprisonment.

Disinvesting Reconsidered—The Version of Culture and Politics

So far I have been speaking of Louise's disinvestment as a result of an actual taste for cooperation. I have been supposing that this taste reinforces, and is reinforced by, her concern for hostages—a concern that may induce her to enter into dealings in which, step by step, she effectively sacrifices her assets of all kinds.

Another way to look at her disinvestment is to make only a weak assumption—to assume not that Louise actually has a taste for cooperation, from which she derives a concern about hostages, but simply that many people share a cultural belief that she has or should have this taste. Perhaps Louise has no use for cooperation and feels no responsibility for others at all; perhaps she does not have children; perhaps she acquires nothing else that could be treated as a hostage; perhaps she is in general a very cool and calculating character.

All the same, the cultural expectations that she will or should cooperate may mean that others will punish her if she does not. How do they do so? The easy forms of punishment are gossip about her or charges that she is unpleasant or peculiar. More importantly, she may face social isolation and refusals to deal with her on an equal basis (or perhaps on any basis at all); and those persons who do deal with her may face similar punishment from third parties, again in the form of gossip and ostracism.

A more formal way that these cultural expectations may result in her disempowerment once again has to do with a kind of investment, namely, political investment. Let us suppose for the moment that Louise gives up no hostages that put her at risk and that she is not losing ground but is only gaining somewhat less from her dealings than Sam is from his. Even on that relatively mild supposition, if the Louises of the world acquire fewer assets than the Sams, they are not likely to have the political influence that the Sams have, because they cannot make the same investment in politics that the Sams can. By the way, they cannot make the same investment in influencing culture either, even when the culture is about "what women are like" or "what women think," subjects on which, as Virginia Woolf noted, men have had a great deal to say.[61] Although I think this is an extremely important subject, I will say more about the political example, which in a way may only augment a cultural regime.

If Louise does not have the assets to make substantial investments to influence either culture or politics, then in the political arena, the cultural expectations about her may turn into legal demands that she cooperate. Those legal demands may take the form of denying her the ability to live independently or to make alliances with others who might cooperate with her on a more equal basis. The law may deny her the capacity to own her own property, to be employed outside the home, to contract on her own, to get an education, or to form associations outside her father's or her husband's family. By the same token, they may give her no recourse against her father's or husband's discipline.[62]

Such laws may mean that Louise has very few alternatives to a prescribed role. They dramatically increase the cost of Louise's noncooperation in her prescribed role, since they mean that she can be punished much more radically; at their most stringent such laws help to keep Louise in a permanent state of subordination. As a child, she may be expected to undergo such "disinvestments" as crippling physical mutilation or—a more likely scenario—inadequate nutrition.[63] As an adult, her most likely role is to marry into a subservient position in her husband's family. If she does not cooperate with her husband, she may be cast out, and of course there is nothing "out there" for her. No matter how much she may hate cooperation, particularly with husband Sam, she cannot make a credible threat of noncooperation. Indeed, she cannot convince anyone else to assist her to escape; it is dangerous for another party to help her or deal with her in any way, and no one believes she can make it anyway.[64] If she is not playing this game, she is dead, because there is no other game for her to play. And of course, even if she is playing this game, she may be dead too, over a slightly longer run.[65]

In a sense, Louise has become a hostage herself. She has no control over her own efforts and cannot turn them into assets independently of Sam, and she has no alternatives to his control. Given a sufficiently domineering Sam, she may be faced with the downhill moves of the losing game in which she can only cut her losses at each step, preferring the temporarily lesser damage that comes from giving Sam what he wants, to the immediate drastic punishment that he and others will inflict on her for defiance.

Obviously, a woman in this position is in a situation comparable to slavery. In slavery, too, defiance is punished and made even less palatable than cooperation; in slavery, too, there may be no game superior to cooperating with an owner's demands—even though cooperating with a master's wishes may be self-disinvesting for the slave.[66] And in slavery, too, potential helpers of slaves may be policed, so that, for example, none of the enslaved class members may be emancipated, for fear that the presence of the emancipated may make it more difficult to control those still enslaved.[67]

In slavery as well, of course, a potent way to enforce cooperation is to deny the slave the ability to own property and to contract on his or her own. Not all slavery systems have had these disabilities, and where slaves have been entitled to own property, however difficult their position, at least some have been able to purchase their freedom.[68] But where the slave—like the subordinated wife—cannot own property, he or she cannot make an exit even from a losing game with the master, because the property-less slave has no alternative games. The person who cannot own property can have no assets; and the person who has no assets has nothing to bargain with, except perhaps bodily integrity, attachments to friends and family, and ultimately independence of spirit.

It has often been noted that the slave's status is that of a person who is also an object of property.[69] Perhaps less remarked is the slave's status as a person who owns no property and can have no assets. As John Locke noted, however, this person is one and the same.[70]

IV. Some Lessons for Louise (and Sam Too)

At the outset of this essay, I noted that women are better off with the ability to own property than they would be without that ability. The inability to own property is a guarantor of some version of enslavement, however benevolent it may be in any particular instance. Property and assets generally are the means through which one may make choices about one's interactions with the world, and property at least gives Louise an opportunity to make *some* gains, even if relatively speaking, she may fall behind Sam in her dealings with him.

A part of this essay has argued that one can see how women fall behind if one assumes a greater "taste for cooperation" on the part of women; but in working through the arguments, we see that a weaker assumption—that women are merely *thought* to have such a taste—is if anything an even more powerful determinant of their relative lack of assets. The weaker assumption revolves around culture, and that is both bad news and good. It is bad news because cultural presumptions are hard to change, since they present collective action problems to those who would try to break with them. But the good news is that cultural change does happen, sometimes through education and conscious effort.

If culture may be changed, what can Louise do about her relatively short shrift on the property front? One encouraging point is that there are others from whom Louise can learn. First, there are other groups, like new immigrants, who have also been in a position in which their needs have required them to accept, at least for a time, the lesser gains from their cooperation with more powerful persons. The escape of at least some immigrant groups from this situation should give women some cues.

One cue is that even the short end of the deal is better than no deal at all. Those who get something, even if it is the short end, can save and invest that sum and turn it into something larger, so that in their dealings on other fronts and in the future, they may not have to accept bad terms from a situation of need. Another cue is that gains can be made by cooperation with others in a like station. Again, get-ahead immigrants have notoriously helped their own, and in so doing, they have dramatically illustrated the way in which cooperation may increase a group's wealth.[71] One can look to one's allies for help in dealing with nonallies; and when Louise starts to deal with Sam, she may do well to make certain that her alliances with other Louises are intact, so that they can give her advice, assistance, and, if necessary, an escape route.

Another group from whom Louise can learn may be the participants in some of the traditional women's crafts practices—those oft-demeaned quilting bees and cookoffs and so on and, in a distinctly modern version, the literary "story trees," a set of complex branchings of plots and subplots that women writers have jointly created in science fiction fan magazines.[72] Modern feminism has made the art world more interested in the aesthetic merit of such crafts, suggesting that such cooperative forms of creativity may attain very high levels, in spite of the often strained circumstances of their creation[73] and in spite of the disdain with which our legal institutions have traditionally treated them.[74] But aside from artistic merit, these group efforts could be studied for what we might call their "politics." If women have a more capacious taste for cooperation, or even if they are just assumed to have such a taste, they ought to be able to turn that real or purported taste to their own mutual advantage in their joint pursuits; it should be cheaper for such groups to maintain cohesion for common projects than it is for groups with less of a perceived taste for cooperation.

I wonder particularly whether these groups might have been able to turn their own limited opportunities, and especially the classic "hostage" problem, into a kind of advantage. The theory of cartels suggests that collusive groups—such as the Organization of Petroleum Exporting Countries or the old railroad cartels—begin to fall apart after the membership rises to what is really a rather low number, perhaps eight at most.[75] This occurs because the members cannot police one another in larger numbers, so that in larger groups, any given member can safely cheat. When several do, the cartel collapses. On the other hand, one way to assure adherence to the cartel—or to some more benevolent cooperative group—is to use "precommitment devices."[76] For example, the members may post bond, or as the practice has actually been dubbed, they may exchange "hostages."[77]

But precommitment devices only work if they are credible, and this is where women's concern for hostages becomes an advantage. If women are thought to be concerned about others in ways that put them at some risk, and especially if their outside opportunities are limited—that is, if each knows of her own and the others' vulnerability and need for the group's support—one might expect such groups to attain a higher level of solidarity (at lower "policing costs") than groups that have more outside opportunities and fewer hostages to exchange.[78]

Hence if Louise does have a taste for cooperation, or even if people merely think she does, she should be able to turn the real or purported taste to advantage and not just be victimized by it. The taste for cooperation could be an asset itself, insofar as it helps Louise to make alliances with others and stick with them, and insofar as it helps others to recognize her as someone who will hold by her deals.

The issue that may be most difficult for Louise is selective noncooperation: she and the other Louises are going to have to learn to enforce their collective deals and collective interests by occasional threats of noncooperation with nonparticipants. In a world that mixes "testers" in with the cooperators, cooperation alone is not enough. One must also be able to police one's deals and to enforce them by exit or even by retaliation. Louises have to learn not to permit shirking by those with whom they deal and not to give the impression that they will. They have to learn to punish slanderers, politicians, or any others who would systematically cut down on their opportunities to gain "assets," whether these are financial, educational, or psychological. Even in this unpleasant task of punishment, however, Louise's alliances with other Louises may help. Together, they may be able to reinforce each other to do these unpalatable tasks collectively, even if they have a difficult time doing them individually.

A rather different point is that Louises might well pay attention to alliances that they can make with sympathetic Sams or even with Sams who are simply indifferent to local customs that might otherwise shortchange women. Such indifferent Sams—perhaps newly arrived employers or entrepreneurs—are at least not hostile; and since they do not necessarily share any local expectation that Louise might accept particularly low wages, they might help Louise get a better break than she would have had under established customs.[79]

Moreover, Louise should not despair of educating the Sams of the world and then making alliances with them. The long history of philanthropy and indeed the modern civil rights movement and modern antidiscrimination law suggest that *some* elements of a taste for cooperation are in fact fairly widely distributed. These historical examples argue that whatever the gender differences may be, it would be a great error to think that all Sams are completely indifferent to anything but their own immediate well-being; or that they are all impervious to what used to be called "self-interest rightly understood," that is, an understanding that one's own welfare is tied up in a common enterprise with others; or that they are all morons empathically, unmoved by the stories of those who are differently situated.[80] We may not think that our own substantial legal changes have resulted in perfect justice, but they are strong evidence of the possibility of cultural learning and change. The married women's property acts, the franchise, the legislation restraining discrimination in employment and education, the laws attempting to enforce child support—all give evidence of cultural learning, no matter how much is left to teach.

Even the "strong" assumption—that there is an uneven gender distribution in tastes for cooperation—is compatible with the point that *some* Sams, or even most Sams, share *some* cooperative capacities and that some are not indifferent to the plight in which women may be caught. Women in turn should not be indifferent to this fact and should be encouraged by the very substantial gains that have been made through alliances, at least in the modern West.

Some of the behavior and relationships I have been describing are deplored by most civilized people and at least to some degree are proscribed by our laws, however imperfectly and incompletely. Where the law restrains the exploitation of cooperative moves, it does so at least in part because all of us need cooperative activities, and all of us, even the Sams, are worse off when the incentives to cooperate are reduced by the punishment and disparagement of cooperators. This is of course a generalized problem with letting the cooperative Louises lose out systematically to the uncooperative Sams. Such scenarios teach a lesson too. They tend to drive down the overall level of cooperation in any given social group. If Louise's cooperative traits (or just her *seemingly* cooperative traits) routinely result in advantage-taking at her expense, we may expect lots of people to get the message that cooperation is personally problematic, and we may predict that many potential gains from wider cooperation will be lost to the fear of exploitation.

It has sometimes been noted that more developed societies tend to be characterized by a greater equality for women.[81] My point is that the correlation is not simply coincidental. From a larger perspective, we must consider the incentive effects of norms and practices that let jerks win systematically, while nice people finish last, also systematically. These norms and practices may have ramifications for a larger social well-being: they discourage the "niceness" that lets cooperative ventures occur.[82] And that, of course, is one of the major reasons why not just the Louises but the Sams too should be interested in figuring out why women do not have much property—and doing something about it.

Notes

1. Virginia Woolf, *A Room of One's Own,* 35–37, 43 (1974).

2. See, e.g., Matt Moffett, "The Strong Women of a Mexican Town Crush Stereotypes," *Wall St. J.*, Apr. 2, 1991, at A1, describing a town dominated by women descendants of a tribe with "Amazon-like traits"; Robert Williams, "Gendered Checks and Balances: Understanding the Legacy of White Patriarchy in an American Indian Cultural Context," 24 *Ga. L. Rev.* 1019, 1039–42 (1990), describing women's extensive ownings in traditional Iroquois culture.

3. See, e.g., Jaclyn Fierman, "Why Women Still Don't Hit the Top," *Fortune Mag.*, July 30, 1990, at 40.

4. See, e.g., Bureau of the Census, U.S. Dept. of Commerce, *Current Population Reports,* Series P-60, No. 163, "Poverty in the United States: 1987," at 118–19 (1989), for tables showing over 34% of female-headed families in poverty, as compared to slightly under 11% for all families.

5. See Viviana A. Zelizer, "The Social Meaning of Money: 'Special Monies,'" 95 *Am. J. Soc.* 343, 352–67 (1989) disputing that all members of a household share its wealth equally and instead noting the relatively minor "pin money" historically available to wives. See also Mary Louise Fellows, "Wills and Trusts: 'The Kingdom of the Fathers,'" 10 *Law & Inequality* 137 (1991), noting the historic and continuing lower inheritance shares of widows by comparison with widowers.

6. For the prisoners' dilemma and its more general application to commons problems, see Jack Hirschleifer, "Evolutionary Models in Economics and Law: Cooperation Versus Conflict Strategies," 4 *Res. in L. & Econ.* 1, 17 (1982).

7. The PD is conventionally described with two players, but the "tragedy" can be mapped as a large-number or "n-person" PD. See, e.g., Elinor Ostrom, *Governing the Commons* 2–3 (1990).

8. See Robert Axelrod, *The Evolution of Cooperation* 19–21 (1984).

9. See Anthony de Jasay, *Social Contract, Free Ride: A Study of the Public Goods Problem* 45–46 (1989); see also Douglas G. Baird, "Self-Interest and Cooperation in Long-Term Contracts," 19 *J. Legal Stud.* 583, 584 (1990), arguing that contract law may allay the "mutual suspicion" that would otherwise prevent some trades. Unfortunately for this contract-law solution, the establishment of a legal system presents another, large-scale variant of the PD problem. See James Krier, "The Tragedy of the Commons, Part Two," 15 *Harv. J. Law & Pub. Pol'y* 325, 338–39 (1992); Carol M. Rose, "'Enough and as Good' of What?" 81 *Nw. U. L. Rev.* 417, 438–39 (1987).

10. See de Jasay, supra note 9, at 65, n. 17.

11. See C. Gilligan, *In a Different Voice* (1982); see also the essay "Storytelling," earlier in this volume.

12. See, e.g., de Jasay, supra note 9, at 58–59 ("singleminded" PD games exclude actions based on collective rationality or attentiveness to payoffs of others); cf. Robert H. Frank, *Passions Within Reason* 14–16, 51–56 (1988) (role of tastes and emotions in overcoming problems arising from real or expected self-interest); Annette Baier, "What Do Women Want in a Moral Theory?" 19 *Noûs* 53, 57 (1985) (issue of trust should be central to moral theory).

13. See Jon Elster, *The Cement of Society* 44–49 (1989), describing a variety of motivations for collective action.

14. This version of noncooperation overlaps with what Gary Becker has named a "taste for discrimination," defined as the willingness to forgo income in order "to be associated with some persons rather than others." Gary S. Becker, *The Economics of Discrimination*, 14–17 (2d ed 1971).

15. Elster, supra note 13, at 35–36. In the "Storytelling" essay, I called this person Malice Aforethought.

16. Tamar Lewin, "Ailing Parent: Women's Burden Grows," *N.Y. Times*, Nov. 14, 1989, at A1.

17. Marcia Saft, "Risks and Benefits in Having Siblings," *N.Y. Times*, May 27, 1990, sec. 12 (Conn. section) at 3.

18. See Charles F. Mason, Owen R. Phillips, and Douglas B. Redington, "The Role of Gender in a Non-Cooperative Game," 15 *J. Econ. Behav. & Organization* 215, 217 (1991), finding that female bargaining pairs began with greater cooperation, although gender differences disappeared over time; see also Lynda L. Moore, *Not as Far as You Think* 140–42 (1986), finding that women adopted more cooperative negotiating tactics while men were more likely to compete with and deceive other bargainers. Such studies suggest that the concerns of current bargaining theory, particularly the way in which competitive tactics dissipate gains from cooperation, may assume a "male" model of bargaining. See Baier, supra note 12, at 54, for the comment that the "preoccupation with ... [the] prisoners' dilemma is a big boys' game, and a pretty silly one too," to which few women have been attracted.

19. Bill Carter, "Children's TV, Where Boys Are King," *N.Y. Times*, May 1, 1991, at A1, arguing that since girls watch everything but boys only watch males, male-oriented shows predominate.

20. For some descriptions of the debate, see Deborah Rhode, "The 'Woman's Point of View,'" 38 *J. Legal Educ.* 39, 42–44 (1990); Robin West, "Jurisprudence and Gender," 55 *U. Chi. L. Rev.* 1, 14–15 (1988); see also Martha Fineman, "Challenging Law, Establishing Differences," 42 *Fla. L. Rev.* 25 (1990).

21. See, e.g., Peter Cramton, "Bargaining with Incomplete Information: An Infinite-Horizon Model with Two-Sided Uncertainty," 51 *Rev. of Econ. Stud.* 579–590 (1984).

22. Axelrod, supra note 8, at 152–53 notes the advantage of reputation for bullying and retaliation in game strategies.

23. See, e.g., Paula England and George Farkas, *Households, Employment, and Gender,* 94–99 (1986). Women's employment also makes little difference in the housework and childcare done by the husband; see Beth A. Shelton, "The Distribution of Household Tasks: Does Wife's Employment Make a Difference?" 11 *J. Fam. Issues* 115, 130–31 (1990). See generally Joan Williams on domestic work differences as "a system of gender privilege," "Sameness Feminism and the Work/Family Conflict," 35 *N.Y. Law School L. Rev.* 347, 353 (1990).

24. For a similar approach to the household economy, see England and Farkas, supra note, at 54; for wider ramifications, see Amartya K. Sen, "Gender and Cooperative Conflicts," in *Persistent Inequalities: Women and World Development* 123 (Irene Tinker ed. 1990); a somewhat more popular version appears in Sen's "More Than 100 Million Women Are Missing," *N.Y. Rev. Books,* Dec. 20, 1990, at 61.

25. See, for example, Martha Fineman's review of Susan Moller Okin's *Justice, Gender and the Family* (1989), pointing out that Okin's discussion of "family" ignores all but traditional heterosexual families, 101 *Ethics* 647–49 (1991).

26. See Julie Dunfey, "'Living the Principle' of Plural Marriage: Mormon Women, Utopia, and Female Sexuality in the Nineteenth Century," 10 *Feminist Stud.* 523, 529 (1984), noting that 19th-century Mormon women thought most men were unwilling to take care of the family. Without romanticizing the institution, modern feminism may suggest a more sympathetic reconsideration of historical "plural marriage"; see Joan Iversen, "Feminist Implications of Mormon Polygyny," 10 *Feminist Stud.* 505, 507, 512–13 (1984). On the attractions of modern polygamy, see Elizabeth Joseph, "My Husband's Nine Wives," *N.Y. Times,* May 23, 1991, at A31, describing plural marriage as ideal for working mothers like herself, a lawyer.

27. See Trina Grillo, "The Mediation Alternative: Process Dangers for Women," 100 *Yale L. J.* 1545, 1603, n. 272 (1991).

28. See Mason et al., supra note 18, at 216, noting that gender differences in bargaining could affect wage differences. I will return later to the issue of Louise's sense of responsibility for dependents, another factor that may weaken her employment bargaining position. Louise isn't the only one, of course, given the traditional breadwinner role of some Sams.

29. See Gilligan, supra note 11, at 164–65. An alternative "on the job" explanation is that women learn to lower their expectations of advancement from discriminatory workplace experience; see Vicki Schultz, "Telling Stories About Women and Work: Judicial Interpretations of Sex Segregation in the Workplace in Title VII Cases Raising the Lack of Interest Argument," 103 *Harv. L. Rev.* 1749, 1827–32 (1990).

30. England and Farkas, supra note 23, at 171–72.

31. See Nancy Zaroulis, "Daughters of Freemen: The Female Operatives and the Beginning of the Labor Movement," in *Cotton Was King: A History of Lowell, Massachusetts* 105, 106–108, 113. (Arthur L. Eno, Jr., ed. 1976). Employers may have benefitted indirectly from these young women's taste for cooperation, too; the women apparently enjoyed the chance to be in the company of other employees and formed a number of educational and social groups.

32. For examples of low-wage immigrant labor around the turn of the century, see, e.g., Ronald Takaki, *Strangers from a Different Shore* 182–85, 274–75, 302 (1989) (Japanese, Korean, East Indian migrants). On the relationship between available alternatives and bargaining power, see England and Farkas, supra note 23, at 56; see also Joan C. Tronto, "Beyond Gender Difference to a Theory of Care," 12 *Signs* 644, 649–52 (1987), criticizing Carol Gilligan's association of "ethic of care" with women and arguing that this ethic may instead be class based, associated with minority or other marginal status.

33. For retaliatory "cooperation," see Jon Elster, "Norms of Revenge," 100 *Ethics* 862 (1990). In the employment context, harassment may amount to a norm and even seem "reasonable." See Nancy S. Ehrenreich, "Pluralist Myths and Powerless Men: The Ideology of Reasonableness in Sexual Harassment Law," 99 *Yale L. J.* 1177, 1205–10 (1990); Jerry A. Jacobs, *Revolving Doors: Sex Segregation and Women's Careers*, 151–55 (1989), and see generally Catherine A. MacKinnon, *Sexual Harassment of Working Women* (1979).

34. See generally Jacobs, supra note 33.

35. For an exhaustive account, see Mark Seidenfeld, "Some Jurisprudential Perspectives on Employment Sex Discrimination Law and Comparable Worth," 21 *Rutgers L. J.* 269 (1990); see also Jacobs, supra note 33, at 190.

36. Even if Louises (or sympathetic Sams) do become employers, they may face a collective action problem: they have to compete and take their bargains where they can—even if this means taking bargains out of their Louise-employees' wage packets. For more on collective action problems, see later sections of this essay.

37. For the role of cooperation in Japanese management, see Jon P. Alston, *The American Samurai: Blending American and Japanese Managerial Practices* 31–47 (1986); for the more jaded view of an American baseball player in Japan, see Robert Whiting, *You Gotta Have Wa* 78–110 (1989). Apparently, however, Japanese men extend this cooperation only reluctantly to businesswomen, if indeed at all. See Mary Brinton, *Women and the Economic Miracle: Gender and Work in Postwar Japan* (1992).

38. Axelrod, supra note 8; for a more skeptical view of "tit for tat," together with some sophisticated and colorful variations, see Jack Hirschleifer and Juan Carlos Martinez Coll, "What Strategies Can Support the Evolutionary Emergence of Cooperation?" 32 *J. Conflict Resolution* 367 (1988).

39. See de Jasay, supra note 9 at 65, and n. 17; Elster, supra note 13, at 5 (questioning how a "rational" player might even contemplate another party's cooperative move).

40. For a famous study, see Edward C. Banfield, *The Moral Basis of a Backward Society*, 83–101, 158–60 (1958), where "amoral familialists" were unable to trust or cooperate outside immediate family, with political and economic ill effects.

41. Cf. Ian Ayres, "Fair Driving: Gender and Race Discrimination in Retail Car Negotiations," 104 *Harv. L. Rev.* 817, 827–36, 850–51 (1991), reporting auto sellers'

disparate price offers and bargaining tactics depending on customers' race and sex, and noting that sellers' bargaining assumptions may be self-fulfilling predictions.

42. See Robert Sugden, "Contractarianism and Norms," in 100 *Ethics* 768, 779–82 (1990)

43. Cf. Ayres, supra note 41, at 855–56 and nn. 113, 114, noting that even small perceived customer differences may elicit widespread "testing" behavior in bargaining.

44. See Susan S. Blakely, "Credit Opportunity of Women: The ECOA and Its Effects," 1981 *Wis. L. Rev.* 655–57, describing the credit discrimination against women prior to antidiscrimination legislation.

45. See Seidenfeld, supra note 35, at 326–29 and literature cited therein.

46. See Gary Becker, *A Treatise on the Family* 180–81, 192–95 (enlarged ed. 1991), observing that families invest more in sons if they think this will maximize the next generation's income. For the relatively low investments in women's nutrition, particularly in less-developed countries, see Hanna Papanek, "To Each Less than She Needs, from Each More Than She Can Do: Allocations, Entitlements, and Value," in *Persistent Inequalities* 162, 165 (Irene Tinker ed. 1990); Sen, "Cooperative Conflicts," supra note 24, at 123–25. These and other authors note education differences, though in the United States, investment in men's and women's education appears to be more equal; see Jacobs, supra note 33, at 41–43.

47. For a particularly dramatic instance, see William Glaberson, "Why Hedda Nussbaum Fascinates: Most Can Identify," *N.Y. Times,* Dec. 9, 1988, at B1.

48. See Elster, supra note 13, at 189–91.

49. She may lose these assets to Sam, in which case there may be no net loss, but on the other hand (a) her assets may be worth less to Sam than they were to her and (b) her example may discourage others from cooperation, which could result in less overall wealth-producing cooperation.

50. See Lloyd Cohen, "Marriage, Divorce and Quasi-rents; or, 'I Gave Him the Best Years of My Life,'" 16 *J. Legal Stud.* 267 (1987); for some variations, see also Frances E. Olsen, "The Family and the Market: A Study of Ideology and Legal Reform," 96 *Harv. L. Rev.* 1497, 1537 (1983); June Carbone, "Economics, Feminism, and the Reinvention of Alimony: A Reply to Ira Ellman," 43 *Vand. L. Rev.* 1463, 1491–96 (1990).

51. See England and Farkas, supra note 23, at 57–58.

52. See, e.g., Dorothy Gaiter, "Pygmalion Story," *Wall St. J.,* July 24, 1991, at A1, A12, concerning a woman who committed welfare fraud when attempting to care for ten children, including four left on the streets and four more nieces and nephews left after her sister's fatal auto accident.

53. E.g., in divorce negotiations husbands sometimes enhance their bargaining position for family assets by strategically threatening to seek child custody; see, e.g., Martha A. Fineman, *The Illusion of Equality: The Rhetoric and Reality of Divorce Reform* 164 (1991); Lenore J. Weitzman, *The Divorce Revolution: The Unexpected Social and Economic Consequences for Women and Children in America* 310–13 (1985).

54. Linda Gordon, *Heroes of Their Own Lives: The Politics and History of Family Violence, 1880–1960* (1988).

55. Kimberlè Crenshaw, "Race, Gender and Violence Against Women of Color: The Intersections of Racism and Misogyny" (forthcoming; manuscript on file with author). Congress has attempted to address this problem in the Immigration Act of 1990, Pub. L. No. 101–649, sec. 701(a)(4), though Crenshaw thinks the problem will continue.

56. On abusers' extreme jealousy, see, e.g., Don Dutton and Susan L. Painter, "Traumatic Bonding," 6 *Victimology* 139, 145 (1981).

57. See generally, "Comment: Spite Fences and Spite Walls: Relevancy of Motive in the Relations of Adjoining Landowners," 26 *Cal. L. Rev.* 691 (1938).

58. See, e.g., Charles P. Ewing, *Battered Women Who Kill* 15–17 (1987); see also Okin, supra note 25, at 128–30.

59. For the argument that wife battering may also cause psychological impairment, see, e.g., Ewing, supra note 58; Lenore E. Walker, *The Battered Woman* (1979). Critical views of this approach include Elizabeth Schneider, "Describing and Changing: Women's Self-defense Work and the Problem of Expert Testimony on Battering," 9 *Women's Rts. L. Rptr.* 195, 208–11, 215–17 (1986); Stephen J. Morse, "The Misbegotten Marriage of Soft Psychology and Bad Law," 14 *Law & Hum. Behavior* 595 (1990).

60. For an excellent review of the precedents and theoretical problems, see Schneider, supra note 59. See also Ewing, supra note 58, at 34–36, noting the much greater severity of abuse distinguishing battered women who kill from those who do not.

61. Woolf, supra note 1, at 33, 38–45. For the "silencing" aspect of this phenomenon, see Catherine MacKinnon's view that First Amendment protections for pornography permit men to talk about women in ways that silence women; MacKinnon, *Feminism Unmodified* 206–13 (1987); for the effects in literature, see the very witty Mary Ellman, "Phallic Criticism," in *Thinking About Women* 27–54 (1968).

62. See, e.g., the description of an earlier Chinese family order in Winnie Hazou, *The Social and Legal Status of Women: A Global Perspective* 185–86 (1990).

63. See Papanek, supra note 46, at 170–78, noting the persistence of inadequate nutrition and mutilation (especially foot binding) of female children in China.

64. For a distressing contemporary example, see Mary W. Walsh, "Pakistan Women Look to Bhutto to Improve a Harsh Existence," *Wall St. J.*, May 3, 1989, at 1, reporting that a woman aiding others in divorce was hunted down by her own brothers and that other women were jailed and mutilated for leaving their husbands; also documenting the lack of women's education, economic independence, or independent property.

65. See Barbara Crossette, "India Studying 'Accidental' Deaths of Hindu Wives," *N.Y. Times*, Jan. 15, 1989, at A10, reporting a growing concern for wife murder. Excess mortality among women is a special interest of Amartya Sen; see Sen, "100 Million Women" supra note 24.

66. See Yoram Barzel, "An Economic Analysis of Slavery," 20 *J. L. & Econ.* 87–92, 95 (1977).

67. Id. at 100.

68. Id. at 99–100.

69. See, e.g., Patricia J. Williams, "On Being the Object of Property," 14 *Signs* 5 (1988).

70. John Locke, *Second Treatise of Government*, sec. 85, in *Two Treatises of Government* (Peter Laslett rev. ed. 1963).

71. See, e.g., Richard D. Alba, *Italian Americans* 48–51 (1985); Hubert S. Nelli, *From Immigrants to Ethnics: The Italian Americans* 115–18 (1983), both describing Italian immigrants' mutual assistance. An extensive discussion of investment funds generated through rotating credit associations, common to Chinese, Japanese, and African immigrants, is given in Ivan Light, *Ethnic Enterprise in America* 22–36, 58–61 (1972).

72. See Camille Bacon-Smith, "Spock Among the Women," *N.Y. Times*, Nov. 16, 1986, sec. 7 (Book Reviews).

73. See, e.g., June Freeman, "Sewing as a Woman's Art," 55, 58–60 *Women and Craft*, 55 (Gillian Elinor, Su Richardson, Sue Scott, Angharad Thomsa, and Kate Walker eds. 1987).

74. See Shelley Wright, "The Legal Protection of Art: A Feminist Exploration of Some Issues in Intellectual Property" 21–23 (manuscript 1991).

75. See, e.g., Richard Posner, "Oligopoly and Antitrust Laws: A Suggested Approach," 21 *Stan. L. Rev.* 1562, 1570–72, 1601–05 (1969).

76. See Elster, supra note 13, at 69.

77. See, e.g., Oliver Williamson, *The Economic Institutions of Capitalism* 167–68 (1985).

78. Here again immigrant self-help is instructive, e.g., the "revolving credit associations" built on trust among persons who are widely disparaged in the larger community. See Light, supra note 71, at 22–36, 58–61.

79. For an interesting case of indifferent Sams as employers, see Linda Y. C. Lim, "Women's Work in Export Factories: The Politics of a Cause," in *Persistent Inequalities* 101, 115–19 (Irene Tinker ed. 1990), noting favorably the role of multinational export corporations in hiring local women in less-developed countries, contrary to local patriarchic practice.

80. See Robin West, "Economic Man and Literary Woman: One Contrast," 39 *Mercer L. Rev.* 867, 874, and n. 28 (1988), citing the work of James Boyd White in describing narrative as a "bridge to empathic understanding."

81. See, e.g., Frances W. Mascia-Lees, *Toward a Model of Women's Status* 112, 119 (1984).

82. Cf. Okin, supra note 25, at 17–22, on the implications of hierarchical relations within the family for the more general understanding of justice.

PART FIVE

Persuasion Revisited: Vision and Property

This final part has only one concluding essay, "Seeing Property." It delves into some of the enormous influence that sight—whether literal, metaphoric, or totally imaginary—can bring to bear on people's conceptions of property and entitlement.

Vision-based knowledge has its detractors, and their reasons eerily echo some of the argument's of property's detractors. But in this essay I attempt to reconsider sight along with property, in order to raise the idea that vision and visual metaphor may be rhetorical modes of great power in the way people think about property, persuading people about the content and meaning of entitlements as these change over time. Even the failures of vision are instructive for the strengths and limitations of property's persuasions.

9

Seeing Property

Introduction

A Personal Vision: Hawaii and Chicago

In this essay I explore the way that *sight,* both real and metaphoric, dominates the persuasive and rhetorical aspects of property. But the impulse that set this essay in motion came from personal experiences of two very different places. To begin with the more recent: after several years as a legal academic, I had the great good fortune to spend a semester teaching property at the University of Hawaii Law School. Quite aside from the expected pleasures of spending a few months in Hawaii in the wintertime, and the extraordinary pleasures of dealing with an especially vital and charming group of students, this visit reminded me of the enormous importance of visibility in property.

While in Hawaii, I noticed that the people who live there seem to take an unusual interest in property law, and they know a great deal about it. An obvious reason is that land seems very scarce and costs a great deal; scarcity and price, of course, have a way of attracting attention. Perhaps for the same reasons, Hawaii's history, which covers the interactions and grievances of many groups, seems to revolve to an unusual degree around control of land and tangible resources.[1] But intuitively, at least one other important factor stands out: the visual character of the place. Hawaii, with its forceful and imperious landscape, has a striking physicality. Its island character, its theatrical volcanic terrain, its inflexible patterns of tides and wind-borne rainfall: all this hits even a visitor in the eye, and it all dramatically affects the way one thinks about what can be done on, with, and to this landscape, and about what is malleable and changeable and what is not.

Those issues are at the heart of property law, but they run in two opposite directions. The landscape has directed Hawaii's property law to an intense concern for issues of land and water; but the intervention of property law, in its various guises, has in turn affected the landscape. Those effects are visible too: the waterworks, the patterns of cultivated and natural vegetation, the tall buildings in Oahu and the low ones in Kauai—those matters are creatures of law, among other things, and most particularly the law of property.

But Hawaii was not the first place where I had to take note of property law's peculiar links with vision. Years before, as a law student at the University of Chicago, I observed that my property teachers constantly mined the city for examples. No wonder: Chicago too has a forceful and imperious landscape, though of a very different character from Hawaii's.[2] There too the terrain itself frames and directs a great deal of what can and cannot be done. The city's flatness makes the street grid plausible; its lakeshore location makes it a meeting place, historically for Native Americans and more recently for successive waves of commercial travellers and transporters; its openness to the brutal winter winds, according to some, makes its beaches and baseball parks assume a critical importance in the summer. But of course law dramatically affects the way this terrain looks too, perhaps as much as its own untouched physical nature. Laws established or permitted the rail and trolley lines, the relentless street grid, the canals and sewer system that have directed the city's once explosive development;[3] the successive building codes and setback requirements have visibly shaped the structures over time; and both public law and private contracts have given the city its long and beautiful open waterfront.[4]

And so, years later, Hawaii reminded me again that public and private property law can interact with physical circumstance in a way that lends the larger landscape a kind of special visibility, a quality that Kevin Lynch has called "legibility" or "imageability."[5] And Hawaii also reminded me that, as in Chicago, one can read the messages of successive generations through the way that property looks: property's visibility, in a sense, is especially attuned to letting people speak to each other, over time, about their relation to place.[6]

Or is it? According to some, vision is not the appropriate sense to support persuasive interactions at all. Indeed, as will appear shortly, some scholars have mounted a rather startling attack on vision as an objectifying, static model for knowledge—an attack that has disturbing implications for the notion of property as a persuasive enterprise, since persuasion is necessarily intersubjective and dynamic. In this essay I argue that vision is an essential part of the rhetorical and persuasive equipment of property, but a nagging question lies in the background: if property depends so deeply on sight and metaphors of sight, can it really have anything to do with persuasion at all? That is the question that I will address here, and in so doing, I will try to do something to vindicate not only property but vision as well.

Seeing and Claiming

It is easy to think of property as a set of rights to *things*—"this thing is mine; that thing is yours."[7] But almost one hundred years ago, Wesley Hohfeld published a pathbreaking article that has been mentioned several times on these pages and indeed made a point that should have been obvious all along. Rights generally, he wrote, even property rights, are not really about claims to things as such. They are about the claims and obligations, or "jural relations," that people have vis-à-vis *other people,* even if these claims and obligations are deployed over the uses and dispositions of things.[8]

In spite of this quite obvious point, property often makes it quite difficult to ignore the influence of things—those inert (or not so inert) objects over which people construct their "jural relations." Several essays in this book, such as those on the comedy of the commons and on the history of eastern water law, revolve about the way that property doctrine often takes at least some of its shape from the material characteristics of the "things" over which property rights are claimed. Much the same could be said of the property doctrines governing claims to wild animals, minerals, trees, or many other resources: the physical characteristics of the resource frame the kinds of actions that human beings can take toward a given resource, and these in turn frame the "jural relations" that people construct about their mutual uses and forbearances with respect to that resource.

In turn, physical characteristics are often visible. Perhaps this helps to explain why, for example, issues of governmental "takings" are so notoriously sensitive when they concern what are called "physical invasions" of property, and why more generally visibility runs through property law as perhaps no other legal area. Another essay in this book, on possession as a claim of title, describes how literally this is the case. A claim of title depends on the claimant's ability to signal dominion to the world, but those signals are notoriously visible. Fences, plowed furrows, all kinds of markers show the world that you are claiming an entitlement. If you happen to use a neighbor's property in a way that leaves some visible residue, like cutting down the trees or driving across it in a way that leaves tracks, in time you may well acquire rights that have the force of law;[9] but if you use your neighbor's land without leaving visible traces—if, say, you "merely" enjoy the sunlight or air across a neighboring lot—your actions may well be treated as a passing breeze, giving you no entitlements.[10]

In modern law, of course, you may acquire an intangible right, like sunlight or a view, particularly if you negotiate for it and record the agreement, thereby leaving visible tracks at the county recording office.[11] But there too, those visible marks are what command the world's respectful response to your claims. In nonliterate societies, in what have been called "performance cultures," the transfer of property is marked by elaborate celebratory rituals and held firm by the memories of witnesses; but even here the boundaries of property are likely to be marked by poles and other lasting visible signals.[12]

For persons interested in property, it is thus somewhat unsettling to learn that the all-important sense of vision has taken some rather hard knocks at the hands of writers who strike out at the domineering characteristics of sight as a model for knowledge. And perhaps it should be no surprise that these critiques of vision, by analogy, find some easy targets in the law of property as well. Any strike on those targets is particularly damaging for the idea of property as an ongoing persuasive activity; if the phenomenological critique of vision applies to property, then this very common way of apprehending property cannot even be conceived of as intersubjective or changeable over time.

Let me backtrack: one might well ask, What could be the matter with vision? The most substantial complaint about vision is encapsulated in the adjective "voyeuristic": vision, it is said, distances and objectifies the thing seen.[13] Unlike the listener or the toucher, the visual observer need not interact with the object of her attention. Instead, vision seems the quintessential sense for cool and uninvolved objectivity: through sight, the seeing subject takes in the thing observed from a distance, and the object need never assert its own subjectivity. Thus vision occurs without the complicating (or, depending on one's point of view, sullying) effects of particular transactions between the seeing subject and the object that is seen. The latter is *just* an object, a thing, observed without its own volition or reciprocal action.

To be sure, in modern times, Heisenberg's uncertainty principle has taught us something different about the effect of observation on the observed, but not until long after those who praised the "nobility of sight" had imparted a dream of objective knowledge.[14] Thus the sense of vision, according to the first critique, eradicates the understanding of knowledge as an intersubjective enterprise between the knower and the known; and by extension, it also undermines the idea that the transmission of knowledge depends on the ceremonies and memories of a community of witnesses.[15]

A second and closely related critique is that vision also eradicates something else: the dimension of time, and with time, the importance of experience and even consciousness. Unlike the sense of hearing, on this account, vision occurs with minimal reference to time, since the eye can capture a whole scene more or less synoptically and need not depend on memory of developments that only unfold over time.[16] In this respect seeing is quite different, for example, from the perception of music or poetry or even from the perceptions that come through touch, since the latter renders an understanding of shape only through a sequence of remembered tactile maneuvers.[17] Moreover, through vision, the subject can observe the object many times over, in a more or less unchanged state. Indeed, unless the object does stay the same (or at most changes in constantly repetitive ways), one might think that one or both or all the observations were faulty—not replicable, as scientists say.

With respect to time, then, vision gives the impression that time does not matter, that the past will be like the future, that experience itself is logically irrelevant to the way events play out. This is because, in the visual metaphor of the "real world," experience never transforms or changes anything. Events may indeed unfold in time, as when a stone drops to the ground, but they do so in ways that are in principle susceptible to prediction—precisely because they can be observed repeatedly. The second "run" of events should not change simply because it comes later in time than the first or because it has been experienced before. So much the worse, then, for any notions that consciousness, memory, and knowledge might be transforming and potentially liberating; for vision, according to such critiques, these are nonexistent or at most "subjective" ephemera, relegable to "unscientific" branches of inquiry.

Clearly such intellectual blasts at the phenomenology of vision are aimed at vision's role in natural scientific inquiry, with all its historic pretensions to objectivity and prediction, and all its slights, real and imagined, to the interpretative and narrative modes of *understanding* human action.[18] Indeed the critique of vision is part of a barely disguised attack on what is perceived as a dehumanizing science.[19]

But though this intellectual artillery is aimed primarily at vision, it also explodes dangerously close to some very common understandings of property.[20] First, there is the central matter of vision's objectification of the thing seen and hence (scientifically) known. The same charge could be levelled at property: in the simplest form, property claims are "objective" in the sense that they are interpersonal in only the thinnest and most abstract form and are said to be good against not just this or that other person but against the world at large. That, in theory, is the formal claim of an "in rem" action to establish a claim to a specific property (as opposed to an "in personam" claim against this or that individual). The successful in rem action supposedly establishes that all potential rivals must yield to the claimant's title to the object in question—the boat or parcel of land or trust fund or whatever—on the implicit premise that all individual claims can indeed be homogenized and dispatched at once, as belonging to one generic "objective" type.[21]

More profoundly, and sometimes shockingly on first encounter, the common law of property at many junctures quite unabashedly refers to property in the language of domination, that ultimate form of objectification. A person claims title to wild and fugitive things by "depriving them of liberty" and showing a definite intent to take them over for his own purposes—often meaning that he kills them.[22] To be sure, there is a transaction of sorts in this reduction to dominion, but it is a pretty one-sided one, in which the perspective of the claimed thing is entirely ignored. At the end of the road, the claimed thing can assert no subjective will of its own. That very absence of will and subjectivity is what it means to be "reduced to dominion"—to be "tame" instead of "wild." Marking and dominating—particularly with visual cues, be it noted—are property law's analog to vision's objectification of the thing seen, and they are analogs as well to vision's disinterest in the seen object's own point of view.

Then there is the second branch of the critique of vision, that is, vision's assertion of changelessness. Common understandings of property also share this characteristic: the very claim of property is that it is something lasting. Indeed, duration is an important element in making a claim *property,* as opposed to a merely temporary usufruct.[23] When one claims a right to something even as changeable and literally fluid as water, one may take water from the stream here and now; but in an appropriative system, what makes this act a *property* claim is the potential right to take the same amount every year, into the indefinite future.[24] To be sure, some property claims, like leases, may be bounded in time by their very terms, but even those claims are supposed to stay the same over the duration of the specified entitlement.

Should it be any wonder, then, that claims to property, those domineering pretensions to objective and lasting entitlement, should rely so heavily on a nontransacting, time-ignoring sense of vision? Should it be any wonder that property so deeply implicates an organ of perception that can treat the perceived thing as an object, and act as if the passage of time did not matter?

All these interrelations between property and vision, of course, suggest that property law is one enormous, brittle structure of antiquated false consciousness, systematically repressing the Hohfeldian perception that rights—including property rights—are embedded in interpersonal relations. Property law, with its reliance on real and metaphoric sight, its urge to look at things and to label those things *properties,* seems to be in a serious state of denial. That is, property law seems implicitly to deny that property is about relations among people, whose institutions necessarily reflect the way those people think, argue, persuade, change their own and one another's minds over time. What is possibly even worse, vision-based property might infect the notions of other rights as well and make other fields of law lose touch with the evolving and persuasive aspects of "rights" altogether.[25]

On this bleak account, then, the institution of property indeed may be a persuasive enterprise, but the reliance on vision suppresses that fact; property, like the vision-based model of objective science that it apes, is falsely supposed to be objective and forever. If all this is so, then we should hardly celebrate vision as a way to approach and understand property. Instead, we should cast it out as the crypto-scientific, antihumane, lying Jezebel that it is.

Now, wait a minute. Things are not so simple—either for vision or for property. As to vision itself: some of sight's rehabilitators have pointed out that seeing may represent a dynamic intersubjective encounter too, and a very intense one at that, as in the well-known experience of "locked eyes."[26] And as to property: true enough, prosaic and conventional property law does make claims of dominion and fixity, and it signals those claims by visible marks; but neither dominion nor fixity is quite so easy as all that. Fences fall in. Boundary markers get lost. Animals—and waters—that are supposedly "tame" suddenly decide to run away and become "wild" and unowned again.[27] Neighbors forget or ignore demarcations; they drive trucks across each other's fields, and they start businesses or place their garages, toolsheds, and entire houses on each other's lots.[28] As I pointed out in the essay "Crystals and Mud," even the documents at the county recording office are periodically threatened with hopeless tangles.

In short, wildness lurks all about in the fields of tameness, and the visible signals of ownership flicker and falter much more than one might suppose from listening to property's brave claims of control and permanence. Those claims are often considerably more aspirational than real. And, be it noted, vision shows that some things are outside the realm of human dominion. One can see what is not claimed—or not claimed any more or not claimable at all—in experiences that are simultaneously humbling and exhilarating: the Grand Tetons look as if they own themselves, whatever the National Park Service may say about them.

Still, these instantaneous impressionistic reactions are scarcely enough to deal with vision's startling public relations problems. It is time now to go through some ways that people really do see property, in order to compare those "envisionings" to the objections about vision, and by extension about sight-oriented property. In the remainder of this essay, I will take up four ways of seeing property, ranging from the most literal to the most figurative. The first "envisioning," through pictures and maps, takes on the complaint that vision *objectifies.* I will argue that on closer analysis, these representational modes of "envisioning" are transactional after all and quite clearly do aim at interpersonal persuasion. The second mode of seeing property—through metaphor—extends the discussion of persuasion, particularly focusing on the ways that property metaphors can relate parts to wholes. A third way of seeing property—that is, seeing property in a kind of unfolding drama—takes up the complaint that vision ignores time and experience; this section suggests that the visual aspects of property are also not nearly so fixed and impervious to experience as they may seem to the critics of vision but instead can inform various kinds of narratives. A fourth way of seeing property is what I call "illusory property"; this involves the imaginative construction of property even where the law recognizes none. Here I will try to show how very consciously people make use of the persuasive aspects of property's visual signals and how quickly they read visual cues as claims, counterclaims, argument, rhetoric. At the conclusion I will return to Hawaii to revisit some historic and tragic miscues in different "envisionings" of property, where one cannot but note the cultural boundaries around persuasions of property.

The larger argument throughout this essay is that "seeing" property is to some degree an act of imagination; and imagination in turn opens the door to rhetoric, culture, and most of all persuasion, with all the capacity to influence action that persuasion entails.

Ways of Seeing

Seeing Property in Pictures

The most obvious and prosaic way to see property, of course, is to go and look. But one step away from that is to see property in pictorial representations. Photo 1, for example, is a quite graphic assertion of a boundary. And Photo 2 is another, no less emphatic, for all the modesty of its materials.

As in some other areas of property law, the law of historic preservation makes pictures essential for laying out the features that conform to a given historic style. Though a verbal description might be concocted, a picture is far more comprehensible, as in Illustration 1, which shows window trim styles thought appropriate for the historic district houses of Rockville, Maryland.[29]

Why do the specifications for historic properties seem to call for an illustration rather than a verbal depiction? Why will words not do so well? Some might claim that words alone will not "do" for *any* form of knowledge and that all knowledge is essentially perceptual (and sight the most privileged perception),[30] but one need not subscribe to such visual imperialism to discern sight's significance in property. Property, even understood as a set of claims against other persons, often revolves about access to some resource that exists in space and extension, and for that reason vision may be the first sense to be called upon in apprehending property. The sense of touch, of course, may do much or even all the work,[31] and indeed touch is used in understanding property, as in the still-used practice of "walking the boundaries." But sight is relatively quick and may also

PHOTO 1

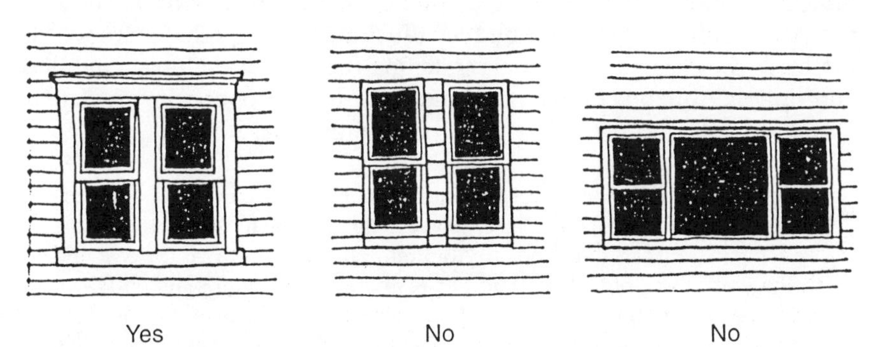

ILLUSTRATION 1

PHOTO 2

serve to synthesize spatial information from other senses;[32] perhaps for that reason, visible markers are evidently important in property even in the nonliterate "performance cultures" that generally suspect the sense of sight as unreliable.[33]

One can get a sense of the awkwardness of verbal descriptions from the examples that appear all too frequently in the legal literature of property. Judicial opinions often describe disputed properties, usually in the first few paragraphs, and in so doing they illustrate the ways that mere words can leave the chagrined readers scratching their heads. Here is a familiar description, from one of the most famous cases in property law, *Village of Euclid v. Ambler Realty Co.*,[34] which upheld municipal zoning.

> Appellee is the owner of a tract of land containing 68 acres, situated in the westerly end of the village, abutting on Euclid Avenue to the south and the Nickel Plate railroad to the north. Adjoining this tract, both on the east and on the west, there have been laid out restricted residential plats on which residences have been erected. ... Appellee's tract of land comes under U-2, U-3 and U-6 [zoning use categories]. The first strip of 620 feet immediately north of Euclid Avenue falls in class U-2 [two-family residences], the next

130 feet to the north, in U-3 [churches, schools, etc.], and the remainder in U-6 [heavy industry].

Here is a judge talking to you as reader, yet the words seem oddly uncommunicative. To make sense of this prickly statement, readers have to sketch their own crude pictures or maps. Indeed, you wonder why the judges, who often have had the advantage of seeing maps and pictures in the documents submitted by the parties,[35] think that readers can manage without such illustrations. You might be tempted to attribute this to some form of subtle judicial authoritarianism—"I know what this is all about, and you do not"—though a more charitable explanation might lie in the printing costs of graphics. For purposes of rehabilitating vision, however, it might be noted that a picture or map, far more than the words, would seem to be oriented toward assisting the audience to comprehend.

I am sliding from pictures to maps; although in a sense a map is a kind of picture, common understanding draws some major differences between them. In particular, a map is more abstract than a picture, and in looking at the map, you clearly let yourself be guided by someone else's version of the key features in a given landscape. But sometimes you can use this kind of help; the map, stripped down though it may be, nevertheless can be a more legible guide than a seemingly more accurate and detailed picture, which indeed may overwhelm by detail.[36]

Moreover, by bringing data together in a single perceptible space, maps may yield unexpected new information.[37] Police departments map the locations of unusual crime patterns to learn something about motives and perpetrators,[38] and in a famous historical example in epidemiology, the mapping of cholera outbreaks led public health officials to understand the relation of the illness to polluted drinking water.[39] To take an instance in property law, in another well-known older case, *Nectow v. City of Cambridge,*[40] one party challenged an odd zigzag in a zoning boundary. The court's verbal description of the boundary was almost impossible to fathom; but a map of the area, showing the way that this peculiar zoning line would have protected a row of existing residences from the noise and sight of industrial uses across the street, strongly suggests the motivations behind the ordinance.[41] The map, far from stifling the imagination, invites the viewer to reflect on the story behind the case.

Let it not be thought, though, that there is only one map (or one story) that can explain property relations. A map, of course, does not include the jagged edges of real life, but more generally, maps can be quite tendentious in directing the attention to this feature or that—so much so that a 1993 historical exhibit on maps chose to display them as "instruments of power, persuasion and control."[42] But on second thought, we see that a picture, even a photograph, also highlights some items at the expense of others, however much it may purport to "tell all." Art critics, including those who insist on photography's special capacity for accuracy, still point out that a photograph is selective and that it reflects the photographer's imagination and intent about what should be in the scene—or, rather, what things you and I should see in it, whether in fact we see those things or something else.[43]

On third thought, we realize that the act of seeing itself has some of the same characteristics of imagination, purpose, and selectivity. It is now well known that in visual perception the viewer's imagination organizes and embellishes the mass of sensations that appear to come from "out there" to "in here," as the viewer persuades herself of the meaning of various features of the object she is seeing.[44] Take, for example, the recognition of faces: in one set of experiments, viewers of simplified or blurred computer images, once having "found" the face, added detail to the coarse images presented to them; moreover, they were unable to "un-see" the face after it was perceived.[45] Indeed, it is not altogether clear that any optical physiological stimulus whatever is necessary for "vision"; formerly sighted persons are well known to have describable visual images of objects perceived through other senses.[46]

And so a map abstracts and reorders what one sees in a picture; and a picture, even a photo, abstracts and reorders what one actually sees; but what one actually sees also abstracts and reorders the light waves that enter the eye. At every step, someone's interests and ideas of meaning (including *one's own* interests and ideas of meaning) guide one's attention and draw one to the "important" things in the picture.

Thus pictures of property, and maps even more, are visual reductions and interpretations of property relationships, and these renditions can make the subject easier to grasp than the great booming chaos "out there." But the eye of the mind is already at work, reducing that booming chaos to something that can be "envisioned" either in one's own mind's eye or in someone else's and directing what that mind's eye is going to see.

All this goes to the point that imagination and hence persuasion can enter into even the supposedly simplest and most straightforward pictures of property. Imagination and persuasion enter even more strikingly at the next level of "seeing property," that is, seeing metaphorically.

Seeing Property Metaphorically

What is a visual metaphor of property? A notable example is a property metaphor now in rather common usage: the analogy of property to a "bundle of sticks"—that is, a kind of visible, physical entity made up of other visible entities.[47] The idea informing the metaphor is that property is not a single unitary thing but rather a group of rights, some of which may be added or removed under appropriate conditions.

A few years ago, the "bundle" metaphor played a prominent though somewhat dubious role in an influential little article by Thomas Grey entitled "The Disintegration of Property."[48] In this article, Grey discussed what he perceived to be the imminent demise of property as a moral category. He took as a starting point Bruce Ackerman's observation that nonexperts understand property as "things," whereas another approach (which Ackerman calls "scientific policy-making") takes as a starting point a Hohfeldian understanding of property as abstract collections of claims among persons.[49] These claims can be envisioned metaphorically in various "bundles," and indeed, the "bundle" metaphor is in some ways an effort to get people to "see" property in a different form.[50]

But Grey argued that this very rhetoric of bundles of rights, precisely because it suggests the infinite divisibility of property into separate non-thing-like rights, undermines the ordinary commitment to property altogether. Although Grey traced the "bundle" conception to the practical and theoretical necessities of modern economic organization, he thought that the metaphor encapsulated the divergence between a capitalist market system and the popular conception of property as entitlement to *particular things*.[51] As such, he described the metaphor as part and parcel of a general weakening of property's grip on the popular moral imagination. The bundle-of-rights metaphor for property, in short, attempted to persuade the world of a "scientific" understanding of property; but on Grey's account the persuasion would self-destruct by hollowing out the popular notion of what property means.

Shortly after Grey's article, Frank Michelman published another article in the same philosophic periodical and made a point that might support Grey's.[52] Among other things, Michelman argued that the concept of private property needs what he called a principle of "composition,"[53] that is, a principle that holds a set of property claims together as one comprehensible package. Since Grey had argued that the "bundle" metaphor suggests dismantling rather than composition, one might conclude, as Grey did, that the bundle metaphor contributes to the "decomposition" of the idea of property itself.

Well, does it? The bundle metaphor has been around a while. Has it doomed the popular attachment to property or made it less central in legal and political discussions, as Grey suggested in 1980? The answer so far is no, not yet—not by quite a long shot. In fact, the bundle-of-sticks metaphor itself has taken on a quite robust new life.

The most prevalent deployment of this metaphor is in the constitutional law discussion of governmental "takings" of property, where landed property in particular is often described as a bundle composed of discrete parts, and the legal question is whether the regulation has taken too many or too important "sticks."[54] But the metaphor has uses in some other private arrangements as well, wherever a single name covers several related interests,[55] for example, in describing private condominium ownership or interests in other varieties of planned communities. The condominium owner normally might have a "fee simple" interest in her unit's living space, an exclusive easement in her balcony area and parking space, tenancy in common in the hallways and the swimming pool, defined participatory rights in the community's governance, and so forth. When she buys the condominium, she becomes entitled to the entire bundle, which is composed of a number of different rights, some exclusive and some shared with other owners. In a somewhat different area, the bundle metaphor might explain the property aspects of contracts; that is, one might talk about contracts metaphorically, as "bundles" of entitlements to this service or that.

The bundle of sticks, to be sure, is not the only visual metaphor for property. Oliver Wendell Holmes, in making the point that a contractual right can be conceived as a property interest, observed that the assignment of a contractual right was just as much a transfer of property as was the sale of a horse.[56] In this analogy, of course, Holmes was also using a visual metaphor for entitlements. Indeed, in some ways Holmes' horse metaphor has some rather more sophisticated features than the currently standard bundle of sticks.

Useful as it is, the bundle has several problems. For one, as a visual metaphor, it suggests that the component entitlements in the bundle are all more or less alike—everything seems to be just a stick, even though some sticks may be bigger than others or have different shapes. In that way, the metaphor distracts from the *content* of the component entitlements. We might be better off with Holmes' horse, especially if we think of the horse as "packaged" with a harness and a buggy. Toys in a toy chest could be a better metaphor too. Such visual metaphors suggest that the component parts of a given type of property might be quite different among themselves but might still relate to one another and might perhaps also aim in a complementary fashion at some larger general purpose.

This brings up a second problem. Aside from the fungibility of the "sticks," the bundle also metaphorically suggests the sticks' separability; perhaps this fueled Grey's comments on the decompositional quality of the metaphor. The metaphor breaks down related sets of entitlements into smaller rights-entities, and each "stick" reifies one separate right-entity, with no particular relationship to the other sticks except proximity. The visual image of the sticks is thus one of separate objects, and in this respect the metaphor weakens the sense that groupings of property rights might be interconnected and interdependent.

This can affect one's thinking about property. To give an example, a 1992 political science colloquium paper on property was based on the bundle metaphor.[57] The paper, at least in draft form, made quite a fuss about the differences between two of what the author considered to be property's "sticks," namely, the right of use (or control) on the one hand and the right of "income" on the other (the latter deriving particularly from alienation). He argued that use rights or control rights are more fundamental, since they depend on the owner's own preferences and plans; income rights, on the other hand, involve transferring some part of the property and are thus conditional on the wishes of others.

No doubt there are important differences in these rights, and yet upon reflection it seems obvious that they are more closely intertwined than the "bundle" analogy might make one think. For example, my decision to *use* my bicycle is clearly influenced, at least some of the time, by the price that someone else would *pay* me to rent it or even sell it. I may love my bicycle dearly (as indeed I do), but given the offer of a cool million, I would dispose of it in a New York minute. Others might divest themselves of the family heirlooms with the same alacrity, for the same reasons, if appropriate offers were forthcoming. Luckily for the stability of property, such exaggerated offers are not forthcoming very often; and even when they are, some people still refuse. But all the same, the decision to use property for one's self takes place over against an implicit background comparison between one's own use and the gains that one would receive from selling or renting to others[58]—which is to say, use rights and income rights are all tied up together. One must wonder whether such sharp use/income dichotomies might result from the mesmerizing character of the bundle-of-sticks metaphor itself, which may induce people to envision these elements of entitlement as considerably more separable and independent than they actually are.

The "bundle," then, is at best a crude metaphor. This is not necessarily a bad thing, of course. In one way, crudity is another name for abstraction and single-mindedness. Those can be advantages for the metaphor, just as the crudity of the map has some advantages over the detail of the picture, or just as the crudity of the picture has some advantages over the even greater detail of unmediated vision. The crude presentation is easier to understand and more likely to highlight particular elements—even though some other elements are lost and even though their loss may give an unspoken tilt to the new "picture" (which of course may be the point all along).

On the other hand, different kinds of things may be lost in the metaphor—or at least this bundle metaphor—from the things that are lost in the map or picture. Actual pictures, and maps even more, are likely to suppress detail, but they do so to show the interrelatedness of the parts within some concept of a whole. That is why people say "oh" when a picture or map illustrates a verbal statement: they see the parts in a whole. But the metaphoric "picture," the bundle of rights, goes in the opposite direction. It is in large part a device for separating the various facets of property and for giving an intuitive grasp of their separateness and moveability rather than their interrelatedness and porosity.

To some degree, all metaphoric pictures may have some of this separating quality, because they make non-things (like contract rights) seem "thingy" (or *dinglich,* as the German philosophers might put it)[59] and hence separable in the visual imagination. Indeed, Jonathan Swift satirized Lockean epistemology for its representational or picturing version of "clear and distinct ideas." In one revealing episode, Gulliver encounters some "sages" who carry weighty bundles of objects around in packs; they say nothing in conversation but instead communicate more precisely by displaying one thing after another from their packs.[60]

It seems quite clear, then, that visual metaphors are capable of conveying a sense of the separateness of the parts of property entitlements—just as fences or other physical markings separate one piece of property from another in actual vision. But this can be a distortion, too, creating an idea of finite and bounded "things" even where people's actual experience suggests much more interrelationship and fluidity. Indeed, the separating aspects of visual metaphor again raise the specter of a narrowly "scientific" form of vision, which supposedly dissects and analyzes objects to the point of losing any sense of the whole. The big question is whether visual metaphors can work in the opposite direction, aiding in *understanding* as opposed to analysis—that is, reclaiming a sense of the whole and of the relatedness of the various elements of entitlement.

The answer to this question must be yes. Even the bundle of sticks is not just *sticks* but a *bundle.* In examples like that of the various condominium rights, as mentioned above, the bundle metaphor acts at least as much to "package" the various elements as it does to give an impression of their separateness.

Moreover, there are many other visual metaphors that relate different entitlements into wholes. A very famous metaphor was mentioned in two of the earlier essays on historic property rights,[61] and it was one that was much used up to the seventeenth century: the metaphor of the "body politic." As I observed in those earlier essays, old political treatises went on at great length about the likeness of the polity to the individual—according to one, the polity should be healthy, like the body, and it should have a proper ratio among the parts (a correct proportion as between craftsmen and farmers, for example).[62] A dominating idea behind this rather peculiar imagery was that each class of people had its own function and its own set of entitlements tailored to that function, so that all groups could play their proper role in the political order.

Such elaborate discussions of the "body politic" carry an implicit message of hierarchy (the king is normally the head), and they are clearly out of touch with modern thinking about desirable political ordering. But they also are an important example of the way that visual metaphor may bring parts together in the imagination into a whole—and, indeed, it may be one of the difficulties of democratic polities that they have no such obvious integrative visual metaphors.

Aside from politics, there are other areas where one can locate metaphoric visual images that bring *parts* into *wholes.* Some of these show up in statistical literature, and though their subjects range rather far from property law, these metaphors do have some implications for property as well.

The political scientist Edward Tufte wrote a book several years ago, *The Visual Display of Quantitative Information.*[63] When he failed to find a publisher who would follow his exacting layout specifications, Tufte published the book himself. This made several million dollars for him and helped win him a feature article in the *New York Times* Sunday magazine.[64] Thus encouraged, of course, he has written a sequel to give some variations on the subject.[65]

Tufte thinks that many statisticians today lack the knack for visual presentations that at least some earlier data specialists had.[66] Why does it matter that statisticians use visual representations? It matters because people really do not understand statistics very well and may not grasp statistical information at all without the aid and impact of some visual representation. Since Amos Tversky and Daniel Kahneman's classic work on the flawed "heuristics" that people use in assessing statistical probabilities, cognitive psychologists have run experiments illustrating in various ways that statistical logic seems to be absent from most people's intuitive repertoire.[67]

Most of us make some characteristic errors in this area. One intuitive reaction is to flatten very large numbers and very small numbers as well. That is, most of us have no strong intuitive feel for the difference between a million and a billion—or between a one-in-a-million and a one-in-a-billion chance of some event occurring.[68]

This brings us back to property. In the modern world, quite a number of resource entitlements are, so to speak, statistical entities. This is notable in environmental law, which can be analyzed as a branch of property law.[69] Toxic air emissions, for example, are a kind of invisible trespass on other people's bodies or territory; we know about these encroachments, but only statistically, as some X parts pollutant per million parts air. If we do not grasp what these small numbers mean, then we really do not have much of a grip on toxics at all.

Suppose that two different sources of air pollution release equally dangerous toxins into the air; the first releases at concentrations of one part toxin per million parts air, while the other releases at one part per billion. Intuitively, at least to most people, these numbers do not seem very different, even though, as statistics, they are very different indeed.[70] Similarly, when pesticides are tested, we may get test results on the incidence of tumors or growth defects, and the differences may be substantial from a statistical standpoint; but intuitively, one chance in a million does not set off a lot more bells and whistles than one chance in a billion.

Naturally, the next question is, So what? What difference does it make if these figures are treated as practical equivalents? They are all dangerous substances, are they not? That is precisely the problem: if all those risks sound alike to us as voters, we are going to regard them all as equally dangerous. If we have no good cognitive intuitions to put them in priorities, we may pressure our representatives to regulate toxics in ways that really waste our regulatory resources and generally waste social resources.[71] We will wind up being too careful about some and not careful enough about others. As a society we may spend equal resources (or make other citizens spend equal amounts of *their* resources) to abate a one-in-a-million risk, a one-in-a-billion risk, or a one-in-a-trillion risk.

Needless to say, if all other things are equal and if risk abatement carries equal costs for different risks, we would be better off expending funds to get rid of the bigger, one-in-a-million risk first, at least until we have brought it down to the same danger level as the smaller one-in-a-billion risk; then we can think about tackling the smaller risk.[72] But to do this in a systematic way, we have to grasp that these risks really are different and that one really is more dangerous than the other. The question is, *How* can we get that sense?

One way to escape from intuitive psychological flattenings is to use visual and spatial representations of statistical information. That is why Tufte's book has such practical importance, and that is why, no doubt, it has earned millions of dollars. Others too have used some ingenious devices to reformulate these statistical entities into visual metaphors. For example, former congressman Mike McCormick, who later became a science consultant to Congress, used beads. He showed a container holding 1,000 beads and asked his congressional listeners to imagine the same beads covering the entire floor of the committee room (for a million); then the entire Capitol grounds (for a billion); the city of Washington, D.C. (for a trillion); and finally the state of Ohio (for a quadrillion).[73]

Now, my own statistical intuitions are as flawed as anyone's, and I do not argue one way or another about the accuracy of these visual comparisons. What I *would* argue is that this kind of visual metaphor can be extraordinarily helpful in conveying information about statistical probabilities and about the entitlements based on those probabilities. Visual metaphors let people "see" what the numbers *mean*, and they permit us to shape our policies for restraining and permitting emissions according to the relative risk levels.

It is also important to note what happens in such representations: the visual, physical metaphor here does not divide but rather reintegrates. The individual beads are not so important in McCormick's metaphor as the comparative sizes of the areas covered by the beads. The visual imagery of beads, placed in imagined spaces of various sizes, allows ordinary understanding to relate the part with the whole and to get a meaningful purchase on the comparative sizes of these different abstract risks.

Visual metaphors of this sort may be critical in citizens' and representatives' ability to come to terms with the problems of environmental law. It is not so much that numbers lie, though perhaps they can. The much bigger problem is that statistical reasoning just does not come naturally for most people (including research psychologists themselves),[74] unless statistics can be put in some more easily imaginable form.

It need hardly be added that the ability to imagine, to use the mind's eye, presents an opening to persuasion; imagining statistical properties, through visual metaphor, can be a first step to taking action on the problems the statistics represent. Hence metaphor in this arena has profound political implications, and the choices of visual metaphor will be important. But then, the absence of a visual metaphor has serious political implications as well, because the lack of metaphor leads to a kind of imaginative disability—that is, disabling us from even "envisioning" the risks that we encounter or the ways to deal with them sensibly. Envisioning is a step toward persuasion, and persuasion is a step toward decision and action.[75]

So far I have been suggesting that in at least some of the ways that people see property relations—from pictures to maps to metaphors—the depiction speaks to a viewer's imagination and attempts to persuade. Insofar as one can understand these depictions as persuasive forays, they suggest that presenting and *seeing,* including seeing property relations, is quite far from a simple objectivizing activity; instead, presenting and seeing take place in a kind of conversation, where a whole array of persuasive gambits may be put forth. For the moment, I leave to one side the question whether these gambits are actually understood as efforts to persuade, but I will return to that question later.

Seeing Property as Narrative

Persuasion tells a story, and in the preceding discussion I was moving from one chestnut to another: from "a picture is worth a thousand words" to "every picture tells a story."

But does it? Indeed, does a picture tell any story at all? Might it be the case that property, with its dependence on visual representation, is merely the *end* of the story, a set of static results that carry on into eternity the completed action of, say, contract or tort or crime? Might those other branches of the law represent the true narrative style and for that reason depend on the senses of sound and hearing, which take place over time, relegating sight to a secondary role at most?

We might note, for example, that a contractual relationship may be quite difficult to "envision," but it normally has a *story*, since contracting entails some transacting that results in a deal; and of course when a contract goes bust, the story develops further. Tort law too is laden with stories, since some sequence of events lies behind every claim of injury; and the same may be said of the law of crimes. Visual effects are not entirely absent in these areas of the law, but they are certainly secondary to the story line. Might it be, then, that property's reliance on sight simply epitomizes the point that the *action* lies elsewhere and that property relations are essentially end states, static and nonnarrative?

The answer must relate to the initial question: *does* a picture tell a story? Well, some clearly can. Edward Tufte, whose work in the visual representation of statistical data was discussed earlier, has a favorite graphic, and it is a sharp reminder of the way that a supposedly fixed picture can give the sense of a story that plays out over time. This graphic is Charles Joseph Minard's mid-nineteenth-century depiction of one of the most famous military disasters in history: the fate of Napoleon's army as it marched into Russia, and then back out, over the fall and winter of 1812–1813. The graphic is composed of quite wonderfully mixed elements. In the background is a simplified map of Eastern Europe; the French army is presented as a stripe, with its width representing the numbers of soldiers at any given time. Broad and commanding as it begins on the left, at the origin of the campaign on the Polish-Russian border, the stripe tapers down steadily (and in some stairsteps at particular battles) as it moves to the right, eastward into Russia; then at Moscow the thinning stripe reverses direction—now accompanied by a depiction of the falling winter temperatures—and retreats in an ever-dwindling width back to the west, where, by the end, the stripe is constricted to a pencil line. The statistics of this military debacle were stunning in themselves—an army of 422,000 at the outset, a band of 10,000 stragglers at the end. But the visual graphic of the stripe, steadily diminishing as it moves across and back over the map of Eastern Europe, "def[ies] the pen of the historian by its brutal eloquence."[76]

There, at least, is a picture that tells a story. How about the signals of property? Well, these may not be created to tell a story, but they can do so all the same. All over New England, there is a certain spooky irrelevance to the battered remnants of the last century's stone fences, meandering as they do through the blissfully resurgent woods. Here vision reveals the impermanence and pathos of property's aspirations to eternity and shows how much can change in the passage of time after all.

Property's ability to "tell stories" is one of the points of historic preservation of older structures and neighborhoods; these are reminders of the lived life of the community in which they exist. Stories are even more the point of many publicly owned monuments, like the lettered black slabs of the Vietnam War Memorial or the flowing waters of the Martin Luther King, Jr., Memorial. These physical locations and visual markers bear witness to their respective tales, providing the viewer with cues that will make their stories ring through the ages.[77] Here, too, the properties, and the narratives that accompany them, are sometimes conscious persuasive efforts in a political context; they are often recognized as such and can be quite controversial—a point that I will pick up shortly.

A particular piece of property, then, may tell a story, just as there is a story about a contract or a tort. But an especially notable use of the dramatic form in property is a kind of "big picture" of property: the story that purports to relate the evolution of whole regimes of entitlements. Oddly enough, these narratives may be more prevalent in law-and-economics approaches to property than anywhere else, and although they are told in various guises, they all boil down to the same story, one that has often appeared in these pages. It is the tale that I dubbed the "scarcity story" in one of the earlier essays.[78] This story is about the way that property rights emerge with scarcity, and in the most abstract and summary form, once again, it goes roughly as follows: (Act 1) a particular resource or other becomes scarce, for one of a variety of reasons; (Act 2) meanwhile, a lot of people scramble to get the resource; (Act 3) for a while, they get tangled up in conflicts over who has what; and, finally, (Act 4) they create property rights regimes, which make the conflicts go away, while the rightsholders happily invest and trade.[79]

This is of course a lifeless and featureless presentation of the story; what gives it life is its mapping on some real-world experience, and that is where the visual narratives come in. Among the influential works in this literature are Harold Demsetz's recounting of the story against the vivid backdrop of an evolving North American fur trade, and particularly eastern Native Americans' development of property rights as they became engaged in that trade;[80] Terry Anderson and P. J. Hill's set of stories about the western settlers and their ever-sharpening definitions of water and livestock rights as their numbers grew;[81] and John Umbeck's story about gold rush miners' creation of customary systems of mining entitlements.[82]

Again, these narratives are really variants on a single analytic theme; it is, by and large, an optimistic drama, and it aims to convince the audience that property is a good thing, showering peace and prosperity on its practitioners. One can agree or disagree with the analytical argument embedded in the various dramatic presentations. But at least, through the example of all the hunting and mining, the cowboys and the cattle and the gold, one can grasp easily what the argument *is* and how it makes sense of the evolution and branching of property entitlements. The underlying argument is much strengthened rhetorically when it emerges in these entirely imaginable narratives, narratives that take place in physical settings with tangible objects in them. In fact, as I also pointed out in the earlier essay "Property and Storytelling," the narrative forms of the scarcity story make the argument almost too persuasive, since the narrative versions gloss over some real analytic problems in the argument.

The scarcity story has taken tremendous rhetorical sustenance from its numerous dramatizations, and, not unexpectedly, other intellectual perspectives on property have started to mimic its dramatic narrative style. Though they are not widespread, there are clearly some efforts to catch up, particularly in what are now being called the "outsider" narratives of law—property tales as told by minorities, indigenous peoples, women, and others whose experiences with standard property law has not necessarily been entirely cheery, to put it mildly.[83] Larceny, by force or deceit, is the dominating theme in many of these "outsider" narratives of property. When such stories are told about the encounters of differing cultures, and about those who gain and those who lose in such encounters, they are particularly powerful challenges to the sometimes aggravating smugness of the scarcity story. These stories spin out a quite divergent evolutionary drama underlying the experience of Native Americans or other indigenous peoples, for whom the introduction of Western property regimes has often meant not wealth-enhancing individual entitlements but the loss of an entire way of life.[84]

Larceny stories seem to be emerging in other parts of the "outsider" literature as well and again very usefully illuminate some aspects of property regimes. Carol Karlsen, an historian of American witchcraft, has used narration very tellingly on a feminist theme in property. In her 1989 book, *The Devil in the Shape of a Woman,* she tells the stories of a number of colonial New England "witches," and in so doing she illuminates how tightly the seventeenth-century witchcraft trials revolved about property disputes, particularly when substantial amounts of property were controlled by some conventionally "improper" persons. The typical improper person was an older women who by accident or aberration controlled, say, a farm, and who did so all by herself because the usual husband or son or other male protector was dead or far away. And in the typical tale, she was self-assured enough not to back down when she got into a dispute with a neighboring farmer; but when by chance the neighbor's heifer took sick, it was clear to all that this stiff-necked woman must have bewitched the animal. If she was lucky, she was "properly" pauperized by the end of her encounter with witchcraft law; if she was unlucky, of course, execution was the last page in her personal story.[85] In the accumulation of these many tales, where uppity women's property disputes slid into accusations of witchcraft, Karlsen paints a larger picture of a world of gendered hierarchy.

Narratives like these involve seeing property too; indeed they enlist the visual imagination to tell a story about property generally. They aim at making the audience understand property relationships—and the social relationships that underlie them—by watching in the mind's eye the changes that occur in the shape and configuration of ownership and control. Not all these outsider stories are pessimistic and dark, because some involve a heartening self-help among seemingly indomitable peoples.[86] But of course some *are* pessimistic and dark, and that too is a part of seeing property relations as they evolve over time.

Indeed, the scarcity story itself has a well-known pessimistic version in which the play never gets beyond Act 3, where conflicts break out over scarce resources. In this version, Act 3 ends the play, and the conflicts go on and on, never resolving themselves into happy property. The name of this dramatic production, of course, is *The Tragedy of the Commons*,[87] set metaphorically among graziers and livestock in a common field. This play too, like any good production, has generated tremendous controversy—especially in environmental circles, since it seems so easily to lead to the larger conclusion that only an authoritarian regime can salvage the common resources of Spaceship Earth.[88] That is a matter hotly contested by some neocommunitarians, who have generated some stories of their own about the successful evolution of common property regimes among persons who collectively use and manage resources such as irrigation systems, pastures, and woodlots—even though these arrangements rely on the seemingly frail reeds of reasonableness and trust.[89] Indeed, two essays in this book, "The Comedy of the Commons" and "Energy and Efficiency," are a modest contribution to that literature of common property institutions. But this scholarly enterprise in some measure takes its start from the particularly vivid story of the tragedy of the commons, which crystallized the problems of common property in a way that made scholars pay attention, if only to argue against it.[90]

These are of course not the only dramatizations of the evolution of property regimes; Marx had his own drama about the unfolding of "bourgeois property" over time and its potential future transformation. It need hardly be pointed out that there are vigorous persuasive efforts in all these dramatizations—often quite consciously so, since the persuasiveness *vel non* of any given property narrative has important implications for political action. Indeed, if seeing is believing, these dramas are aimed at seeing the whole institution of property in sharply different perspectives; and believing, in this instance, may not be far removed from acting.

Seeing Illusory Property

The preceding discussion suggested that sight in property is not so timeless and static after all, both because particular properties give visual reminders of past events and because arguments about the institution of property are often embedded in visually rich narrations of transformation. This present section will go on to suggest that the visual aspects of property not only serve to persuade and argue but that people are widely aware that they do just that. All this will appear in the context of yet another way of seeing property—that is, seeing property where the official law of property would deny that there is anything even like property.

People sometimes act as if they were asserting and acknowledging property claims, even though it is quite well known that these claims really have no legal status at all. This is what I call seeing illusory property or what one might call "un-real estate." There are various places where one could begin to explain the notion of illusory property, but I will start with an early guru, Jane Jacobs. Her justly famous 1960 book, *The Death and Life of Great American Cities,* very tellingly described how the physical and visual features of an urban area may lend the sense of security and control that is normally associated with property. One of her well-known phrases was the "eyes on the street"; this referred to the numerous trusted storekeepers, the "public characters," and the other residents in city neighborhoods who keep the street under a certain benevolent surveillance—particularly in the neighborhoods where accidental contacts bring the residents together in casual, multilayered transactions.[91] In several chapters, Jacobs discussed the actual physical characteristics that promote such transactions—short blocks, densely packed and mixed uses, old buildings scattered in with the new.

The gist of Jacobs' argument was that configurations like these give the residents a sense that the streets are "their" streets. Officially speaking, of course, the streets are owned by the public at large, but the "eyes on the street" act as proprietors of this un-real estate, and the presence of the "eyes," taken together with the physical characteristics of places, let other residents feel that they too own the neighborhood, if only in some informal and nonlegal sense.

Oscar Newman, among others, picked up on Jacobs' ideas and extrapolated some of them in his own book, *Defensible Space* (1970). Newman was interested in the way that architectural features might relate to crime prevention and especially the ways in which the appearance of "defended space" might deter crime. With that goal in mind, he compared the architecture (and crime rates) of two public housing projects, one a high-rise project, the other a set of garden apartments. The latter had the physical features of low height, semiprivate doorways and entrances, marked sidewalk configurations, and distinct yard spaces; all of these apparently gave tenants a sense of proprietorship about the areas surrounding their apartments. Outsiders as well understood these features to mean that a given area was under a kind of imagined proprietary control. By contrast, Newman argued that the high-rise project's larger building sizes, expansive surrounding lawns, and more open and impersonal configurations made many spaces look as if they were unowned and undefended "commons," with the standard tragic outcome—anything goes, and the strongest party rules.[92]

Newman's work stressed the element of *exclusion* in illusory property. Safe spaces in public housing are those that give off the impression of some "owner's" ability to exclude interlopers; on the other hand, on Newman's analysis, where things have the look of the unowned commons and where the physical features do not lead one even to imagine a fictitious exclusive private property—there lurks violence and danger. One can hardly help but hear some eighteenth-century echoes in all this: Blackstone too regarded the ability to exclude as a most wondrous aspect of property, while Bentham described the absence of exclusion—using the example of the great unexclusive "commons" of America—as murky, miasmic, and dangerous.[93]

But a rather different aspect of illusory property emerges from the work of William H. Whyte, who stresses the more positive aspects of publicness or common usage. His exuberant *Social Life of Small Urban Spaces* details the kinds of physical configurations that invite city people to "make themselves at home" in public places—sitting spaces, water fountains, food vending carts, accessibility to the street, and so on.[94] Clearly none of these features transfers official title to the users, yet their physical appearance can let people imagine a certain phantom property and feel themselves "entitled" to claim "their" spaces, however temporarily, amidst great crowds of others who are equally comfortable in adjacent spaces of their own.

In the realm of illusory property, Whyte's interests lie at the borderline of the exclusive and the shared. It seems quite clear to Whyte that the most enticing public spaces derive their allure in large measure from their combination of protection and participation; he notes, for example, the way people seat themselves outdoors just at the edges of the most heavily travelled footways and seek out the best perches from which to see the crowd of passersby.[95]

An earlier writer in this vein was Kevin Lynch, whose interest in the "legibility" of space was mentioned at the beginning of this essay. Lynch focused even more than Whyte on the shared aspects of illusory property. He too was looking for physical features that let people feel "at home," but he quite clearly meant "at home" with the rest of the public who share these spaces. In *The Image of the City,* Lynch was interested in a very simple set of phenomena: what do people speak of when they describe a normal trip, such as going to work?[96] What features stand out to make the surroundings "legible," and, perhaps most important, what helps people *not to feel lost?* The respondents' answers led Lynch to generalize about the kinds of visible features—landmarks, "edges," "nodes," and so forth—that let people know where they are and that by extension give them a sense of mastery and control in the larger landscapes in which they find themselves.[97]

Interestingly enough, several aspects of illusory property have worked their way to formal recognition in the "real" legal world of property law and land use regulation—perhaps illustrating the way that popular understandings and formal property law are in continuous dialog. After the formal law (in the guise of urban renewal) ignored and flattened the kind of fine-grained housing construction that might have been visibly "defensible," modern public housing statutes seem to be in the process of doing an about-face and in a muted way refer to Newman's ideas of defensible space in public housing design.[98] Much more overtly, after a generation of urban land regulation encouraged the construction of tall, forbidding buildings located in shadowy, windswept plazas, New York City changed its mind and now puts Whyte's bubblingly sociable places at the center of its open space zoning law.[99] And finally, after tax and development laws long encouraged the destruction of older buildings, the modern historic preservation statutes now speak, echoing Jacobs and Lynch, of the importance of older structures in securing a sense of "orientation" for the citizenry.[100]

In a way, the legal imprimatur on "orientation" recognizes a conception of property lying somewhere between individual private property on the one hand and the tragic commons on the other. Even though Lynch was interested in large, officially public spaces, such as cityscapes, some of his ideas are quite similar to Newman's. Like Newman, Lynch notes the jarring and frightening psychological aspects of disorientation and the vulnerability that one feels in featureless surroundings. The relatively unmarked and blank public space, though it officially does belong to the public, is imagined to belong to no one at all. Lynch contrasts those imaginings with the sense of security, harmony, and intensity of experience that can accompany environments that are "not only familiar but distinctive as well."[101]

In the scholarship of common property, some theorists draw a distinction between "open access" and "common property regimes"; the latter are owned, even though they are owned in common. Lynch and others implicitly suggest that this distinction lies in the visual imagination, too. Lynch illustrates how certain visible physical configurations lend a sense of security and mastery in common spaces; this is a sense of *belonging* as well as owning, and as such this imagined property is both public and participatory—but it is not perceived as an unowned wasteland, open to the first one who can grab it.

In one way, of course, the sense of property that Lynch describes is not merely the illusion of property, because many of these areas—like streets—actually do belong to the public in a quite official way. What is interesting about Lynch's work, however, is that it suggests that some officially recognized public property strikes the *imagination* as "owned," while some does not; that is, in some cases the official "story" seems believable but in some cases not.

From the perspective of property as a persuasive enterprise, perhaps the most interesting aspect of this perception of ownership is that members of the public *know* that visual characteristics may be part of an argument—and sometimes they may not agree. The public, for example, can become quite irked about the private "appropriation" of public spaces through visual signals. This can lead to some interesting conflicts over "ownership." Take graffiti: some graffiti artists no doubt consider themselves as the just appropriators of the spaces for their grandiose murals, though some no doubt revel in a sense of furtive theft; in any event, they use the language of property in describing the places for their work. But so do objecting members of the public, and that is what the argument is about, quite aside from the artistic merits of the work.[102]

A particularly interesting battle erupted in New York City in 1981, when the artist Richard Serra installed a controversial sculpture entitled *Tilted Arc* in the Federal Plaza at Foley Square. The *Arc* was a 12-foot-tall, 120-foot-long rusted steel wall, and the controversy swirled most around its location straight across a favorite outdoor lunch area, which, as one reporter put it, the sculpture "bisect[ed] ... like the business end of a giant cleaver."[103] Outraged office workers dubbed the sculpture "the Berlin Wall," and the ensuing public uproar ultimately led to its removal in 1985. In the meantime, both sides explicitly used the language of property.[104] Quite aside from aesthetic and expressive issues, the controversy did suggest some points about a public sense of property: first, artworks, like other visual features, can have very much the quality of assertions of proprietary claims, and, second, in public spaces those claims may be contested hotly and met by counterclaims, including visual ones. The visually aggressive *Arc,* for example, very quickly acquired some graffiti. This comes back again to the point that visible property claims are a way of talking to other people—and although people may sometimes be persuaded, they sometimes may also quite consciously argue back.

Perhaps this is the place to return to those critiques of vision that seemed so applicable to property: that vision is both objectifying and insensitive to change over time. Property, dependent as it is on vision, should supposedly share these rather unattractive characteristics. But whatever may be the character of vision in scientific investigation, the visual aspects of property are not that way. Visual markings are social statements, often consciously so, and they are subject to interpretation, misinterpretation, and furious debate.[105]

But if visual markings are "statements," they may give rise to different stories among different audiences, just as texts generally may acquire a certain life of their own and may sometimes escape the control of the text-giver as well as some preferred "audience." Historic preservation law, for example, has a place for what amount to accidental landmarks—the rather unheroic and idiosyncratic structures, like the shell-shaped Shell gas station in Winston-Salem, North Carolina,[106] or the birthplace of Al Capone in Chicago[107]—that have willy-nilly become the loci for stories, controversies, and remembered experiences, for better or worse, of people who have seen them over time and who have woven their own symbolic networks around the visible objects. Even the purposefully memorializing icons, the monuments to this event and that, may acquire quite different and sometimes jarring meanings under the reinterpreting gaze of new audiences.[108]

Seeing property, then, like hearing a tale, depends on imagination; and the role of imagination in turn means that the interpretation of visible things is quite open-ended—indeed, imagination opens a role for culture, sociability, persuasion in the understandings of things seen. But the more one "sees" property through a lens of meaning and culture, of course, the greater the chance that people's visual statements can talk straight past each other, particularly when one sees the property of unknown others. That is the subject of one last example, in which I return with the reader to Hawaii.

Conclusion: Seeing the Property of Strangers

The first European explorers to reach Hawaii came with Captain James Cook in 1778, during Cook's great mappings of the Pacific. Cook and his men saw a great deal when they looked at Hawaii. This was not just a blank landscape but a place with huts, temples, irrigations works, cultivation, aquaculture fishponds—all arrayed within more or less natural topographically bounded areas running from the mountains to the sea. In short, they saw great numbers of visible features and improvements that would suggest "dominion" under the English common law of property.[109]

Cook, and slightly later the early European and American settlers, did in fact treat all these things as property, and indeed the property of the kings and chiefs, or *ali'i*—that is, they thought that the Hawaiian landscape was under the dominion of these native aristocrats. There is an interesting contrast here to the settlers' actions in North America and especially Australia, actions that are described briefly in the first essay of this book. In those places, many European settlers simply did not see anything at all that signified indigenous entitlement, except insofar as they themselves might claim title through some purported "purchase" of land from the original inhabitants. Even without such purported claims, European settlers moved into North American and Australian lands, and many justified their moves by what they said was the emptiness of the land. Their answer to any charge of trespass was that this land had not belonged to anyone; the natives had done nothing to signify their proprietary claims according to what was straight-facedly called "the law of nature."[110] The chief exceptions in North America were the agricultural plots of the Native American women, which did indeed signify property to Europeans, because their cultivation visibly marked the land in an enterprise familiar to European conceptions of property.[111]

In Hawaii things were rather different. European and American settlers moved into the islands, too, but they recognized indigenous ownership, thinking that the islands and their geographic regions and subregions belonged to the kings and chiefs in a sort of feudal tenure. Over the first few decades of the nineteenth century, the settlers directed increasing efforts toward getting these kings and chiefs to make the land alienable. One reason was that they themselves wanted to buy land and enjoy the security of property ownership instead of the uncertainty of a status that could more or less be described in Western terms as tenancy at will. But another reason was that some of the Westerners, particularly the missionaries, thought that property would be good for the dwindling and dispirited Hawaiian common people and would, as in the classical story, turn the Hawaiians into thrifty, industrious, and prosperous yeomen.[112]

The Westerners succeeded in these persuasive efforts, though not without the aid of real and threatened force; and once Hawaiian land became legally alienable in the mid-nineteenth century, non-Hawaiians bought a great deal of it.[113] And so, in Hawaii, the answer to any charge of trespass was not "nobody owned it," as it often was in North America or Australia. It was rather, "They sold it to us."

The story went on, however. What Western settlers did *not* see in Hawaii, or at least did not see very clearly, was something very similar to what they had not seen earlier in North America. To the settlers, the native Hawaiian's common gathering rights—tremendously important to ordinary Hawaiians for foodstuffs, textiles, building materials, fuel, marine products, and so on—were more or less invisible, as were the understandings of land as part of a reciprocal trust relation between native nobility and common people.[114] The Western settlers were thinking of their own land practices when they looked at the islands, and what they did see, again similarly to what they saw in North America, were the native Hawaiians' cultivated patches of taro plants. And so, among the Hawaiian commonfolk, the introduction of Western law treated as property chiefly the Hawaiians' agricultural plots; whereas the Hawaiians' own understanding of their entitlements extended out to the varied vegetation and animal and marine life throughout the areas in which they lived, including a certain patriarchal relationship to the governing figures who also lived there. Needless to say, the outsiders' land purchases and clearings, particularly for intensive sugar cane cultivation, very much disrupted the earlier gathering rights and trust relationships of the indigenous people, because to the new settlers, these were not rights at all.[115]

Such culture-conflict stories, upsetting as they are, must reinforce the point that seeing property is an act of imagination—and seeing property also reflects some of the cultural limitations on imagination. Different peoples see the signals of the surroundings through very different imaginative lenses, and they put those signals together in different property stories; they persuade themselves that the things they see can yield the security of entitlement, whatever that may entail, and then they act on the visible signals as if the signified entitlements were permanent, solid, objective. And to some degree they are—so long as everyone, or most everyone, is persuaded.

Persuasion, of course, is what makes property available to action: even in the classical utilitarian story, the persuasion of security allows one to invest in one's property, safe in the expectation of reaping the rewards. Moreover, a persuasion that property arrangements generally are just and useful—and that they are so perceived by others—may well influence one's decision to refrain from running off with the property of others, and lead one to try to prevent others from such transgressions. But finally, a persuasion of *in*justice or relative *dis*utility lies behind the efforts to alter particular property arrangements or even whole property regimes, and persuasion in some cases supports what is described as a "justified" use of force to turn imaginings into quite different legal entitlements.

These latter events are necessarily infrequent occurrences in any given property regime. Property regimes cannot bear very many or very frequent uses of force; force and violence are the nemesis of property, and their frequent use is a signal that a property regime is faltering.[116] What is much more important to any property regime, and to the material and psychological security it may bring, is widespread and peaceable consensus, even where that consensus changes over time.

In property, vision and visual metaphor are essential modes of persuasion in the ways that human beings think they can and should interact with their environment. Vision mediates between what is given by the surroundings and what the viewers think that they and others can do, either to accommodate to their surroundings or to shape them anew.

There is an old adage, told of plain people and plain things: what you see is what you get. Property seems plain in this way too: what you see is what you get. But things are more complicated than that. With property, the nature of "things" imposes their own quite fascinating constraints. Yet even with those, *what you see* in property is what you and others have talked yourselves into about those "things"; and given some imagination, you may always talk yourselves into seeing something else—with all the effects on understanding and action that a new "envisioning" may bring.

And that is why, with just a bit of exaggeration, I could have named this book *Property* Is *Persuasion*.

Notes

1. For a general history, see Gavan Daws, *Shoal of Time: A History of the Hawaiian Islands* (1968); see also Lawrence Fuchs, *Hawaii Pono: A Social History* (1961). For one continuing land controversy, that over native Hawaiian land claims, see *Native Hawaiian Rights Handbook* 26–65 (1991); Linda S. Parker, *Native American Estate: The Struggle over Indian and Hawaiian Lands* 168–72 (1989).

2. The sight of Chicago has elicited strong reactions from many writers. William Cronon relates a few (including his own) in *Nature's Metropolis: Chicago and the Great West* 5–19 (1991).

3. For ample illustrations, see Harold M. Mayer and Richard C. Wade, *Chicago: Growth of a Metropolis* 14–26, 138–44 (1969). Cronon, supra note 2, at 55–93, 249–50, discusses wider rail and canal links as well as the bold sewer canals, stressing the human manipulation in the city's growth.

4. For a famous case reversing the Illinois legislature's attempted sale of Chicago's lakefront, see Illinois Central Railroad v. Illinois, 146 U.S. 347 (1892); for an account of the impact of private lakefront controls, see Allison Dunham, "The Chicago Lakefront and A. Montgomery Ward, 25 *U. Chi. L. Sch. Rec.* 11 (Winter 1979).

5. Kevin Lynch, *The Image of the City* 2–3, 9–10 (1959).

6. Cf. Patricia Nelson Limerick, "Disorientation and Reorientation: The American Landscape Discovered from the West," 79 *J. Am. Hist.* 1021, 1048–49 (1992), on the invitation that "layered" landscape presents to historians.

7. Bruce A. Ackerman, *Private Property and the Constitution* 97–100 (1977), discussing lay understanding of property as things.

8. Wesley Hohfeld, "Some Fundamental Legal Conceptions as Applied in Judicial Reasoning," 23 *Yale L. J.* 16 (1913).

9. See, e.g., Cushman Virginia Corp. v. Barnes, 129 S.E.2d 633 (Va. 1963).

10. See, e.g., Fontainebleau Hotel Corp. v. Forty-Five Twenty-Five, Inc. 114 So.2d 357 (Fla. App. 1959). British law is different; see the distinction in Parker & Edgarton v. Foote, 19 Wend. 309 (N.Y. Sup. Ct. 1838). A controversial American exception is Prah v. Maretti, 321 N.W.2d 182 (Wis. 1982), discussed earlier in this volume in "Crystals and Mud."

11. See, e.g., Petersen v. Friedman, 328 P.2d 264 (Cal. App. 1958) (easement for view retained in deed); for a survey of modern legal developments, including sunlight access laws, see, e.g., Adrian J. Bradbrook, "Future Directions in Solar Access Protection," 19 *Envt'l L.* 167 (1988).

12. See Bernard J. Hibbitts, "'Coming to Our Senses': Communication and Legal Expression in Performance Cultures," 41 *Emory L. J.* 873, 902 (1992), citing an ancient Irish poem that referred to the ruler's activities of "measurement by poles," "marking out fresh boundaries," "planting of stakes" in connection with land law.

13. Hans Jonas, "The Nobility of Sight: A Study in the Phenomenology of the Senses," 14 *Phil. & Phenomenological Res.* 507, 514–19 (1954).

14. Id. at 507, 519, relating vision to Platonic philosophic realism; cf. Evelyn Fox Keller and Christine R. Grontkowski, "The Mind's Eye," in *Discovering Reality: Feminist Perspectives on Epistemology, Metaphysics, Methodology, and Philosophy of Science* 207, 210–13 (Sandra Harding and Merrill B. Hintikka eds. 1983), arguing that modern science's objectified version of nature derives from the seventeenth century and ignores other aspects of the Platonic understanding of sight.

15. Hibbitts, supra note 12, at 905–21, attacks vision particularly in its association with writing; this interesting piece laments that vision and writing displace a "performance culture" operating through a much richer array of sensory experience, ceremony, and memory.

16. Jonas, supra note 13, at 507–508.

17. Id. at 508–11. Hibbitts, supra note 12, at 906–24, argues that in "performance cultures" visual information itself is kinetic (gestures occurring in time, remembered over time by witnesses).

18. For a brief survey of the division between predictive and narrative knowledge, see "Introduction: The Crisis of Understanding," in Fred R. Dallmayr and Thomas A. McCarthy, *Understanding and Social Inquiry* 1 (1977).

19. See the interesting account of Keller and Grontkowski, supra note 14, at 218–21; these authors, however, argue that the objectifying understanding of vision itself displaces an earlier communicative aspect of vision and suggest that the displacement was part of a more generally de-eroticizing and misogynist epistemology. Id. at 220. See also Carolyn Merchant, "The Theoretical Structure of Ecological Revolutions," 11 *Envt'l Rev.* 265 (1987).

20. See, e.g., Merchant, supra note 19, at 265, 273, sweeping capitalist property into her critique of objectifying vision and science.

21. See the discussion in Tyler v. Judges of the Court of Registration, 55 N.E. 812 (Mass.), writ of error dismissed, 179 U.S. 405 (1900). As this case suggests, the typical conundrum concerns potential claimants who may be excluded without notice.

22. The classic case is Pierson v. Post, 3 Cai. R. 175 (N.Y. Sup. Ct. 1805).

23. 2 William Blackstone, *Commentaries on the Laws of England* 3–4 (1979; reproduction of 1766 ed.).

24. See Coffin v. Left Hand Ditch Co., 6 Colo. 443 (1882).

25. On the "myth" of property as a general symbol for rights, see Jennifer Nedelsky, *Private Property and the Limits of American Constitutionalism* 246–54 (1990).

26. See Keller and Grontkowski, supra note 14, at 220. For Native Americans, locking eyes with an animal signified the moment in which it "gave" itself to the hunter; see Richard K. Nelson, "The Gifts," 57 *Antaeus*, Autumn 1986, at 117, 122–24; for a very different "gift" by an animal, see id. at 127–29.

27. See, e.g., Conti v. ASPCA, 353 N.Y.S.2d 288 (Sup. Ct. 1974) (repossession of runaway parrot).

28. See, e.g., Van Valkenburgh v. Lutz, 106 N.E.2d 28 (N.Y. 1952).

29. Rockville Historic District Commission, *Architectural Design Guidelines for the Exterior Rehabilitation of Buildings in Rockville's Historic Districts* 49 (1977).

30. See Rudolf Arnheim, *Visual Thinking* 97–115, 229–33 (1969); for some more modest variations, see Stephen S. Hall, *Mapping the Next Millennium: The Discovery of New Geographies* 18–19 (1992) (maps may be a prototype for thinking); Mark Hollins, *Understanding Blindness: An Integrative Approach* 52 (1989) (discusses theory that vision gives a framework for other spatial sensory data).

31. The philosopher George Berkeley thought that touch was developmentally prior to sight in spatial perception. For his and some modern opinions, see Hollins, supra note 30, at 50–55.

32. Id. at 51–53, 57.

33. Hibbitts, supra note 12, at 902, 906; see also that note.

34. 272 U.S. 365, 382–83 (1926).

35. E.g., in *Euclid*, a note referred to maps of the property; see 272 U.S. at 382.

36. Cf. Hall, supra note 30, at 18, comparing map to mass of sensory data. Jesse Dukeminear and James Krier, the authors of a very widely used property law casebook, must have noticed this comparative advantage of maps; compare the somewhat opaque aerial photo accompanying *Othen v. Rosier*, 226 S.W.2d 622 (Tex. 1950), a complex easement case, in the first edition of their *Property*, to the highly stylized but much more comprehensible map substituted in later editions. For the photo, see 1st ed. (1981), at 983; for the map, see 2d ed. (1988), at 850; 3d ed. (1993), at 814.

37. See Hall, supra note 30, at 25–27, discussing the unexpected revelations emerging from astronomical mapping. Perhaps somewhat similarly, stunning computerized "mappings" appear to have stimulated further work on fractal geometry and chaos theory; see Benoit B. Mandelbrot, *The Fractal Geometry of Nature* 22–23, and C-2 (rev. ed. 1983).

38. See, e.g., Sabra Chartrand, "Random Shootings on Capital's Streets," *N.Y. Times*, Mar. 27, 1993, sec. 1, at 6, reproducing map of crime sites in seemingly unmotivated shootings in Washington, D.C.

39. Edward R. Tufte, *The Visual Display of Quantitative Information* 24 (1983).

40. 277 U.S. 183 (1928).

41. Several maps of the properties at the time of litigation appear in Norman Williams, 6 *American Land Planning Law*, plates 13–15 (1975).

42. Diane M. Bolz, "'Follow me ... I am the earth in the palm of your hand,'" *Smithsonian Mag.* (Feb. 1993), at 112. The 1993 exhibit at the Smithsonian's Cooper Hewitt National Museum of Design was named after the book by the curator, Denis Wood, *The Power of Maps* (1992). See also 1 J. B. Harley and David Woodward, *The History of Cartography* 506–507 (1987), noting association of ancient and medieval maps with elite control; Gregory H. Nobles, "Straight Lines and Stability:

Mapping the Political Order of the Anglo-American Frontier," 80 *J. Am. Hist.* 9, 30–35 (1993), on the place of maps in the (rather unsuccessful) effort at frontier social control.

43. For an interesting discussion of what it means for photographs to be "realistic," see Kendall L. Walton, "Transparent Pictures: On the Nature of Photographic Realism," 11 *Critical Inquiry* 246 (1984). Walton's claim is that photography is a "contribution to the enterprise of seeing," id. at 251; on the photographer's influence, id. at 261–65.

44. For perceptual organization of visual sense data, see generally R. L. Gregory, *Eye and Brain: The Psychology of Seeing* 219–25 (3d ed. 1978); see also Glyn W. Humphries and Philip T. Quinlan, "Normal and Pathological Processes and Visual Object Constancy," in Glyn W. Humphries and M. Jane Riddock, *Visual Object Processing: A Cognitive Neuropsychological Approach* 43 (1987), describing various theories about the recognition of objects in different spatial orientations.

45. Leon D. Harmon, "The Recognition of Faces," *Sci. Am.*, Nov. 1973, at 70, 74–76.

46. See Hollins, supra note 30, at 83–87.

47. See, e.g., Kaiser Aetna v. United States, 444 U.S. 164, 176 (1979), describing the right to exclude as "one of the most essential sticks in the bundle of rights that are commonly characterized as property."

48. 2 *Nomos* 69 (1980). Grey's usage was "bundle of rights" rather than "bundle of sticks."

49. Ackerman, supra note 7, at 23, 114–19.

50. Id. at 115.

51. Grey, supra note 48, at 76–77.

52. Frank I. Michelman, "Ethics, Economics, and the Law of Property," in 24 *Nomos* 3 (1982).

53. Id. at 8–21.

54. Kaiser Aetna v. United States, 444 U.S. 164, 176 (1979); Loretto v. Teleprompter Manhattan CATV Corp., 458 U.S. 419, 433 (1982); Nollan v. California Coastal Comm'n, 483 U.S. 825, 831 (1987).

55. See the rich discussion of private arrangements in Robert C. Ellickson, "Property in Land," 102 *Yale L. J.* 1315 (1993), with several arrangements specifically described as "bundles," id. at 1362–75.

56. Portuguese-American Bank v. Welles, 242 U.S. 7, 11 (1916).

57. John Christman, "The Importance of Ownership," delivered April 28, 1992, to the Faculty Political Theory Seminar, Yale University; manuscript on file with the author.

58. This is the reason why economists talk about the ways that *income* may be imputed to one who *uses* her property for herself. See, e.g., Richard A. Posner, *Economic Analysis of Law* 465, 479 (3d ed. 1986).

59. Martin Heidegger, *Sein und Zeit* 67–68 (1984; 1st ed. 1923), using the noun form *Dinglichkeit.* To my great regret, this has been translated into English as "Thinghood" rather than "Thingyness"; see *Being and Time* 96 (John Macquarrie and Edward Robinson trans. 1962).

60. Jonathan Swift, *Gulliver's Travels* 198–99 (Arthur Case ed. 1938); for Swift as satirist of Lockean sensationalist epistemology, see W. B. Carnochan, *Lemuel Gulli-*

ver's Mirror for Man 122–23, 133–44 (1968).

61. "Property as Propriety" and "Ancient Constitution Versus Federalist Empire."

62. J. W. Allen, *A History of Political Thought in the Sixteenth Century* 141, 145 (rev. ed. 1957).

63. Tufte, supra note 39.

64. Phil Patton, "Up from Flatland," *N.Y. Times,* Jan. 19, 1992, sec. 6, at 19.

65. Edward Tufte, *Envisioning Information* (1990).

66. Patton, supra note 64.

67. Tversky and Kahneman, "Judgment Under Uncertainty: Heuristics and Biases," 185 *Science* 1124 (1974). For more recent literature, see Paul Slovic, "Perception of Risk," 236 *Science* 280 (1987).

68. See, e.g., Paul Slovic, Baruch Fishhoff, and Sarah Lichtenstein, "Rating the Risks: The Structure of Experts and Lay Perceptions," in Christoph Hohenemser and Jeanne X. Kasperson, *Risk in the Technological Society,* 141, 144–45 (1982); Chauncey Starr and Chris Whipple, "Risks of Risk Decisions," id. at 217, 227–30.

69. See, e.g., Carol M. Rose, "Rethinking Environmental Controls: Management Strategies for Common Resources," 1991 *Duke L. J.* 1.

70. Health effects may diverge further if toxicity is not related to concentration in a direct linear pattern; i.e., toxins may have thresholds below which they are harmless, while higher concentrations are exponentially more deleterious. For a brief discussion, see David Doniger, "Federal Regulation of Vinyl Chloride: A Short Course in the Law and Policy of Toxic Substances Control," 7 *Ecology L. Q.* 500, 512–14 (1978).

71. See Roger G. Noll and James E. Krier, "Some Implications of Cognitive Psychology for Risk Regulation," 19 *J. Legal Stud.* 747 (1990).

72. For a description of this "risk portfolio" approach, see Richard B. Stewart, "The Role of the Courts in Risk Management," 16 *Envt'l. L. Rep.* 69 (1986).

73. "Current Developments," *Env't Rep.,* May 27, 1988, at 101.

74. See Tversky and Kahneman, supra note 67, at 1125–26.

75. For a similar treatment of narrative, relating narrative to the theory of action, see David Carr, *Time, Narrative and History* (1986).

76. Tufte, supra note 39, at 40, quoting E. J. Marey, *La Méthode graphique* (1875), at 73. Maps often seem to stir mental journeys; Hall, supra note 30, at xi, notes that "one of the supreme joys" of reading a map (in his case, tracing the travels of Lewis and Clark) is the way the map tells "a wonderful human story."

77. See U.S. v. Gettysburg Electric Ry. Co, 160 U.S. 668, 680–83 (1896), describing the memorable impact of seeing the battlefield at Gettysburg.

78. "Crystals and Mud in Property Law."

79. A gloomier fifth act follows in some of the more modern versions, in which interest groups capture government and then intervene and mess up the perfectly adequate arrangements that had emerged earlier. See, e.g., Mancur Olson, *The Rise and Decline of Nations: Economic Growth, Stagflation, and Social Rigidities* 17–35 (1982).

80. Harold Demsetz, "Toward a Theory of Property Rights," 57 *Am. Econ. Rev.* (Paper & Proceedings) 347 (1967).

81. Terry L. Anderson and P. J. Hill, "The Evolution of Property Rights: A Study of the American West," 18 *J. L. & Econ.* 163 (1975).

82. John Umbeck, "A Theory of Contract Choice and the California Gold Rush," 20 *J. L. & Econ.* 421 (1977).

83. Richard Delgado points out that "outsider" voices have to compete against a crushing number and variety of damaging "insider" narrations; see "Images of the Outsider in American Law and Culture: Can Free Expression Remedy Systemic Social Ill?" 77 *Cornell L. Rev.* 77 (1992).

84. See, e.g., William Cronon, *Changes in the Land: Indians, Colonists, and the Ecology of New England* 58–68, 77–81 (1983); Arthur McEvoy, *The Fisherman's Problem: Ecology and the Law in the California Fisheries, 1850–1980*, at 41–62 (1986). Cf. Robert A. Williams, Jr., *The American Indian in Western Legal Thought: The Discourses of Conquest* (1990), for an extensive study of the historical "discourses" used to justify these divestments.

85. Carol F. Karlsen, *The Devil in the Shape of a Woman: Witchcraft in Colonial New England* 77–130 (1989).

86. See, e.g., Ivan Light, *Ethnic Enterprise in America* 22–32, 58–61 (1972), describing "rotating credit associations" among immigrant ethnic groups; for a "borrowing circle" among low-income women, see David Wessel, "Two Unusual Lenders Show How 'Bad Risks' Can Be Good Business," *Wall St. J.*, June 23, 1992, at 1, col. 6.

87. This is the famous name created by Garrett Hardin, "The Tragedy of the Commons," 162 *Science* 1243 (1968).

88. See William Ophuls, *Ecology and the Politics of Scarcity* 145–63 (1978).

89. See, e.g., Susan Jane Buck Cox, "No Tragedy on the Commons," 7 *Envt'l. Ethics* 49, 55–56 (1985); Elinor Ostrom, *Governing the Commons: The Evolution of Institutions for Collective Action* 88–90, 94–100 (1990).

90. An earlier and in some ways more intellectually satisfying version of the story was less noticed, perhaps because it had a considerably less striking name: H. Scott Gordon, "The Economic Theory of a Common–Property Resource: The Fishery," 62 *J. Pol. Econ.* 124 (1954).

91. Jane Jacobs, *The Death and Life of Great American Cities* (1961); see "The Uses of Sidewalks: Contact," ch. 3, at 55–73.

92. Oscar Newman, *Defensible Space* 1–50 (1972). Cf. Robert Sommer, *Personal Space: The Behavioral Basis of Design* 22–23 (1969), associating strong spatial markers with efforts to compensate for blurred social distinctions.

93. 2 Blackstone, supra note 23, at 2; Jeremy Bentham, *The Theory of Legislation* 118 (1987; reprint of Ogden ed. 1931).

94. William H. Whyte, *The Social Life of Small Urban Spaces* (1980). Whyte also made an equally exuberant film of the same name, using the film footage from which the book's photographs are drawn.

95. Id. at 32–33.

96. Lynch, supra note 5. For examples of the questions and responses in Lynch's study, see 140–81. For more recent scholarship, see Harvey J. Miller, "Human Wayfinding, Environment-Behavior Relationships, and Artificial Intelligence," 7 *J. Plan. Literature* 139 (1992)

97. Id. at 46–49.

98. See the "Public Housing Security Demonstration Act," reprinted at 12 U.S.C.A. sec. 1701z, n. 6, at 1048–49, requiring that housing officials consider "social and environmental design improvements" along with other measures to enhance public housing crime control.

99. See, e.g., Carter B. Horsley, "Radical Midtown Zoning Overhaul Proposed, Giving Greater Diversity," *N.Y. Times,* July 13, 1980, at 1, quoting Whyte among other consultants.

100. See Carol M. Rose, "Preservation and Community: New Directions in the Law of Historic Preservation," 33 *Stanford L. Rev.* 473, 489–90 (1981), and authorities cited therein.

101. Lynch, supra note 5, at 4–5.

102. On graffiti, see, e.g., Craig Castleman, *Getting Up: Subway Graffiti in New York* 12, 25, 46–48 (1982), describing "writers'" sense both of public service and of theft; see generally Donald Appleyard, "The Environment as a Social Symbol" 45 *J. Am. Plan. Ass'n* 143 (1979).

103. Grace Glueck, "What Part Should the Public Play in Choosing Public Art?" *N.Y. Times,* Feb. 3, 1985, sec. 2, at 1.

104. E.g., id. (official cites "public's ability to live with the space that belongs to it"); Douglas C. McGill, "Office Workers and Artists Debate Fate of a Sculpture," *N.Y. Times,* Mar. 7, 1985, sec. B, at 1 (*Arc* likened to a wall in front of one's house); Douglas C. McGill, "'Tilted Arc' Removal Draws Mixed Reaction," *N.Y. Times,* June 6, 1985, sec. C, at 21 (defender of sculpture likens removal to eviction from rent-stabilized apartment). Serra, in his fruitless suit to prevent the removal of the sculpture, also claimed a property right in having the sculpture in a particular location; for this and a reprise of the controversy, see Deborah Solomon, "Our Most Notorious Sculptor," *N.Y. Times,* Oct. 8, 1989, sec. 6, at 39.

105. The artist Christo even regards the arguments and fights as part of the artwork; see "Esthetic Terrorism," *Newsweek,* Aug. 9, 1976, at 78 (artist's reaction after vandals attacked work on his *Running Fence,* a 24-mile-long temporary sculpture); Calvin Tompkins, "Onward and Upward with the Arts: Running Fence," *The New Yorker,* Mar. 28, 1977, at 43, 54.

106. Karen de Will, "Landmark Status Can Serve More Than History," *N.Y. Times,* Sept. 28, 1980, at 22E.

107. Blair Kamin, "Capone House Landmark Status Fought," *Chi. Trib.,* Apr. 14, 1989, sec. 2, at 1.

108. See, e.g., Garry Boulard, "New Orleans Battles over a Monument," *Christian Science Monitor,* Apr. 19, 1993, at 12, concerning controversy between modern civil rights organizations and Ku Klux Klan over reinstatement of old monument to white supremacy group.

109. Parker, supra note 1, at 8–15 (1989); Jon J. Chinen, *The Great Mahele: Hawaii's Land Division of 1848* 1–6 (1958).

110. Johnson v. M'Intosh, 21 U.S. (8 Wheat.) 543, 569–70 (1823) (brief for defendants). Justice Marshall's opinion in the case mentioned this argument but skirted it. Id. at 587, 591; but cf. the debates over Indian ownership of land, Williams, supra note 84, at 271–75, 288–89, 308–317. For Australia and the absence of any recognition of aboriginal entitlement, see 1 C. D. Rowley, *The Destruction of Aboriginal Society: Aboriginal Policy and Practice* 14–16 (1970).

111. Cronon, supra note 84, at 56–58, 62–63.

112. Parker, supra note 1, at 94–104; Daws, supra note 1, at 124–28.

113. Parker, supra note 1, at 96–115.

114. See Lilikala Kame'elehiwa, *Native Land and Foreign Desires* 8–12 (1992); for a similar ignoring of Indian gathering rights in New England, see Cronon, supra note 84, at 63–68.

115. Parker, supra note 1, at 109–11. There were some efforts to protect gathering rights for tenants, but many were lost, particularly as large land areas were cleared for sugar and pineapple. See *Native Hawaiian Rights Handbook,* supra note 1, at 224–25.

116. For a current example, see Juan de Onis, *The Green Cathedral* 19–20 (1992), on the devastating effect of violence in disrupting preservation efforts in Amazonia.

About the Book and Author

In an era in which socialism has been widely discredited, the moral and legal status of private property is crucial, and property theory has become one of the most active and exciting battlegrounds of contemporary political and social thought. In this important contribution to the theory of property, Carol Rose sympathetically examines the two currently dominant traditions—neoconservative utilitarianism and liberal communitarianism—acknowledging the strengths of each and laying the groundwork for a theory to bridge the gap between them.

By insisting that community norms must underlie any property regime, she expands the horizons of property theory, exploring the role of narrative and storytelling in the establishment of these norms. The result is a study that credits the insights of rival views and breaks new ground both substantively in its implications for understanding property and methodologically in its application of the study of narrative to property law.

Property and Persuasion is a valuable contribution to legal theory as well as to political and social philosophy, and it is essential reading for students and professionals in all these fields.

Carol M. Rose is Gordon Bradford Tweedy Professor of Law at Yale Law School. She is the author of many articles on the law of property and natural resources.

Index